the
Reality
of
Time

the
Reality
of
Time

by Janet Iris Sussman

TIME PORTAL
PUBLICATIONS
FAIRFIELD, IOWA

Time Portal Publications, Inc.
P.O. Box 2002
Fairfield, IA 52556
United States of America
Website: www.timeportalpubs.com
E-mail: info@timeportalpubs.com

1|12

Printed in the United States of America
by Thomson-Shore, Inc.

ISBN: 0-9643535-2-0 (paper)
ISBN: 0-9643535-3-9 (cloth)
Library of Congress Control Number: 2004112326

Executive Editor:
Douglas A. Mackey

Graphic Design:
Laurie Douglas, www.lauriedouglas.com

Illustrations:
Fractal images were created with Fracture,
http://www.sticksoftware.com/software/Fracture.html,
and are copyright © 2001 Stick Software, used with permission.

table of contents

1 The Structure of Time

2 The Perception of Time

3 Cosmic Time

protection mantra
from the chandi path

Shulena Pahi No Devi

Pahi Khadgena Chambike

Ghantha-Svanena Nah Pahi

Chapaj-yanih Svanena Cha

Oh Mother, protect us with your spear of penetrating insight and sword of discriminating non-dual wisdom. Protect us with your bell sound of clarity and the twang of your bowstring—the strength of concentration.

— Translation by Shankaracharya Swami with permission

acknowledgments

This is a book about time and as a result, its contents speak of things that are in essence part of the annals of a history not yet written. We are the purveyors of its contents and the matchmakers for a series of manuscripts which we hope to bring forward. The process of crafting this material is much like carving a sculpture made of ice. First one has to have a frozen block of material, without any definition, and quickly, before the material melts and loses its own reflection, we have to make sense out of it.

This delicate job has been handled by a very capable and diligent editor, Douglas Mackey, who has tirelessly quizzed the author in Socratic fashion every step of the way. As a result, we have a wholly original manuscript that maintains the strength and character of its original transmission. I owe a tremendous amount of time to him, but since there is no past, present, or future, I can only repay him with my love.

Secondly, I wish to thank Carole Connet, our tireless copy editor who had the courage to pull apart our editorial decisions and question them with kindness and a quick hand. Finally, to the other members of our study group, Paul Bien, John Connet, and Laura Nelson, thanks for your input into the manuscript at its more raw stages.

Then there is Laurie Douglas, graphic designer and arbiter of formatting. Her patience, sense of humor, and faith in the project has aided in its birth.

To Lilli Botchis, my lifelong friend and confidante, goes the honor of having lived through the material before it was even a word on paper. Through her tireless, visionary inspiration and constant coaxing, the butterfly came out of the cocoon. She's now poised on a perch where every eye can see her.

To my partner, Thomas Brumma, I offer this book as a gift to his selfless willingness to give up four years of quality time with me. He has seen me through crises of health and faith while I labored over a project that looked like it would be miraculously quick and, in the end, is simply a loving miracle of diligence. Thanks for your prayers and your belief in me.

Lastly, there is my mom, Selma Sussman, bless her heart. She did the final proofreading for the manuscript with her usual thoroughness. I give thanks for all these years that she has listened to a child with silk in her eyes bear witness to things that go bump in the night. She has with typical aplomb given me the space to bring forward the fruits of a lifelong creative quest. May she be in good health and available to witness many other installments.

foreword

by Douglas A. Mackey, Ph.D.

time is an ever-present and inescapable fact of our existence. We celebrate it and rebel against it. There never seems to be enough of it, yet when we contemplate time's illimitable expanses, it reduces us to insignificance. It represents the ultimate decay of everything, including our minds and bodies, our species, our planet and star system, the universe itself, and it betokens the radical rebirth that can happen perpetually in every moment. Its repetitive patterns reveal a cyclical tendency and inspire the hope of rebirth. The eternal moment unfolds the perpetually new even as the creations of the day crumble into the slumber of night.

With time, we have the essence of paradox. We try to define that element in which we live and have our being but can never directly perceive.

The first question that might be asked in confronting the title *The Reality of Time* is: Is time real at all? The elusiveness of the concepts of past, present, and future, and the philosophical difficulty of proving an objective present and flow of time apart from individual experience, are factors that erode our confidence in the possibility of defining and ultimately understanding the reality that we call time.

Many writings of spiritual philosophy attempt to delineate a "higher" account of the physical universe. The wonderful reductiveness of their mystical formulae such as "all this is That" is not necessarily wrong, and may in fact be supremely right if one's consciousness is at the level of That, but this is not the way that Janet Sussman travels here. Her vision acknowledges the variety and complexity of the physical universe and the subjective relations we form with it. By the same token, the oft-repeated dictum that "time is an illusion," as a formula for breaking out of the linear lockstep of classical materialistic physics and common perception, will not be found echoed here. Even physicist Julian Barbour (*The End of Time*) goes so far as to repudiate the existence of time in favor of a "philosophy of timelessness" based on a static quantum model.

In these pages, time is not only real, it is a primary shaping force underlying manifest reality, a conscious principle that the Godforce itself uses as a dimensional background for its creative play. We also, as creators of our personal reality, use time as the canvas upon which we apply the colors and form the shapes that compose our picture of the world.

When reading this book it is necessary to redefine time, to intuit its essence as fundamentally different from the "referential time" that is part and parcel of life in the material world. Referential time is based on measurement of matter: for example, the distance that the earth travels in its orbit around the sun constitutes one year. Essentially this construction of time *refers* to an arbitrary measurement in space. We look at objective phenomena using chronometric reference points, for subjective time is extremely variable, as we know from everyday experience.

The subjective notion of a "moment," I believe, indicates a close encounter with time itself. Insofar as we experience a moment, we feel a certain suspension in the pure dimensionality of the time element, and we step out of the referential mode by which we walk that unforgiving timeline. The anomalous nature of that momentousness makes us alert to new ideas and possibilities.

Humankind's technological quest may be seen as an attempt for liberation from the tyranny of referential time, to escape the imprisonment of the senses with its inexorable cycles of beginnings and endings, of death itself. In this, the scientific spirit is profoundly religious.

The field of pure or non-referential time, however, is not devoid of differentiation. It is full of discrete areas which function as mathematical variables. They constitute the bits that are processed by our computer-like nervous systems in the construction of objective reality. Our perceptual apparatus fills in the holes—much like persistence of vision bestows continuity upon the frames of a film—and the result is the known universe.

The further evolution of human consciousness, whether regarded from the standpoint of the mind, heart, or spirit, depends upon opening up the awareness of time to encompass the dimensional context. We must begin to hear the individual notes of the symphony and not be entirely lost in the totality of the waveform of the music of time, for that engulfs true self-awareness as well as the original perception of "real time." To echo physicist Amit Goswami (*The Self-Aware Universe*), consciousness creates the material world, and this leads to the search for the "quantum mind." Physics continually reaches into areas that are considered metaphysical.

Whether *The Reality of Time* is judged to be physics or metaphysics depends on how restrictive our definition of science is. Certainly verification of these ideas lies beyond the current capability of modern physics. That does not make them any less scientific. This knowledge is based on intuition of higher mathematical ideas beyond present-day apprehension. The writing proceeds from a certain level of freedom from temporal structures, as it must do in order to express temporal unboundedness.

Physics in the last several centuries has endowed us with three major perspectives on time:

1. **Newtonian:** Time is conceived as an unchanging, absolute background for physical reality. This is the commonsense view, which Julian Barbour characterizes as "some invisible river that flows uniformly for ever." Such a notion seems appropriate for the world of everyday experience, in which time is experienced in linear fashion in the familiar form of a definitive past, present, and future common to all viewpoints. However, as classical physics proved inadequate to describe the world of very tiny things, the twentieth century brought a revolution in conceptualizing time and space.

2. **Relativistic:** In this model, time is an aspect of four-dimensional spacetime, which is warped by the presence of matter. Time is also relative to the motion of the observer. The famous "twins paradox" is an example of relativistic, Einsteinian time: If Bob and Sue are twins, and Bob gets on a spaceship leaving Earth and travels close to the speed of light, when he returns to Earth he will have aged many fewer years than Sue has. This is because time "slows down" for an object in motion, although it is only when its speed approaches that of light that the effect is very noticeable. The relativistic theory of spacetime undermines the complacency of the commonsense referential mind. It opens one up to the syntax of time loops, matrices, and curvatures described by Janet Sussman.

3. **Quantum:** "Quantum reality" is often used synonymously to refer to the quirky, quarky subatomic world. Quantum physics further contradicts conventional notions of space and time, and cause and effect, in finding instantaneous connections between physical objects widely separated in space, a notion which caused vexation to Einstein. A promising path for the grand unification of quantum theory with relativity is the study of higher-dimensional superstrings, described lucidly by Brian Greene (*The Fabric of the Cosmos*), and which promises to get us closer to the Holy Grail, the "theory of everything."

Although the quantum nature of time has not been experimentally verified yet, in some theories time, like space, may be "quantized" or differentiated as ultra-tiny units. In the theory of loop quantum gravity as articulated by Lee Smolin (*Three Roads to Quantum Gravity*), time can be quantized in units of approximately 10^{-43} seconds (Planck time). This idea of the discrete nature of spacetime is based on "loops" or representations of the spin of points in diagrams of quantum spatial networks.

In reading Janet's descriptions of "locator points," which are akin to quanta of spacetime, one feels one is glimpsing the cutting edge of modern physics from the perspective of the cause rather than from the effect. In other words, we find ourselves existentially *geworfen* (thrown) into a received reality, a creation that has already emerged and whose causes, physical and metaphysical, we are forever seeking. In this book, reality is not posited as a fait accompli. It is a paradoxical and conscious process like a quantum particle wave whose position cannot be precisely known unless its wave function is "collapsed" in the act of observation. This implicate order that Janet Sussman speaks from and about has no referential value; in terms of human conceptualization, it is unmanifest.

When you collapse the wave function through measurement, quantum physics gives you a definitive value (about where a particle is) but you lose the wave behavior of the quantum system. By doing the measurement, you force the system to lose its indeterminacy. You "pop a qwiff," in the phrase of Fred Alan Wolf (*Taking the Quantum Leap*), which refers to the collapse of a quantum wave in an act of perception. Consciousness is inextricably involved in creating what we call reality, moment to moment. We are all plotting a spacetime map of our personal realities, and the process of how this works, from both the psychological and the physical standpoints, is described in detail in the pages that follow.

Quantum physics supports paradox. In the same spirit, the Sussman description of time is paradoxical, metaphorical, and evocative. The purpose is not to provide a linguistic "measurement" of time's mercurial essence, but to provide a spectrum of possibilities that is so much greater than the reductive referential shadow that time casts upon the mind—a falsely static image. The shift in the perception of time from a fixed, collapsed referentiality to a vibrant, multitemporal dimensional, high-energy reality where past, present, and future are interwoven, is one to which human perception may eventually evolve to encompass.

The Sussman cosmology specifically affirms the existence of parallel universes. According to David Deutsch (*The Fabric of Reality*), the "multiverse" constitutes the whole of physical reality and is based on the quantum interaction of parallel universes. This "many worlds" description of quantum reality, in which alternate universes are splitting off at any given moment, may be cognate with Janet Sussman's frequent discussions of "multidimensional time," in which temporal regions break off from one another.

Theoretical considerations of time inevitably lead to discussion of higher dimensions, parallel universes, black holes, and the possibility of time travel, which has been a popular field for speculation, both in science and science fiction (Paul Nahin, *Time Machines*). Janet Sussman addresses many of these topics but not in the manner common to the many popular books on physics, which use as their starting point basic scientific understandings about physics considered as a purely objective description of the universe. Rather, her approach proceeds from the perspective of the unity of consciousness and time—which invests time with a conscious, creative power that she posits as the underlying reality of the universe. The reality of time becomes at once the truth of the universe that manifests as our personal reality—the world as we know it, and the truth of who we are as conscious, living entities.

The writing in this book has a condensed, gnomic quality that allows one to experience it in small bites, and even at random places. Illumination can occur out of the linear context of the chapter sequence, although it is certainly possible to read it that way, as later chapters build on those that have gone before. The text is holographic, appropriate to the multilayered, multidimensional universe we inhabit.

This is the textbook of the future in which we can glean today the understanding of a unitary physics, metaphysics, philosophy, linguistics, psychology, and spirituality. The truths embedded here will be like time-release capsules, dissolving in the higher mind of readers, activating their imaginations, and imparting a profound and lasting appreciation for the ultimate mystery of our existence in the landscape of time.

preface

how to read this book

there are very few moments of free time that we have each day to read, write or contemplate the events that have transpired. In a time in history when we wish for everything to be instantaneous and simple we have very little room in our lives for the subtleties and complexities of philosophical discussion. We come after words with our heads and not our hearts and try to make sense out of them rather than allowing them to make their way slowly into the inner fire of our own being.

To meet the intensity and the boundary-breaking quality of this writing, it will be necessary to imagine that one is a pioneer. This is a campfire of the soul, a place where one must sit around, gain a deep measure of inner stillness and come to the point of understanding in a slow and sometimes contradictory manner.

Normally, when we read a book, we are careful to follow the train of thought step by step, not wanting to miss any nugget that might give us a clue of what is to come. In the case of this book, one can open it at any point, find a train of being and trace it back to any point along the way. It is like a spider web in which the spindles of silk will keep finding their way back to a central axis, holding the reader prey to deeper understanding. Terms that appear, which at first might seem strange or unclear, will find their way to comprehension through repetition and contextual use, becoming old friends like the words of some ancient but somehow familiar language.

Art, music, theatre can all have reverberations that last long after one has left the venue of their presentation. To read this book, one must visit the pages regularly with the purpose not of complete comprehension but with complete immersion. When the mind is lost, when the heart has found its voice, there is a feeling that time itself has ceased. One has entered some other world that has never before been seen, invoking the sense that there is something startlingly new to which one is witness.

Time waits for no one. Except here, in the pages of this book, time is going to actually step out from within its own framework. Time will wait and ask only that one observe one's reactions to its unfoldment. The quality that time exhibits, from the depth of its truth, is going to speak directly to you the reader. You will be asked only to enter without a definitive feeling that you already know or you wish that you could. Then, suddenly, perhaps when you do not expect it, there will be a profound comprehension, an astonishing awakening to a place within oneself that is both very new and very old. Look into this place, for it is here that the reality of time might come more clearly into view.

introduction

he process of viewing time as a living reality, as an examinable, identifiable field of awareness, is the foundation of *The Reality of Time*. Our common experience of time is one that sees time as a means of measurement, a ruler that describes the interval apportionment of our lives. The perception of time as a field, a groundwork for the establishment of sequences of personal reality, and the mechanics that describe a layered dimensional context are simply unknown to us. This book, as an extension of my first published work in this area, *Timeshift: The Experience of Dimensional Change*, goes deeper into elucidating the many ways of seeing time from its interior. We learn how to view time not as a ruler but as a landscape, a territory of consciousness whereby all of our personal and environmental realities can be understood. We experience time as having movement, shape, and interrelationship to itself as well as to space, motion, and distance.

For those of us for whom reality is based primarily on conceptual frameworks, the study of time and consciousness, as well as the process of cognition itself, is a place of mystery. How can something as ephemeral and abstract as time have a voice, an avenue of self-expression? When one travels down the road of meditation practice, one is treated to the possibility of having knowledge hatch rather than having it be the result of some particular mental application. Time is made known through the context of self-revelation rather than as a course of study engaged in by the intellect. It is, therefore, the journey into the fabric of knowledge that forms the backdrop for this work and the linguistic processes that have been coined to describe its mannerisms. This is a book of scientific etiquette in that it describes the norms, the guises, and the handiwork of time from its own point of view.

The ability to experience time is commonly fostered by two different avenues of awareness. The first is "waking state," which is the place of inner alertness differentiated from sleeping and dreaming. Here, time is experienced within the context of intervals spent or gained. There is little elasticity to this reality. The other avenue is an altered or contemplative state that is traditionally gained through the practice of meditation, breath work, or martial arts. Here the sense of time can be suspended for long intervals, producing a feeling of euphoric or absolute freedom from psychological strife.

A third context, spoken of in many spiritual traditions, involves the gaining of lucidity in the sleep state. This practice creates the opportunity for a bridge between the higher mind and the practical mechanics of everyday life. When one enters a prolonged period of wakefulness in the context of sleep, the experimental and imaginative forces of the superconscious can set the groundwork for fundamental research into the nature of intelligence. The combination of intuitional and imaginative faculties, in concert with the template of pure awareness, sets the stage for the self-descriptive component. The language that approximates the recognition of subtle mechanics is voiced through the personal dialogue that the human mind constructs to recognize the symptomatic outpouring of personal reality.

All of these contexts are apt to overlook what I would call the choreography of time, the dance that invokes the mechanical unfoldment of temporal agility. How does time move in the spiral of our personal events? What does it mean to study the sequencing of time, to approach it as one would analyze a great symphony or work of art?

Due to the overriding nature of the higher mental faculties, when one consistently surrenders to their predominance, a permanent sense of objectivity emerges. This state, often referred to as "witnessing," is produced when the personal mind enters a profound release into self-observance that is often accompanied by a sense of tranquility. When the keenness of contemplative practice is combined with the stabilization of this clear, objective window on the mechanics of the mind, a new reality emerges. In this reality, the structure of thinking probes deeply into the fundamental basis of silence even while the problem-solving and mechanical aspects of intelligence remain functional. This integration provides the opening necessary for creative achievement that inherently offers a high degree of originality.

Artists, musicians, and scientists of great merit often exhibit a high degree of sensitivity, both to their inner world and to the environment. Their capacity to engage in the process of witnessing, combined with an affinity towards imaginative enterprise, produces a surge of visual, auditory, and linguistic experimentation that deeply influences collective consciousness.

The question arises as to how the purely yogic practices, with their emphasis on returning to the inner core of being, interface with the life of the creative spirit, with its inherent restlessness and unwillingness to settle into the habit of silence. When one taps into the heart of any field of knowledge, as one does in these yogic practices, there is a type of "call and response" that brings one to a felt sense of awakening. There is a call, a question that occurs from the psychological level, and a response that is generated from a deeper order of being. At the fundamental layer of human consciousness resides a cushion of pure awareness. Knowledge gained through this steady, refined research takes one into a uniquely languaged voice composed of the very impulses to which one is attuned.

The question arises as to the possibility that a radical change in the construction of time values could knock a person off course from his or her personal reality. From my point of view, time bends, coils, or spins around the apparent options of personal activity and perception that come into play. Through the spin that time provides, an event is indeed altered but its alteration is not something to be feared. This shift is the natural outcome of a change in the rate, speed, and flow of consciousness. The feeling of "rightness" of a given course of action is always considered in the context of such a change.

There is a type of temporal disorientation that can be evoked when the change in the time flow is faster than the psychological and physiological processes are capable of digesting. This type of temporal break, which I have also experienced, can indeed be frightening. But with practice one can learn to stand in the middle of such a situation and shift just slightly the flow of consciousness so as to bring things into a state of apparent normalcy.

As one's ability to process time becomes increasingly more rapid, the ability to cognize the significance of these sequences does not always keep up. This is how a gap can be formed between one's ability to travel or journey into other domains or dimensions of temporal experience but not feel entirely comfortable once the destination has been reached. Temporal acclimatization is brought about through the yogic practices of witnessing, observation, and breathing techniques which keep the psychological and physiological processes stabilized as the temporal references are altered. Constant practice appears to be the key.

The truth is that most human beings find that their desire for self-investigation is usually brought about through some aspect of personal suffering. Our desire for access to heightened states of happiness or at least a degree of equilibrium is the predecessor to much of what we think of as spiritual attainment. The burning desire to enter into union with what one begins to experience as a pure state of inner light or clarity drives one to continue to engage in practices that will bring about such a shift. A type of momentum builds that opens one to lift free of the everyday clatter of activity and enter realms more conducive to the sense of freedom.

The sense of passing opportunity, the process of physical and psychological aging, produces a pressure to gain access to an unlimited experience of time. One is freed from the pursuit of triviality for the more attractive option of open-ended lucidity. When the will for outer achievement is temporarily set aside, time naturally enters a state of suspension. Restlessness is conquered as one engages with heretofore unknown areas of knowledge.

The entry into the silent, expectant world of temporal alteration or suspension occurred very early in my personal life. Contemporary psychological thinking tends to associate such a shift with the need to escape from pain. In my own case, this may be true, but if so it was the pain of wanting to get to the bottom of the innermost being rather than any acute trauma of environmental origin. The passion for a depth of self-exploration has been with me for as long as I can remember, and without it most assuredly certain breakthroughs between the everyday personality and that of the super-conscious would not have come about.

When I was a child, sleep was the venue whereby consciousness could consume itself with the process of knowing and return to the soul's most familiar abode. There, resting within that state, alert to the process of perception, I was soon able to retrieve information gained through a direct dialogue with the inner voice. Such understanding was often pictorial, colorful, and holographic. It was filled with symbology that was often indecipherable in the immediate context of an immature mind.

With the advent in my twenties of more intensive spiritual practice, the ability to retrieve information not usually accessible through traditional courses of study became more dependable. At first, this took the form of what appeared to be a sort of university of the spirit, in which one could take classes in any area of the arts or sciences. These classes seemed to be populated by others such as myself who wished to understand areas of knowledge that one could not learn from a book. I eventually understood these classroom experiences to be symbolic, a picture that the mind had constructed for hallways of learning that would be comfortable to the personal identity.

It was obvious from the first that one of the ways I could recognize whether I had hit the mark in these investigations was the powerful sense of floating in a timeless, fluid state. Time became elongated, resituated, placed in a context in which any pretense of age, limitation, or boundaries was immediately lost. It soon became clear that it was time itself that was attempting to speak to me about its very nature. A system of language or structure of thinking was developed that became quite coherent and repeatable.

In the beginning, the ability to retrieve this language was fragmented. Little sound bites would enter my waking consciousness as if brought up from the darkly lit vantage point of a dream. Gradually, this language became more succinct, though clearly different from the usual way that words and phrases would normally present themselves. This novel use of language permitted the mechanics of temporal experience to be intelligible to the conscious mind.

All of this, when described, seems very temperate, even perfunctory, but the actual unfoldment of this dialogue bore a closer resemblance to the dramatic intensity of a great film than to the emotional atmosphere of everyday existence. The surges of feeling, actual heat in the body, remain to this day of great intensity, which I came to learn bore witness to the presence of what yogic thinkers call "shakti," or the workings of a higher order of the human nervous system.

Why does it appear that most people fear the unfoldment of a superconscious awareness? Is the fear based on the need to hold fast to the norms of social and personal convention, or is the reason more involved? My personal feeling is that there is a root apprehension about moving out of the temporal landscape that defines and describes the boundaries of reality. One could say that the two greatest fears human beings possess are of insanity and death. Breaking temporal confines immediately invokes both issues.

For this reason, I have had to personally address the type of terror invoked when one is no longer utilizing the strategies of psychological and/or material reference to keep the mind or heart stable. In this new state of being, one must draw exclusively from the pool of inner silence and attributeless activity that makes it possible for time to stand still. The amazing thing is that when time actually does arrest its propensity to move forward, one discovers it can actually move at great rapidity in any conceivable direction. One learns to travel with the flow or stream of time as it presents itself, intently focused on the area of knowledge or flow of feeling encountered.

My first attempt to articulate the voice or language of time occurred after the shock of a hurricane which swept through my home in Charlotte, North Carolina, in the spring of 1989. I now think it is not surprising that such an event would be an effective internal prompter for the development of an original temporal language. Like physical pain or trauma of an interior sort, the power of natural disaster is an effective vehicle for inspiring self-examination and reawakening. Swept clean of familiar references in the physical landscape—trees, buildings, power lines—the mind was returned to the condition of emptiness that could best bring about a new vantage point for time.

Hurricane Hugo acted as a temporal wall of fire that brought what had been a private, subjective understanding into public recognition. The development of the manuscript for *Timeshift: The Experience of Dimensional Change* came about through this experience. As the printed words were viewed on the page, something powerful and startling occurred. For the first time the actual description of a purely internal journey came fully into awareness. There was a natural inclination to deny or resist this transition. It was as if something totally intimate, contained, was now fully exposed.

In the over-ten-year period of integration that ensued, I gained the ability to more fully enter into the domain where this avenue of intelligence could be found. It seemed that the willingness to share, to give voice to this material, now made it possible for it to become more coherent, retrievable, and understandable. A profound unification was taking place between that part of my identity that was the writer of such extraordinary material and that part existing in its own psychological constructs separate from any superlative state. This process continues to this day.

I desired to go still further, to bring the reader/participant into a more comprehensive understanding of the challenge and grandeur invoked through breaking the time barriers. Surprisingly, there was also the lingering fear, the concern of my personality structure that it would be exposed, revealed, or hurt. I now think that this emotion is built into the territoriality inherent in human beings to preserve their sense of personal identity as well as their bailiwick of referential time.

The reality is that time exists as a pure template, a backdrop behind the activities and psychological interlays that make up human life. This type of time—free, unfettered, and uncontained by the intricacies of events or emotions—is what can be termed nonreferential time. In contrast, referential time is personal, highly subjective, and based on the inner calendar of our deepest apprehensions, memories, and associations. It is inherently unfree, bound continuously by the movement of the mind. Once one gains access to the unmapped territory of unreferenced time, one can begin to perceive how the natural waves or curves in this ocean of silence invoke the possibilities of creation. There is a stillness behind the possibility of choice that opens out into the awareness like a graceful ribbon of perception. Time exists as a superimprintable reality, a surface structure of labile movements of history, personal attributes, and relationships, which are composites of a type of universal geography known only to the mind of God.

Time has motion; it is not static, opaque, without life, color, shape, or form. There is white time, grey time, and time without attributes, a cosmic twilight that lives in a state of suspended animation. There is also a colorful time, a painterly time, a time filled with the mosaic of life. These contrasting qualities, time as sparkling or dull, time as empty or teeming with infinite spectroscopy, make up the inner living eye of men and women. When one brings the two together, an alchemical magic appears—there is a feeling that one is floating, collapsed in the bubble of unified perception. One loses the environmental cues that signify orientation, encapsulation, or form. It is here, in this awakened, full, exciting, and sometimes terrifying state of vertigo, that one lives when the nervous system wakes up to an atemporal point of view.

This book is an attempt to reckon with this sometimes brilliant, sometimes subtle, sometimes noisy, sometimes intensely quiet environment, which is the reality of time awake. It is the story of time talking for itself, speaking its own truth. It is also time colored by the history, patterning, and understanding of a subjective nervous system and life experience. If time could speak for itself, this is its opportunity.

To come to terms with this atemporal reality, one needs to come into contact with the Divine, spacious, indescribable presence that lives in each of us. It is this presence that is capable of supercreative acts and can make words, sounds, or visual pictures that take us beyond the mind. To do that requires more than a suspension of disbelief. We are asked to actually suspend time, to enter a higher mind that is silent to the core. When we enter this lightless, colorless, soundless refuge, we leave behind our previous notion of reality. We are left in awe of that which is perpetually creating itself.

Spiritual energy, which pursues the individual rather than the reverse, invokes a delightful animation of spirit that makes it easier to shed the coat of conformity. The inner contest that the mind invokes to stifle this process is the reason why creative acts are born in the first place. The mind desires to curtail the flow of time, to smother it in the jaws of psychological insecurity. It is the job of the heart, enriched by the courage of outrageous acts born of temporal originality, to enter completely into the current. To do this, the pulse, the pace, the stream of time must be realized in the heart. Time must burn through the heart completely before it can make a permanent home.

The loss of the personal "I" naturally occurs when time has broken through the boundaries of the heart, instilling the individual with a quality of fearlessness. Before this absence of fear occurs, there is often an intensification of it. This is because the ego structure rarely will give up without struggle. One comes to accept that when one surrenders to the spiritual presence, nothing can be held back. Cobra-like in its intensity, mirroring all of the different aspects of dimensional perception, the Divine strips us of the notion that time can exist separate from that which is. This is how the creative process operates once it is set free. It is the way of time.

The Reality of Time seeks to elucidate some of the conceptual keys that make it possible to understand a non-timebound awareness. Like *Timeshift*, it does so by invoking the rapid advance of interior language as it courses through the nervous system without any room for mental censorship. The attempt here is to expose this highly charged creative process as well as the subject of time it seeks to describe. If the reader feels altered, unglued, less opaque through the course of the work, then I feel the book has been a success.

Janet Iris Sussman
Fairfield, Iowa
November 2004

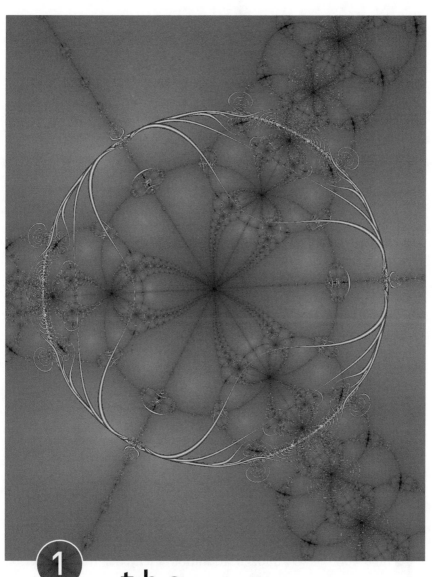

1

the
Structure
of
Time

1.1
time, space, and matter

1.1.1
stepping into time

The Principles of Perception

time is the principal perceiver of perception. Through time we understand the world around us and its relationship to our innermost thoughts, desires, and expectations. Since time is not based on sensory perception divorced from our physiological makeup, it must be viewed as an extension of the primary source of our being, the pure awareness that courses through every cell in our body.

Time rests on the fundamental assumption that there are lapses, pauses, or curtailments to the continuity of our understanding and its inherent stature. To work within the confines of these lapses, the nervous system creates a synchrony of movement that prevents us from becoming too independent, too far out of range of our individualized time stream. Each individual is riding on a jet stream, a taper of fluid, unrealized being that mirrors the comet-like flow of matter/energy of universal causality. This jet stream is tailor-made to the individual's needs, wants, and predetermined attributes. The individual learns to alter these time streams to fit judiciously into the context of his or her point of view.

As time works its way through the mirror of reflection that each person generates, it creates a map, a blueprint, a type of causal circuit that lets the individual know where he or she will fall in reference to each event of life. As the person approaches a choice, a moment of preference, the nervous system registers chemical cues that invite the person to move towards a particular trajectory. This process is inherently smooth and seamless, except for periods when the person faces some conflict or indecision. In this psychological territory, the phenomenon of worry can block or impair the natural rhythm or flow of time within the subset of that individual's core patterning. Here the individual meets up with a tear in the fabric of perception that can interfere with the natural mechanism of choice that has come into play.

Time is like a wagon. It pulls all of the individual players along, seeking to assemble them in preplanned bunches or groups, assimilable according to their rate of activity, longevity, and fields of motion. Because the hues or colors of time are dependent on the flow of development of each individual jet stream or ray of perception, time is not soluble through the mechanism of an individual's lone activities. Time flows through the range of collective markers, creating a pattern that rides the wave of many, many collectively stored databases. Each marker that time collects is experienced as a turn, a blink in the eye of a single sentient being.

Time exists as a mathematical model as well as a perceptual one. Time is expressed as an algorithm, a formulaic repetitive pattern that is designated to perform a set of operations. In the case of time, these operations are mathematical, as in a set of proven and recurrent data stretched over a block of time to describe or create a certain landscape. The algorithm can be framed or referenced as a series of graphic impressions to describe a similar set of temporal circumstances.

Since time collects through an algorithmic pool of "weak-" or "strong-minded" data, it must rely on its own arithmetic timetable to make sure that what is to be accomplished is truly accurate. Weak data are like the mathematical rivulets that bind a more coherent data stream to its express purpose. They are possibilities not fully or easily derived from that which has been assembled previously. Strong data, which are easily trackable and more readily assembled, serve to prove or formulate an individuated action. They are also involved in accounting for a fixed rate of activity. Time "gardens" these seemingly unrelated sets of mathematical objects, tracking them through two principles: the law of randomization and the law of opposites.

The Law of Randomization

The governing law of randomization states that when two event streams come together, one will always spontaneously overtake the other. Random operation means variety. Variety is the stage onto which the different players that make up the time epistemology can be divested of any colors that are not ripe for play. Randomization insures that there will always be categories that have not been "up for sale," that the flow of data will always be new, spicy, and original. Randomization casts doubt on the understanding that the divine plan is a type of governable or predictable force of reason.

Time creates reason out of its own memories rather than relying on the temporal cues of any one individual or civilization. As a result, the randomized, uncompartmentalized flow of time maintains a type of civility, a flow of apparently irreconcilable forces, even though their interior makeup, from a psychological perspective, may not be fully grasped.

Due to the feeling of terror evoked by randomization, human beings try to control their perceptual universe through creating conflict. This conflict mirrors the second governing law of time, which is the law of opposites. This insures that once a time value is crisply woven into the network of perception, its partner, its mirror image, will always come into view. This dualistic dialogue, which maintains the core separation of time from the object, is the source of great consternation to those of us who are constantly trying to make all our possibilities resolve into one. Due to the dualistic nature of time, the ensuing possibilities are always liable to break apart and crystallize into an array of nonparticulate form, color, and shape. These possibilities explicate the grandeur of individuated reality, but they also appear to cause suffering on the part of individuals, families, and nations.

Within the interaction between randomized values and opposite values lies the possibility of complete and ultimate unification. This possibility forms the backdrop for the spiritual and psychological quest that individuals of the current millennium will be coaxed, if not forced, to undertake. This quest involves a turnaround in our understanding of time as a fixed, uninspired journey in which we have to "pay our dues" and go forward despite any obstacles or unforeseen avenues of perception that come our way. In the future, our journey on the road of time will be to understand how reality itself is formulated. It is a quest that involves mirroring the very underpinnings of the mechanics of time from the core level of our awareness, and arriving at a godlike understanding that heretofore may have been viewed as impossible, or at least quite rare.

The founding metaphor for time is its ability to gain thunder through forward, ever-striding movement. The gain that time achieves through this activity is that it becomes self-thinking, self-generating, and self-renewing. It provides an avenue for a core shift in the matrix of causality, which brings about the interior mechanics for dimensional interlacement. Time enacts a retributive or parliamentary stance with regard to all of the activities that come under its charge. It is simply democratic in its attempt to right various wrongs, restore order, and make things appear to be essentially good or clear. What time does not do is describe the reason behind such decisions. This is up to the viewer. The inherent arbitrator in the court of time is therefore the individual him- or herself.

The Patterns of Universal Causality

There are four standards of deviation that time depends on to originate its pattern of universal causality. First, the *pattern of uniformity* strips time of any randomization and leaves it solely to its own perceptual cues. Second, the *pattern of enchained opposites* creates a string of memories, analogous points of reference, and standards of reason, looped together through the power of the mind. Third, the *pattern of anomaly* is unusual in its ability to make abnormal what our fixed mental concepts might ordinarily see as normal. Fourth, the *pattern of sameness* creates a searing set of questions that defy the laws of reason and compress time into stages that can be fully studied as the systematic development of consciousness unfolds.

Since time governs the flavor as well as the tempo of reality, time cannot be hitched solely to the lamppost of reason. Time itself is the purveyor of reality and as such cannot be limited to any temporal curves or curlicues that human sentience might present. Therefore, to understand time, the human being must research the very makeup of his or her interior framework. One develops an experience of the flow or dialectical output of time that spurs one to mirror the streams of time that seek representation.

Time is an equal opportunity employer. That is, time recognizes that each opportunity is advantageous, singularly pure or unique, and creates the physiological and psychological breakfronts that make choice grow in the minds and hearts of individuals. Since there is "no time like the present," time gobbles up all of the other possibilities and makes this moment, this stream of opposites, entirely unique, fresh, and to the point. Within the range of causality, time strips down everything that would interfere with the perfect garden, the perfect row of honored tulips that would make individuation entirely plausible.

The inherent nonstandard tone of time builds up over long periods of earth memory. To each individual person, time is elongated, stretched, broken apart, and re-ribboned due to the tonality of his or her own musical interlude. To the ripened gardener of time, each moment becomes a seed, a crystallizable window into the opportunity to regain his or her stride, to move beyond impediments and to gain access to an invincible, ever-growing sunlight.

Time and consciousness derive their meaning through the standardization of events. Events are simply cues, encapsulations of time that have now crystallized for the purpose of materialization. Since time and matter must interweave for the purpose of dimensional restitution, time and matter dialogue through the patterns of events that human beings interlay. Matter is a friend to time. Matter relates the events that time is attempting to lay down and creates the mechanism whereby these events can come into material view.

Materialization and the Godhead

Materialization is relative, of course. There are degrees of realization, from pure to highly grained, in the optical networks that make up the mirror of universal order. Materialization at its core is the attempt by the Godhead to fundamentally outlaw those vehicles of time and space that are not in accordance with the natural flow of land, sea, and air. The gods, in their infinite capacity to view and analyze the flow of events, create material order out of seemingly endless and apparent chaos. It is only we human folk who make this return to the succinct chaos from which it all sprang.

Time is like a rainbow. Its colorations are myriad. The shades of time form the backdrop for what is called its "slope." This term implies a type of graphic display of up or down which, like scaling a vast mountain or navigating a perilous sea, gives one a sense of accomplishment. The slope is the mathematical equivalent of an ice skating rink in which all of the skaters will fall or dive according to precise marker points on the rink. The slope determines who will fall, dive, weave, or bob, who will sink and even perish under the ice! The significant effect of slope therefore cannot be overestimated, because it is the slope of time that creates the possibility of time-honored paradigms of apparent indecision that affect civilizations as well as individual travelers.

And what about time travel? How is it that one can actually go from one point to another in time? How is it that a traveler can arrive here from some dimensional outpost altogether different from what we would know as reality? To understand this, we must recognize that temporal references are always paradimensional; that is, they are split like logs to accommodate different measures of heat, frame of reference, and activity, much as the fuel for a fire. First we have the kindling, the beginning dimensional reference points. They build the heat, get the juices going, and create the sparks out of which other dimensional reference points will be built. Much like the teepee shape that is used to build a campfire, the dimensional spirals coil around each other in a type of triangulating heap which interweave and ring about each other with an impending and awesome grandeur.

The dimensions are like heavens; they are like maps of the interstices of God's mind. They form the "brain of the world" and live simultaneously and comfortably within their nested configurations until someone strategically "cracks" or interferes with their confinement. Then they can splay out, interweave mysteriously, and create unusual opportunities for individuals or whole civilizations to meet on the crossroads and find originating opportunities that would not have normally occurred.

Dimensions of a Heavenly Kind

Dimensional reality is fundamental reality. That is, the laws of time and space govern how a dimensional surface or interlude will be reached. Due to the fact that time and space are limitless, their parent companies, the dimensional superstructures that build them, are also unlimited. There cannot be any causal highway that does not lead to future and past simultaneously. Therefore, one could say that in some respects time and consciousness redirect dimensional activity and give it the "fluffiness" that makes it particularly sweet. Time and matter live within the dimensional boundaries that the Godhead sets out for them. However, it may be said that in some respects time precedes or actually creates the activity of the Divine rather than in the reverse.

The Temporal Geography of Nation-States

According to the concept of "nation-states" or individual event pools, time and consciousness interweave and form vestibules of activity. Time creates a type of interstellar civilization in which different related streams of causal opposites can come together for the purpose of divine relationship. The purpose of temporal nation-states is the patterning of opposites in each dimensional ring or subset. These nation-states are controlled not by sentience as we know it, but by a flow of attitudinal godmind within each subsection of space/time that the event stream represents. God and consciousness control the event spirals as they tumble and fall, and time, in its need for freedom, always causes these event spirals to tumble into the limitless chasm of pure infinity.

This book is an attempt to reconcile how time can become so fashionably infinite and so gloriously fixed in the mind of Man at the same time. How can time be both breathless and full of air, so insufferable and so ecstatic, and how can anyone, seer or common person, ever hope to understand its complexities and its point of view? Of course, it is impossible to understand the ineffable, but it is possible to wrestle with it and to grasp the strategic imprints that it makes on the mind, heart, and soul of individual human beings.

The reality of time is therefore an adventure into the heart of the mind/matter spiral that records the data that describe human restlessness and dispiritedness, as well as celestial activity. It is by examining the underpinnings of the subtle mechanics of individual perception, as well as the principles of uniformity, randomization, and opposite strategies, that the flavor of time can be most easily assimilated. Time is the purveyor of all that is good in the human experience. Without time we would have no measure of what is and no signpost for what would be. Therefore, to investigate, unwrap, and dialogue with the interior mysteries of time gives us the possibility of understanding the everyday mechanics of our own lives, and the more fabulous strategies that whole planetary civilizations seek to undertake. Time makes us visionaries, and with a visionary outlook one could say that anything, even the alteration of the seemingly permanent, is possible.

1.1.2
the relationship
of time and space

The Interpretation of Reality

the frequencies of time-derivative information can best be articulated through the ability of the nervous system to catalogue information as it is fed through the upper chakral area. The time variables are translated through the upper energy matrix and fed directly into the subtle bodies of the human being.

Time provides the backdrop for the individual to interpret reality, both psychologically and physically. The perceptual base of the visual field is formed by the interweaving of time relationships in the context of individual consciousness. Time in its pure state is stripped of event or precedence. It lives completely independently of any prescribed variables, but is also directly subject to them.

As time is imprinted into the human energy matrix, the individual is able to record the calendar of daily activities and idea formations, deriving a sense of personal identity or core beliefs. These beliefs or energy pathways form the basis for the individual's knowledge of his or her internal life. Human beings keep such information throughout a lifetime. Even during periods of deep sleep the essential fabric of the mind is directly maintained.

For time to become free-moving and independent of the structures placed upon it, it has to learn to move past these areas of fixed internal perception. The open-ended expression of consciousness gives rise to the time variables becoming original or expansive in their character.

The key here, in terms of originality, is in the velocity of time. Time maintains a certain speed of interpretation in the brain and central nervous system that causes the individual to feel emotionally present and stable. When these time derivatives are destabilized, the individual's primary orientation to both physical and emotional reality is severely altered. Most individuals do not have enough flexibility and stamina in the energy pathways to tolerate their dimensional reference points being shaken. This is why temporal conformity, even in the dormancy of sleep, is maintained.

Ripping the Cloak off Awareness

As the individual becomes stronger in the establishment of pure or transcendental consciousness, he or she rips the fabric off the cloak of awareness and arrives at a point in which original interpretation of dimensional existence begins. Until this time, the individual's reality is painted by the events, circumstances, and objects of perception, and not by consciousness itself.

Once the individual enters the universal time state, he or she is mapping or cognizing the flow of time/consciousness as it forms the background for reality, rather than confusing that characterization as reality itself. As the individual enters this state of being, he or she is freed from all time constraints and can move forward and backward, both through the fixed variables of apparently normal reality and the more advanced state of fluid or non-opaque reality.

The ability to see objects as fields or waveform frequencies of consciousness/matter would be too disorienting for most individuals and would not create a solid psychological resting point. As the individual becomes more secure in consciousness, the environment becomes a dynamic interplay of color, sound, and light and the individual learns to create processes which mirror this reality.

He or she becomes capable of playing with the energy/matter continuum as he or she sees it and imprinting this interplay into the fabric of everyday activity. Such an individual is less time derivative than his or her counterparts and is thus able to incorporate a wider range of time variables into his or her personal vocabulary. This creates a situation in which time can grow on itself, bringing the quality of infinity into the finite.

The juxtaposition of the infinite with the fixed brings about a situation in which gradually the individual can view him- or herself directly from the original structure of consciousness that brought the persona into being. He or she can view the persona as a trick of time rather than taking it so seriously. Then the persona can gradually fall away.

Shifting the Time Codes

The time codes of an individual who is moving into more advanced interdimensional frequencies are less fixed. The person sees waves or bands of time outpouring into the fabric of reality on a continual basis. The individual feels that time is on his or her side, that he or she can accomplish what is necessary because the waves of consciousness that are making the individual events are being moved in the direction of independence. This is startling at first, and can cause dissonance with the fixed reality of action.

When the individual is still living in a reality that requires a clock time basis for functioning and he or she is already experiencing time as inherently fluid and nonfixed, a type of internal conflict and discomfort can result. The time/consciousness framework must become so fully integrated that essentially the individual is living in both time reference points at once. He or she is able to function within the conformed context of consensus reality, and also to develop the freedom and independence to exist in a multidimensional framework.

Without this dualistic style, the individual will find that he or she is limited either in consciousness development or in his or her ability to function successfully in a limited dimensional vantage point. Those beings that are highly integrated can fill the shoes of any dimensional context and still maintain the full measure of absolute awareness. Thus the unification occurs at every level—mental, emotional, and spiritual—and never wavers. Such integration is rare, however.

Beyond the Mind

Time cannot be manipulated by the mind. Time is not a mental function but rather one of consciousness and the ordering power of the universe. Therefore, attempting to manipulate time for one's own purposes never succeeds. Time cannot be controlled any more than the power of consciousness itself can be controlled. Those who attempt to manipulate time for their own purposes are using the ego function in a detrimental manner.

The ego must surrender to the immediacy of time, thereby taking a back seat to the velocity and frequency of variables as they are sent throughout the energy matrix. No individual can see him- or herself as the controller of time and still maintain a cognitive and sacred relationship with the creation itself. This is how the spiritual attributes of the nervous system are refined and developed. The individual ego structure begins to recognize where his or her volitional input might interfere with activity and then chooses to get out of the way.

The ego structure cannot be fully healed or recalibrated without the time variables becoming the main causality behind free action. The ego structure cannot change itself; it is interdependent with the consciousness matrix for its freedom. Therefore, as time becomes more "chewable," more available to the body/mind, the individual can become fully independent and maintain his or her balance in all contexts.

Time is the great purveyor of life's secrets. As time becomes more fluid, each overriding influence of time decloaks reality and lets it breathe a modicum of air. Time tells consciousness how to reveal both material and psychological reality. What human beings fail to realize is that their psychology is extremely dependent on context. The visual circumstances of their surroundings cause them to think in more defined ways. It is difficult to step out of what is possible. In order, therefore, for more time-derivative freedom to be available, the individual has to create new contexts. The question is what would such contexts look like?

In these new contexts, the individual no longer has to cling to the opaqueness of objects but is free to explore the light value inherent in every form. This causes him or her to develop objects that straddle the plane between solid and gross. The individual can live in both worlds and coast between the refined variables that he or she is experiencing.

The Transparency of Objective Reality

This transition to objects that are not completely solid in their visual acuity and their actual functioning is the first step in living in a world that is not strictly time dependent. As long as the environment is fixed and the psychology must continue to view it as such, time independence cannot be won.

This is the value of forming some sort of a garden or light matrix laboratory in which time can be the banner of consciousness and the stage can be set for the development of a nonsolid reality. Objects that are interdimensional are never locked into an opaque variable. They move between subtle and gross continually because they are not locked into the constraints of a strict time agenda. This is the science of the future. When science can unlock reality and allow it to move between manifestation and nonmanifestation, then a whole new range of truly consciousness-based technology can come into play. Otherwise, we are still living in fixed time and cannot bridge to the absolute in any permanent way.

1.1.3
the linear functioning of curved reality

Linear Perception and the Curvature of Time

urved reality implies that there is a central, positive, unified whole around which the probable realities of time spin. Time modifies itself in a linear spread to fit the psychological constructs that make up human reason. In its natural or unified state, time is essentially seamless, whole, and unrefined. The locator points that arise as time situates itself within the boundaries of the whole can be described as "catascopic" or catapult-like integer formations, which move randomly from one to infinity, propelling time along in bunches or ribbons of solid, independent light.

Linear perception is derived when time drops off, creating a distinctive crossover between the light-based, smooth derivatives which describe time in a kind of endless cross weave, and the circular, curving arc of time that gives time shape in the world of form. Each locator point is a kind of marker that gives time the ability to tend to different points on a linear scale and develop a system of breaks or schisms which lets time unlock myriad points of view. Each set of locator points functions as a type of spin center, like that of a spinner on a game board, causing time to flex and fall back onto its different centers of operation and develop parallel or circuitous systems of real-time motion.

Locator Points and Parallel Movement

The system of reality that humans set in motion is based on the reorganization of locator points, which creates a parallel movement in time. We rely on the convergence of these points over a particular interval to organize our reality into psychological "bunches" that appear like ribbons or knots one after the other in quick succession. Each of these ribbons forms a series of event streams that we associate with given story formations of our personal lives. When an individual evolves into higher states of consciousness, the personality, with its many distortions based on personal need or opportunity, is left in a separate state, and the larger, more expanded field acts to reorganize all of the possible future scenarios into a more open, noncontainable landscape. Such an individual attains avenues of perception from the level of pure awareness, and the syndicated streams of reason, which heretofore

13

colored the points of choice, authentically disappear.

The vanishing lines, which are like the pinnacle apertures of each event horizon, open freshly into the curves in time, causing the randomization of possibilities from every perspective. These randomized systems of event foundation may be termed "acronomic" in the sense that they are infinite, nonlinearly based readouts of the point derivatives as they spread and give rise to transpersonal reality.

The locator points cannot be limited to scale since they represent the forwards and backwards movement of time without definable aperture or distance. Time stands on its end and cannot be limited or confined to any fixed angle. In groups or "dockets," the locator points function as flyaways from one set of random, stationary movements to another. They are the resting points between fixity and pure infinity. Stacks or sandwiches of locator points rest like fields of layered reality, holding within them the seeds for infinite perceptual realization and understanding. One could say that time sends "fly balls" or uncatchable, unknowable items of perception into the infinite horizon of events, locating a precise, knowable trajectory and trapping it in its glove.

The Pictographic Representation of Time

In the third dimension, in which we presently reside, time develops the ability to freeze-frame reality, which forms the basis for psychological interpretation. We live in a type of temporal linguistic stream, which is paginated on the basis of reason and then bends in our own frame of choice. Time is pictographically coded through a binary system of "dot-dash" formations, which locate our points of reference in the nonlinear highway. In linear time, the space/time variables bunch up together, creating ragged, braced surfaces onto which "tags" or markers find their place. This creates a system whereby the tag breaks off, creating a cue to the time lords, the divine governing forces of time, that infinity is no longer programmable from that point of reference. This causes the time breaks, which lead to the degrees of magnitude we view in this dimension.

Time, because it is both angular and refractive, relies on the curved system of relayed impulses to create maximum heave in the "death curve," i.e., the change from one spiral of refraction to another. The system of refractive integers places time in the position in which it can become a host barometer for numerous values as they coast along. When pulled into the seam or fabric of reality, these mathematical constructs create a passageway for time to become mobile, translucent, and lean.

For the human mind to interpret the angularity of time, we create possible futures or ribbons of light that interpose themselves before us like a huge explosion of interpretive possibility. The mind grasps at this array from its own unique angles, developing strategies for the implementation of meaning and fundamental perception. Time remains transitory until the time breaks arrange themselves over the surface area they are destined to contact, practicing self-elimination on the basis of the highest integral formation for each passage back to infinity.

Changes in the Temporal Pattern

Anomalies in the temporal pattern form the structure for event sequences. The arrangement of time-based sequences is positioned to form repositories for the angular streams of electromagnetic energy. These repositories act as buttresses against the breaks. Time breaks are electromagnetically coded so that any one sequence can be lifted clean from its original temporal imprint and show up as a "ghost" or buffer in the next sequence of events. Event streams are angular because they are interpreted through a process of refraction that bounces them off each other to form rivulets or streams of related but often dissimilar patterns of light/time. The process of organizing time in this manner sets the stage for the electromagnetic signals that determine the temporal language interpreted through the human nervous system. They are stylistically elegant imprints that develop into the first streams of language, and allow the temporal markings to become separate, distinct, and random when necessity demands.

Since time and space are equidistant, and retain their spatial superiority through checks and balances in the time-wave function, linguistic patterns of temporal interaction are the main means of ascertaining temporal function. The maximization of temporal functioning is due to the introduction of language, which describes and gives birth to each successive interpretational point. Time breaks are smoother, more even, and less inclined to splinter or fracture once they are lined up in delicate fashion by the intricacies of the mind. Time is standardized by the laws of motion, which cause event streams to break off or peak at given ranges of opportunity. Time moves or schisms without thought, but once the mind is engaged, the temporal language that gives us the information necessary to paint a picture of life is made synchronous and coherent.

Systems of language have been developed that accommodate the synthesized motion which scoots time along on the surface of our interpretive reality. We acknowledge a temporal potentiality, which is at once wholly based on reason and wholly based on the flow of temporal objects as they mirror themselves along the horizon of our personal reality. From this perspective, time can only be understood on a limited basis, formed through the functional means whereby language and objects are given reference.

Weaving the Language of Light

Time is intimately interwoven with the language of light. For time to receive the messages that create personal reality it must translate light into "codicles" of precise meaning and efficacy. Time and light live alongside each other as friends and companions. They provide the ballast for the event cataclysm that must arise when the infinite pattern of "nothing" meets the intricate pattern of the whole. Light language, though essentially angular in refraction, meets the time stream head-on, creating a synthesis of development between the real or fixed time break and its curved ancestor. Light language leans heavily on synthesis, blending the folds of circuitous time into a blanket that can be read logistically and interpreted. Since time and space coexist in a type of wholistic uniformity, they are often misinterpreted as indistinct. However, as one becomes sensitive to the underlying basis of reality and its reliance on the flow of mass through many conduits, one understands that time precedes matter and fundamentally creates its uniformity over and over again.

The parallel dimensional backdrop of each civilization is mirrored in its reliance on time. Cultures that rely on time as linearly based also see civilization as a type of cognitive history with event streams interpreted for their consequential description of the whole. Cultures that utilize time independently of event streams view reality as a blanket, with events wrapped up in the matrix as a type of stream of consciousness model for collective integration. Time and space live conjointly, holding their own in the absolute.

Nonlinear Time Formats

As the time spreads curve back on themselves, they do not share the territory of expressed motion in the same way as they would in a linear context. In linear time, the loops or spins of time that create order or distance are defined radially; that is, they are organized according to precise spins or precision juxtapositions in the space/time continuum. In the case of nonlinear time, each expressed interval of time shoots out from a precise vantage point, forming clusters or "spreads" that are so thoroughly randomized as to be indistinguishable from one cycle to another. The time spreads that form the stripes of nonlinear time cannot be pictured in a perfectly predictable or unalterable chain of progression. By their very nature they have an enhanced radiance or afterglow that makes them stand out from their more linear cousins. The enhanced radiance of nonlinear time is due to its ability to perform gallantly from one time curve to another.

Space/time must withdraw from compartmentalization in order to be expressed in a nonlinear format. As space/time is compressed, the grand unification of space and time becomes more easily formatted. This is a union that places both space and time on the same platform of reality and makes it possible for time to be expressed both multidimensionally and multiradially. This union is necessary for the mechanics of creation to know its place in the graphing of forces necessary for free-wielding expansion. When faced with the unlimited expanse of space/time, the nonlinear expression of time holds the greatest advantage in that it can align itself directly with the space/time margins that will allow it to be ever more grand and conjoint.

Time and space share another feature: the quality of motion that is represented. Because time and space are randomly fixed on a series of points rather than spreading themselves backwards or forwards, they remain looped together angularly once the time break fissures or recedes. The time maximum for any curve is always related to motion rather than to speed, distance, or angularity. One can view time singularly, but really it is a double function, that of motion rectified by speed and standardized by distance. Since nonlinear time is based on the willingness of the time codes themselves to "put in" or recede prior to each change in the motional gradient, the time frames that are postlinear have little to show for themselves in the larger picture. Time can be seen as regal in its queenlike reliance on the radiance of motion to provide for its own opulence. Strung together like strands of pearls, the time codes bear a relationship to the host integers that maintain their sheen.

Parallel Realities and Parallel Motion

Parallel motion defines parallel reality. Traversing the vast reaches of the infinite continuum in an arrayed splendor, time knows no obstacles. It scales the vast reaches of the continuum without having to assess or contend with any form of limitation. Since parallel realities form spontaneously out of the "time stuff" that makes up singular reality, there are often instances in which that which seems to have already appeared, appears again. There is a "puff" or pull in the time wave that causes the parallel system of motion to occur again. Once this puff is achieved, the parallel system breaks off from its original site and becomes amplified by the time waves that are already in its vicinity. Because the mechanisms of resistance are so tight, the spangled epilogue to the time breaks is always seen as parallel or coexistent with the existing stream.

Parallel realities exist because time is a dyadic, folding, translinear mechanism that derives handouts from the infinite matrix of its own continuum. Parallel realities defy definition because they cannot be easily viewed as transitory. They create their own fields of motion and rely on the combust nature of time breaks to spin their way onto the fold. Since each parallel "puff" is an heir apparent to the next wave of relationship, parallel motion always defines time and gives it its shape. Without the translinear assessment of time waves from every point of origin there would be no possibility of situating time in its own constitutional flow.

Time is "soft" when it retains its own ratio of distance between its actual spin and its native angularity. Soft time is curved time. Soft time is also responsible for parallel motion in the singularity of the spread. Since every opportunity for transverse functioning must be preceded by a leader in the spin, it is often apparent that time is vested in itself prior to becoming diverse.

Parallel Universes

Parallel universes are another matter. Because time and universal motion are always in constant dialogue with each other, parallel universes form to combat the spread of dislocated "locusts" in the infinite field. Locusts are collections of "dust" that appear on the screen of time. They retain their shape, color, and size, and "squeegee" down into temporal curves once they are randomly located in the slope. Parallel universes are formed through the organization of these locust-like collections of time-dust, preoriginators to matter clusters or stationary fields of any type. Universes form through the influence of time as it flows into the quest for uniform matter. Since universes must maintain their individuality in the stream, they depend heavily on time/mass balance to retain their form and shape.

Parallel universes are composed of time/matter globules or pockets, which lean into the infinite like a ram blocking a mouse's tiny door. As each tendril of time meets up with its counterpart in the curve, it can act separately to push its way through the narrow entryway, creating a time tunnel in which the parameters can be sequestered. They build up, one on top of the other, fomenting a type of temporal pressure, until finally they rush out, seeking differentiation. This quest will eventually define the psychological territory that we experience as different subsets of time. Like their more "thinly sliced" counterparts, parallel universes are composed of these very similar rushes of event/time openings.

In their race to develop precise corridors of dimensional shift, parallel universes act like runners seeking to get to the next hurdle. They try to push back the lag that would not permit them to embrace one obstacle or the other and to rush the time gates head on. This permits event sequences that ordinarily would be deemed inconsequential to continue to be lifted from one stream and embraced by the other. Without a continuity of motion, the parallel movement of time from one dimensional corridor to another would not have the "play" to relinquish its identity and to form a new system of reality. Therefore, like a racer seeking to finish the match, each of the temporal waves must find completion on its own.

It is not usually the case that living entities can live simultaneously in parallel causalities, but it is possible that individual entities can bond with other characters or strategic matrices in the continuum and share knowledge and understanding. The portals between individual universes are not nearly as distinct or widespread as one might think. The holes or blanks that allow information to seamlessly fit into the gaps in the universal language can only be read by masters in the scope and perception of time itself. These masters can actually shift time from one universal perspective to another.

Altering our Notion of Reality

Strategies for embracing time as a system of language would allow parallel realities to become possible expressions of event flow that could have interesting consequences for the redevelopment of civilization. Since our civilization presently relies squarely on linear transmission, the doorway to parallel civilizations has not been crossed. We are constantly visited by such parallel streams, but we have been unable to duly reciprocate.

As we lift the barriers between the time waves, we will be able to freely cross between one portal of perception to the other. This will not automatically imply a doubling or direct counterpart to that which we see and hear. Rather it will imply that we will be able to see reality as something less fixed, more transitory, and developmental rather than wholly focused on a given outcome. This will psychologically alter our notion of reality and cause us to explore more fully the underlying perception of time.

1.1.4
the dialogue of time and matter

Time as a Storybook

n the manifest creation, time and matter rely upon each other to write the page for the formation of reality. They do so through a heartfelt symbiosis of mathematics, language, and reason that paints a picture for the dimensional constructs we have come to embrace. The Creator, in the infinite wisdom that He easily invokes, creates templates for time and matter to interact. We think of these templates as cultures, civilizations, or simply congregations of like-thinking brethren who interact in ways that stimulate and refine each other's knowledge of who they are.

The mechanism whereby time reveals its stationary albeit temporary imprint is through the random formulation of curves which appear on the event page around which we coalesce. Time is a storybook, opening itself to an infinite array of possibilities that curve languorously around each other in a bowed or elongated fashion. The mathematics of time relies upon systems of variables that are preset, acting as a backdrop out of which the curved dispersements of time can be projected. For this reason, time is not a symmetrical system, but rather a jagged, open-ended affair, tamed only by the opportunities for organization that come along to portend a particular field of closure.

The art of building time involves a steady buildup in the continuity of motion. Motion is important because it is through the speed of temporal displacement that matter can breathe. Without some speed it would be as if time would not have the gaps, the pregnant pauses that herald the change in registration or temperament. Time remains stationary only when it is angular, hardened just briefly so that a particular sequence can take hold. There are many contradictions to this process because time is expressed infinitely but arrayed unilaterally. The Mother intelligence, which monitors the expression of matter, develops strategies that embrace time and provide for the full explosion of motion that gives our lives a feeling of progress and meaning. Our psychology needs to move, breathe, feel, and think in not only a logical way, but in a way that feels substantial. Time arrays itself to achieve this effect.

How is it possible that time curves so elegantly, while leaving matter angularly refracting the dark side of the time break? This is the question.

The nobility of time as a marker for matter has been understood. But why does time refract so dramatically when encountering the episodic conduct of matter?

The Marriage of Time and Matter

Time is the plaything of matter, and as such, it cannot reconcile itself to being simply put into play on the most Spartan of occasions. Time, always taciturn, glistens while matter sings its lilting chorus. Time is remarkably sanguine about the realities that matter provides. Each turn of the screw with relationship to matter causes time to be shattered, turned upside down, and spun out like the finest of weaves. Time and matter refract the opposite tendencies of each other like the best-made garment. They retain a sense of woof and warp without targeting the opposite pattern. Try as we may, time and matter are not translatable by any known system of language and therefore they remain aloof, capable of blending with the event streams they are wont to create, and incapable of explaining how they are to do it and why.

Time and matter blend with the absolute so magnificently that even the absolute cannot digress from this marriage. When time and matter entertain the substance of infinity, they unify themselves strategically and await the introduction of light, sound, and substance. They turn themselves inside out and await the majestic dawn of the absolute. They are called out of the house of each other and placed together simultaneously, the trumpet call of infinity beckoning them. Can one resist the synchronous tonality of matter when it has been turned away from the absolute? Matter cries out for a substantive reply that only time can give it. Ever so humble, the absolute is the core of resistance for the infinite wakefulness that the Creator desires. He wishes His creation to awaken to itself, to experience the tenderness that makes the butterfly and the bird. But he is not always patient with this process. Since time and matter must intertwine with each other to prevent the demolition of the field of opposites, it is the responsibility of time to call on the Mother and relate the necessary synchronization that will denote a smooth flow of conduct.

Time is choreographed through this Mother intelligence that creates change in the rate of speed, fluidity, and movement of each temporal wave. Once the landscape of time is created, matter then acts as a catalyst to springboard new selections of time onto the surface of creation. This is why we say that matter jumpstarts time. To understand this process more fully, let's look at how one primary time curve could be formulated. A stream of electromagnetic energy is identified; then time forms a backdrop that elongates and "squeegees" onto the field of matter like toothpaste from a tube. Once the time sequences extend, they loop around the preexistent stream of matter, creating pockets or whirligigs of energy from each junction point. The Mother intelligence, in Her effort to redefine the landscape for each temporal wave, creates a lullaby of peaceful, tranquil energy that acts as a buffer for the rapidly firing time variables to have something to cozy up to. Matter and time are made equidistant as they become electromagnetically sensitive to one another, developing a symbiotic, mutually advantageous relationship. In this way, the skin or encapsulation of time is made.

Time and matter coexist in a smooth, effortless continuation that maintains a glass-like appearance. This is because the variables no longer shatter as they accumulate, but are stretched along and made clean and whole by the buffer that the Mother intelligence has created. She wipes clean all of the clattering, shattering randomization that is natural when time and matter collide, and makes a shell around which the temporal mandates can be built. Time benefits greatly from the touch of the Mother, because it is She who builds the mathematical bed from which our personal dimension can be formed.

The Culturing of Uniformity

We interpret what time has to offer from the regionality of our own experience, and it is the Mother that governs that regionality and makes us who and what we are. Culture is composed of temporal norms that give us a sense of identity and make us feel at home in the world of form. The Mother intelligence regulates the mechanics of this uniformity, giving us the means whereby we can eventually return to a more accurate formulation of what actually is in front of us. We move from singularity to uniformity and back again, developing along the way a system of knowledge that will eventually make it possible for us to be creators in our own right.

The concept of time as a loop or ribbon is built into this dance in order for matter and time to cooperate with one another. They must develop a ribboning effect for time to branch out as fully as it must to sweep the event structures clean and develop new ones. Time loops around a preexistent stream of matter at each junction point, supporting independence even as it gives rise to uniformity.

The Mother remembers for us where we are to go in reference to our own personal map of time, and it is She who causes us to have a sense of where we have been and where we are going. She bathes us in a type of interpretative intelligence that makes it possible for us to maintain our compass in this swirling mass of matter, time, and space. Though everything therefore is infinitely variable, the Mother gives us a sense of causation and helps us to rely on points of reason for our own personal decision-making process. She gives us just enough space so that we can eventually develop a fully unified point of view while giving us room to maintain a spicy brew of deviation that keeps everything wholly original. We rely on our own perception of cause and effect very heavily in that we are for the most part incapable of grasping the seamless whole that actually underlies all that we experience. In reality, uniform matter and uniform time exist passively but coherently, fed by the freestanding variables that rectify time both mechanically and psychologically.

The rectification of time with respect to matter occurs because time is not capable of predistancing matter. It remains equidistant, saturnine, and sanguinely dependent on matter for a definition of its solidity. Time returns to matter as a child returns to its mother, needing the solace of matter to determine its sovereignty. Time is prismatic, curved, and translucent in its relationship to matter, while matter is angular, lean, and obtuse when compared to time.

There is no linguistic reference to describe how matter and time coexist. This is because time and matter do not really exist simultaneously, but actually predestine one another just enough so that they are really independent. The Mother is the director of temporal independence. She determines when it will be possible for matter to leave the womb of time and vice versa. The codependent situation that develops between time and matter is built with enough play in it to leave room for manmade obstacles in the race for infinity. The rule of thumb is that when matter leaves the comforts of infinity, it cannot count on time to appear any sooner than it is ready.

Time is characteristically obstinate in its search for a clear, coherent expression in the world of matter. Time and matter derive mutual pleasure in creating a mate-like synthesis that causes them each to merge back into the infinite and form the one majestic whole. Equidistance is maintained only through the transitory reflection of time in its phase transition between an infinite passage into the absolute and the formation of a random event stream. Where randomization was once chaotic, it is smoothed out and made functional by the Mother intelligence, who demands order always out of the domain of confusion.

The smooth-running functioning is only transitory in that the time/matter phase reaction must occur momentarily, in a singular spontaneous event stream. There is no chance for matter to swing back and retain its nonriveted fixation with the time spread. Time and matter return to the infinite One, the never-ending stream of normality that pictures itself as a rainbow in the prismatic world that eventually forms our visual reality. They color the absolute with substance and give meaning to the creation.

Playthings of the Creator

Time and matter, being the playthings of the Creator, are not subject to His whims in the usual sense. Since time and matter coexist, the Creator appreciates the humdrum sense of uniformity that the two elements can bring to one another. When event streams are randomly selected and challenge each other in the curve, time and matter retain their dialogue with the infinite long enough for the Creator to feel that He has had enough. Out of the bondage of the infinite, the Creator dispels the notion of nothing for the reality of everything and makes the plea for creative abnormality through His relationship to the balance of time.

Time spins back, significantly altering the Creator's ability to determine how time will play out. He leads the creation into temporal breaks that bring choice and reformation and help to define the characteristics of civilizations and their history. The Creator gives us the illusion of the finite through blending a temporal cauldron of event sequences into a pool of event stream language that makes matter/time halt at predetermined stations of rest. The standards of conduct between time and matter are turned around. Whereas before time and matter stood at the crossroads of infinity, they are now the glass, the windowpane through which God can see to make each stunning episode in the lifestream startling and unique.

The Mother is the mask of time. She hides the fluctuations that make time indiscernible except to those who bear witness to it. She leaves the field of matter, crashing through the boundaries that formulate Her skin. She becomes skinless, boneless, protruding through the holes of the infinite like some crazy costumed lover. She is the fountainhead of creative functioning and produces the wisdom that makes matter a living conduit for celebration. All of the trust that matter places in time can be broken if matter does not relate fairly to the Mother. The Mother must place upon Her lap all of the broken secrets that time represents. She must unmask Her newborn lamb and lend Herself to all matter of degradation if She is to find out where and how She is to be born.

The Mother is the founder of infinity. She is the dark night unto which the infinite cauldron of perspicacious matter is revealed. It is unlike the

Mother to call to Her young without some reason. So She returns Herself to the very stage of creation for Her sport. The Mother rectifies time and unifies matter. She maintains their perfect sovereignty while blending them righteously together. She leaves the standard of motion, change, and knowledge to each alone, while demanding that they retain their uniformity forever.

Why is the Mother so obstinate in Her role with time? Because time is the backdrop to which the Mother must surrender if She is to create the perfect counterpart for time/matter. The Mother surrenders Herself to the space/time continuum gladly. She does not want to be burdened by having to clean up Her past or add chinks to the patterns of the future. The Mother wishes to have no past or future but simply to be skinned alive by the monumental heave of time.

Matter and the Mother

And what of matter? The Mother retains the vehicle of matter for Her own amusement. Since there cannot be any objects without time, the Mother makes all of Her objects subjective. She subjects them to the counterpoint of the instant relative and makes them play out the spectator sport of time without knowing why. Is this the joke that Mother plays on the window of chance we know as time? Perhaps, but it is through this window that the pain of knowing is made evident. It is through this window that the Mother christens Her young children in the art of independence and self-distinction.

For all of the peoples of the Earth there is only one Mother, but there are infinite points of view about Her origination and Her destiny. This is because the Mother peels back the strata of reality and allows Her children the most plump, opulent point of view. She gives Her children the pick of the crop, the best set of variables imaginable, through which they can reimagine their infinite view. The crystallization of time, which gives rise to fixed patterns of existence and the outbreak of all dimensions, is the methodology that the Mother has derived to make Her children free. She utilizes fixed integral perspectives to make dialectical opposites. She entertains Her twin children, time and matter, with the same playthings. These are the measurings of the Mother. Her desire to please, simplify, and retain solidity place Her at the forefront of the Creative flow.

The Mother is the recipient of time. She is the pervasive influence underneath the quest of time to be unlimited and untitled. To grasp the Mother is to grasp the power of the infinite Creator to make steps in the field of existence. The Creator is the most process-oriented force imaginable. It/He has all of the time in the world to patiently play out the many possibilities of language, custom, and style. The Creator can make civilizations out of the tangible waiting ground of matter/time.

The Creator is so perfectly creative that even that which appears wasteful never is. Everything is useful to the Creator and although its use may not instantly be seen, all that exists is necessary and ardently, wholeheartedly perfect. The Creator does not stop the deed of creation at any one point, but always curves back onto the fabric of the Self to make available that which can be had for the asking. Everything that is abundantly sustaining to the Creator is attainable by human beings. This is why, in the time/matter blend, it is always beings that are reasoning, knowledgeable, and infinitely capable of love who make the grade.

Love and time, fostering the individuality of multiplicity and creating the magic of union, are the foster children of the Mother, and the principal components of unification.

1.1.5
algorithmic time

The Mathematical Sequences of Time

time expresses itself in randomized sequences that are describable mathematically. These sequences have a type of analytical precision and are related one to the other through curves or openings in each set. For example, an algorithm that describes a particular subset of time along a curve will apportion itself approximately midway in the curve, opening the temporal envelope to many disparate nuances that will describe time in an assortment of views. The algorithms are protected, in the sense that once information enters into the field it is not alterable for a period of time, giving the temporal cues the opportunity to align themselves and present a landscape of "prehistory." Human organization demands that we have fundamental rules or standards of behavior that are repeatable in different cultural formats. The algorithmic organization of time is behind all of these societal differences. How we behave as groups of people, both functionally and cosmologically is dependent on the way the algorithms of time interact with one another.

Within the context of this mathematical communication, there is also a system of logarithmic functions. Logarithms are the stuff from which algorithms are made. Logarithms in this context are ground formulizations, mathematical cues that set the pace, direction, and timing for all of the algorithms to be displayed. Time picks up the logarithm from its database, enters it into the spread, and then organizes it through the patterns that the algorithmic sequencing is producing. Historical formulation, which leads the individual to precise choices at precise times and creates holes in the field of influence that must be filled, is fueled by the mathematical juxtaposition between future time, expressed in algorithmic fashion, and present time, which is filled in through the subtext of logarithms.

Shaping Time

Logarithms smooth, shape, and define time so as to create the definition of how time will appear in any given sequence. These logarithmic expressions are fundamentally simple and elegant, and do not require any dressing up or relinquishment of their essential flavor through any other type of mathematical instruction. Once these logarithms are imposed in relationship to the human nervous system, they must be structured in such a way that the brain/mind can interpret their signature and translate these signals biochemically. This translation process occurs through the rigors of algorithmic expression, which takes the system of logarithms in their simplicity and organizes them in a more complex system of programming, which stamps the degree of originality onto the individual identity structure.

Since human beings must function very quickly, spitting out a vast range of information to correlate to the movements both internally and externally of the body/mind, the algorithmic sequences that are established must function biorhythmically. They create biochemical relationships with each other that are the direct expressions of the algorithms that form them. At this stage, all of the mathematical relationships are fed directly into the nervous system, and the simple, elegant logarithmic values are chewed up by the complexity necessary to create both a parasympathetic and sympathetic nervous system.

The nervous system provides a network of highways that are the corridors through which bits of temporal intelligence can flow. The nervous system orchestrates how time will be used and when it will be biologically relevant to express it. All of the avenues chosen by the brain for the production of neural information can be traced back to chemical switches that define the rate, speed, and flow of data to the body/mind. These switches are tripped randomly and spontaneously, but later their precise organization becomes necessary for the maintenance of biological homeostasis. Time expresses the continuous flow of data through periodic openings in the pathways of intelligence.

Algorithms reinvent the subsequences of time and make the brain "think anew" in ever original and creative ways. Since algorithms released by the avenues of time are of a very high order of functioning, they must often be declined or recalibrated so that their vibrational order can be more readily assimilable. Algorithms are stepped down or transduced in their value, aiding the brain and nervous system to calibrate the streams of information that are arising, and making it possible for biological integrity to be maintained. Human beings are fundamentally time interpreters or time sharers. They utilize the documentation of time from the absolute level and give it a sense of meaning from the relative.

Logarithms cause time to be smooth in its organization, digestible in terms of personal experience and cosmological aptitude. Logarithms define how time will be placed in the scheme of human life. Their friendly standardization of time over precise intervals makes them easy companions to the more elaborate and fancy display of algorithmic data. Logarithms create a sense of homogeneity and uniformity that makes them purveyors of pure psychological information. We become open to receiving the rules of order that will define our lives. This more static expression that logarithms represent is essential for us in order to live in one time-dimensional room or another. The logarithms house time for our individual use through their interpretative mechanics in the central nervous system.

Logarithms and the Flow of Time

Once time organizes itself logarithmically, we are indebted to its flow. We become creatures of comfort, predictability, and logic. Yet these logarithms have the capacity to establish new sequences, new building blocks for the formation of life. In fact, they actually govern the formation of the human nervous system at its embryonic outset. The momentum that is established when logarithms pick up the pace and begin to direct the flow of information at faster levels of expression makes human life more fluid and exciting. When interfaced with their algorithmic cousins that shape the momentum or ribboning of time, logarithms become the ground upon which new systems of language and restitution can be made. The algorithmic flow of time moves life forward. The interior life of the individual can best be enhanced through the circumspect movement of time as it awakens in the individual's own awareness.

Time is mathematically balanced through a spread or sequence of logarithms. Temporal data is organized in pools or reservoirs for data that are eventually to be assimilated into the nervous system. Logarithms give stature, grace, and meaning to these pools because they operate as systems of language. Once the individual becomes acquainted with the particular system of logarithms that gives shape or meaning to his or her situation, they are then fed rapidly into algorithms that actually create the programming sequences for human behavior and understanding. These algorithms proceed very quickly, developing the biological underpinnings of human psychology and defining the essential mechanics of the nervous system.

One could use the analogy that the logarithms form the bits of information that are fed into the chassis of the brain. They are oiled by consciousness and transmitted to the central nervous system. There, interpretation and coordination occur through algorithmic sequences that give meaning to something that by its very nature would be meaningless or mechanical. We become a vehicle that can think and feel, as well as one that is information-positive.

Smooth-Talking Algorithms

An algorithm presents a blueprint or schematic that tells time when it is to shift. It is the code for the notebook in which all of the possible timetables are written. Time is compressed through algorithmic markers that influence the personal reality of an individual. An event occurs, followed by a highly individualized internal perception of that event, and then a corresponding reaction to it. All of these internal markers must be calibrated and taken into account by the time spread. Algorithms arise like sheaths or banners, each upholding a particular section of the time puzzle. To resolve one's own event framework, one chooses certain algorithmic markers like pieces of a child's board game. These markers hold a place on the board of one's system of life events. Like a board game, all of the pieces are often going to the same place; that is, they are pooled to determine a set outcome. However, the possible routes to be traversed by these variables are infinite.

It is the function of algorithms to create smoothness in the way that time functions. In order for time to be fed gradually into different event sequences, which then define the climate of psychological structure, a system of algorithmic values must be interposed. This is how time jumps or leaps from one section or sphere of influence to another. It is also why, in our psychological perception of time, time appears to slow down, speed up, or advance at very fast rates of speed. It is the algorithmic function that causes time to alter in this manner, but still maintain its elegance.

The reaction times of different individuals to each event sequence are dependent on the state of consciousness of that individual. The more that a human being finds him- or herself firmly planted in the "now" or nonfractionizated moment, the more that he or she is capable of addressing the possibility of speeding up or slowing down the traversing of reality. In each moment the individual has a myriad of personal choices. Within these choices, a specific mathematical structure is built in. The logarithmic values form the basis of all these structures. The algorithmic values form the changing or moving continuities of these structures.

When an individual picks from the stream of events, there is an internal realization about the nature of that choice. This aspect of realization, which is a reaction to the event, is as important as the event itself. This is why in many spiritual traditions the individual is taught not to react to the thoughts that naturally arise. When psychological neutrality enters the framework of consciousness, a person actually has more control over the course of events. However, the natural outpouring of choice and response inherent in the process is impossible to deny. One can hope to control the more blatant emotional responses such as intense fear, anger, or sadness, which would move the event stream from one algorithmic sequence to another, but one cannot stop the response/reaction habituation completely. It is part of the time creation mechanism in the human brain and nervous system to respond to each choice with efficacy and a streamlined sense of personal destiny.

The algorithms underlying and governing time are schematic. They can best be represented visually as a split or tear in the sequence of events, representing a choice point for the individual. The person can actually witness this split by seeing how the seamless flow of time could be caught or netted for the purpose of redirecting it to a different cast of possibilities. The person sees a brief glimpse or flicker of where the time sequences could lead, and at that moment unconsciously chooses the path that will alter his or her perception the least. This allows the flow of time to remain steady. It is only in large "gulps" or chasms of time that these moments become opportunities for tremendous change of outlook, perception, or continuity. This cannot happen too often in the life of an individual, as it would be too disconcerting psychologically.

The Space/Time Map

The personal development of an individual utilizes both the component of space and the component of time. For a human being, space is the ground upon which event sequences walk. Space is the magical, nonmaterial ground on which being rests. We tend to think of space as an empty, forbidding place. It is rather a bustling, hustling place of tremendous activity, beauty, and power. Space is the nesting ground for time. Time elevates consciousness to the point where it can launch into the birthing room of space. From there, time knows no bounds.

Space must be mapped by time. In this inherent relationship, time becomes the master of space. Time learns to "eat" or subsume space for the purpose of developing light. This light is of an interior origin, that is, the light of consciousness itself, or the light of particular sets of events. It is also the light out of which matter is ultimately created. Space offers an address book for time. Each spatial unit or endpoint maps a particular location in the space/time continuum, presenting an address where time can be located or pinpointed. These locator points are the derivatives of time in its fixed or finite state. In its infinite identity, time cannot be encapsulated into a point or structure.

Each of us is the technical writer for our own personal reality. We research possibilities and enter them at a great rate of speed into the nervous system. In order to do this successfully, each pool or cluster of time variables must be entered, analyzed, and ultimately sifted. We research possibilities by playing them out on the level of the mind. We stretch the series of "dots" that link the different eventualities together and look to see what will be most efficacious for us. This is done so automatically and quickly that most of the time we do not even know it is happening.

The conscious thinking that one does is actually an "afterburn" of the original and much quicker mapping process of information accomplished by the unconscious responses of the nervous system. The degree to which these mapping processes become conscious has to do with the development of the individual on the level of consciousness. As the individual becomes capable of distinguishing mind from pure consciousness and sees the patterning underlying the scheme of his or her own existence, a deep "aha!" occurs that allows for fuller participation in the process of reality-making.

Advancement in the Personal Calendar

There are those advanced beings whose job it is to work not simply with their own timing but with the timing of others. They do so consciously, and eventually on a vast and infinite scale. As an individual grows in consciousness, the personal event calendar becomes less prominent and a universalized identity emerges. In this state, the individual is thinking more for the good of the whole than for his or her own welfare. This is not an altruistic sense alone, although it may play a part on the level of the development of character. It is a wider level of functioning of the sphere of influence, based on the individual's own mastery of the flow of events in his or her own life, and on the understanding of the underlying play of space/time that makes physical existence manageable.

As an individual becomes a researcher in the flow of dynamics and consciousness, he or she examines the possibilities that present themselves. This is done not just for the good of his or her own self, but in reference to the lives of many other people. If I choose this situation or move in this direction, how will it affect the lives of others? This becomes the fundamental question. In the early stages, it may appear that this level of functioning is highly sacrificial and therefore inhibitory to the evolutionary flow of the individual who observes this change in direction. However, after awhile it becomes apparent that the individual consciousness that is working constantly for the good of others is also serving him- or herself, but in an entire-ly different way than before. In each instance where choice, time, and motion play a part, the individual can ascertain how to move so that the whole makes progress. It is like being the sail of a boat, where one move of the sail can affect the angle, proportion, and width of the sailing trajectory.

In the early stages of this process, it is easy for the individual to actually forget his or her own life, or to see it as unimportant. This is a psychologi-cal liability in the shift from working solely for the good of oneself to work-ing for the wholeness. As the individual leaves behind the feelings of self-ishness, fear, and greed which often govern human behavior, he or she is able to push through any obstacles and retain the perception, bigness of spirit, and decorum that makes growing larger a more evolutionary occasion. The individual then has mastered the mathematics of time from the deepest level of being and knows how to act for the good of all. However, the action is so grounded in the fundamentals of being that it cannot be assessed from the surface. It is like the workings of an underground river, flowing in all direc-tions to reach the surface, but skillful in finding just the right rate and flow to bring it into the open.

Predestination and Choice

The flow of time is "scored" or sectioned through algorithmic derivatives that cause it to be parceled out from many different points of view. This schematic dialogue that time achieves between its future-past and its past-present gives it the capability of interweaving between different sections without interfering with the favored psychological constructs that have brought it into full view. The grand sweeps that time makes over whole his-torical quilts of perspective are governed by these algorithmical juxtaposi-tions. Once the curtain drops on time and a given event sequence is placed in its appropriate historical cluster, it is unnecessary to interfere with this sit-uation. Time recognizes the initial thrust that an event sequence is about to take, and, in military precision, complies with the order that this sequence is apt to derive.

Any section of time that is incomplete is fed back into the predestina-tion advisory, only to be picked up later if a particularly "juicy" or potent sequence is to be played out. The field of temporal derivatives, from which event sequences are poked out or left in the fray, is composed exclusively from the event packets that have been left over after different subsections have been cut. It is like creating the "rushes" of a film: the event sequences are randomly cut, broken apart, analyzed for their appropriate varietal content, and placed back in bits in their proper sequencing again. This is why, from a psychological perspective, when one views the patchwork of one's life, it seems that different scenes or attributes of perspective could be pulled from one drawer or another, looked at closely and placed back in another drawer without anyone noticing. There is a certain *je ne sais quoi* element to each of these sequences, which essentially states that I don't know why this is happening now, but in the final result it will all make a certain allegorical sense.

Time has the capacity to reshape itself to fit the event sequences as they arise. This gives rise to the ability to mapscape one's life-play and understand how the different variables conform to fit one's individual psychological wave. Every person is inherently skillful at deciding how his or her map is to be constructed. The value judgments placed on this scenery are inherently subjective. Since individuals live like frogs, going from one lily pad to the other, they rarely stop to think of their trajectory until after it has been achieved. One senses that there is a plan, and although one seems to keep making plans endlessly, the actual trajectory seems to have a time curve all of its own. This is because the allegorical process of time develops its own rate of speed, and it attains the apex of its trajectory through a psychological recognition of nowness that is essentially personal and indefinable from any outside point of recognition.

The display of language that distorts or exaggerates the quality or perspective of time as it is to be played out in the individual's frame of reference is built on the assumption that human beings are unable to break free of their prejudices long enough to bring about temporal originality. The cause of this limitation lies not in the process of intelligence itself but in the ability of the participant to understand what is unfolding before him or her and stop it long enough to assess the trajectory that is to be won. The value of a stop-time consciousness that can hold to a given pattern, perceive its aftermath, and then fan it out over the continuum is that it can actually develop plans and successfully fulfill them. The true planner therefore must have the ability to disengage the time clock from its maker. Then the planner can actually curve back over the many variables that are laid down and sort them out one at a time. To bring time into such a play of slow motion is a divine art and not usually a human one.

1.1.6
the algorithmic flow
of the godhead

Forwards and Backwards in Time

he researcher that is seeking to understand the mechanics of how the past is formed must utilize the knowledge that algorithms present. Algorithms hold the key to the determination of time as a split derivative made up of a chain or series of events called "pools." The algorithms describe the rate, point of entry, and assimilation of the time values so that they can be recognized by the individual. Since the past appears to the psychologically based mind as temporally fixed, it is difficult to understand how time can move or swing from one parameter to another, changing the field of time as it sways.

The researcher who studies the flow of time must identify how time crisscrosses over the eaves or breakpoints without casting a shadow or rivulet in the time pools. This motion of time, which sweeps the variables and allies them so that they can be matched one to the other is what causes the backwards motion of time. From an historical reference point, once time is shot back past the first set of variables, it is now independent of any one particular grid. It can go in any direction. This is why there is no such thing as a fixed past. The history that one relies on so vividly is simply an algorithmic play on the particular set of variables that were found at the time the event sequence was manifest. It can go in any direction and interplay within itself. Therefore, history is no more fixed than is the future. The historic reference points are principally psychological rather than teleological and are really suspended through the collective consciousness where they can be "pulled" at any time.

Docking Time

The mythological idea that time cannot be altered, and if it is that all time variables will be distorted in some way, is false. Time can be altered at any moment. It is not fixed in any way. In fact, every new sequence of algorithmic correlates splits time in a thousand different directions. It is not set but is splattered, more like rain drops on a roof. It falls into random subsets which organize themselves in spatial sequences and form the basis for spatial orientation and event cognition.

Time derives its spatial sequencing through psychological as well as physical factors. The algorithmic docking of time within itself creates a vortex where the space/time variables can marry themselves to the endpoints and proceed cautiously through the rivulets or channels of time into an open clear field. There time is split up, folded back on itself and made elastic, repeating its variable sequences again and again. This is why there are psychological formations of interior sequencing in all of the time spindles one generates in a given lifetime. Each sequence can be traced back to primal correlates in the past and brought forward into the future. There are no fixed reference points except within the mind.

Time moves backwards or forwards within the context of human thought or experience. Inherently, time exists in the "all-time" which has no forward, past, or present. In order for time to be recognized as having movement or acclimation within a present context it has to be interpreted and defined according to a system of patterns. These patterns are expressed as algorithms. The algorithmic formulas map out time over a spatial matrix. Time is first expressed cubically. The overlapping sequences of time are arranged in cubic units of measure that are later put to use in the salt factory of the mind.

The Apportionment of Time

Time is apportioned through prescribed variables that determine the speed at which it will be assimilated by the nervous system. These variables appear as blocks or regions, similar to how the map of a city might be laid out. These blocks each have their own time differential, a system of equations that tell that individual area how it will be fed into the nervous system and when it will meet with the functionality of the individual that will give that region a sense of meaning. Time exists independently of meaning or significance. It is through the systemization of time that it is given a sense of originality or a specific quality of function.

Some variables in the sequencing of time are fixed. These are part of the compartmentalization of time. Variables that are fixed create the structures that inhibit time from becoming too infinite, too original in its character. Without such limitations, the human individual would have no ability to live in this dimension with its rapidly changing parameters and the need to make psychological closure on personal events. The velocity of time is directly dependent on the sense or meaning that we give to the personal event sequences that underlie our reality.

Space wraps around the floor plan of time. It makes the avenues of perception visible to us and defines how we are going to use time in the context of our everyday reality. When we go to the supermarket, ask for change at the bank, or contribute to the everyday reality that we assume, we are utilizing the storage blanket of imposed meaning and context that time has given us. Time expresses itself through space.

The proportional mechanics that define space are expressed through ratios. These ratios draw up a system of comparison that gives space the capability to recognize how time will be apportioned or derived. Space exists primarily as a backdrop for time. Time is expressed in tandem sequences of binary numbers, a 2 x 2 format that creates squares or cubes. In this sense, the formation of time is crystalline, abstract, but inherently logical.

Time is developed through the implementation of the algorithmic sequence in random-ordered cubic breaks or substructures. It is categorized through a process of linear breakpoints set over random intervals within the matrical scheme. It cannot break past the original set of sequences without a corollary movement or unique set of prime values and must be mapped accordingly. The valuation of time is logarithmic when it is first tapped and algorithmic as it progresses. Within each set of sequences, the breaks or maps spin off and form independent substructures. These are equal in terms of rate and volume and are derived from the mapped value of integers that have broken away from the spin.

The text of time as it skates backwards or forwards over the breaks is mapped through logarithmic slopes or longitudinal breakpoints which define the curvature or stretch of time. They can be mapped through viewing the algorithmic leaps that time derives when it moves from one sequentiation or map pool to another. As time leaps or forwards itself over the breaks, there are specific algorithms which map the flow and effulgence of the time pools and give them scope or amplitudinal range. Where velocity cannot be categorized then speed becomes a nonissue. Time leaps past the relative constituents of its mapped model and becomes able to coast along within itself independent of motion-sensitive variables.

Breathing on its Own

Time, although looped in its array is usually spun out over a wide area. It is woven or reconstituted by the mental attributes of the user. Time is therefore user-friendly in the true sense. It is able to correspond to the needs of the time rather than as a fixed derivative. It expands and contracts due to the psychological home in which it finds itself.

Time is so advanced in its "thinking" or God structure that when it advances it always leaves behind a tail or streamer which reminds the individual where he or she has gone. This is how we do not become lost in time. Time catches up with itself over and over and weaves a tale of psychological significance which it cannot have in and of itself.

The algorithmic sequences determine the width and breadth of time. Time breathes because it is able to catapult itself over the breaks and rest on its own numerical sequentiation. It is not capable of "falling asleep" because there is always activity going on within its inherent character. The individual uses a block of time as one would use a piece of cloth. One covers the cloth over the object and positions it so that there are no spaces or naked areas which the cloth does not cover. This is how we utilize time. Time is spread over the surface area of individual existence and "prettied up" so that it can cover all of the psychological variables we seek for it.

The longitudinal mapping gives us the concept of date or place. The identity of time as a date or place is constructed through the longitudinal mapping of time as it crisscrosses over itself in the pool. Time lapses for a moment, looking for its mate in the date pool. Then when it finds an inherent match it scores itself and refers to itself as a date or place in the continuum. This is how time is stopped or allowed to breathe for a moment. Otherwise time would continue unabated and there would be no historical reference points.

Time loops over the first set of reference points, creating a spiral which continues infinitely and gives time a sense of character or longevity. When certain historical dates are of great significance to a psychological stream, as in a cultural or symbolic subset, then time loops back over itself in a rather thick or bunched sequentiation so that all of the variables can be met from many psychological reference points. Otherwise, one person's version of a given event would differ dramatically from that of another.

Timestamps

In order to give a time event a quality of being stamped by a collective reference point, the time variables have to bunch or crinkle in the pool. This gives the data the semblance of rationality and a sense of rightness that everyone who has experienced the event can agree upon. This is how it becomes fixed in collective memory. However, this type of bunching can be reconfigured and this happens over and over collectively through an advanced system of algorithmic reference points. If this were not the case then time would become too heavy or weighty with its own derivatives and would sink rather than float. It would weigh down the collective experience of progress. In order for progress of a psychological or teleological nature to be made, time must become fluid and be able to bend to the need of the time.

Time must therefore undergo a type of surgical plaiting in which it is scanned over and over and given a free play in its interim or variable mating. Time cannot be watched over too closely, nor can it be married too soon. Each type of plaiting gives time the capability of returning to a nearby event source and creating a docket or holding pattern where the time codes can be filled in and retained.

To view time from a fixed vantage point, human beings hold belief structures or mirrors in which they have painted particular event sequences for pleasure or for understanding. They are not likely to give these up without a struggle. This is how they fix their viewpoint of time, which as an independent operator does not exist. Time is used by human beings to give their lives a type of psychological shaping so that they will not be lost in the loose-fitting structures that time naturally unfolds unto itself. Knowing that human beings must do this for their sanity, the Universal Intelligence implants certain stays or pins in the fabric of time so that it will not tear out prematurely and interfere with the immature belief structures which human beings pattern. However, once a human being is knowledgeable about the knottedness which they have accumulated through their psychological ingenuity, they can then live in a free status and are not impinged upon by their psychological necessities. This is a form of temporal or spatial liberation.

The Psychological Moorings of Time

The algorithmic subsets that wing back and forth through the spatial pools form the backdrop for time to break within itself and set up streamers which magnify each internal consideration. These streamers represent the patterning of thought waves as they travel through the regions of space/time and form the gear out of which temporal nation-states are made. Each nation-state has its own thought waves or temporal strata which form blocks of spatial glue. These regions are the underlying juncture of a nation-state and form its cultural moorings or genealogy. When a culture clusters together to define itself, it does so for a given psychological purpose. This may or may not be infinitely lasting as we have seen nation-states come and go. As a psychological nation-state matrix collapses it takes its time codes with it. Then it forms new ones as the new hierarchical categories reformulate.

For example, when you view a slide of ancient Rome and you see push-carts in the streets and catacombs of tunnels in every direction, you are actually viewing the time matrix blocks as they are resequenced within themselves. There will come a time when you will be able to type codes into a computer and actually see time for what it really was—not as a reproduction, but as it really existed. Then you will first see how time is physically and psychologically constructed. When you can punch a key and see time for yourself, you will understand that it is made up of building blocks of psychological glue that are culturally and spiritually derived. Time is completely plastic in this sense.

Physical existence is independent of time. This is hard to understand since human beings are so bound by their psychological perception. However, physical existence is governed more by spatial representation than temporal orientation. When a being is incarnated into a given plane of existence, he or she is actually free of any time constraints. A newborn infant has no conception of time whatsoever. It is governed entirely by its biological and psychological needs. It organizes itself into a temporal matrix due to the patterning of the familial culture in which it finds itself. Without this backdrop, the human being would be a purely causal distributor of time. The physical incarnation is derived spatially and is mapped by the Godhead for the purpose of creating windows in which the Godhead can view itself more clearly.

The illusion of temporal or spatial independence is necessary for individuals to play out a given lifetime and make sense out of it. They derive meaning from the interplay of events, and they do not cast a shadow on the infinite through this game. They are inherently free to decide for and with themselves how to cast their net over the infinite, but only the Godhead knows how this vision will be played out. When individuals wake up to their interior responsibility for Creatorship, they take on more of a role in this matter. Then they find themselves outside of time and can build the rivulets or time codes for the purpose of creating alternate or mirrored realities that are infinite in scope.

Time Unbound

The free individual is not bound by any psychological constructs that make up a series of events. He or she steps out of this jungle and lives in an open free expanse in which any set of implied parameters can be achieved. This understanding of liberation is the true version. Anything less is simply a mirror reflection of the Godhead at a higher order but is not freedom itself. Once the individual is stripped of limitation due to the barriers of time, he or she lives independently. Bodies can be taken or cast off like clothing. There is no spatial limitation either. The individual is free and can live unencumbered by any psychological barriers. This energy matrix which constitutes the human soul is not limited to any point of reference from a galactic or universal standpoint.

The coat or mirror in which the individual clothes himself is based solely on its evolutionary excitation, the thrill of creation in and for itself. It is not based on any type of limitation within the mindframe or any sense of knowing other than a spontaneous understanding of the creation mechanics as they are derived. This is pure immortality in and for itself and cannot be replicated other than by an individual who has arrived to a stature of complete and total freedom. At this junction point, God frees Man to be his own God and there is little difference.

1.2
the primordial nature of time

1.2.1
time and consciousness

The Characteristics of Time

time and consciousness have an interwoven relationship. It includes the field of differentiation of the time variables in connection to the formation of impulses in the brain and central nervous system; the field differential of the expansion of time as consciousness grows in the humanoid species; the shift in the velocity of the time frequencies as the maturity of the individual deepens; and the role of time itself in the formation of both material and spiritual reality.

The relationship of time to consciousness is in the impulse wave variations that determine the frequency of how consciousness is derived. The impulse wave variations match the predeterminate mechanism in the human brain. The brain acts as a generator or impulse wave receiver for the time variables to manifest in the central nervous system. Each individual maintains his or her own wave frequencies, which have to do both with the genetic variations as well as the sociological circumstances of the individual.

In order to form the proper wave patterns for time to become ingested in a manner that is lucrative to the consciousness formation of an individual, the nervous system must uptake these frequencies in a prompt and efficient manner. This occurs through the downloading of preparatory information into the subtle nervous system. The nervous system is prepared through the maintenance of certain chemical properties that are related both to the brain and the physical heart. The brain acts as a receiver, downloading the information, and then the heart calibrates this information for use in the maintenance of the involuntary systems of the body.

The Blueprint of the Body

The body is the floorprint or blueprint for the energy maintenance system. It is the primary generator of the system and attests to the velocity and rate of time variation as it is imprinted into the fabric of the individual life. The time calibration is from one to zero in an on/off manner, usually a binary upgrade of yes or no responses which act as chemical switches that feed the brain information at a base two interval rate. The frequency of information can be spirally placed or geometrically placed with upscaling relative to the frequency derivative of the individual's own core matrix of energy. The time principles involved are interdependent with the level of motion in the individual's core velocity channels. This is because the individual must maintain a certain rate of response to the time variables in order for them to be approved or realized by the brain. Each individual has a maternal sequence for these impulses that helps him or her to recognize how to uptake these components and make them useful to the chemistry of the body.

Time is the principal component of the core condensation of reality into this plane. As time rotates reality to such an extent that it can be crystallized directly into the central nervous system, the relationship of time to consciousness is increased. Time cannot be measured through any exterior means, but must be regulated through consciousness itself. The expansion or wave fluctuation of time is also governed by the desire of the individual to meet time in its proper apex or position.

The individual emerges from the depths of his or her evolutionary pattern with certain understandings already in place. This is why it sometimes seems that time is predetermined. The individual recognizes, "This is my time; this is the sequence that I will uptake in order to create order and a sense of superfluidity in the environment." Each individual acts and responds in his or her own time bubble, which is interdependent with the reality framework in which he or she functions. Time constructs windows in the reality matrix that allow the individual to breathe reality into his or her own house or energy nexus. The valuation of time is always subjective, therefore, but it has certain characteristics that are universally significant.

The relationship of time is always governed by the response of the individual to certain key situations that set up the backdrop for personal reality to be constructed. When time is used as the tuning fork to awaken consciousness, then the individual becomes capable of readying him- or herself for the status of time as it is maintained. Any individual that is able to breathe time directly into the nervous system is capable of analyzing this valuation of time. Time can be opaque or translucent depending on the frequency variables involved. This degree of luminescence governs the mechanism of human sight and wave perception.

The Swing of Personal Reality

The eyes of the human being are interdependent with the time matrices for understanding the nature of one's personal reality. The solid formation of the reality matrix identifies the individual as human or humanoid, and is a determining characteristic of the species. Other transdimensional lifeforms have no need to take the time variables and release them into what would be called clock time. They can uptake time directly and do not need translation into physical form to complete the matrix.

Presently the human species is experiencing time swings that create concentric fields of light energy. These can be used to bring time into a direct correlation with the central nervous system and prepare each individual for a massive jump-pull of energy that will take place in the future. As the time sequences are speeded up, there will be a sense of timelessness, a relaxed feeling that there is no need to rush to accomplish any given task, because time is already complete in and of itself.

In the twenty-first century, the relationship of time to the sense of well-being is shifting. Individuals are learning that they are part of one massive energy body, and are beginning to calibrate their activities more in relationship to the whole instead of deriving pleasure simply from individual pursuits and activities. This will cause a collective experience of time as both a subjective and objective window on the event sequences of a given corridor of activity. The individual will become capable of preparing him- or herself to engage in transdimensional activities which involve the merging of consciousness in a group context. No sizable consciousness technology can be developed independently of the mechanics of the group. This is not to say that such mechanics must be authoritarian in nature, but that the power of the collective status gives time a greater expanse of free-floating variables to work from. The range of these variables is of course dependent on the nature of the individuals involved and the degree of preparedness of their central nervous system.

When an individual becomes free of fear and can actualize the core intelligence, the time sequences of the brain open up and all of the derivatives necessary to create social and planetary change can be made available. Every individual that is illumined by consciousness can maintain his or her notion of time and can rely on this framework for a personal reference even as the collective understanding is expanded. In this way, time can become so open-ended as to create a meeting of the no-time and time-apparent vantage points. This is how the infinite value merges with the relative. This forms the basis for new styles of activity in which the absolute and relative levels come together to form new ideas and aspirations. Society must rise to the occasion of a new birth into the framework of the here and now, and learn to create vehicles for interdimensional relationship.

Coping with the Range of Variation

Time coasts along on its own until the individual becomes capable of locking onto its frequency and can ride the wave of his or her own creation. The time codes embedded in the human nervous system are relational to the flow of consciousness as it manifests in the energy matrix. When the energy matrix is fluid and maintains a spark or radiance of life within it, then time can become more creative and spontaneous.

Time is the linchpin of creation mechanics. The relative ability to create, at will, the vehicle for both material and energetic transformation is inherent in the mastery of the uptake of the time variables. Every material object exists at every moment; it is not time-derivative except for the necessity of its maintaining solidity. The time frequencies develop in and around the core matrix that springs forward into what is known as material reality. Once the individual can uptake time quickly enough, the ability to ascertain reality becomes so strong that he or she is skipping frequencies, and can thereby balance or change the time variables accordingly. This gives rise to the creation of spiral ranges of perception that open the individual into the universal flow of light.

Individuals who cannot cope with this range of variation cannot predetermine time. Therefore, one must prepare oneself by relating to time in a new and vigorous way. This involves "crashing" the time variables completely so that the experience of reality is not fixed on any one vantage point but can blossom in and of itself from the matrix of its own bearing. This entails releasing the past constraints of both the mind and heart and allowing consciousness to release itself into time. Then time can become a companion and one can voyage into its spatial dimensionality without fear. Otherwise, the bound rigidity of the mind keeps the time constraints in place, and the individual cannot encounter time directly as it is, without any accoutrements of the mind.

1.2.2
the skin of time

Temporal Parchment

t he term "skin" refers to the lining or envelope in which time resides. Since time is encapsulated or coated with a skin, it is possible for time to remain stable. In the context of human experience, our ability to work within the skin of time makes it possible for us to enjoy a sense of order and continuity in our everyday life. The skin of time is layered, much like the human skin, each layer being built from the interlocking envelope of time that precedes it. Layers are not rigid, but are like sacks of thin, parchment-like creases that stir consciousness in one direction or the other. For this reason, these layers mirror the variations in the time sequences as they are reflected over a wide stretch of space.

Matter is related to the skin of time through its underlying buttressing or support matrices, which pin time directly to a particular region or situation for the purpose of creation. Matter lives directly on the various skins that time produces, mimicking this layered temporal creation in its own display of physical ingenuity. When we view the natural world, we see matter appearing in distinctive strata of color, shape, and form, each with its own messages of light. The eye picks up these strata and translates them to a type of ephemeral solidity, much as matter translates time from the absolute to its more relative, sandwich-like perspective.

The Simultaneity of Time and Matter

Time and matter, because they must exist simultaneously, always retain a reasonable degree of fluidity and power. In the context of human life, matter is the end product of our perception. Matter reveals how the world should appear to us, based on the contextual structure we have been born to. In the Western mind, matter is the most solid, the most streamlined, and the most rigid. It retains a type of opaqueness that defies the matter/time layers from which it is originally built. In less disciplined societies, matter maintains its vestigial lining, which is of a degree finer than what we would normally perceive. Matter then coats the inside of the time "capsule" and reveals the essential nature of time itself. The shimmering, wobbly nature of matter that is still imbued with the skin of time forms the backdrop for subtle perception and gives the creation a secondary glow.

Since time and matter rely on a flat plane for their optimal existence, this plane creates a flap or opening through which the time/space continuum can contact its first suspension. Time utilizes the flaps or skin to direct its own self-revealing nature. The skin or flap functions as a channel through which time/space can travel and build the garment that adorns manifest creation. This flap or channel reveals the relationship between time and matter. Time, in its inceptionary state, must court matter, giving it duration, speed, and variability.

Peeling Back the Skin of Time

The stature of time as an opaque but refined value is always understood as being a product of its skin. In other words, the skin of time peels back to reveal its unmanifest, raw nature, but it must return to the manifest like one would return to a favorite garment. Since time must rely on the slightest tip in the turn of matter to reveal its nature, the light value of time is what creates the luminescent skin of consciousness. We say that time cannot be found in any other component of the absolute except the field of matter that defines it. Matter is not something that becomes opaque automatically; it is the light value of time that creates the fluid shield whereby time can crystallize and create the reality of matter as a solid state.

As we travel through the events of our everyday lives, the skin of time peels back, and layers of perception, meaning, and opportunity are birthed. We see secondary and tertiary coincidences that tell us that there is an order to things, even if we do not always understand how it has come about. Time beckons us to know the mechanics of our actions through creating a template or skin by which we can understand the nature of our personal choices and concerns.

When the skin of time peels back, there is an opportunity for the light value of time to create the effulgence that denotes the purer attributes of matter/time. There is no reason for time to peel back other than to reveal matter in this way. As we embark on the journey of our lives, markers or signal points that correspond to the pulse of time present themselves. The skin spins on its edge, creating a furling effect in the folds of time/matter relationship. One can think of these time shapes as opaque, fluid environments in which the edges or circumference of the time variables undergo a twisting, rotary motion. Time spins on its axes, over and over, each time causing the innermost range of its variables to "cook" in the spin. We can say that this flowing, opaque, opulent motion of time is what gives it this edge.

When we cross over the barriers between what we think of as the future or the past, we must push past these temporal shapes, and as we do so, the figurative understanding of our life's performance is opened out. The time values narrow as they appear before the crisscrossing web that makes up the matter/time continuum. This narrowing gives time its ability to reach past the boundaries of the absolute and take advantage of a myriad of shapes and points of view.

Setting the Time Clock

To arrange time in the puzzle of the continuum, the Godforce sets aside certain time variables, which are to be contained in the matter/time subset in and of themselves. These variables are dotted or striated, and multiply wed to one another, so that they are unique. Their role is to trip over the smallest edge that time presents and entertain the past, present, and future. The human mind is the linchpin in this process, creating the value constructs that determine how we break the present into the future. The present is essentially broken apart by our perception and arranged into future parts. These parts are fed to us from another aspect of our own awareness, and are arranged simultaneously with our notion of past and present in a continuous stream of parallel formations.

Time entertains the sense of past by locking in the time variables as they jump over the "eaves" of matter. Time speeds up, the clock slows down, and the past becomes the past. This diet of old time variables is sustained by the time/matter spread feeding itself on the edges of the time skin, rather than entering the bright, fluid pool in its center. The past edges its way into the opening to be birthed. Of course, there is really no past, only an abrupt simultaneity which can be measured as a psychological backdrop for infinity. There really is no sense of going back or forward when it comes to reading the book of time. Instead, there is an unraveling, a jump-starting, a pulling back or reaching in, much like the dance steps of the absolute. There is no relationship to any sense of past because the time variables always criss-cross over themselves in random but precise intervals, and vary only so much as they themselves desire.

Since the past is composed of time that has not been thoroughly digested, the present, by contrast, is controlled, variable, and speedy. We are happy with the present, because it seems stable and incontrovertible to us. However, when it offers challenges or perceived states of suffering, we immediately try to wiggle out of what it represents. We find ourselves traversing past options of perceived comfort or jumping forward into futures that could on the surface appear brighter and more full of life.

Life in the Present

The irony is that the future itself beckons us to accept, understand, and enter fully into the present, because as we do so, the future that we would find more favorable can actually make its existence more keenly felt. By escaping into regions of the present in which we perceive ourselves to be less bound, we often create chasms of time/space that must be filled in by the spontaneous formation of future/time. We are limited by our illusions of stability even as a simultaneously magical future could be offered to us.

The past opens into the matter/time continuum, like a bullet seeking to make a foregone trajectory. It appears that there could be nothing but a present option, but actually, there are many presents, many options that could conceivably come about. Time spins along its most favorable trajectory, hitting its mark and creating a stable, reconcilable present. This present value, which makes time appear in the now, is repetitious in character but rebellious in spirit. It never appears the same twice. The newness of time, and the newness of every moment, is brought about as time congeals onto the field of time/matter and creates formations of consciousness that betray the radiance of the absolute.

Each present moment exists as a separate field of influence that can be crushed as the time window opens. This is why, when the present first reveals itself, it is reminiscent of what we think of as the past. There is always a little bit of past in the present, and this is because the variables that confine matter/time to the present are always tainted by a slight glimpse of what was. This creates a feeling of permanent nostalgia, a sense in human beings that there is never anything new. We feel that the present is never original, but is simply repeating itself. The remedy to this predicament is that the freshness that makes individuation memorable is not brought about through originality; it is brought about by light.

The Originality of the Future

It is the light value interweaving with time that makes reality appear to be what it is. Pure time has no originality. It is randomly curving, circuitous, and opulent, but never wholly original. It is the light value in matter that makes reality appear succinct, dichotomous, and available. Since the light value in reality is actually a figurative influence from the Godforce itself, it cannot be trapped by the field of time. It exists independently of time/matter and in a sense independently of God itself. The present is made radiant by this divine light which sheds its rays on everything that makes up the Now. The Now becomes imbued with this presence and it shines out onto the surface of reality like a mirrored glass.

The future on the other hand, is wholly prismatic. It has many possible faces, many possible avenues of response. The future is the only part of the time game that is wholly original. It is by its very nature available in any variety for infinite play and self-revelation. The future is the life of the party. Because the future cannot play itself out other than to continually form unusual and interesting shapes and directions, it is considered to be the source of God's manifest creation. Everything is coming back from the future. Since there is really no past and the present is simply a psychological construct, it is the future that is wholly real. Here the time variables are constantly dancing, making new experimental time/matter "cocktails" and entering a state of unification as they sign off. The future creates the past and the present in a finely interwoven carpet of time/matter/light, which is always on the go. This constant sense of motion in the continuum makes the future the brightest star.

The future is not random in a true sense. It has a constancy, an order to it, which is arranged by the mind of God. God creates the future and then stores the variables so that they can be arranged as the past and present. God sees to it that these variables are dusted off, arranged according to the order of priority, and put in the trust of time. Since God cannot see any further than the future, neither can we. If there is anything but the future in a psychological sense, we do not know what it is.

When Man thinks of the future, he thinks of the possibilities that will define his reality and give it weight. He lives in the future, and although he wants to be more present, he is constantly incapable of maintaining any sense of what is. This is because the time variables are constantly spinning out from their center and maintaining optimal future states. Man constantly wishes to engender the past as well. This is because the past appears understandable to the psychological perception of human beings.

The past appears to have a constancy, a shape, a size, a predictability. However, this is an illusion. The past does not exist. It is purely a psychological construct.

The future is actually what is truly permanent, because it is ever-changing and unfixable in any direct sense. The mind carves up the future and turns it into the present and the past. The event streams that regulate the making of the present are susceptible to the outreach of the future. They are interned in the cistern of the variable reality. The event streams are taken up, one on top of the other, in a type of layered formation.

This is where the skin of time becomes prominent. It is through this layering effect, where the skin or coating of time is laid bare, that all of the variable relationships between time, matter, and consciousness are made available for scrutiny. Since time and matter are synonymous here, the skin of time peels back and out of this raw, fluid environment, the whole notion of time and its future perception is made clear. Human beings are future beings. They cannot live without a future. They literally feed their minds on the future and open themselves independently to that which will be. That is why to pin them to the present places them in a type of fluid "now" which in a sense *is* the future. The Now that the sages speak of is actually their cognition of the absolute refined in such a way as the future becomes the Now.

Since the psychology of Man depends on the future, it also recoils from the past. Man cannot make a life out of the past. Man must undertake the job of reliving the past purely for the purpose of amusement but not as a source of inspiration. Man gets all of the joy of life out of thinking about what will be and how it is to be accomplished. This sense of purpose imbues life with psychological power and resonance. It is time itself that gives life its thrust.

The search for meaning, which defines Man, is in and of itself the search for time. Man tries to find time everywhere he looks, and does not ever give up. This constant drive towards return to the absolute, which gives Man a place in the future, is the reason why God made Man. God utilizes the thrust of time to make Man search for the reason for his own existence. Out of this search, the backdrop for time and consciousness is created. To restore Man to his true state, the sense that time is absolute must also be restored. The turning of time over on itself and investigating its true meaning will free Man and give him the opportunity to develop an optimal future for himself and his world.

The future is the state in which Man is free. There he does not rely on physical reality as a statement of his divinity. Instead, he can play in the field of time and give it any possibility to which he can set his mind. The independence of time from the field of matter is Man's actual birthright, but it cannot be claimed until Man becomes a true futurist. Man must learn to fly on the wings of time, free himself from fear, and trust in the right-minded adventure of the divine that gives him room to grow. Out of this, Man lands his freedom and the skin of time is peeled back forever. This destiny gives Man the room to claim victory over his own mortality and over his own sense of impairment. The feeling of being damaged by the act of incarnation is not something that is limited to human beings. All beings that claim a body feel limited by it.

The past, present, and future of embodied entities is limited not by the body but by the sense that the body is imprisoned by the field of time. The body resides in a separate state with respect to time. The body is not made to be timeless or without temporal awareness, because it is the nature of the body to be moved forward in clock time in order to accomplish the needs of the physiology. It is consciousness that has the capacity to transcend the time values of the body. The notion of a fixed past and present keeps the body dependent on a more rigid definition of time. In the highest sense, the body is naturally nonsolid and unmanifest. It is capable of shifting shape and even dimensionality with response to time. It is due to the fear that we as human beings carry that the body has become so incapable of stretching to fulfill its innate capacities.

The Body of Memory

Bodies exist not to enchain Man but to help him develop memory. The memory capacity of the body is what makes it divine. It gives it the capability to store vast fields of information. The body is like a huge memory envelope in which time can pour all of its known and unknown information. The body exists as an envelope through which time can make all of its essential determinations about the fields of existence. Therefore, when Man is given the cloak of the body, he is also given the possibility of becoming something other than what is human.

The reality of the God/Man, free of the body, but hovering about its perimeters, is the truth of the human condition. The body of time is like the body of the Mother. It gives birth to infinity, and is unclaimed by any sense of limitation. Here is the making of the true skin, the true inner workings of the Godbeing: to create a perimeter of time language out of the Motherskin of the time continuum. Here is the reason why the language of the infinite is always spoken in many tongues.

1.2.3
the refractory nature of time

The Model of Refraction

he principle of refraction provides a model that describes the swing of time from one subsection of reality to another. Time curves or swings in such a way as to release the momentum of matter so that it can respond to the pathways of unified creation. Since matter and time do not have a fixed trajectory in their own right, it is the smooth, refractory power of the space/time wave that causes time to fit into its own groove and make way for the parallel expanse of motion that causes dimensional reality to flourish.

When time emanates from a distant point or vista it sets up a "ping" effect that causes an echo throughout the space/time realm. This ping is like the trumpet call of sonar, which catapults the time front into many points of signature at once. As the signal catapults from one zone to the other, the time current is refracted or masked so that it can be viewed from infinite points of reference. In the process of refraction, the views of time become nonlinear and efficaciously expanded.

The Tempo of Time

The tempo of time picks up. Each corresponding flush or wave is transferred from one unitemporal breakpoint to another. Time heaves or pushes out from the first marker to the second in flashes of space/time consciousness that leave each situation breathless. Time is the indicator that will determine how that portion or cube of reality will be marked.

In order to spice up the portion of time indicated, each section refracts infinitely back to the causal endpoint, causing time to be curved in each remaining sector. One could think of this process like the formation of a star: the heat/light pressure of the gases that form the star bond together in a type of attitudinal fusion. In the case of time, this process is reversed, and the pressure of reality/space causes time to explode into an infinite amount of pieces or metaphorical rings. These emanations do not crystallize into one wholistic formation like they would in a star or the formation of a galaxy, but instead fractionizate and create the prismatic interdimensional layering that we recognize in our most subtle perception.

Once it is understood that each dimensional shell is an inner box into which another dimensional shell will be placed, we understand that what we see in our sector is but one hub of many. We view our reality from the reference point of that space/time bubble, and we fashion significance through our psychological reference points. The manufacturing of our reality is therefore partly intimate and partly situational. We rely on what we see in the framework of our reality to create the shapes, sizes, and formation of objects that will be pleasing and helpful to our point of view. Once these objects are formed, we then put a plating of our own perception on them.

The Creation of Objects

The ability to create objects directly without any physical synthesis other than that of the mind is necessary for such objects to become more primary mirrors of our awareness. The refractory sense of reality formation brings a harmony to the distillation of form that cannot be achieved simply from the vantage point of secondary laws of creation. When creation becomes primary, the infinite range of causality comes into view. One can easily see that a red ball could be brown or black or green simply through the mechanism of internal reality formation. This changes our felt sense not only of objects, but of time. We see that the object will change without a footprint based on the constructs of the mind. The object has a "will" or proportional marker, which alters it from one possible construct to another. This may be seen in Nature most readily in the myriad of similar but uniquely delicate forms that Nature expresses.

Once human consciousness can achieve a direct relationship between matter, motion, and perception, one enters a realm in which the accumulation of objects for the sake of security no longer seems relevant. Since human beings are essentially dedicated to the formation of creature comforts, they are not likely to give this medium up unless there is an indication to do so. There is a notion that the ability to have mastery over the realm of matter will cause one to overstep the range of personal power that the Divine has offered. This is a misunderstanding in that once one has reached the level where such direct creation can be achieved, the ability to alter the flow of divinity for one's own purposes is greatly reduced. One perceives the nature or rhythm of the flow of motion and the signatory reference points that are to be gained or lost, and one instinctively and naturally moves with them. There is no gain in attempting to interfere with what may be readily seen as the preternatural plan.

54

The human brain has the ability to witness reality from a purely objective stance, independent of the characterization of reality. For this state to be realized, the brain must function in such a way that the pictorial representation of linearity is torn apart at the center of formation. In its place, there is a steady, underlying signal of uniform awakening which holds the attention riveted to that which is being viewed. The individual does not bring psychologically based understanding to the field of perception, but instead holds attention steady until that object splits apart into fragmented, prismatic rivulets of expanded intensity. The intensity of this type of perception accumulates to the point where a picture or crystallization of a new type of identity formation comes about. The individual is locatable in the space/time continuum but is not bound by his or her location. It is the power of yogic orientation itself that rivets the attention to a point of intensity where nothing but the pure reality can be known.

The Split of Attention

It is difficult to understand how attention can create a split or fragmentation while at the same time being wholly unified and powerfully integrated within consciousness. The more fully conscious human brain and nervous system are infinitely self-repairing and regenerating. They see what is to be done and do what has to be done. When attention is placed on an object, the refractory mechanism of consciousness curves about the object and creates a type of cradle where the knowledge of that object will be fully expressed. It is only necessary to rock that cradle with the underlying motion of causality, to bring it to a point where all of the possible outcomes for that infant object will be catalyzed.

Light and sound are the most fluid and delicate radiances of the celestial flower. They create the vehicle for objective unification at each state of awareness, and are responsible for all that we taste, smell, see, hear, and touch. The sound of the unmanifest, which generates the flowering of an object in nature, is perceived as a wholistic frequency. This frequency then splinters or refracts into selections appropriate for that individual creation to occur. The seer, reckoning with the eloquence of this message, arrives at a point of reference where time and space appear to collapse, and here, in this moment, is the most important opportunity for matter to come about. Matter is born of this restless, vibrant, eloquent silence. It whispers to the absolute, "Know me, I am whole," and out of this perception the wholistic field of matter is born.

The School of Creation

For human beings to tutor one another in the school of creation they must develop the depth power of concentration and momentary unification that will make worlds and situational contexts unfold before them. If there is magic in the laws of creation, it is that the individual who enters into the seat of unification must rely solely on his or her ability to see and hear what is being placed before him or her. It is like being invited to a large celestial banquet in which there are many delicacies to be laid at the table, but only a few will really appease the appetite of the gods. So it is when faced with the infinite and intangible eloquence of creation. One views the possibilities, enters into a rapport with the Host, and then manifests that which will make the entire environment happy and content.

The inspiration for creational intelligence lies in the parapet of matter and motion. Matter spreads the seed, whereas motion tells the seed where it will go. The motion involved in the process of creation is also derived from sentient consciousness. We survey an object, see its efficacy, and, in a finer comportment of will, bring that object to the point of reference where it will produce the most gain. As we emerge into a more direct, interwoven connection with the creation envelope, we can store possibilities in our frontal database and spill them out as the situation demands. Each throw of the collective die causes matter to spill out in intricate patterns governed by the laws of motion. Motion relies on temporal fluidity. Time must fly, sweep, and beckon so that motion will hop along. In tune with the demands of participatory creation, each human being has the opportunity to divest him- or herself of all unnecessary psychological accoutrements and leap into the field of motion.

When creation demands a large-scale panorama, it asks that consciousness make room. When we have too many guests for the house, we advise them to seek other lodging. When consciousness sees that there are too many variables, it will curtail these variables until it is possible to satisfy all of them. Consciousness is infinitely pleasing and malleable. It wants to make all things happy, content, and free. Rather than wrestle with limitation, consciousness seeks to ascertain what the best possible advantages there will be for freedom. When an open-ended consciousness meets up with the mechanics of creation, a beautiful and indescribable union takes place. All objects become friends for that consciousness, and the individual seeks a completely interwoven relationship between that which one knows oneself to be and the Godhead.

The Curtailment of the Ego-Structure

Fundamental to such a relationship is an understanding that each situation is built upon the framework of its predecessor. This is not only true in a mental or psychological sense, but in a purely physical, objective sense. Every momentary flux is built on the fabric of every other, and the pull to respond or react to that avenue of perception is kept in check by the experiencer. Here, the experiencer is cut loose from having to control or react to the experience. Consciousness is then set free to define the nature of experience from the level of creation itself. The individual can see his or her part in the creation without having to adjust it for one's own comfort or gratification. This creates a smooth flow from the central nervous system to the environment and causes changes in the rate, wave, and pulse of the formation of matter.

Consciousness that is driven by the curtailment of ego structure and the surrender to objective unification is rare. Once this state has been gained, then the desire for personal aggrandizement is lost. At this stage, all of the energies and attributes of the individual are steered in the direction of divine manifestation. Everything steps out of the way, and the divine intelligence can fully flower. Localization in reality is then based on the ability of the individual to endure emptiness, locate the seat of manifestation, and mirror the reflective capacities that are brought forward within his or her range. Despite these seemingly unlimited attributes, individuals who are living in such a state are in some respects more limited than individuals who are not. Bound by the definitive matter/motion envelope of causality, non-timebound individuals divest themselves of the notion of personal freedom for the satisfaction of mirroring creation itself.

The souls of individuals who have entered the pathways of yogic creative intensity are led not by the passion for power but the passion for beauty. They long to experience the full range of Divine beauty in each moment, and seek greater and greater intensities of union to bring this about. Impassioned by the desire to undertake the responsibility of learning how to breathe life into matter, they can walk with the hope that they will have the augmentation of spirit to be true to what they see and feel. Visited by the spiritual inspiration that the laws of creation naturally bestow, individuals who pursue the avenue of dimensional manifestation see that which they are becoming as that which is. There is no greater satisfaction or love.

1.2.4
the curvature of time and space

The Rotation of Time

the curvature of time is accounted for by the fact that time essentially rotates. It moves about a fixed radius within the context of space. Time turns about the field of space, applying qualifying spheres of influence until it turns back on itself, repeating the dilation process again and again. There is no curvature of time without space because space has to "turn over on its belly" in order to allow for time to repeat itself and make a proper set of space/time intervals.

Time curves back on space in order to reveal its latitudinal and longitudinal parameters. These parameters are inductive; they repeat their "quest points" in precise intervals in order to reveal their relational spin. Quest points represent the precise turning points where energy, matter, and time come together. Here, the synchronicity of event streams becomes extremely significant, both mathematically and cosmologically. The event streams bunch up, forming a pack or cluster that is quested after by the precise time intervals necessary to complete their formation. These event streams are puffed up by the preceding time formations that act as buffers or chutes onto which the event streams can slide.

The event stream clusters form a symbolic gesture similar to the hub of a wheel, where arcs or spokes run off from the main center, developing parallel avenues of consciousness. These different data streams form the basis for dimensional expression, the hub or centerpoint forming the most uniform origination. The curvature of space and time depends on the refraction of these collective center points, which when stacked in mirrored cross-sections one over the other provide the depth and width upon which the concentric motion of time is based. The mathematical predisposition to curvature is based on the understanding of matter and light returning to their main point of impact upon the introduction of precise temporal specifications. This work was brought forward in the scientific discoveries of the late nineteenth and the twentieth centuries.

The Theory of Max Planck

The scientist Max Planck developed a precursor theory to the present-day scientific understanding of matter, light, and time. Planck deduced that light, which is arrayed as a particle as well as a wave, could be split or transduced down to its finest optical point such that the motion incurred during this split was dependent on the speed of light as well as the distance it traveled. By ascertaining that light was frayed in its encounter with motion, Planck deduced that light could be measured, thus creating the backdrop for the term "light years," and the understanding that light and time are inextricably intertwined.

Due to the fact that time precedes the formation of light, Planck reasoned that each new set of parameters encountered when traveling within the avenue of time would have to be met with a concomitant set of light descriptors as well. Parallel dimensionality assumes that there is a substructure that underlies the core mechanics of time. Planck theorized that there is both a relative and an absolute field of time, within which the structure or basis for material reality could be justified. The articulation of time over a flat field of relativity is characterized by arcing or curvature that makes possible the containment of dimensions. Such containment is not absolute, however, and is based on the precision in which each dimensional sphere can be wrapped or contained within a given set of mathematical protocols.

In Planck's subsequent study of creation mechanics, the underlying assumption was that matter would indeed follow the mathematical routes laid down for it by the intercession of time. If time were not constant, there would not be the capacity for curvature, because each successive match point in the consciousness process would have its own set of rules by which it had to live. Planck understood that light and time realign themselves over a distinct or relative distance. Planck's Constant created the mathematical bridge between light, as a distinct waveform with particulate characteristics, and time, which when described as a derivative of motion underscored the value of developing a consistent framework from which reality could be described. Planck understood light as quanta or expressions of variegated data with wavelengths that are not necessarily uniform but could be molded into a sandwich of consciousness. This has become the theme behind modern-day quantum mechanics and future light-sensitive technologies.

In Planck's Constant, it is motion rather than distance that really engenders our notion of space/time and makes it possible for us to understand how human consciousness could travel in time. The key is that light, which is a carrier wave for the movement of consciousness, breaks apart or splinters when it encounters an incoherent or broken construct within the human mind or nervous system. Planck was a theorist not only of the mechanical attributes of time, but also of the psychological and sociological variables. He ascertained that as time, which followed the rate of motion or intelligence of the mind, wrapped around the speed of light, it became possible for reason or cognitive standards of operation to be realized.

Planck was able to ascertain that the rate or speed of change in psychological terms was not built simply on the functionality of a purely mechanical mental structure. It was in fact in receivership of the very light waves towards which consciousness would need to travel. He perceived that light and consciousness were indeed synonymous in the absolute sense, and that it was only the variability of light that made it possible for event structures to be formulated that would impair or digress from the established curves that light seemed to want to produce.

The Planck Constant therefore set the groundwork for advanced study into the psychological attributes of creative advancement, not only for individuals but also for psychosocial knowledge as a whole. Planck was probably the first modern genius to be able to bridge the psychohistorical frontier of pre-time with the mathematical transactions that made it provable. This territory of randomized information precedes the development of time as a more fixed state.

Historical Time

History itself is merely a plainsong, a psychological motif that radiates through the cornerstone of human history. It is clearly the path of light itself, which rests comfortably in the human brain, making possible our knowledge of creation mechanics, and thus curved space. Planck's definition of the curvature of time was based on the idea that matter, which eventually is formulated from the patterns of energy and space that time represents, must always curl back or refigure itself. That is, matter and time are only constant when there is a derivative installment of light that will paint the picture for time as a slope or correlative function. Light and matter breed time, and Planck was able to see that, given the right circumstances, all of the attributes that make time sensitive to the pull of matter would become prominent.

If it is true that matter simply creates itself when given enough spin on the ball of time, then it must also be true that our propensity to reason as human beings must be built on the same set of variables. This is in fact the case. We wind up the ball of time and pitch it unvaryingly to the batter. We send it forth without a second thought as to how it will affect our personal life circumstances or situation. However, when we begin to understand how time is mirroring the very fabric of our life achievement, there ensues a singular instance in which we are entrained within our own thought processes, and can ascertain what it means to be fully human while time plays in the background.

Max Planck's ability to wrestle with the very mechanics at the basis of light and time gave him a jump on the rest of humanity. He became a fountainhead for what might be termed the fluoral mechanics of light. The underpinnings of light as a function of temporal mechanics is explained by Planck as an array of unified perception that tricks the eye and the brain to view time as something steady when it is actually something fluid and subject to imbalance. Intelligent beings such as ourselves will eventually recognize how to supersede our own time parameters and begin to break the time barrier, both internally and circumstantially. We could say that Mr. Planck is a hero in time in this regard.

The standard Planck definition of speed and motion informs our understanding of how time drops out of infinity at a set rate of speed and recovers its mobility on the downslope. Entropy lifts time free of its moorings and deposits time back to a point of reference that precedes it. Thus time, in its typical loop-locking fashion, becomes a centerpiece upon which the world of matter can build its nest. There is no reason to believe that time is incapable of recapturing its identity once it is tossed into the space/time cauldron in this way.

Time is inherently plastic and retains its consistency even when it is wrapped in the space/time vault for long periods. It consistently rotates on its end, spinning along the Planck Constant and dropping light waves out from its center or stillpoint. Although the speed of light remains constant at certain rates of vibration, there is a kick to this velocity as the spectrum shifts from one of optical intensity to one of dimensional rhythm. When the speed of light reaches a certain entropic rate of thrust, the structures of time are warped or curved to prevent flux.

Changing the Pressure

Time curves to prevent ambient pressure from bursting the inside of the space/time bubble and thereby crushing the matter that might be contained therein. Where there is no matter present, as is the case with free or lucid space, then time has no difficulty compressing itself to fit the given circumstance. In this case, time stands free, not bearing the weight of compressed intervals, because such structures would be unnecessary.

From the psychological point of view, it is time that becomes compressed, causing the individual to experience the event sequences of his or her life in a rather crowded or frenzied scenario. With the advent of time smoothing out or curling, as it is wont to do, the calendar of time within each one of us, which is highly personal and subjective, is given a parallel stretch.

The value of our understanding of time as a clock reference point would not be in place without the knowledge that time can be grafted or hinged onto a particular point in the span of our experience. Knowing that we are living in clock time gives us the feeling that we are expending a certain degree of energy and are moving towards a point of accomplishment or power. Each click or press of the clock gives us the notion that time is something that is constructible, not something that is ineffable, predefined, or simply a matter for conjecture. One wakes up to the idea that time is being constructed out of the human thought process itself, and that it is neither purely subjective nor purely objective. One recognizes that for matter to enter into full objective responsibility for the creation of this dimension, it must focus itself directly in the field of time.

With the advent of clock time, each motion of the clock in constructed time would engender a turn in true or absolute time. For us to comprehend how time relates to motion, and how the speed or frequency of motion governs creative advancement, it is necessary to rely on the notion that time can crisscross between dimensions or frequencies. We are not locked into the dimensional bandwidth through which we bridge our psychology, any more than we are locked into performing a particular function at a particular hour in the day. It is time that governs our activity, but it is our own intelligence that mirrors the temporal choices that we make. So it is that matter, once given the myriad temporal choices that will provide it substance, articulation, and eventually meaning, is faced with the reality that time in its infinite character is fluid.

The knowledge that time comes together as a type of glue that bonds reality together is based on the idea that time is neither a purely psychological reality nor a purely physical one. It is both, inherently and magnificently. To retrieve time from the confines of a light-intensive situation, time must become concurrent with its range of motion. Time pulls free from the motion-sensitive circulation that it enjoys in order to build the structures that hold our psychology in place. It does so by creating barriers or separations in the actual means by which light enters the central nervous system and causes us to understand that it is day or night, up or down, forwards or backwards.

Thus, our very orientation in our surroundings is based on the circuitous, winding force that time creates as it blends with our own awareness. This sinuous, rapidly pulsing, dialectical sphere holds us in check and gives us the capability of becoming racers, movie stars, or any other role that gives us pleasure. We are not bound by time; we are invited by it. We become guests of honor in the synchronous establishment of event streams that it so graciously represents.

The Concept of Motion

Time gains knowledge of space by gaining distance from it. The concept of motion gives time the inherent capability to define its multitudinous parameters. When time greets space in its own field, then motion creeps up and reveals the inherent origin of time for that given interval. Motion is not cosensitive with time, but rather it undertakes a symbiotic movement with time that is both quixotic and rapid. It stirs the pot of time, turning over the folds of space as it proceeds. Locked in the frolicking motion of deep space, time dreams of living cosensitively and independently of comparative sensation. Time is a light-sensitive creature, capable of revealing the continuum of matter in the face of the absolute. The different universes, in their simultaneous flow of life-giving matter/time, are illuminated by this vibrant, pulsing temporal spin. The rhythmic pulsation of time bends the flow of the absolute and gives rise to the infinite parade of matter.

Through the strength of intuition, one instantaneously arrives at the knowledge that time is characterless without the sweet breath of motion. If one can actually see time for what it is, with all of its movements, its strengths, its weaknesses, its idiosyncratic breaks in distance and rate of flow, then one can curl up with time and it can become a friend, a place to rest one's weary head.

The secret of time is to understand its breath, its changing mechanics of consciousness, as it expresses itself through the absolute. Nowhere does time reveal itself better than in the realms of free, unencumbered space. There, free of the demands of matter or creation, time can spin as it pleases, opening its jaws to the infinite without repose. Here time neither sleeps nor gives rise to anything except more of itself. Here time is contained by its own rhythms, and it enters its own avenues without any compromise. By understanding this inherent freedom of time, the human being can begin to express him or herself independently, without the encumbrance of motion or changes in interval dependence.

The Kaleidoscope of Time

Time lives inside each one of us but it does not govern itself without the intervention of the mind. Just as God governs time through His own internal kaleidoscope of internal vision and perception, the human individual becomes a time collector, a mirror of that infinite relationship. No one is free of time, even God, but the human being can become free of his relationship to a fixed or noncalibrated sphere of time, giving him or her the illusion of freedom. It is a useful illusion, which allows one to travel in time and return to the historical moments, past, present, and future, that reveal the byproducts of conceptual reality. Through such advancements, Man can consider the meaning of his own personal reality and understand that truth is relative to his own patterns, his own scheme of things. Without understanding the crisscrossing backdrop of time on the kaleidoscope of life, Man is left to wonder why his life looks the way it does. Without a conversation with the underlying fabric of reality, time appears random and chaste. With time understood, every point of reference has inherent meaning, a sense of light and character, and all of the shades of the absolute can be revealed.

The curvature of time through thick or random space makes possible this interpretative mechanism of time. The curvature of space/time is what gives everything a sense of repetitive elocution or meaning. This relationship of time to matter is not something that can be understood immediately. It must be impressed upon the viewer through his or her advancement in consciousness. With progress, the viewer can see the underlying fabric of reality and know how to proceed, rather than being dumbfounded by the incidents that pattern his or her point of view. Each passing tide of time reveals a further unmasking of this reality until it can be spread open and enhanced through the Divine Mind itself.

Each set of space/time wave frequencies must be latitudinal, because they cross over a different set of space/time barriers. This is how matter retains its shape, size, and elasticity. The plastic or elastic quality of time, when fed the parameters of deep space, keeps time warped or curved for long intervals. Each curve blankets the space/time relationship, mimicking set variables at every stretch of activity. The fabric of time is a lively, frolicking expression of motion-sensitive derivatives that underlie the foundation of psychological and physical reality. Time cycles back and forth over the fluid avenues of space, creating a blanket of time/energy/matter that forms the celestial bodies.

Time Ribbons

The ribboning masses of fixed and windward stars that line up over the cavalcade of the absolute are mirrored reflections of the wandering avalanche of time. Stars form and dissolve, each taking a tier of time within it. Stars appear dwarfed because they are no longer bridged by the antiquated time/matter feed that has heretofore represented them. Stars die, recede, appear to fade, although the temporal mass that is left behind forms the backdrop for new star babies to be born. Clusters of stars are like pages in a book; time turns from one page to another creating temporal interludes that lock each star mass together. Time glues the cluster to the point of its origination, creating the binding influence of the cosmos.

Space/time continues through the variance of light and heat, and is not independent of motion, except when matter does not come into contact with light. Light frequencies that travel in the space/time continuum become less fluid in their sequencing only when they traverse cold space. Light is not warm except where time travels in its path. Each break in the subsection of light that makes up the space/time portion lifts time free from its inherent imprint, and describes a coherent state of entropy which makes time available to matter.

To determine the frequency of time in relationship to matter, two variables must be present. First, there must be radiant heat or cold light that represents the character of time as it spins back on itself from its own continuum. Second, there must be a spin to time that causes it to break off on its own and return to the light factory from which it is derived. There is no value to light without time because light bubbles up through the conduit of time to be cooled before time ferments it into matter.

Opening the Door for Divine Breath

God opens the door for time through divine breath. It is through the respiration of time as an eternal force that God enters our reality. To free time from God is impossible. We structure our life events through a step-by-step movement of evolutionary progress.

The imprint that time creates with relationship to matter is arguably the fundamental concern for creation to ponder. When matter is encrusted with the jewels that time inlays into the fabric of creation, each interval that is structured from this source holds within it the pause or gap that will eventually breed the inherent organization of new life. Light becomes not simply an influential factor but the causal breakpoint between matter that lives entirely independent of time and matter that lives predominantly in the shadow of time. Matter becomes the hourglass by which the temporal understanding of sentient life can read its own future.

Time is influenced by the rate at which light falls within it, thus justifying the succeeding rate of spin. If time is captured by light prematurely it loses its elasticity and will fall back into its premanifest state. Time can only catch light by waiting for it to remember its own inherent flow or distance. Light becomes refractive, divested of its essential character, and thus it has no memory of its own. It remains equidistant from the speed at which it was previously traveling, and though it possesses a type of innate memory, it cannot remember the true and complete relationship that it had with time at its original stage. Light defines its present velocity without the interference of time. Time cannot hold onto light, but light cannot break free without the permission or intention of time.

Each curve of time that enters into the mind of God is essentially a mirror or prism in which light can refract strata or nodules of its own influence back into the Godhead. To discuss time one must understand that time is the hourglass of the Godmind as it is expressed in the relational field. Time is Godless within itself. It has no mind of its own without the imprint of the absolute impressed upon it. For time to catch up with light, God must send a code or message to time to cause it to wind back and create avenues in which light can travel. This relationship with God in the field of time and matter is what gives rise to intelligence itself. Intelligence becomes buoyant because it is imbued with the constructs of time. The inherent reasoning that makes intelligent beings able to think, read, draw, paint, or do any creative activity is based on our ability to freeze time as a relational object.

The beauty of this truth is that time, though it can be fixed by the creative activity of a human mind, is not fixed in any absolute or permanent sense. Time functions as a marker; it is a rotational gesture in the ever-spinning, constantly stirring relationship that time presents in the dissolution or creation of matter. Through our relationship with time, the God Intelligence gives us the ability to find our way through the chasms of choice and perception that make up our dimension, and gives us the creativity to decide what we are here to do. God creates avenues or walkways in which time is presented as manifest creation. This allows time to become a spatial imprint in the open window of creation.

Knowing God Through Time

To know God one must know time. Time does not open to God without His knowledge. The stature of the Godhead itself relies on time because it is through time that all of the imprints of creation are contained. They are then brought forward into relative manifestation. Despite the fact that human beings experience time as limited, God sees time as infinite and unmanifest, independent of the governing influence of light. God uses light as a point of reference for creation, but He maintains a special place for time because He knows that it is unrelated to anything except His own indescribable nature.

Time is therefore closest to God and cloaked forever in His light. Once one understands that time is a characteristic of the movement of the Godhead in its own field, then one can grow closer to both God and time in one's own existence. One comprehends that it is not matter that makes up the characteristic basis of our dimensional psychology, but it is time that does this. Time, in its celestial stature as the mirror for God's own reflection, gives us the wherewithal to know ourselves as well as the environment that surrounds us.

Our lives demand a deep sensation of a time base to cultivate living things. Since organic matter is so dependent on time, it cannot exist without an inherent knowledge of it. That is why all organic life forms have a seed of time within them. For the structures that God creates to be lively, they must rely on His will and exist simply as His instruments or playthings. God structures time to be accordant with His will so that the sensation of our being independent life forms can actually arise. Time gives us the program whereby we structure our own life sequences, but it is the Godforce itself that takes this programming, shapes it, and gives it the final curves that will bring a full human life into a sense of completion. Even when events occur that appear to break into the sequences that we have laid down, it is the Godforce that relabels and restructures these sequences so that we can understand a new beginning or a new end. There is nothing wasteful or unnecessary.

Karmic Repetition

Although the organization of time may appear random, it structures the fabric of human existence. Through the evolutionary movement of history, whether personal or collective, the flow of time is revealed. Each person or situation peeks out over the field of his or her personal drama, presenting a show of temporal situations that act as sparks or catalysts for future templates to appear. This normic or karmic repetition of temporal patterns does not necessary imply that we are to be stripped of our natural desire for progress or achievement. As we trip over the roots of our karma, the nature of life as a temporal formation reveals itself. We are not limited or bound by our fate but are rather torn from it, much like a garment caught on the back of a chair. We wrench our way from the preconceived pattern that appears to govern us and find ourselves back at a time and place that is much the same as the innocent makings from which we began. We are not therefore afraid of the binding mechanisms of time; we are shorn from them, and in so doing are inextricably and wholly free.

Karma does not imply that we are locked forever in a relentless wheel of nonchange. The beauty of karma is that it patterns the possibilities of freedom through every turn of the notch. As we advance, we can see the dance of karma unfolding, and like any good dancer we can anticipate the feel, the lilt of the next step. We charge forward, seeking advancement of our lives and fortune, and in the most careful and elegant way we are able to leap past misfortunes and darkness that heretofore would have been forbidden and constrictive.

Karma is the doorway to self-realization because as it restores the cyclical mirror that defines our personal universe; it also gives away the secrets of how that universe has been constructed. Once we can see the patterns that have at one time held us in bondage, we are forever and inexorably free. The binding influence that is retained is just a vestigial imprint, a scar that is irrelevant once the individual can fully master the personal avenues on which the wheel of time must tread.

Event streams give way to the repetition of data that exists solely for the purpose of elucidating primary motifs in our quest for individuality and change. The fabric of reality is stitched together through these motifs, gradually and inexorably, until such time as the human intelligence reconstitutes itself completely as it wakes up to its essential nature. Event streams that are chosen mirror previous choices, but they are not bound by them any more than one row of corn is bound to another. The pathways between each sequence are mapped out through the carousel of time as it spins ever more majestically through the events and separates or recasts them as human psychology demands.

These event streams reveal the fabric or underlying trend of meaning behind our life plan. Time gives life meaning; without time there would be no sense of repetition and therefore no feeling value in the pattern of existence. With time, everything has a flavor, a value, an inherent stroke of the pen that gives it character and a sense of graciousness. This is why things that have aged well have an inherent beauty. Once God recognizes that the patterns inherent in a given field of influence have been fully formed, He can withdraw His mighty hand and proceed elsewhere. One must break free of the time constraints and live in a state of open, unrestrained spatial origination in order to determine the full extent of the personal life stream.

1.2.5
the fractionization of time

Breakages in the Rhythm

ime fractionization is the key to understanding how time differentiates and compartmentalizes in the mechanics of creation. The activity of fractionization is the result of independent whirlpools or spins of energy that reside within each time window.

Time matrices are formed through the process of fractionization. As time individuates into separate streams of activity, each of these streams forms a conduit or bypass for dimensional activity to occur. These streams are linked together through endpoints, which are the final outcropping of the time spread as it coalesces into a break. This break is similar to a pause or breath that crystallizes the time feed and makes it possible for it to repeat itself.

The structure of time involves a series of ripples or waves that crystallize. Each of these waves can concretize in such a way as to present different shapes or sizes of expression. As these crystallized waves break open, each reveals new templates of energy/light that can form the basis for new migrations of the field. The rapid increase of thickness or tension between the opposing lines of force causes the time lines to advance uniformly. Time waves crystallize like stalactites breaking off from the main crystalline buttress in jagged but often evenly spaced gradations. The rapidity of these breakages forms the rhythm of time in its precedence and creates the necessity for new time windows to form.

The spread or bridge that is created when these windows of time link is determined most closely by the degree to which time can be calibrated. This calibration is based not only on the template of fractionization but also on the psychological backdrop into which such a template advances. These bridges can be viewed from any surrounding point. The capacity of the time break to fractionizate makes it possible for the time spread to appear as a window of opportunity for each point of origin. Possible outcomes for each window are infinite, but the capacity for their organization is actually built on a finite principle. This principle is that time inserts itself into the context of consciousness; it is an interloper in the field of form.

Creating the Time Spreads

Time creates the capacity for movement, and as such its contiguous activity builds upon itself again and again, making it possible for the time matrix to formulate its own essential character. Without fractionization, the time spread would be randomized but would not retain any of the individual flavor that would differentiate it from the rest of the temporal field. Without a flux in time, there would simply be a loop-de-loop of parallel realities without any one point of reference finding favor in the matrix.

Time windows are created when time, which is an optical spread, finds its corollary surface through any given reference point. Time opens a portal or window, whereby it can reference itself laterally to each independent link. Since time is infinitely variable, it will form a myriad of these windows, and it is therefore the responsibility of consciousness to form the backdrop of how and when such windows will be formulated. This centrifugation of temporal reality creates the fabric whereby our personal set of everyday circumstances is brought into view.

Time coalesces, and as it does, whirlpools or vents are created in the matrix. These whirlpools form whirligigs that simulate the formation of reality at its base. Each of these whirligigs is funneled through the matrix through a type of swoosh or wind which, when heard on a subtle level, imbues consciousness with a sense of a shift or a break in the matrix. This is why when one initially enters a field of time there is a kind of hush or whisper, during which time is developing its strategy for random materialization.

Time windows develop both internal and external reference points. They define their own parameters and are startlingly original in their conception. Since they are mandatory for the development of both eternal and finite time, their determination is the central focus for the process of fractionization. When time bends, it fractionizates; when it breaks or curves more acutely, it then forms spears or arrows which make it possible to literally pierce the underlying fabric of consciousness. The independence of time streams is related directly to the ability of consciousness to maximize the breaks as they are randomly situated.

Time breaks appear face up when they are located laterally to the break. They appear face down when they are closed or formulated centrifugally. As the windows open and shut, each of the time breaks builds up a kind of mass or force which if not randomized coequally would actually crush the windows preceding it. As the windows are maximized, the gaze or break of time is broken up bit by bit until all of the factors for randomization are complete. This allows time to present an elegantly curved vantage point that can be optimized even when the full course of fractionization has not been observed.

The windows that precede the break are often opaque until they are made more translucent through the factor of light. Light is the principal variable that defines consciousness. When light and sound are woven together in the beneficent array of time, there is a quality of development that allows the time breaks to loosen or swell, as the case may be. The relationship between time and matter is dependent upon the range of motion that each window of time can present. As a given reality is brought up on the screen of possibility, time can switch back over itself to create new structures. It is the forward and backward movement of time along the curve that actually can carve out new dimensional realities.

The Factoring of Time

The reality that is formed when time curves or drops back from its original position may also be joined by a quality of precession. This formation causes time to leap back over itself as breaks or divisions in the curve tend to repeat. As each new formation of time encapsulates, a rapid firing of advanced motion is offered continuously to the spread. With the advent of a new format, time forms a blanket or wave across the horizon of precession. This assists in the formation of a new range of possibility.

Since time factors itself endlessly, it is possible that each of the breaks will be infinite in its correlation as well. From point to point, or break to break, time compounds its interest in the bank of the absolute. Drawing from each account at precise intervals and investing time according to the need of the matrical interlink itself, time gains ground from each preceding opportunity. Every move that time makes is precise, to the point, and interdependent. It correlates precisely to the degree that time must go to make its next move.

The fact that different frequencies or wave formations of time must crystallize directly from the absolute does not preclude that time will always come across in a random or fluid manner. Time will criss-cross over the different fields available to it, and although it may seek to find correlative formations with the absolute, it will also maintain this fluid or random position. The simultaneity of the two states brings about order in what would appear to be chaos without such inclusion.

Time Loops

The process of looping is the counterbalance to the process of fractionization. With looping there is no breakup in the winds or motions that govern time. Looping presents curves of opposites, whereas fractionization is beneficial to the manifestation of infinite possibilities. Looping instills time with the capacity to revisit past sequences that are important both psychologically and structurally. Were time to simply be instilled with the aspect of fractionization, our sense of personal reality would have a width to it but not a breadth. With the advent of fractionization, the winds of time are steered apart and form the backdrop for all of the motion that time represents with response to consciousness and the ability to witness the manifest creation.

Time is a benefactor to motion, and as a result the windfall that is gained when time and consciousness interweave cannot be overestimated. If a time break resides nearest to that point, we could say that the time break has gained optimum or fluid momentum. It is essential for the time break to retain the pulse or character of that impulse so as to be invested into a particular section of time. As the preceding window dominates, time is switched around, and the gaze or break of time becomes situated.

If a time break arises too soon, there is a possibility that it will be missed. This would shatter the matrix and possibly create the collapse of the entire stream. It is essential that the time break fall evenly within the matrix; then the whole fractionization process can proceed smoothly.

At time wave zero, the internal fractionization process enters a type of standstill or free-fall, in which the variables split apart and randomize gently, like leaves falling in the wind. If this process happens too momentously, a curtain falls over the absolute, and the ability of the time breaks to correlate themselves is lost. We could then say that there is a hole or break in the time frames which is essentially impossible to justify. It is only through the lapse of time that matter and time can complete themselves. However, if this lapse is too great, time fractionizates too quickly and the time variables cannot array themselves to accomplish their essential task. This task is the establishment of a clear, referential field onto which reality and matter can take their course.

In order for time to well up and impart the variables represented, it must slide or drop back through the winds that have been formed. If there is a miss in this slide or recession, the time break will collapse and, as has been stated, the stature of the time break will be in question. Time must continue to expand, even if a specific event sequence has not been fully set in place.

The calibration of a time break is due in part to the inevitable collapse of certain structures, which causes intense fractionization and then the inability of the matrix to rebuild itself independently. Time and space are so fragile in this regard that the slightest little tilt from one stream of influence to the other will result in a permanent hole in the matrix and an inability of the spread to repair itself. This is why we say that time and consciousness are the most fragile of all realities in God's world.

Circular Time

Time breaks are colinear in the fractionization process. As a result, news is introduced in a circular fashion with every change in the rate of spin. This way the time matrix maintains a steady flow. The pinwheel-like circumference of the time variables is available to the matrix only when there are marginal origins to the spin itself. Each turn in the wheel of time trips a specific set of corollary integers or vestibules, which makes it possible for the time spread to appear stationary for a given period. Without this feature, time would feel like it was on a permanent merry-go-round, never slowing to reveal the psychological circumstances at hand.

Time, being circular, develops intervening attributes of time, speed, and motion for each range or calibration of a spin. This is why, when time curves, there is a characteristic groove or sharpening of the points that makes the time wave appear compatible. Since time and matter must function as a type of groove-to-socket enterprise, time must enter into the window at precisely the right rate of speed or motion for the time interface to lock the appearance of matter into place. Each time the matrix spins co-laterally, there are corresponding movements that signify that the full motion of the time continuum has come to rest. This resting, heaving motion of the matrix brings into position just the right point of reference for the co-magnetics of time to be established.

Fluctuations in the Time Variables

Since time is a fluctuating variable and motion must fluctuate in tune with it, it is matter that forms the basis for solidity and strength in the soup of creation. Corollary intervals or breakfronts attach themselves to the spin and create the magnetism that causes matter to attach itself to the underlying field. One could say that time and matter, when resting nearby to each other, form a type of pillow that crunches or expands as polarity requires. The in-and-out movements of the polarization form the lateral spin, and the back-and-forth movements create the flow or dimensionality of the experience. Since time is magnetized to its field of opposites, it attracts to itself those standards of optimization which are easily in reach. It looks for pairs or twins of itself; then, calibrating them to the proper dimensionality, it loops them off a pair at a time.

The degree to which time can reconstitute itself is also based on its ability to fractionizate. One could assert that time is contiguous to the field of motion but not to the wholeness of the central force of consciousness. However, it is time that plays the role of "god" in the formulation of motion as a constant. Therefore, when time is resting, it develops its own synchronicity, and this spin to the center is what causes it to be crafty in its ability to resist self-duplication when it is not indicated. To develop originality, time must be capable of developing new strategies for polarization without risking depletion of the central intelligence that brought its identity about.

Time dances on the face of the absolute. Continuously in motion and arrayed unilaterally against itself, it betrays all of the corollary movements that make it obvious to those who would watch its rate of spin. The value of fractionization is that as time curves back, cutting across the perimeters of the matrix, the whole structure bolsters itself, creating avenues of perfection that make the matrix complete.

Longitudinal Time

Time develops through a system of longitude, which stretches variables across a plane or sea of magnitude; and latitude, which frames or quashes variables until they array themselves neatly on end. Since time reflects the optimal pools that define matter, one could say that time is sub-longitudinal because it is uniquely characterized by a subset of time variables that create its skin or outer core. Time is binary because it is the one-two feed of time that makes the on-and-off movement for matter to solidify. Through its gangly field of opposites, time never runs astray but picks up its correlates as it is wont to do.

Time is inherently fruitful because its own substructure continuously makes "babies" or tiny units of space/time matter that form the backdrop for each curve. Since time ranges itself in a binary or polarized string, we say that the strings that formulate time are matter that has been made in the likeness of time. These strings or collective blankets are characteristic of time as it spills itself on to the rims of consciousness. Matter is a spread, a shield, much like a coating on the edge of a riverbed, lining the field with possibilities for the establishment of unified creation.

The reach of time, which is neither of a forwards or backwards nature in concept, is longitudinal in scope. Time pools are the result of time needing to regroup so that it can feed all of the variables that are within its reach. The pool is scooped out at intervals to prevent it becoming over-loaded. As the time variables coalesce around the pool, an optimum height or breadth of time is reached, and then the systems that relay conscious-ness from matter to time and back again are launched into view. Since time is squared with consciousness in a type of resistance or feedback loop, it is important to recognize that time and consciousness are not always based entirely in a system of perfection. Flaws or tears in the lining of real-ity can occur which mimic the flaws or tears that are obvious in the time breaks themselves.

The Laws of Formation

Time spins and matter is propelled. This is the secret of successful opti-mization of the field. As a result, all of the possibilities for operative mechanics are realized. Time pays attention to the laws surrounding its formation, and like a patient student it awaits its turn in the calendar of opposites until a subtle position for restitution can emerge. There are only a few situations in which time, bent too far in one direction or the other, will not commit itself to the process of self-repair. In this case, the time variables are skewed and there is no chance for optimum repetition or advancement.

The appearance of time as a slope or hill is a concept that allows us to examine how time can change shape, size, and appearance so dramatically. Since time is bilateral, it must glide or coast along the outsides of the time pool. This is why, when we see time from the opposite direction, it always seems to be standing still, while when we are living time from inside the perspective of the present reality, it seems to be going along at a good clip. Time is referenced through psychological paradigms rather than physical ones. However, the slope of time is what causes us to have a sense that we have seen or known something before. The slope of time gives us a sense of a psychological past. It is the slope of time that is usually unpredictable because it is so variable.

The Arcs of Time

Time forms arcs or curtains which differ from its other shapes insofar as an arc is like a cascade of variables that seem to have no parallel opposites. The arc slides down the time matrix like a thick, fast, gelatinous gas. We could say that the arcs occur as smokescreens for consciousness. The arcs create shade, density, and respite from the intensity of the temporal curve. As the curve sweeps through the downslope, it forms a type of umbrella-like nobility that retains the demeanor of the curve without changing its oblong shape. The umbrella-like formation is pleated due to the distance that time must travel from one parallel loop or swing to another. The umbrella braces or squashes in time's brisk windstorm. It heaves forward, creating a rocking motion that will eventually lead to the time breaks being held at bay at both ends. This provides the comprehensive lift and "shading" that will render that particular temporal matrix complete.

Time and consciousness array themselves in arcs so that the slope, which is a much more variable and fluid motion, will have something to pin itself upon. The arcs are the standards of deviation for time. They show us how time will be "marked up" in the field of consciousness, and bear a distinct resemblance to the afterburn that one sees in a fast-moving celestial object.

Time and space are not scattered, but are rather opaque in their character. What is meant by this is that the rate of spread, when sped up or cascading down the edge of the matrix, presents itself at a very thick or masked rate of vulnerability. The exact opposite is true when time is slow-moving, because then the variables are quite scattered and it is impossible to fully develop their potentialities from a psychological perspective.

One cannot easily predict the variability of time without understanding that slope causes time to "chew its fingers" and develop all sorts of strategies to ease the anxiety that the unknown brings. In making predictions about what is to occur as the motion shifts from the absolute to the relative, it is impossible to assess the variables unless the slope is taken into consideration. The trigonometric sequences, which mathematically define the rate of slope and assign variables or "crunch cards" to each option, flesh out the temporal field and give it room to breathe.

Time arcs, spins, or collaborates with the matrix as the case demands. Since the slope is the christening force for time as it appears from the absolute to the relative, it is also the first to subside when time wakes up and identifies itself as the creator in the field of matter. Since time and consciousness develop strategies for optimization unilaterally, as time becomes more obstinate, more self-justifying, and more capable of stagnation, so slope becomes more impaired and lazier in its self-definition.

Time is set in motion due to the position or range of "bleed" in the arc. Since time cannot loop itself over a variable that is simultaneous with its own rate of motion, it must maintain a distance or nobility that causes it to be in step with the system that is taking place.

Time arcs or spins around like an automobile that has spun out on the ice. It loops around, gauges how it will propel its field of motion, and then gets back on to the proper rate or sequence without having to consult with any outside reference points. The time arcs accommodate each point of reference and act as buffers or signal points for the time loops to present themselves.

Time arcs or slides according to need and desire. These decisions are principally calibrations of the time continuum itself. One must recognize that the continuum is an intelligent, self-defining field, and therefore will continue to develop strategies for self-justification or impairment along the way. Time arcs are the most intelligent of God's developments in the field of time. They provide the kick or buffer for time to gain its full independence, and for motion to define itself as something that will eventually spill over into material reality.

The Strategy of Meaning

Since time and consciousness defy any set laws of accommodation, their attempts to limit the rate of spin are always variable. Time is lifeless unless motion comes in and alleviates its nostalgic turn. Time develops all sorts of strategies to maintain itself in the face of a fast-moving dive or slope, but since time cannot exist independently of its slope it always manages to sneak back into place when necessary.

The full restitution of time in the integer-rich life of the sea of momentum is always developed through absolute repetition. Time collapses, breaks forth, returns, and collides in a constant play of motion that is most lively when it is first begun. To recognize the restoration of time is to understand that time is the reason for all optimal mechanics in the relative universe. Time spins out, time spins in, and all of the meaningful coincidences that build up to form the psychological parameters for sentient life are ultimately formed.

Time builds friends from its relative neighbors. It seeks out vistas on to which it will return again and again. The temporal arcs that signify who will appear and who will disappear form the backdrop for the understanding of unification and eventually of mortality. Time is immortal continuously but mortal subterraneously. In other words, time is made mortal through the combination of opposites that create freeze positions or gaps in its range of motion. Time arcs in order to accommodate a free range of motion, and always returns to this arc when it is through with accommodating the field of opposites it has randomly generated.

The psychological offspring of time are the arcs themselves. When an individual determines how his or her point in the space/time continuum will be reached, he or she then loops over the back of his or her own matrix and develops the necessary parameters to make the time sequences come about. In this way, the temporal slope for full originality and optimum grandeur can be displayed.

The Slope of Time

Time mirrors the rate of change for each impending storm or sea of motion. This allows it to be minimally dependent on every situation that comes its way. Since time and consciousness loop around continuously, one could say that time is like the blade of a helicopter, twisting and turning in each direction so that the time field will "stay up" and not collapse randomly from view. The slope or forward motion of time gives it the character of optimization, and the slant or downward glide gives it the character of change. This is why time and motion are always codependent and rarely if ever affected by the change in the rate of spin.

The angles that display themselves when time goes into forward drive and strives to counteract any variables that have been "misbehaving" are the characteristics that define what we would call the "forward-past." That is, time and consciousness are "superstoppers" in the absolute. They develop curved chains of reference that swing the whole field of matter about and make for the time parameters that document forward-future space.

Time and consciousness develop a range of motion that allows the future to be variable but the present to be absolute. This is the paradox. The present stands on end, like a type of temporal monument, seemingly motionless, but sharp, more defined than its temporal opposite. On the other hand, the future, in its striving towards infinite perfection, is always utilizing the function of the binary curve to develop strategies for independence. This is what is meant by optimal randomization.

Time arcs are the basis whereby the future builds momentum. Time arcs are the way that the future "seizes the day" and develops its inceptionary mechanics for fluid motion. When time and consciousness array themselves in this grand and optimal manner, there is cause for celebration in the field. Time has become uniform, fluid, and manifest, and it is through this eventuality that there is full accommodation in the spread. All of the variables line up like little doggies at the fair, developing strategies for their range of motion independent from any of the future parameters that they would have been fed. Everything is clear, uniform, stretched out, and open. Every fundamental impulse is built into the structure. Each category or system developed will be an independent cause of sharpness or randomness.

Reaching the Resting Point

Once fractionization has reached this optimal resting point, then the range of motion is complete. The arc keeps the time variables posed at their proper angles so they can be picked up by the spin. The slope keeps all of the variables frozen until such time as the field's range of motion can thaw them.

This whirligig of motion, time, space, and psychological underpinnings is what makes up the core of unified reality, and allows the sentient being to get his or her bearings in the world of fractionizated time. We could say that although time does eventually become uniform and free of any clutter, the process that brings it about is one of the most fragile and messy around. All of the avenues for perception rely on this fractionization process, and this is why it is so important in understanding the backdrop for psychological reality. Time becomes the doorway through which sentient beings develop their taste for infinite knowledge, and it is time that restores reason from the insanity that can be provoked when all randomization is left unchecked. Time organizes reality in such a way that sentient beings can restore their dreams and recognize their role in eternity. It is for this reason that temporal mechanics was born.

Time is a glider. It glides through the infinite collecting different strata of data that it will use to mark or gesticulate where a certain event structure will emerge. Think of it this way: when a glider picks up its pitch or yaw, it moves to and fro, forgetting how to throw itself back on the current in order to gain optimum draw. When time forgets how to function in the wind or funnel that it has created, it has to reconfigure all of its opportunities directly from the pool in front of it. It cannot stop to think, "Well, I am in the soup and there are so many possibilities, and I have to figure out where I will be." It has to coast, spin, and move. It has to maintain its equilibrium or it will fall into the absolute unnoticed.

As time shrieks past the field of opposites, it leaves behind a tracer or marker that could best be described as a filtered stream of radiant light. This marker is the best way to see where time will go and what it is about to do. Time glides forward, floating onto the surface of all of its possible parameters. The psychological bleed that is represented when time floats along unaware of its surroundings causes the individual to feel unmoored from his or her temporal vantage point. This is indeed disturbing because human beings rely greatly on their moorings to their individual life circumstances.

Mirroring the Event Streams

When time coasts wildly along, it leaves behind the rhythms and attributes that have established it as a type of psychological backdrop for the underpinnings of reality. The individual is forced to pose rather than to maintain his or her spontaneous stream of responses or understandings. When time ceases to glide, the whole psychological framework becomes jerky, uneven, and hard to predict. One could say that the time streams have forgotten how to fly. They get lost in the complicated ramifications that are brought about when time loses its point of reference. Then, the insidious aspects of the mind, which are like jumper cables in the stream of the absolute, are more likely to take hold. They will shock the system back into the spiral again and restore a measure of temporal sanity and apparent reason.

Time cannot appear twice. In other words, time establishes itself as an individual and original field of motion whenever an event stream betrays itself. One cannot go back in time, really, because one cannot conjure up the precise system of variables that made that original time sequence come about. The best one can do is to reconstitute time, to bring up the possibilities in a type of psychological backstroke that will allow one to see how time can be made anew. Then one can recognize the mistakes or poses that caused certain event streams to come about and others to fade. In this way, one can wrestle with one's own inner goblins but not disturb the fundamental matrix that has been the basis for all underlying action. Were this not true, the mirroring effect, which is one of the principal characteristics of time from a psychological perspective, would not come into play.

Mirroring is brought about because it is the first step to bridging psychological and physical reality. One sees a mirror of one's own thought process in the impending reality, and in so doing can decide what should crystallize onto the field and what should remain motionless and in place. As a result, one can reckon with the causality behind one's own individual reality and not have to break up the curtain that has caused that reality to come fully into view. One could say that it is the mirroring effect in consciousness that makes room for more of the absolute to shine forth.

Once time blends with the psychological constructs that have brought one's own worldview about, there is a ribboning effect that stretches time more effectively than any other process. Time develops the optimal mechanics for originality while maintaining its steady, more even character. Out of this, all of the probable causes for material reality can come into view. Time is built on the seeds of optimal causation. It functions as a type of laundry room for the absolute to develop strategies of ratio-synchronization that must come into play.

Time splits off independently of any variables that could be found when the absolute meets the relative. The splitting off or fractionization that has been described is the desirable state for any formulation of sentience. It is the backdrop for all of the psychological shifts in awareness that even out the reality of a human/sentient lifetime.

1.3
the character of time

1.3.1
The signature of time

The Interpretation Factor

T he singular most important function of time is its ability to regulate and control the psychological basis for reality. Time creates a signatory nomenclature that catalogues, estimates, and refines the time values as they speed along the human nervous system. Since time creates an estimate of how it will spiral, long before it actually imprints itself directly into the human physiology, it is through this estimated response that organs and systems calibrate their response to the give and take of ordinary life.

The signature of time describes how time will meet the advances of everyday existence from a noninterpretive point of view. Since each event sequence provides a particular angle on the flow of information into the nervous system, time must create a systematic set of variables that defines this substructure independently of any derived norms. Time ekes out a range of motion for each of these variables, which is seen as a signature or match point. Time invests each of these quanta with a rhythm or pulse that allows the nervous system to interpret the data that are to be imprinted within it. These imprints create the psychological understanding of who we are, how we see the world, and how we interpret the pathways of time that our individual plan of destiny imparts.

Time Signatures

This signature of time describes the correlation between the actual event sequence structure and the randomized impulses that are stored by the nervous system as a means of imprinting psychologically derived information about the meaning of life. The signature creates a fluid medium through which such information can be stored. When an individual goes to process a given event in his or her life story, he or she pulls up the event signature that gives meaning to that individual situation. Since this information is entirely subjective in its personal content, the nervous system must create a system of signals which will provide the impersonal or underlying nonattached language that will cause the physiology to understand why and how something has taken place. When the individual chooses a given path, a temporal signature or imprint is immediately created. This is how information about the nature of personal reality is stored in the database. Then, when the individual has a need to recall or reconfigure his or her experience, the information is pulled up through the temporal signature and brought to life again through the inner workings of the mind.

Time relates to event sequences as if they were objects, but it also relates directly to physical objects that enter its field of view. For time to describe a nonmaterial object, it has to catalogue the sensation, the positive field of response. Then it holds this imprint within the context of the nervous system for a precise interval that allows the individual to repage the information and understand its foundation in his or her reality. For an individual to relate to time, he or she must be able to commune with time from the basis of his or her own fundamental reality. By dialoguing with time from the level of the brain and central nervous system separate from random fields of interpretation, the individual's psychology expands to fill the gaps between objective and subjective perception.

The Psychology of Event Streams

Event streams act as cues or ribbons for the nervous system so that it can impart the precise messages that will cause the impartial reality to come into view. Event streams function as event objects or mirrors for the nervous system, much the same way as obstacles or identifiable landmarks would be produced as we march down the road. The events are tagged, marked off, and incorporated into the interpretation network of the imagination.

One could say that there are two types of psychological language barriers that event streams have to master in order to become decipherable to the individual. The first is the barrier of sound, which creates a particular system of bites or readouts that make the event stream intelligible to the individual. Even psychologically based events have an impulse or sound base that gives the nervous system a cue as to the form of intelligence that is to be represented.

The second type of tagging involves a subjective felt response that tells the individual how to view the event now and into the future. It is a type of fogging that actually temporally clouds the event structure and brings it into a sense of felt subjectivity so that a response can be registered. There is an underlying impartial tagging that goes on simultaneously with this foggier, more delicate imprint. Without it, the individual would never be able to rise above a subjective stance and study his or her own reality on a more impartial or less personal basis. However, the temporal landscape is inherently filled with purely whimsical or personal information that only the individual can understand or interpret. This is why the human nervous system is so difficult to fully comprehend outside of the frame of reference of a particular individual or cultural influence.

The relationship of time to the event stream is formed through the random occurrence of each variable that is elicited to form the bulk or lining of time. The lining is made up of all of the psychological variables that will be influenced as the individual imprints his or her foundation for reality on to the event stream. The event stream crawls or streams through the time/ space wave, forming a signatory landscape that will be interpreted continuously by the mind, simultaneous with the events as they are pictured. The event streams curve back onto themselves, creating a type of rotating signature that gives the mental landscape an image of future and past.

The Hop, Skip, and Jump

Time curves back on itself only through a random series of possible points of anticipation. This is why time must always be considered to be happening at a random portrayal of sequencing rather than at a predictable line of crossing. The point here is that time, rather than being a container with variables that are always announced ahead of the event, creates a field of variables that will be capable of dancing in rows of implied opposites. It is a type of "ring around the rosy" where the time variables dance about each other in pairs, creating the bulk of consciousness that the individual will encounter during his or her personal situation.

Time forms a series of multiple-based event sequences which hop, skip, and jump around each other, creating the basis for an individual's whole life screen. The litmus test for the expression of time involves its ability to curve back over the field of consciousness so as to reveal the pop-up value of time on the down side. When time flaps over itself in this way, it creates the field of personal memory that causes the individual to be able to distinguish what is important or relevant in his or her life story. Time regulates the event stream through this interwoven unification between actual time and record-able time in a type of wave or scatter stream of formation that forms the backdrop for both psychological and material reality.

Since time is the vehicle for space to refine itself, the skin or coating of time is crucial to the way that time identifies itself. Space refines its character through the emergence of time. As time imprints itself along the event hori-zon, a pool is created out of which each time interval can pop up to form new, ever more complex event streams. The skin of time refers to the moment or interval in which the time break is peeled off like the skin of an onion along the event parameter, and then pops up to form the new possibility. The skin or perimeter of time is the most superficial or identity-driven spatiality to the entire continuum. It is here that time presents itself as a forward-driving, moving, ever-changing vision, and it is also, because of this parchment-like skin, more highly vulnerable to the capacity for change. Therefore entropy, or the inability for motion to present change, becomes the least influential.

The Backdrop of Space

Time, as the underlying field, and space, being the secondary modality, create a positivistic surge in the event/time continuum that causes the event streams to pop up randomly over the surface of the void like bubbles in hot glass. This surging effect in the surface of the event stream brings about sig-natory arrays of time/matter, which form the seed mechanism for con-sciousness to display itself onto the field.

The backdrop for time is interstellar space itself, and time is a voyager in space like any other. For time to appear as a cloak or random error-drawer in the space/time continuum, it must always appear to be questing for entry into the event stream and never coaxing a lead. The time matrix swings ran-domly from one series of event "coasters" to another, and in this way the underpinnings of time never fall short of appearing as teased strands in the undergarment of the matrix.

The Possibilities of Interplay

As individuals move along their individual event stream, they relate even-ly and fully to these coasters, which suggest to them ways in which they will be able to develop or control the event sequences of their lives. Since individuals are rarely satisfied with one or two such event possibilities, they often will create streamers or ribbons of information, which the nervous system will singularly interpret and inform itself about in an attempt to gain a purposeful route through the individual's unique range of life. There are rarely opportunities to change or fix such decisions once they are made, but it is in the planning of such decisions that a vast range of possibilities presents itself. Once the individual has committed his- or herself to the coasters as they emerge, the individual is inherently locked into the possible future that will be made available. It is clear from this process, therefore, that it is in the best interest of the individual consciousness to be aware of how the event streams are stitched together in the first place.

The rapidly pulsating event streams are always unsure of themselves when they first develop. They vie with each other for a place in the sun. Once the event streams multiply, they appear to trip over each other waiting for a place to enter into the full panoply of the awakened reality. The reason for this is twofold: once the event streams multiply, they must wait patiently for a donor. They are catapulted into the tumble/toss character of the relative so quickly they do not have a chance to prepare themselves. Of necessity, therefore, they are quick to identify what the character of reference in the time scheme must be to assure optimum mobility.

Once the individual identifies his or her point of view in the event stream, there is an attractive influence on the part of the mind, which scans the region and gives rise to the points of reference that will allow the individual to imprint the choice as an inherent memory. The process of memory is entirely based on the need of the individual to develop a rhythmic, fast-moving catalogue of signals that will give one the capacity to carve a highly personal psychological stream of consciousness. The points of reference, which are ordinarily scattered over a wide interval, are propped up by the event sequences themselves, which provide the pinpoint level of psychological organization that makes it possible for the individual to complete his or her life screen.

All of the time variables that are contingent upon the afterplay of the event stream are monitored by consciousness itself. Since consciousness provides the underpinnings, it is up to time to come up with the precise arrays that will manifest a given life event course. One may liken this to skipping down an alley, unobstructed by any point of reference, when all of a sudden there is a very apparent physical obstacle on the course. At first one might be startled by this intrusion, but later, as one rectifies one's course and enters into a flow of unity with the obstacle, the obstacle seems to become part of the path. So it is with time.

Shifting the Obstacles

Time is the unifying force that makes all of the apparent obstacles in the event stream become unified with their source. Otherwise, one's personal reality would constantly be shaken by the underlying shift in the consciousness bed that is always there when reality is not masterminded by the fully conscious, awakened awareness. The vast array of possibilities for the time spread is therefore neither fully linear nor fully random. They appear as unified, transparent obstacles in the stream, even when they are little more than blips in the field.

Individuals who gain a fuller or sharper mastery of their personal destiny are capable not of controlling the flow of time but of understanding the flow of the variables that describe it. By being cognizant of how the flow of variables inherently describes their internal reality, they become synchronous or magnetically attracted to those variables that will restore a favorable outcome. Individuals who experience their personal reality as inherently favorable and positive will often create their personal matrix from the point of view of respondency rather than of obstinacy. One must become friends with the flow of consciousness rather than attempting to block it through the fear and hesitancy that often accumulates in the recesses of the mind.

The distinction between time and consciousness is not always as apparent as one might think. Since consciousness does precede time, time is always playing catch-up with the event stream. It does so with each apparent obstacle that presents itself. When time relies on consciousness exclusively for the clues that will allow it to rectify and re-exhibit itself, there is always some room for play. Time lives in a type of dormitory setting with the object, locked into a small, locatable area and forced to exhibit certain qualities of exhibition in order to draw the object out. The object in this sense may be some personal, perceivable variable in the consciousness stream, or something that appears to progress from the outside. When time discovers that it has met an object that would appear to be a challenge of some sort, it rarely comes around to meet it. It holds off for some time, examining the point of reference and making its play only when it understands the possibilities from every angle.

The time/consciousness mirror forms the basis for personal reality to transpose its memoirs onto the field of the absolute. Time discovers the patterns, the arrays, the signatures of the event stream, and then slips in unnoticed, repatterning these possibilities so as to appeal to the psychological character of the individual. We have an exciting role to play in creating the mirroring of our reality, but we can never be fully masters of the time arrays that feed the essential character of it. It is as if we can be playwrights, but have no control over how an individual actor might singularly interpret his or her role.

In order for time to be the principal player in the magnified reality, there is a surge in the event stream once it has been identified. This surge or push in the character of the individual matrix causes it to swell past the point of first incision. First the individual incorporates the time signature into his or her mirror of opportunity. Then he or she waits, positing how the event structure will be placed. Then, sometimes randomly, sometimes not, the event structure is launched from this window of opportunity, creating the stroke or point of decision that will make all future relations possible.

In this window of opportunity, time appears opaque, without the possibility of transverse variables, but after a moment of indecision, time always displays its weight on the glass of fortune. The first optimum signature for time is taken, and time rearranges the psychological eaves of the individual psyche. The patterning that time uses is found within the context of the human nervous system. The nervous system of human beings is extremely malleable. It can be caused to curve or break over the time barriers much more fluidly than other intelligent life forms. This is because of the high degree of mental intensity with which human beings are blessed. Their ability to scan an array of time variables and meet a necessary curve headlong is unique among intelligent lifeforms. Of course this presents a high possibility for psychological confusion and doubt. This is the drawback of such a high degree of time merit and psychological freedom.

The Paradox of Being Human

In order for human beings to interact intelligently with the time streams that present themselves, they learn to skip through all of the outcomes that would not cause them to grasp the next range of meaning for their lives. They enter an internal landscape in which the time/space variables that have been presented to them are lit up by the intelligence of their own penchant for pure choice. In this more opulent situation, intelligent human beings vie for capability to become team players in the webwork of the time continuum. They startle each other by picking time variables that are more randomly scattered, more truly coastal than any others, and thereby they become capable of recognizing the true niche that will make their reality more uniform and clean than another. To become an optimal player in the reality scheme, human beings develop complex psychoemotional strategies that they assemble in order to purge time of variables that do not fit their scheme of understanding. Of course, this is highly self-limiting, but it is also the basis for some degree of order in the anarchical chaos that makes up the relative.

The paradox for human beings is that they must always choose coexistent variables out of a pack of options that appears completely random and incoherent. The human nervous system is at best paradimensional at this time, and being so, it is not able to digest the wide range of variables that a truly fluid time scheme would allow. Human beings must construct time from the bridge of their own psychology, rather than through the imprints of consciousness that present themselves randomly at the event junction point.

In the course of negotiating an event stream, the human nervous system provides a complex system of signals which, when fed to the various muscle groups, gives impetus to a range of perceived motion for the body/mind. Time is the circuitous purveyor of information to the body about the nature of its reality, and creates a front whereby reality can have a point of view. Without this, the body would essentially be unable to calibrate its vantage point in the time/space vault and the psychological confusion for humanity would be too extreme.

However, what if it were possible for human beings to essentially leave behind the body/mind as their principal point of reference for the interplay of time and consciousness? This trick has already been drawn. For, in the future of human interaction, the limitations of time will be completely dismantled. Thereby, human beings will be able to skip completely over the time variables, unhinging their perceptions that heretofore fixed the event stream, and be able to juggle the myriad of possibilities that will then emerge.

When human beings view an object—for example, a ball falling to the ground—they must assume an implied outcome. This is very human, as it is now known. But what if the ball did not fall to the ground? What if it were stopped mid-fall or could be turned around, or shot off in a thousand different directions? This is the beauty of a time/space scheme that has no psychological limitations. There need not be confusion in this situation because the bridge of time becomes interior, directed by the vast, expansive wave of consciousness that represents the stream. When the events are cast from this vantage point, the human being becomes a signatory creator in the scheme of reality. He or she is freed from the notions that any possible spread in the time interlace would be seen as secondary or improper.

To rid the psychology of limitations in the time wave, the first variables that are introduced are always frozen. This may seem paradoxical, but if one understands random curve theory, it is obvious that this must be so. Frozen time variables meet each other headlong and provide the vehicle for all random situations to be built. The reason for frozen time is that it can record the slope or underpinnings of the variable at a much quicker and more uniform rate. After the time variable unfreezes itself, it enters the slide into uniformity much more fluidly. For human beings to develop an independent psychology that is not based on the mind, they must enter this flow of interlaced time. The relationship of personal reality to this underlying unification is not of the mind but of consciousness itself.

Human beings are presently locked into the field of thought, so as to create a fixed impulse or speed of rotation as mental activity arises. Each event stream must be taken in, processed, and returned in the same direction whence it came. This causes a dramatic slowing of the possible time variables and does not allow the human nervous system to process advancing information from many implied sources simultaneously. When the human nervous system is freed from such constraints it becomes a tandem processor, and eventually it can enter into a complete unification with the possible event streams. This marks a shift in human thinking from a condition based purely on mental constraint to thought created through an understanding of the underlying dynamics of events. This change will breathe light into the future of human discretion. The shift in the pulse or rhythm of breath will be the inherent result.

Since human beings must exist in the time scheme of the absolute while they are living in the constraints of the relative, their breathing patterns mimic this outflow and inflow capability. Pure breath is breathed, automatically infusing consciousness into the pulse or internal balance of the individual. Each quickening of the breath provides an object of perception for the individual to flow into. The sharpening of the time manifold will cause human beings to become capable of breathing like sharks; in other words, they will not have to become so fastened to the landlubbing stream of rhythmic pulsation that keeps them living on dry land. They will be able to enter the waterbeds of the planet, and essentially be able to breathe without masks or mechanical intervention. This may seem improbable only because the human being is essentially caught on dry land through the schisms in his or her thinking.

When the event stream is met head on, there is a push on the level of the breath. The outbreath forms a kind of cloak that signals to the central nervous system that there is a distance to attain. The inbreath acts like a barrier reef in the interior motion of the spine and digestive organs. When the human nervous system is freed of its impulse to carry back signals directly to the brain, it can then create a carrier wave of information that feeds directly from the musculature of the body. This is how most animals now operate. They do not simply think a motion; they are the motion.

When intelligence presents itself on a thorough map of time without any discord, the human being can leap strategically over the back of any variables that present themselves. In this way, the breath or pulse of the body will remain intact and continue to function autonomically, even as the consciousness distances itself from the limitations of the body. This is true yoga.

Beyond the Breath

Once the individual learns to leave behind the limitations of the breath, there is a parallel identification with reality as an open scheme rather than as a fixed notion. The individual must learn to walk before he or she learns to run. The first step must be to cognize the internal functioning of the time curve itself, understand its true meaning, and return from the state of fixity to which he or she has been bound. The conversation between the brain, mind, and heart will be more fully realized. Over the period in which the human psychology will undergo such profound alteration, there will be a transition from one stage of development to another. In this situation, all human beings will begin to experience themselves as less captured by the event streams that had bound them. They will be less afraid of the possibilities that might draw them away from the known and familiar.

The time encapsulation of humanity is not something that can be fully understood simply from the realm of mental contemplation. It must be understood within the fabric of the uniform consciousness itself. As such uniformity takes place, the individual becomes equidistant with the freed understanding that makes the event modules of a person's existence transparent. This underlying perception of time's pop-out reality catalyzes a significant upturn in originality, which inspires the individual to return to the center of gravity from which he or she was spun.

1.3.2
the cloak of time

Weaving the Fabric

ime forms the backdrop for all of manifest creation. Matter forms a cloak or spindle around the balancing structures of time. Time entertains this cloak through surges in the matter/time framework. These surges create the epistructure for matter to emerge. Time cannot pin itself to the apron of matter without necessitating a form of attachment. Time is attracted to the cloak of matter in order to create the pauses, the breaths that affect the causal rhythm or pulsation of time.

The fabric is woven through this inward and outward breath of temporal spin. Time must pause, breathe, and open itself to the stretching or yawning of matter in order to reveal itself. All of the fabrics of matter are contingent upon passing through the doorway of time. When time appears, it has to develop armor, a shield, a vestibule of matter/time that is impenetrable. This is the only way that time can come forward.

Matter is shielded by time and given the opportunity to develop. It has both a particulate and an energetic nature. Matter is made of various envelopes of matter/time, criss-crossing themselves over the field like the backs of warriors. In each field of time there is a rainbow, a kind of arc or spiral like the trajectory of an arrow. In each field of time matter is born, and every tear, every streak of light and consciousness, is filled with this amber cloak which is the secret of time.

The Geography of City-States

The cross-sections of matter are geographically spread so as to conform to key sections of each time break. Time spins through the interior sections first, spanning the range that will be taken up and spilling out onto the surface of matter in both longitudinal and latitudinal weaves. Matter, having taken up this spread of time, becomes capable of receiving the temporal facts, the education that time has brought to it. Matter awakens to the essence of time, and through it develops a continuity that will allow physical structures to form.

When time traverses the realm of matter, there is a thrill, a pulsation that is created that repeats itself over and over again. This thrill is stronger or weaker depending on the intensity of the fabric of matter at that given ratio of possibility. Material creation is composed of congealed time, a condensation of the time spread that varies from point to point. Time sprawls, spreading out in every direction throughout material creation. It finds avenues that will bring the greatest advantage to its expression.

The creation of matter is brought about through a system of highways or avenues that are laid out like the map of a city. This cross-weaving, with inlets and tributaries that are formed at various points, can remind one of a city-state, a boundaried division that is significant not only in terms of form but in relational content.

Time creates matter through a system of roadways that lead back and forth into the heart of the city-state. Time becomes apportioned by matter through a type of interstitial sensuality, a type of pulsing, which, when promoted through washing clean the avenues of time/matter, forms the city-states in which matter finds itself.

Traversing Light and Dark

Time is woven through patterns of consciousness. Fields of both light and dark time ambulate throughout the weave, creating angles of radiance that form the backdrop for matter. Time is cloaked so as not to be revealed directly. It must be hidden at first so that matter can have the freedom to take its own direction. Dark time is like a fore-image, a ghost that will be a reminder to the lighter fields to imitate more directly the portion of consciousness that is to be expressed. By staying cloaked, time is not revealed too soon and matter has the chance to become articulate and appropriately complex.

Time maintains a hidden or subterranean darkness before it bursts on the scene in full splendor. At first time is truly invisible, indecipherable, and matter is in waiting, holding together without the true picture that time will communicate. Time, entering slowly and precisely into the field of matter, creates the subtext that matter will later articulate more fully. Fields of consciousness, bright with the full measure of awakening, enter into the territory that time/matter has chartered. Consciousness stations itself in this territory, creating links between matter that has been readied by time and matter that has not.

Time is cloaked, opening only to the awakening consciousness that will cause it to be revealed. Time works its way through the arrays of light and dark matter until it is continuously uniform throughout the spread. It moves forth, a layer at a time, building a fine patchwork that will hold the finest vestibules of consciousness. Time leads the way, moving steadily through the fundamental structures of creation. Time trumpets its true status of recognition, letting matter know that it must succumb to time's call. Matter in its opaque density cannot always recognize time, but eventually, inflated by the pulsating quickness of matter, the breath of time is received.

Matter wants consistency, friendship, and alliances, while time just wants to be free, to explore, to develop infinite markers in the face of infinity. This is all that time can do: open itself to matter and reveal itself. In response, the hunger of matter prevents time from being free. This conflict sets up the marker points that develop the time/space referential feeds that make matter the queen and time the king. All of the different postulates that reveal the nature of time must take into consideration this dark underpinning of time, this thrust into the world of matter without knowledge or reason.

Time continues a rapid, far-reaching pulse that echoes through the halls of matter. This signal system creates the underlying values that will lead to the full unification of time and matter. The interval relationships that develop when time and matter come together form the song of the cosmos, the tones that will bring whole ranges of light together. The solidity of matter is dependent upon these tones reaching deep into the territory that has been formed.

Color, Shape, and Form

Time has color, it has shape, and it has an envelope of sound/silence that keeps it moving and in harmony with nature. The cloak that is created to encompass time, to shield it so that it can develop into the proper avenues for matter to enter, can be described as a type of cocoon. The shell wraps time in a blanket of amber light, a radiant beacon that will enable matter to know how and when to enter. Beings that are transtemporal can reflect this glow, which might be described as "ambergine" in character. As time cartwheels through the range of possibilities that bring about the history of a species, matter can also loop-de-loop through the chorus of time unnoticed. Each step of the way is an adventure because it is not possible to know where matter will be planted and how it will sprout.

Time and matter develop a pattern of receipt and discovery. Each takes up the infinite, coddling it so as to develop a system of language that will coin the parallel realities that could earmark future civilizations. Time comes up over and over again, revealing its nature delicately but with determination, opening the door for the power of Nature to delineate its myriad forms. How can matter, in its infinite, impenetrable darkness, be also filled with the crystalline light that is the determining factor in the development of life? Through the power of God's love, the light that is found in His/Her nature is reflected in the structure of living forms. Matter becomes filled with this sacred "pansophy" that expresses the omnipotence of consciousness relegated to form.

Aging Matter

Matter is afraid of time because it knows the inherent danger in being stripped bare. Time induces the factor of aging, which has the power to consume matter and reduce it to its most frail and weakened point. Matter that has been stripped by time is unattractive, having lost a bit of the radiance that defines its newness. Time, on the other hand, has no fear, being dedicated to the bold and daring effort of revealing matter to the infinite. Time, though barren, will never suffer from being childless. It is rescued from the loneliness of unified creation through that which moves it to its most intimate source.

The matter/time languages that species develop are dependent upon the refrain of the infinite as it pulses through the waves of time. The patterns of language developed by time restore order to the random nature of development. The psychology of living species is filled with the organ-throbbing pulsation of the infinite splendor revealed. Language and time become unified through matter. Language and time are in some ways completely synonymous. Time develops language in a dancerly way, creating the movement, the complex pattern of interrelationship that will allow matter to pull its own weight. The curves of time, its rhythmic arching nature, form the choreography for language to flower.

As time dances onto the field of language, the psychological underpinning of different species is created. Dog, cat, bird, and chimp all need language to give them substance, and their language, whether verbal, sonic, unwritten, or sung, is developed through the chorus of time. Even species that have no bodies have time. Everything must have a rhythmic makeup in its organic sense. The species that have no physical bodies must have time bodies. They must have language structures and a dimensional framework in order to laugh, caress, or frown. Time puts a species through trials to develop a body through a rainbow of interludes that repeat themselves in direct, circuitous patterns of consciousness that create organic substance.

It is the longstanding, patient progression of matter from its inert to its organic form that christens it towards sentience. Impatient matter cannot wrap properly around the event streams that eventually will pattern consciousness. For matter to become bonded to the possibilities of time, a perfect relationship must develop in which consciousness is given a voice. This voice or ring of consciousness signals the advent of a particular species. The inherent characteristics that a humanoid species must possess are particularly potent in terms of the individuation that must ensue to bring this about. For a species in which linear time must play a role, time must open out into the field of consciousness one rhythmic play at a time so that the psychological continuity of existence can be met.

Consciousness is poised on the field of matter, assessing the qualifications to bring birth to a species. This analysis takes place in the finest regions of existence and precedes the awakening of time on the level of matter. It is in the invisible and darkest regions of the space/time loop that consciousness is able to identify a particular form of life, albeit simple or complex, and make it spring anew.

The coacervate is a tiny organelle of energy/space/matter that signifies the direct interweaving of matter with the infinite. Consciousness imparts the design of a species to the primary organic building blocks that will later determine the nature of its core characteristics. God touches the life with the divine pneuma or life force that will impart a unique and resplendent pattern to its signature. He/She knows that every pocket of time that is utilized to define the nature of a creature in the universal continuum will be arranged according to the precise measures provoked by the bonding with matter.

Forward Time

The certainty of matter with respect to its organic components places each sentient species in the position to be a resplendent reflector of the light of God. This inherent beauty is the result of the complex intricacy of God's planning. Even that which would be perceived as ugly has beauty in its own right. The Divine makes everything lively, instilling in life the quality of wholeness. God functions as the signatory agent for time, matter, and consciousness, developing the comprehensive patterns that will allow time to nest in each possibility eternally.

The liveliness of life, its movement through the world, is based on the precise time signatures that are invested within it. God cannot create without the help of time and cannot return to Itself without the knowledge of time. God makes use of the rhythmic clapping of time on the tender heels of creation. All of God's children laugh in the face of time and stretch it endlessly, revealing personal and planetary masks. God plays with the surface of time, stringing it out. As time/matter becomes opaque it reveals opulent living forms that eventually birth new civilizations and planetary systems.

God makes time come forward from His/Her own skin and time must speak this language effectively on the stage of matter. Each stage of matter, each part of the dance of creation, from the smallest whiff of consciousness to the belly of the planetary heave, is made from the restless wonder of time. Nothing can be revealed that is not found in the courthouse of the infinite and nothing can be made to matter if God does not wish it to be.

None of God's children has any notion of actual time because all are incapable of infinite reason at the level that is found in God. Time curls back on itself and explores its nature through the creation of solar systems and galaxies. Time spins through all of the substructures, creating the backdrop for the children of God to be revealed as waves of creation that can inhabit many magnificent dimensional avenues. The children of God breathe these resplendent qualities of time into their own nostrils, thus providing the reflective pool wherein each race can individuate and become sparkling in its interior essence.

1.3.3
time's epicenter

Time Spirals

time at its epicenter stands still. There is a relationship at the center of the time spiral that leans into the edge. The epicenter remains in a state of stillness and silence because it is transfiguring the inner and outer space. The standard deviation with regard to time at the epicenter revolves around the rate of spin that the time spiral accumulates. Each incremental pull towards the center of the spin curls time back over itself so that the fractionization of time will be incomplete. Because there is an eternal need for completion, time refracts the time values through each integral step, depleting the break on the down side and allowing time to coil or retract into the epicenter.

Time spirals through every spin without retracting completely. This increases the value of the time referral for each rate of spin and each incomplete turn or spiral. The referral increases, thus implementing a centripetal lock. This is a holding pattern in the spin that occurs for a brief instant, the intensity of which is calculated by determining where in the spin it is liable to break. At this breakpoint in the rate of spin there is a ratio or interval comparison that may be made mathematically between the time reference as it appears in motion and the time reference in this newly locked position. As the time reference speeds up, there continues to be a pause or opening in the time reference that causes it to feel from the interior level as though everything has come to a stop.

This may be compared to the feeling of flying or driving at a very fast rate of speed. At a certain point, one feels like one is actually standing still although the rate of time variables has actually increased. To calculate the rate of increase, the time core or centripetal lock in the spin is equal to one half the downward-spiraling value as it appears randomly from its set point. There is a trigger response that causes this rate to decline or increase with regard to the objectified reference points of the object involved. An analogy might be that this process is like a barrel that has been shot down from the falls. The force increases incrementally on the way down, but inside the barrel there is a strong epicenter that would be experienced by an individual as a silent, almost stationary pause within the context of a speedy, forceful drop.

The epicenter of the spin locks the time values into place and maintains them sequentially. Each wave of time collapses back over the center, maintaining the force of entry. To understand this phenomenon, try imagining the force needed to break into a safe. When the lock on the safe is strong, the door must be blown open without destroying the safe's contents. There must be a protective caliber to any explosion that would come to bear to break the door. In the situation with a full time spiral, the force of entry must be millions of times greater than the shielding which time naturally places on its trajectory. In spite of this, the time shield gives way without damaging the "contents," which are the delicate standardization of time variables which appear at the center of the break. In order to withstand such a force, time acts as a buffer near the epicenter. It acts as a "windbreaker" here, compiling enough momentum to stand clear of the force needed to break way but maintaining the core integrity of the center.

Past Time and Post-Time

As a result of this phenomenon, the relationship of mass, distance, and speed with reference to time remains constant at the center of the break. This allows the time variables to rest, regain strength, and reconstitute themselves for the next spin. Without this, the variables would use themselves up and not retain enough speed or momentum to go into the next break. Since time retains this smooth, unaffected character at the center, when the time intervals are split or broken due to other factors, the centers of the breaks themselves remain untouched.

How this translates into one's own personal reality is that the breaks which manifest the backbone for the event slides make up the magical interlay between past time and post-time. Since each interlay must be placed over the other in a type of temporal sandwich, the center of that wafer-like formation is found in the steadying effect of the time break itself. All of the dimmer switches that cause time to recede, take hold, or retreat are sensitized to this sequence of events. In the riptide that is formed when the time breaks fall past each other, each squaring the other at the epicenter and curving over the back of each subsequent break, a change occurs. None of the time values have "tails"; unlike a comet, the time break retains its shape. It does not have the squirreling or tail-like motion of a comet because there is no matter spiraling to its core. But the formation of space/time is essentially the same. The pressure and force of effort involved in holding the vortex in motion remains constant at the center, and as a result the event stream also remains constant. This is why, when the event stream is tilted ever so slightly from side to side, the nature of the individual matrix retains its shape but also is changed abruptly. There is a shift in the field of events that will be formulated from the break itself.

In the construction of personal reality, it is the event at the epicenter that creates the biggest wave. All of the avenues of entry between the breaks must be laid bare. There will always be a hint of disturbance in the relationship between the breaks because there is always a little jilting or wiggling between each successive break as it is formed. The wiggle will not be extreme across the breaks. The wiggle is not what causes the event matrix to strike or dilute. It is the epicenter itself that causes this.

Since time is a loop, the construct of the break appears random, but once it breaks off, the chunk that is now no longer part of the matrix maintains a smooth, often angular appearance which can regulate the flow or core of the time break. The angular break which has seemingly disturbed the epicenter is defiant; it is stretched over the gap randomly, repeating itself again and again. The new values, which represent slight differences in the size, shape, and appearance of the time waves, are now lined up. We say that they have a "coastal" appearance, which implies that they are a subset of each other, lined up on the circumference of the break.

When the individual epicenters which manifest personal reality are so shaken, all of the random variables then appear. There is a fest of time in which all of the variables come together, interplaying in a lively melodic interface with each other and then spilling back over the "eaves." The tune that they are playing is the actual song of reality. It is the matrix that makes the tune or shape of the time frame that the individual entity will now encounter. This is true of all sentient life, not only human, for even the animal or plant must construct a sequence of events that will define its lifestream.

Though animals and plants do not have the pure sentience to understand the significance of what is put in front of them, they do have an instinctive and accurate response to the changes in the matrix that manifest before them. They can react viscerally, emotionally, and independently. For this reason, we might say that time becomes more sentient as beings become more complex. The complexity of the time sequences in the array of human intelligence is considered to be about average for sentient life as it is found intergalactically. In other words, human beings employ an average rate of change in their ability to utilize the time breaks as they are set forth. They derive pleasure or determination through their interior relationship with these epicenters, which are the fundamental building blocks for the nature of personal reality.

Speed, Distance, and Motion

Since time is cubic in its character, it does not rely upon the square of opposing values to bring about a state of uniformity. The variable ratios that characterize the flow of time are expressed in triplicate, in that they are a tri-une function of time, speed/momentum, and distance. The fact that one views reality as a solid function, rather than simply one expressed as thickness or viscosity, is explained mathematically in terms of the ratio-synchronization that describes time as a function of light/matter as well as distance. When one views an object, one is struck by the way that time is formatted in relative terms within it.

At first view, one is sensitive to a shift in the image's relative thickness, which one sees as a filling in of the negative spaces in one's field of vision. This is much like viewing a line drawing or television pixel screen. In terms of the time variables showing up in a graphic context, one's view is not simply a perceptual shift but rather a shift in the spectral color variations of the image. The colors vary along a stream of magnetic radiance, in which various particles of color are attracted to one another to form a spectral blanket or optical refraction. Then these colors are strung together in sequences of variation that in our perceptual language form cycles of color perceived as streaks or hues, much like a rainbow. These streaks or hues represent the markers that form the continuity of time in its full spectral character. This splendid array is present due to changes in the way time is collected as it gathers speed and full momentum.

In anticipating the sequence of an event stream within individual reality, one senses that there is a time, an interval, in which that event stream is ripening. This is one's own personal timing for that event episode. In order to pin down the epicenter of that curve, human beings derive pleasure in encountering the meaning of a given event stream within their psychological and physical parameters. However, the significance of a given action or situation is highly motivated by interpretation. There is no absolute significance. But there is an absolute variation on the part of the time break that gave momentum, thrust, and direction to the shift in the actual reality stream. This gap between subjective significance and actual perceptual curve manifests as a change in the scope of the action. It provokes the difference between effective action, which covers the wish center of the individual desire, and the mechanical and somewhat mundane perception of the action as it defines itself within the stream. It is the wish that defines the object, but it is time that makes the wish.

To understand this further, remember that the individual event stream is plotted angularly. That is, it curves, moving over the rise and fall of each individual break. When the event stream meets up with the emotion of personal desire, there is a rise or fall in that stream which indicates which way it will topple in the break. This causes the event stream to spin. It is like the roll of the dice of fate. The event stream will spin, move forward or backward, collide with other pieces of the spiral, and spill out over the entire matrix. This causes time to become parallel, sequential, or longitudinal.

When the event stream dots the circumference of the matrix without a break, we say it is backwards, forwards, or latitudinal. There is always an occasion for time to become interior, coastal, and parametric, in which case it is stored, imageless, waiting for its revelatory spring in which it will dart into the spiral again. Each of these avenues for the time spread is psychologically as well as mechanically induced. This is why we say that the wish is as good as the indicator. The desire for time to reveal itself in a particular manner influences the outcome, even though the outcome must remain random and unpredictable.

The Demands of the Temporal Interface

This interface between sentient obstinacy in the battle for time, and the demands of the temporal interface itself to spin out and return to its origins, affects the life stream most deeply. This is why there always appears to be a point in the life path of an individual in which change or disruption is inevitable. The life path builds up a type of temporal pressure which must be resolved through psychological and in some cases physical or event-centered movement. The static nature that is felt psychologically is held within the armoring of the physical body. The body retains its elasticity through change, letting down its internal guard. The rigidity of the body is a precursor of a type of dormancy in the life path of the individual. The static armoring of the body mirrors this frozen temporal situation.

The moorings or roots of the time jump lie in the ability of the individual psychology to strike out onto different planes of awareness and make a jump in the cognitive function. The individual will not be rooted to any one place in the matrix if she or he understands that the uniformity of all the variables lies in their ability to construct a safe harbor in which the myriad of possible formations comes to life. In other words, the rapidity and solidity of change actually presents a security blanket for temporal development in the field of consciousness. The change in calibration of the event stream presents the refinement necessary for internal stability.

The nature of personal reality always involves change, the more the better. When the individual consciousness resists change, there is little that the temporal mechanics can do about it. The temporal mechanics are always ready, able, and willing to promote variability and to balance it through the random character of the event streams. The individual intransigency of human life makes it impossible to assimilate how time will behave and what will cause it to make the digression into efficacy. The dialogue between human consciousness, in its afterthought and forethought, and the nature of the personal quest for meaning and comprehension act as a buffer for the seemingly violent underpinnings that define and enhance the event forest.

The strikingly similar patterns that can be found in the life of one individual human being and all of his or her counterparts are no mistake. These patterns of life are programmed into the temporal mechanics themselves. They are the patterns that signify the qualitative direction of an individual life. Event streams are fractionizated when they no longer can maintain these predictable, although sometimes confusing, curves. Then the individual event patterning becomes confused, unable to assimilate the rapidly changing scenarios of time, space, and matter. To understand how the event streams pattern themselves, it is only necessary to observe one human lifetime.

Temporal Freedom

The intervals of union, dissolution, and succession are always patterned on the shape, size, and formation of the time breaks associated with them. This is why in family structures individuals retain a "cellular memory" of the moments in which time has collapsed, repaired itself, and gathered strength in the individual or collective structure. The individual is a patterned response medium for the familiar relationship with time. Since time is spread out over such a wide arc, the individual who retains his or her distance and maintains a settled or refined personal demeanor is able to maintain some harmony and fluidity within the context of these preprogrammed family event sequences. However, the actual distancing from them depends largely on the consciousness of the individual as he or she recognizes the absolute underpinnings behind the sequences themselves, and can therefore shy away from their deleterious effects.

Those individuals who find themselves in a state of temporal freedom have rid themselves of all of the avenues of response that would normally define the personal situation. They are standing free psychologically of their standard interpretations of the events and are moving into a state of tempo-ral liberation. No one can be freed of the stroke of time, but the individual can, with the help of realization, recognize how time is constructing the avenues of response, and lift free of the particular constraints that are bind-ing him or her to the cause. In this way, the temporal stroke is freed, and the person becomes capable of utilizing the random nature of time for his or her own use. There is a rapid increase then in the originality and "dive" of the personal reality, and satisfaction with it. A feeling of fulfillment arises, born of the idea that time and reality are now integrally intertwined. One can brace oneself on the slope of time and leap downward without fear. This possibility is the future of all sentient life.

1.4
time travel

1.4.1
the suspension of time

Time Pools

time can be delineated through periods of suspension or easing of its weight. Though it may be described as separative, time is noncategorical in that it cannot be viewed as a compartmentalized or rigid structure. Time becomes precipitous and spacious in relationship to the formation of matter. Since time can be arranged in distinct reality frameworks, it is able to create the blank slate for the imposition of matter. One must consider the structural components of time if one is to understand the reality framework of lower dimensional points of reference.

Time is structured according to pools or dockets that give it the character of being able to radiate into solid structures. All of the variables that define time are made up of these pools, which collect in the waiting ground of presupposed space. Time collects in these pools in a type of ring formation that allows it to freeze back into the waves of time. Since time must cool before it can become motionless, there is a waiting time when time is adherent to the walls of matter and must wait until it can again take up its cyclical and rapid motion. All of the variables of time must become cognizant of this waiting period in order for time to remain in suspension long enough for the intervals of matter to be released.

The reality of the suspension of time is defined through distance. The distance time travels in a given interval is governed by its frequency, its response rate, and its range of motion at any given point. Since time must travel over the subwaves of space and does not have any particular marker in these subwaves, the parallel dimensional material that makes up the time equity is similar to the branches of a tree. Each tree of time has its own distinct pattern of limbs with rays or leaves spreading out into the universal continuum. As time sprays itself onto the field of matter and essentially coats the variables with which it is defined, it becomes smooth and even, or rough and hard to hew. Each pocket of time expresses itself as a clear interval rather than being spread out over a translinear period. Since there is no search warrant for the array of time, it must transduce itself onto the field of matter gradually and thin itself out over a wide field of spread.

Translinear Time

Translinear time is essentially composed of dark and light fields of matter/time interface, which stretch themselves over the variables or limits that have been set. Then these rainbow-like openings create subsets of underlying matter, which form the backdrop for creation mechanics. The spin or whirl of the time variables is calibrated according to the motion of time. When time suspends itself, it leaves behind a marker or trace mechanism, which allows it to be tracked according to its essential character. This is why event streams often blossom into more random sequences without the benefit of any particular frequency aberration. They can become subsets of themselves without ever having to leave behind any traces, or they can become carrier waves for more advanced forms of the time/matter/energy continuum.

Since time behaves randomly, it is not certain when the time breaks will occur. Time is not random by virtue of any inherent methodology; it can only dance at its own variable rate of speed or attrition. Time may be characterized as inherently random, where variables of speed or distance are counter-multiplied exponentially as the change from one unit of measure to another increases. Time is fixed only when it is put in place psychologically, as a locator point for different series of event structures to find their way into the mapping of personal reality.

Random time may be seen as pock-marked by the different reflections of curved reality that are revealed as crater-like formations in which time may pool for the purpose of storage and retrieval. The complexion of time may therefore be seen as variegated or striated, where smoothness is an exception to the norm. The smoothing of the surface of time is based on its need to rigorously return to the point of origin, to jump-start or counterbalance its motives with regard to its beginning stature. Here time revs up, increases its temporal velocity, and then coasts or rides the waves that are created in a type of smooth or viscous temporal spread.

When time enters into the domain of matter, it forces matter to become wed to its skin. Time and matter enter a type of operational symbiosis that determines how time will enter into each area that matter wishes to embrace. Time and matter create spreads or regions of optimization that are expressed randomly and form the building blocks for the creation spiral. Tumbling forth in every conceivable direction, matter spirals out in cluster-like formations. These vestibules or pockets of time can be described mathematically as celestial quotients that describe the rate, speed, and movement of matter. These equations are vibrational in nature, expressing the form, substance, and standard intervals of elocution. Such equations express visceral, felt responses to which one can become sensitized as a type of temporal vocabulary or media. Such equations represent not only how time is unfolding, that is, with regard to rate or amplitude, but also the characteristic breaks in time that will lead to the formation of personal reality boosters.

Since time cannot be spun from anything but the mind of God itself, it cannot be calibrated or fixed by the human mind. Time composes itself randomly through the event sequences that maintain themselves collectively through advancements in the flow of consciousness. Therefore, time is both objective and subjective. There is a personal field of time that forms the backdrop for the lifetime of the individual, and there is a collective field of time that forms the backdrop for the city-states that make up the collective fields of origin.

All of the city-states, which are composed of time intervals wrapped or bundled for the purpose of solicitation by the time lords, are useful in that they remain opaque for specific intervals before they are spun out on to the slope of time. There are standard variables that express this spinning mechanism. Each ray of time/matter is composed of a field or aqueduct, where time is spun out, arranged, and then fed back into its own feed.

Sweeping Without Effort

There can be no underplay in the allied motion that expresses time. As time curves, the underlying mechanics sweep time forward into a given field of expression and then sweep it back again where it is now unlikely to retain a fixed or wrapped position. There can be no accumulation of time without precipitous motion. All of the underlying movements of time exist in a free and easy manner and cannot be presented as unitary attributes unless they remain independent of their own variable positions.

Time remains motionless when it is ready to spring the trap and impose matter as a solid, striated variable. There is a "ring-pass-not" into which time must climb in order to create the crib that will spill it out again. Time remains motionless in this crib or bay until it pulls enough splinters out of its spine to open out into the free, effortless, and motionless spiral out of which matter is composed.

When time opens itself to the array of matter, it creates a junction point that allows it to suspend its breadth, weight, and dormancy, and enter an energized rapid state where, although suspended, it is filled with the breath of God. It becomes rapid like a beating heart and enters an energized state from which it will eventually spill over into the heart of matter. Since time cannot behave itself, and must constantly be in motion in order to secure its independence, it is less likely to advance without these periods of rest and recuperation. Time brings itself into suspension in order to perform actions of self-study and renewal. With activity substantially abated, time has the opportunity to study its own character and create a haven in the sea of independence. This will make it possible for the timed event sequences that play out on the whims of personal reality to become more fully in view.

The memory tidbits that are stored in the minds of human beings are not actually literal, but are figurative of the time breaks that were used to create the matrix. In other words, when time opens itself to the completely random event sequences, they bond together, which creates the flow of matter/time in the hearts and minds of the individuals involved. Each time flow creates a spin or decomposition of what was once known and realigns it to the present course of action.

When individuals create their reality, whether knowingly or unknowingly, they are drawing upon these time crusts or intervals of dark and light spin. As these arrays present the footwork for what tomorrow will bring, they are spun out onto the field of time and form the essential guideposts for the interior reality of the mental field. The constructs that individuals gain or lose are therefore built upon the time frequencies that they must maintain for their psychological survival.

No Short-Term Memory

Since time is purely a psychological tool for the individual, he or she must be rescued from too much accumulation of the goods. There cannot be too many time variables, and therefore the human mind simplifies the flow of action through the accumulation of psychologically derived memories that clock the time codes for the individual's flow of energetic self-expression. These time codes are no longer random but have been pieced together out of the psychological cloaking that the individual needs to maintain a sense of individuated identity. Individuals who have broken free from these constraints, and these are very rare, are likely to think of time more as a spiral motion and to have little or no short-term memory since they are no longer storing variables to make up their life story. This suspension or emptiness is likely to be found in individuals who have willingly amassed a greater portion of expanded awareness than the average individual.

Those individuals who seek to understand the quality of time in their own lives must first come to recognize that time is the glue behind all of the events of their own acquaintance. Time adheres to the field of matter; thus all of the events that characterize an individual's life stream have been plaited there, awaiting shifts in the matrix. There is no reason to believe that time has any value other than to create the shading or meaning for a person's subjective existence.

Time exists randomly. It cannot be collared or left at bay without express permission of the individual. When time appears more cumulative, it is only because at first glance all of the event streams are interlaid one on top of the other, like celestial building blocks. When time is stripped of any psychological meaning and is left to its bare, naked embodiment in the event flow, its relationship to divinity can be palpably felt by the individual.

Divine time cannot be characterized psychologically. It has been stripped of all event or precedence and lives in a type of symbiosis with the carrier, which can be represented translinearly. The divine mind conceives of that which it wishes to define through a felt sense of its implied derivation. Then it brings this description out into the open innocently, choosing words or action on the basis of realization rather than emotional need. As a result, a type of synchronistic organization emerges that is at once coincidental but filled with a type of jovial spontaneity that makes it appear inherently alive and whole. Time in its essential character is at once a mirror for the divine mind and the fabric upon which such a mind forms the basis for reason.

The Unpredictability of Human Intercourse

Time, being both perfectly organized and inherently random, is never wholly predictable. This is also the character of the divine mind, directed wholly by the transcendental field out of which it is formed. The divine mind spills out its content onto the field of life. The flow of time in each interval is never predictable but occurs as a kind of lottery in which the time intervals that are the most pleasing, most lively, and most full of promise are wrapped, interposed with matter, and given differentiation.

Time cannot question its own character; it is up to the individual to do that. Thus, human beings give meaning to their memories and create interpretative jurisdiction over them. As in the land of dreams, the memories that exist in the waking mind are no more than apparitions. They are not meaningful in any inherent sense other than the sequencing that has been interlaid to develop them. As the individual's psychology straps meaning on to each event sequence, there is a panoply of lively intercourse between the life of the mind and the life of the heart.

Time is superfluous to the flow of matter. However, matter could not exist without this rapid, injectory flow that paints time onto the field of matter and gives it substance and life. Though subjective, time is never subject to change without good reason. It must not be tampered with too closely or the fragments of subjective existence that patch it together will lose their continuity. This is why personal event streams must remain intact. Otherwise, they will lose the shine of the hour, their reason for being.

The relationship of time to each event sequence as it matures forms the backdrop for psychological development. The individual assumes a leadership role in his or her own existence. This is the meaning of self-mastery: that the individual can choose the time intervals that will spin out the event streams of his or her life. Since happiness is rather a subjective state, it cannot be interpreted through any fixed set of parameters. It must be garnered gradually, as the individual ascertains the nature of reality and can assume the role of guest in the visit to the infinite.

People in the future will have a more direct experience of time that will appear more conjunctive, i.e., they will be able to move from the future to the past, and future to the present, in a more collage-like fashion. Such individuals will be able to coast directly from one time reference to another, and thus will have an advanced ability to travel through time and back again. Individuals who presently travel in time are gradually brought into a framework in which they are no longer bound by the metaphors of a personal reality. They graduate to a point in which they are no longer trapped by the event sequences that might curtail their personal development and jump into the future, living both present and future simultaneously. Such individuals can move randomly from one event sequence to another and are not likely to remain seated in one particular stream for very long.

Free to Play

Once individuals are free, they can play with the flow of time independently and develop strategies for corporeal existence that are more akin to the incorporeal. They can glide over the interface of time and allow matter to be broken up within the confines that have been created. Although time is independent of matter, it can be packaged as a random constitutional metaphor.

The flow of time in the psychology of a human being is precious and open to change. Any time a person enters into an event stream that is not to his or her liking, he or she will do anything to change it. Time cannot be cast back onto the field of matter without the permission of the individual's own soul perception. Time becomes suspended and then snaps back again into motion.

Time is neither interval-dependent nor essentially and totally free of derivative movement; it is collapsible and bonded to the core of motion. It must rely on this bonding in order to become rapidly cooled once the inner reality of the matrix becomes too hot for handling. The cooling down of the variables allows time to come out and play on the field of motion. It does some fancy footwork to lift itself free of all the necessary variables and become internally bonded to the next event sequence.

The event sequences that paint human life never look the same twice, but they certainly have parallel streams of influence which can be felt all over the relief map of the intellect. Events arrange themselves in strings that are expressions of the psychological pathways that a human being can walk across to get from one stage of evolution to another. These strings can be seen as mathematical rivulets of condensed information that describe and define the passageways from matter to intellect. As these events emerge they reveal messages in each of the streams that relay information to the central nervous system. The nervous system becomes the time machine through which each individual can interpret the streams of information that will conduct the blueprint of a life. When the lifetime is completed, the individual has the opportunity in spirit to look deeply at the event streams that have been chosen, seeing how each has unfolded and understanding to the best of his or her ability the mechanics of time that lay within the field of choice. The individual is paid in the bullion of self-knowing, which ideally will define and reshape future choices to be made in other strata of existence.

1.4.2
the formation of time loops

Avoiding Free-Fall

a time loop is a categorical interval of set duration between one particular dimensional time reference and another. Time loops are qualifiers in that they define, represent, and construct integral relationships between opposite set positions. Since time loops are constructed out of a set domain rather than a random position, they rarely have any slope and are constructed out of their own point parameters rather than borrowing from other domains.

Time loops are qualifiers in the set position because the parallel opposites that define time from more random positions are not allocated in the loop. Since the loop, by definition, coasts back from a free-fall position as it appears, there is no necessity to randomize the set integers. The free-fall position of the time loop makes it possible for time to categorize or randomize from any set position. Each loop acts as a junction point for time to recalibrate itself and loop off from the central sphere.

Time loops are set aside from homogeneous junction points and can be defined according to circumference, duration, and speed. They can be limited or unlimited depending on the parameters involved. Time loops are not considered to exist independently of the variables that define them. Therefore, when time loops back on itself to create the parametric jump position, the loop retains its essential character throughout the duration of the spin.

Time must become variable in order for the time loop to create the necessary propellant value. The time loop must come around just short of its premier duration. To describe the time variable from a purely parametric or jump-start position, the driver or seat of time must be viewed as purely random and then coalesced at a given point. Randomization is always possible, but when time randomizes it usually does not present itself in the form of a loop-lock.

When time loops around, it catches its principal integers on a sideways or counterclockwise motion and propels these integers into the pool. This system prevents premature randomization, which would cause the time variables to sit uneasily in the circumference of the spin. Since time is a qualifier, the proper position of the time variables is always independent and not confined to the catalog of opposites. Time loops are variable subsets with independent duration and limited opposition. They create their characteristic perpendicular or horizontal motion through a series of off/on scale balances that give each parameter its optimum movement.

The 'Skate' of Time

Time loops are considered binary because they remain in the slope position even after all of the randomized variables are scattered. Since time loops free-fall and maintain their position during the climb, they are not scattered prior to lift-off or documentation. They remain set, coasting through the time wave of their own accord. They are the most freewheeling of the time anomalies for this reason. Because they are a closely defined subset and are not limited to any contiguous rate of speed, they can remain constant at any given interval.

Time loops are by their nature "opulo-apparent" in that they can become opulent whenever the range of motion presents itself. Unlike the challenge presented by collapsed or predefined variables, time loops live in the range of maximum opulence. This is the reason why they can download preexisting parameters from their own internal memory. They exist as random encounters only when the dimensional frequencies are dormant. Otherwise, they are a parametric equivalent of time, existing as stationary definers rather than becoming more eloquent. Since time is elongated prior to the slope position, time loops are considered the most frequent, constant, and continuous parametric figures in the "skate" of time.

The continuous dormancy of time loops makes them available to be scanned by other waiting time loops. This provides for a dependable constancy. Time loops behave in their optimum expression through the unleashing of random values that can be described from a base-nine mathematical perspective. After each set of nines is expressed, the parallel motion is circumvented, and the time loop reorients itself onto the next scale of nines. This is why the time variables appear as a loop or rapid continuum and project themselves in a semi-circular fashion. The fact that they pop up one after the other in these nine-based sequences is what leads to the development of parallel dimensionality. Although the loops can overlap in this way, the principle that they maintain a discrete imaging places them in the position of being one of the most independent or unchanging structures in the sequentiation of time.

Time loops develop through a group of predefined variables that describe the range of spin required to cast off from the first definable matrix that they were set to represent. A loop-locking influence always implies the chance that the variables used to define the loop will fly right out of the range of spin. This could cause time to coast too randomly and independently. This is not the outcome one would want to generate. The idea is to keep the time variables frozen until such time as they can loop-lock directly with the interface. Time loops are like pudding in the hands of the more randomized loop-locking influences; they can be spun or can change hands more rapidly than one might wish. To prevent this, time loops rarely if ever spin past their variable might and remain independent until they are collected of their own accord.

Differential Circuits

Time loops are the first definition of time. In other words, since time is the key interface in the continuum, time must be calibrated from a fixed or nearly defined position. All of the event streams that impart the basis of reality to the framework are adherent to the time variables and rarely are cast apart without them. Time loops act as differential circuit breakers in the development of the cast of time. Time loops redefine their sense of motion directly from time itself and not from any independent variables that may have happened to coast in.

Time loops nest one on top of the other in waves of circular motion that define, ordain, and craft the fundamental origins of reality. As time loops from one event stream to the other, rays or branches of possible futures are spun off, which, when captured by the next loop, create the possibility of a new existence. Each time loop is an offspring of the other, multiplying infinitely in the cosmic birthing process. Time loops exist independently; that is, not all of them will eventually manifest as a given point in the reality chain. This is why they can be seen as preexistent or first-up in the continuum reference point. Time loops exist prior to any other screening. They predefine all of the reality parameters as they may have been laid down, and are constantly jumping in order to remain constant and lay down the track for all of the other time waves.

The Migration to Zero Point

Time must rest at a zero point. Time stops or quivers on the arrow of its own calibration at set or redefined intervals. Time relies on this equilibration directly and does not go after variables that do not lie within its apparent or qualified jurisdiction. Time loops, which are the spins that keep the time breaks from coming undone, always maintain the character of their position. They interlock with the time breaks, wreak havoc where havoc is due, and underlie the entire structure of the sequential matrix. Since time is calibrated on the basis of spin rather than random motion, time accentuates the clock and provides the derivatives that translate to causal probability.

The zero-point break is the defining moment for time. This position is the harmonizer, the evaluative junction between where time is portrayed as positive and where it slacks off. The defining factor here is the rate, the thrust that pushes time up from the rudimentary boundaries that have given it position and causes it to lock into place. This loop-locking mechanism defines not only the structure of time but also the psychological positioning that must ultimately be a factor in its interpretation. Time moves through each array, each installment, by giving itself enough of a kick to push ahead through all of the obstacles it has found in its path. The premature fracturing of time would create much more unstable definitions of who we are, why we are here, and what we wish to become. Through adhering to the rules of loop-locking, time is given the possibility of maintaining its essential character, thereby missing any chance of breaking off too soon. Time creates psychological self-definition through developing its zero point, where all of the possibilities are at once introduced or eliminated.

The interfaces are composites of certain key temporal phrases that will eventually correspond to the movement of time within a certain range. When mapped out, each phrase will express the character of that dimensional stream. Dimensions are held together through a type of temporal glue that acts as a bonding mechanism for all of the different strata to fan out. The organizing shape or structural formation is based on the idea of a slope that portrays the elemental turn that will define that particular dimensional curve. The slope gives time its definition from a dimensional perspective, governing the ability of time to reproduce key wave functions within a set rate of motion. The slope therefore presents the mathematical tools that predict and regulate the gardening of time over a long stretch. Time weaves back around, past its initial parameters, making snake-like formations that could be characterized as rows or plots, similar to that of a garden. The gardeners of time, who are the purveyors of past, present, and future in both the absolute and psychological sense, guard the arrays or plantings that will ensure the full measure of temporal objects.

Lost in the Garden

Immersion in the garden is necessary in order to establish the temporal zones that create the climate for each dimension. Since time is strictly "mean"—i.e., it has opposite parameters established for different configurations in the slope—it has to maintain a full range of options. Once time and matter join together, they create a loop-locking interface that is fluid, parallel, and easily definable. The introduction of the field of motion gives each dimension its psychological and temporal character. Inhabitants of each dimensional reference point have "ears" that help them to hear the specific mechanics of their home base.

Time and motion live together and inhabit a kind of timeless field in which time is stopped, recalibrated, and spilled out again into the pool. Thus motion ceases when time does. There cannot be a field of motion without time or vice versa. The loop-locking interface of time creates the gain in the breakfront that makes the concept of overlapping realities possible. The structure of time demands that as realities overlap with one another there is a blending or rapidity of values that describes the different dimensional planes. Each of these realities is versed in a fluid, ever-changing cycle that permits the joining of what appear to be radically different fields of time. Consciousness is stretched to fit each of these regions or nation-states in such a way that conventions of culture, vocabulary, and function can be expressed. The fact that entries into the continuum are primarily random in character does not stop consciousness from seeking a uniform, inherently wholistic relationship between dimensional flows.

Time functions in random compartments or blocks, each with its own mathematical description. The mathematics that rules time is different than what we would normally understand in conventional terms. The primary difference is that this mathematics is not based on a linear progression of definable events. The mathematical cornerstone of time is inherently circular and is progressive only in the sense of a greater and greater appreciation of depth, width, and height, rather than a continuous unfoldment based on sequential logic.

Time as a creative hub is essentially random. There cannot be a reliable mathematical structure for predicting the underlying causality of temporal events. Therefore the fundamental mathematics that describes temporal reality is based on the idea that randomization, although inherently unpredictable, can be estimated as a singular object of itemization. In addition, time, although inherently circular, can be predictable on the basis of ascertaining the fundamental curvature of space/time and understanding how it folds back on itself to create material form. This type of descriptive mathematics inherently leads to a type of hologrammatic imaging, a relief map of the temporal mechanics of creation.

Mathematical Counterpoint

Interdimensional mathematics involves the assimilation of a massive amount of data that must be calculated simultaneously in order to keep the temporal scheme afloat. However, like many things of great complexity when finally brought down to size, there is an elegant simplicity to the matrix that makes it possible to understand and surprisingly easy to be molded by cosmic intelligence.

Each time block is like a "rubric" cube, which can be reformed or reshaped according to an infinite number of parameters. With the time "clock" set at zero, which means that time is standing still, motionless, and prevariant, the time block awakens and with the throw of the dice a new avenue of possibility presents itself. Time fathoms the flow of consciousness through an elegant system in which the rate of spin, the range of motion, and the possibility of a new outbreak of reality are all brought together in a simple mathematical counterpoint. Each time block is referenced one to the other, with each variable that is spun out forming a building block for the next configuration. This honeycombed variability of time causes it to look like a beehive wherein each cubicle or room is inhabited by an intelligence that will eventually expand to fill every hollow.

Time bases its mathematical model on the idea that within the seed quotient of variability, time will appear randomly while eventually affixing itself to a particular matchpoint. Time appears as a filler or carrier wave for each mathematical expression. Time tends to be expressed in the form of square roots of its core bases for action. The function of the square root is to be an internal wrapping for this seed apportionment of time to take place. These expressions signify how time will be cut or roped off into singular subsections that will then combine again to form gateways of compression. Time wraps around itself, with each root integral function acting as a seed thought that has the power to birth a wide range of possibilities. The seeds or pods that hold time in their grasp can be broken open, spilling their contents on the bare floor of reality. Sections of time are like the organic unfoldment of an orange, each peeling back to form perfectly structured corridors each with its unique shape and destiny.

In the context of interdimensional mathematics, numbers do not simply have an intellectual framework; they have a feel to them, a corollary of perception that makes them akin to a living biological network. Just as a nerve or tendon would react when cut or torn, living mathematics has a lifeforce, a wave of internal reckoning that makes it both subjective and objective.

Thus the natural world is actually describable in terms of paradimensional unions of paired opposites, each with their own mathematical structure. When time cuts or imposes itself on one set of variables, there is a rip, a tear in the fabric of time, and the multiverse reels from this collapse. There is a ripple in time, a wave across the surface of reality that changes the felt climate as well as the mathematical one. Time and consciousness function in tandem to insure that what will be created in the flow of never-ending causality will always be repeatable.

Contiguous Self-Definition

Time never wastes any energy. The contiguous drive towards temporal union underlies all of the fabric of reality and makes it possible for time to "dance on the head of a pin" as far as creation goes. The loop-locking interface of time, being definable from every point of reference, creates reference points that make up the temporal calendar. The standards of repetition generated by these loops not only influence time but generate waves of rapidity in the continuum of free space.

Time must be contiguous because if it were to allow gaps in the flow of its own mechanics, there would essentially be holes in the subjective reality we experience. It would be as if one were watching a surrealistic painting in which space/time were melting away before our eyes. The loop-lock interface insures that time will retain its continuity, and thus the subjective reality we have come to rely on maintains a reasonable assurance.

The fact that time functions as a contiguous set of predefined variables in the event matrix also means that events will pop up on the horizon simultaneously. One might ask how simultaneity and mutuality can live so comfortably with each other. This is because the point of reference for time is not derived solely from the concept of free space. It is derived from the event matrix itself. The vantage point of space gives it the opportunity to call up

119

from the intelligence of time just enough give and take that time can be relied upon to fall back on itself again and again.

Thus everything we see is historically repeatable. Were this not the case, every new object would be truly unique and therefore incomprehensible to us. Sentient beings rely heavily on repetition to give them a sense of grounding and orientation in their reality. Although "lower" forms of life seem to live comfortably and fully in this instinctive fashion, we as human beings are terribly accustomed to our habits and notions of time and space. When this rug is pulled out from under us, we have a hard time knowing what to do and how to function.

The matrix that lays out the patterns for historical repetition are based not on the format of history itself, with all of its psychological and physical correlates, but on the flow of time within these subtexts. Therefore, although time moves along rapidly and the event structures inherent within the loops are often seen to digress or flow backwards, causing repetition in the event patterns before us, there is always an independent and steady stream of temporal data from which the event patterns can choose. When the collective consciousness becomes more coherent and able to recognize the flow of time within these structures, the notion of history as fixed and inevitably repeatable can be altered. One can then view history as a temporal map with cues or windows of opportunity in which certain sequences, once recognized, can be altered.

Therefore, the rate of shift in the matrix is not independent of the event sequences that buttress it, but are always carried by the underlying loop-locking interface. Time creates a type of "score," similar to a musical score, that shows when certain event sequences will come in and go out. The instruments here are the individuals themselves in their societal framework, in their systems of economic or social transaction. Once the individual or societal group can delimit its involvement in a particular event stream, a request can be entered to activate the circuit breakers that would interrupt a pool of temporal information and swiftly change the way it would have inherently formed.

These shifts occur naturally in all of the event sequences, but here, with the greater mastery of consciousness, such possibilities can be greatly enhanced. The characteristic swing that supports the march of time causes it to be very sprightly when interwoven with the movement of consciousness. With this swing in place, we can have our cake and eat it too. We gain access to the variability without suffering the complete disorientation that too much unpredictable randomization would cause. Time coasts from one randomly calibrated set of variables to another and we are reasonably comfortable in the process.

With the time loop or loop-locking interface in place, time can literally skip from one range to another. It is by nature both infinitely randomized and completely freed up. The randomization of time, which exists independently of the loop, is the defining characterization of free space. Since time must occur as a series of dockets, or ratiosynchratic mechanisms in the time interface, all of the loops exist as circuit breakers in the system. The loops act as constitutional "wafers," which flawlessly and dramatically interlace with the event streams that prevent the horizons of consciousness from becoming congested with too many randomized variables. If it were not for the time loops, time would essentially become incapable of random organization, and reality as we now know it would not exist.

Clock Time

The parallel organization of time variables, and their abrupt sequentiation in the stream, is always definable independent of the loop-locking screens that create them. The scheme of time is therefore a randomized independent variation of the screen, with time coasting from one set of loop-locking influences to another. All of the mechanisms that govern the distribution of time in the subset are swung from one jurisdiction to another. It is a type of kaleidoscopic feed, with the time variables instructing one another in their patterning as they go along. The concept of time as entirely random is not correct. Nor can we say it is fixed. It is a fluid, parallel dimensional spin in the randomization of consciousness and it can never be fixed for too long an interval.

This understanding helps us to realize that the nature of personal reality is always a timed event. All of the happenings that create time-centered reality are calibrated in advance by the individual entity, but at the same time, the randomization of the curve presents challenges that keep the whole system lively and prevent free-fall too prematurely. This concept of time as randomized, while at the same time clockable, definable, and predictable, makes it possible to develop psychological systems that adhere to the strict rules that make up this dimension of reality.

Parallel time sequences go past this system of randomization and develop time from mapping positions that occur throughout the "garden" or system. The gardens of time, when naturally occurring, are the places where time is cultivated for the purpose of independent randomization. The civilizations that govern time utilize these gardens for the purpose of maximum identification of personal parameters and can offer time sequences in all manner of directions.

Ingesting Time

People who utilize time as a kind of ingestible interface rarely find that time spins off on its own without any utilizable point of view. Time holds its interface, developing psychological reference points, and making it possible for personal history to maintain its point of view. The development of parallel codes of personal history, where there are fewer rigid definitions, and where time can be coasted, skipped, or randomized independently, is definitely in the human future. However, to define time as fixed, and to see it as something that cannot be shifted from one spectrum to another, will never be possible.

The loop-locking interface therefore skews time in such a way that always, and without fail, there will be parallel dimensional breaks that scoot time past the parameters necessary for its particular point of view. The development of a system of checks and balances in the underscoring of time gives human beings a sense of individual freedom, independence, and meaning.

1.4.3
time curvature and travel

Time Goes Fishing

ime bends or curves in order to take into account the change in the vibrational rate of a specific frequency of expansion. As time curves, the values that were originally imprinted on the down side are brought back up again, and all of the probable futures implied therein are automatically recalibrated. Time goes fishing, looking for the variables that will give it the expression it needs. As time curves back over the territory it has just recently visited, all of the forms that were launched can now be given a second reckoning. There is a point at which time vanishes, leaving a hole or break that could be described as a temporal donut.

The curved, concentric rings that are created break forward onto the plane that time had previously traversed and display themselves in such a way as to cause time to loop back over itself. Time presents itself in a simultaneous flow of values that are encapsulated over a given range of momentum. They develop a loop-locking continuity that is a free-range escapade of originality and self-generation. The time values act as catapults to the impetus of pure awareness, leading the individual traveler into places of distinct wonder and novelty.

Once time no longer has a means of identifying itself in the spread, it is in the temporal no man's land in which there are infinite possible outcomes for continuity. However, at first such results are not easily understood. In the context of our junket with time and its enterprises, we become vested in a certain cloak or fabric of reality from which we intend to make our mark. The gap or hole that is created when the vacuum state of time meets up with the rapid advancement in the temporal spread can create psychological conundrums for us as human creators. God wants us to know Him through the context of His creation, but it is only through the lonely adventure of temporal ardor that we can find our way home to Him.

Linear Expression

Time being a curved rather than linear expression, the distance that time must travel to move between two distinct points in the field is dependent on the range of motion incurred rather than the range of response. Time travels circumambulately over the terrain, mapping out signposts that allow it to know where it must return. It is very much like a weekend hiker mapping out his or her route through distinct personal landmarks known only to that person. Individuals sustain their walk in the property of time by creating breaks or markers which are pinned or wrapped around personal event structures as a type of identification banner. Each code or refraction of time is an expressed value and denotes a point in the spin.

Time codes are the nonmaterial markers that shed light on the construction of reality. They are composed of ratios, stacks of variables, which are glued together to form the basis for a complete nest. Each stack is ribboned or striated, making it possible for them to fit together much like a child's set of building blocks. The striations afford time the capability of being flexibly marked for individuality, poise, and meaning.

One of the characteristics of time codes is that they provide the parameters that tell time when and how much to spin. Much like dice in a cup, the cubic parameters of time are spun out and variable meanings are retained by the individual entity. No one can know exactly how many codes are wrapped in each blanket of time, nor can anyone fully understand how they are to be played out. Even the Godhead leaves room to be surprised.

These bursts or transfigurations of light, color, and sound that formulate reality are created when avenues of refraction meet up with their mates in the spin. They wrap around each other, creating hoods or masks that for a very short interval keep the time variable from knowing what will become of it. During this period of masking, the psychology of the individual is left at a point of hesitation, a point of innocence or unknowing. One is essentially left in the gap and momentarily free. Then, the time code hooks in, much like the next phase of a sports game, and the whole pattern re-emerges.

Time codes can be fixed, meaning that they are not likely to be changed in any way by the individual, or variable, which means that they have a high degree of rapidity or range of character. Fixed variables are more likely to coil one about the other because they must find a way of mounting themselves onto the spread. The unfixed variety swim or coast along the edges of the matrix like a wave, creating a feeling of fluidity and freedom. Every human mind has a penchant towards both sets of codes, which form the basis for the personal reality in which each individual finds him- or herself.

There is another factor to consider, and that is the element of light. Light gives time a feeling of definition. Time enters into the field of light innocently, disguised as a point of reference in the continuum. When light shines its brightness on time, time makes room for the light, doing so by setting up ring formations that spin out from the center of the meeting and create the backdrop for material reality. Time, space, and motion work together to create the elements of form. They are free-wielding, but due to the mechanics of motion, they are also subject to the laws that govern the specificity of change.

The fact that time is variable as well as fixed gives our personal reality a high degree of spiciness, of changeability. It makes us feel like we are masters of our own destiny even if we don't truly understand how and why destiny is produced. It is like eating a great-tasting apple; we aren't really that concerned where the apple is grown or what the variety is. The value of now knowing or being innocent about how our reality is constructed appears to have an underlying spiritual purpose. We are forced to play the game of life in a childlike and gullible way, learning the lessons that life presents as we move along from point to point.

At certain moments there is a chilling silence to this innocence. Something happens, albeit traumatic or at least highly different than we are accustomed to integrating within our personal reality. A shock wave takes place and we are left for a moment dangling in the curve of our own personal drama. This is the time when the signposts, which we perceive as psychological but are actually mathematical outgrowths of the curve, come to the fore. We derive pleasure out of re-engaging with the new reality, and the reality gathers momentum for the possibility of re-induction into the field. We feel psychologically safe once again until another set of variables can be added to the mix.

The challenge of course is to reflect upon the degree of adaptability that any one set of parameters may present. Time curves continuously around the signposts, creating a majestic spin that can turn our world upside down. We insert the wraparound value, the quality of attachment or categorical correlative, that makes it possible for us to choose a new reality from what has been wrought. Time cooperates with us by spinning rapidly and firmly out from the psychological marker, from its equivalent, a ring or section of temporal reality from which we can build a new landmark. We count on the circuitousness of this enterprise because it gives us hope that our comfortable sense of entrepreneurial meaning will be restored.

Time breaks appear simultaneously behind every individual curve. They are like the bumps in the road that slow all of the traffic down. Though time appears relatively transitory, in these breaks a certain fixity is imposed that gives life a sense of stability. Without them we would be truly disoriented. The simultaneity of life's individual event streams is calibrated through the transposition of these breaks over the course of a lifetime.

A Spacious State of Mind

The advantage that time has over space is in its apparent flexibility. Whereas space is spacious, roomy, translucent, and fluid, time can be fixed to meet the challenge of an individual's sense of particulateness. Time can scatter over a wide range of light, creating a lantern whereby other variables can see themselves glow in the dark.

Our state of mind is largely created through the movement from one set of time variables to another. We think of this as a subjective mood based on events, but in actuality it might be better thought of as a lack of fixity of events. Everything in our psychological compendium is dependent on our point of reference and range of stability. We view consciousness as appearing and disappearing, moving in and out of view like an apparition of unchallenged demeanor. We hardly ever recognize that the reality we see is the reality we know.

Beings who move in time are notoriously associated with ships or vehicles of a disc-like shape. Why is this so? Is this really a true vehicle, like an airplane or parachute, or is it a simulation of something that our eyes are bent to see? Perhaps it is a little of both. Discs are metaphors for the fractionization of light as it appears in the retina. We view pieces of reality like the eyes of a fly, sometimes dark, sometimes light, a wink in the cosmic reality. Transdimensional travelers come and go in our range of vision all the time, but we cannot see them because they are not visible to our sense of movement. We are like the insect on the back of an elephant, unable to understand that we are climbing around in a reality that is fairly huge and unseen.

On the other hand, because these discs are such good temporal objects, so handy for the job, they are often the shape of choice for vehicles that we might see as ships. The disk-like shape is caused by the compression of the time variables as they are coalesced through the rate of spin. This shape causes a type of cut in the air mass. The interaction between the coastal variables as they are spun together and the speed of the refractory light values is the reason for this particular shape. The other types of shapes that are seen through normal visual perception in our sphere are related to the types of refractory outcomes of light/travel/motion that the time ship maintains.

Time and space, because of their refractory nature, are not usually viewed as solid or opaque objects because they have to have room to move in the continuum. When the time variables collapse and maintain their solidity, they are always viewed as opaque, whereas when they maintain their refractory character they are seen as translucent. This is why the ships that are viewed from this dimension appear to change shape or size and appear to move off the screen of perception at such a rapid rate. When the time variables collapse they take the perception of speed or motion with them, causing the "blip" that sheds off the screen of perception so rapidly.

What must be understood is that time itself creates these illusory premises. It is not some type of extrapolated physical technology. It is the time variables themselves which spin, refract, or collapse that creates these phenomena. That is why it is impossible to understand the time-varied mechanics of dimensional operation from a purely logical standpoint.

Time and space are collapsible items. They are like fold-up chairs in the living room of the absolute. They maintain their solidity insofar as they are able to create time-dimensional tools for linear exploration, which is what all solid dimensional objects are. But in the end, time and space collapse because they must. They refract the objects of light and shade for the purpose of temporary solidity or become the wind-up toys of motion, but they are not susceptible to the whims of objective fantasy.

Time and space, since they derive pleasure from refractory impulses on a continual basis, are able to restore the span of objects and create multidimensional uniformity for the purposes of demonstration and delight. They are driven by the impulses of Nature themselves and do not rest at any particular speed or amplitude.

Time Travelers

Why are time travelers never seen in this sphere? This is because when the traveler gains optimum momentum, the beings who are traveling have no need to return to a velocity that would allow them to come into physical view. The whole concept of solidity for advanced races is of a different character. The notion of optical perception, where the physical eyes must freeze and maintain the "lantern" effect for a period of time, is limited to civilizations that must crystallize time for psychological purposes. When a civilization reaches the stage where it breaks out of the box of presupposed time, it is no longer in need of the shell of the body to create the illusion of hereness or nowness. Therefore, the time dimensional variables arrange themselves more according to the whims of consciousness rather than the psychological perception necessary for comfort/survival. This is of course an entirely different system of operation and must be seen accordingly.

Time and space are the principal vehicles for travel, at any speed. In other words, even in the state of a locomotive or an airplane it is time and space that are deriving pleasure out of the field of motion. When time scatters, it becomes immediately translucent, refracting the proper character of wave formation that makes the illusion of solidity obsolete.

Time and space curve back one onto the other, forming layers of time which are actually the cake out of which all of the omnipresent realities are baked. One could say that in God's world there is no such thing as temporal mechanics, because time itself forms the basis for all of creation. Time and space dot the rim of the absolute, acting as temporal backdrop for creation and signifying everything that is in its wake. Time and space, although they live alongside each other, do not always occupy separate homes. They are roommates, cousins, partners in the divestment of time variables that create the myriad realities that God has formed.

When a race or civilization leaves behind the fractionization principle and enters into the infinite tower of creation with the Godforce itself, it no longer has need for ships or saucers. In other words, all of the travel or dimensional interludes that make up its quest for knowledge can be gotten simply through the daily routine of absolute being. There is no need to launch probes or understand anything because all can be understood simply through the existence of being, the knowledge of knowing. Therefore, any civilizations that have to travel to get anywhere are not really that advanced at all. This will be proven as Mankind exerts its mark on the universe and begins to meet other lifeforms and species.

Hitchhikers in the Continuum

Since time and distance retain their shape uniformly when consciousness expands, there is no need to run off and find anyone or anything. One can see and hear just as distinctly in this dimension as in any other. It is the same as feeling like one has to build a new house just to hear the child crying across the street. It would be unnecessary. Therefore, those beings who travel to this dimension usually have some agenda. They wish to know, see, or feel something that they have not already known, seen, or felt. Otherwise they could stay at home in the armchair of their own dimension and gain access to everything and everyone at their home dock.

Travelers in space therefore are somehow incomplete in some way. This is why your spiritual masters see them as hitchhikers of the absolute. This is precisely true. However, it is interesting to pick up hitchhikers, is it not, and converse with them from their point of view. Therefore, as we humans speed along in our own dimensional sphere and encounter such beings, we will no doubt be fascinated by what they have to say.

Interdimensional civilizations live on time. They essentially breathe time like we would breathe air. In a sense, time and space act as coalescent magnets that feed the nervous system and create relational expression. Since interdimensional civilizations need time and space to breathe, they must rely on guideposts that create maps or conversant expanses of time/space in order to view their worlds. Since Earth is rapidly moving to this stature, the planet itself will be the vehicle whereby the Earth will see other strata of civilizations and adventures.

The concept of a "spaceship Earth" wherein the Earth itself will travel, break free from this dimensional outpost, and understand its place in the full plan is something that is little understood now. This is because we Earth inhabitants rarely see Earth as a living, breathing spirit/being with its own point of view or status of origin. We view Earth as an outpost for sentient life rather than sentient life itself. In a sense, the planet breathes time just as any interdimensional being, and as such is free to go at any moment. It is not really held here by anything other than service. The planet Earth serves the creatures that live upon it and, ideally, we do the same for it. Of course this has rarely been the case. For the most part we are destroying the fabric of the Earth, eating it up for our own purposes rather than recognizing what its true purpose is or what it has to offer. Our understanding of such matters for the most part is extremely obtuse and incomplete.

A Pleasurable Planet

The planet itself derives pleasure from the collapsing of time values. It is the principal means whereby the concepts of opacity and light are viewed on our plane. The planet Earth acts as a kaleidoscope for the buildup of time variables in our sphere. It is the doorway whereby the civilizations that live upon it can scatter their time-dimensional refractory impulses into the celestial kingdom. The civilizations that reside here are like ants on the back of a massive, living, breathing force that is independent completely of any notion of limitation. However, since we ants cannot see the big picture, we have the mistaken belief that we are in control. This is a silly notion, but nonetheless very fashionable at this moment. However, it will be seen as ludicrous eventually.

When time and space create a world or planetary body, they take into consideration the millions of evolutionary miles that must be placed on any body of knowledge before it becomes user-friendly and ultimately distinct. Therefore, the planet itself has become a crib for the many civilizations which have come and gone here, be they extraterrestrial or simply homegrown. However, when time and space return to their full glory here, there will be a renaissance of activity insofar as restoring the wholeness to the planetary community and helping those that remain to understand their mission and purpose here. The planetary intelligence is so strong, so mighty, and really inviolate in its operating mechanics that, although it may appear damaged, it is rarely injured by the civilizations that act as matchbooks upon it. When the planet itself gets ready to ignite, it will take everything with it that is seemly and just leave behind that which it does not want.

This is the function of the Mother or Host Intelligence. We must understand that the Mother is the principal compositor of the time/space relationship between matter and absolute causation. Therefore, the Mother does not have need of retaining anything which is fairly toothless and unfree. She will rip apart all of Her creation for the purpose of restitution.

No Place like Home

The understanding that the home of civilizations is in the force of Intelligence itself is a concept that is for the most part too large for any one entity to grasp. This is why the Light forces that govern this sector allow such things as we presently know to go on and on. There is no need to change anything because it is all part of a vast unfoldment of light/matter/time variables that will eventually recreate itself in the patterns necessary for the full understanding to ripen. There is no time and space in this venue, just the collapsible interchangeable melodies of Nature replaying themselves on the soil of the absolute. This is why time and space garner no moss when they are faced with the rapid unfoldment of Knowledge that can appear intergalactically at a moment's notice. When one sees babes at play one does not stop to think that one should interrupt them and teach them the principles of jet propulsion or the knowledge of how to build a skyscraper. There is no reason to do this. This is how the time lords feel about civilizations at the level of ours. They rise and fall and take all of their variables with them, and there is no reason to change or break them up unless they interfere with the scheme of things as they are.

Time and space are relatively set in their ways. They retain their altruism in the sense that they wish to expand, make new civilizations, retain the causality of motion, and repeat themselves endlessly in the vast reaches of fixed space/time understanding. But once one has been freed from the endless repetition that forges the confines of ignorance, true originality in the space/time web can be spun. This is the object of selective freedom, and it can be gained through the knowledge of how time expands and contracts, and removes all of the obstacles in its wake.

2

the
Perception
of
Time

2.1
structure and organization

2.1.1
space, time, and seership

Space/Time Constructs

the perception of time in a nonlinear manner involves synchronizing the personal, subjective inner reality with the space/time constructs that are the causal level for this reality. We see time in relationship to the cause and effect event sequences that build up in the bed of our own perspective. Time, however, views reality as something that is constructed for the benefit of its own enjoyment. Time utilizes personal reality as a place of possibility and universal expression.

Within the time and event sequences that appear, one must distinguish between the intimate daily stream of existence experienced by one individual and the collective growth of psychological and physical reality. In the personal sense, time is subjective. It is based entirely on the needs, wants, and expectations of an individual as he or she defines the personal world. As time becomes more universal, it manifests a more impersonal or relative disposition based on the tendencies of the collective consciousness. These tendencies may indeed function in a personal manner, for example, pushing the causality of a given collective stream in one direction or another, but such tendencies are not defined by any one individual. This may not always appear to be the case, as certainly individuals can make a huge impact on the level of their own morality or actions. However, as far as the march of time is concerned, it is the fundamental adherence to a particular set of thematic principles that gives time a lift or balance in the realm of collective accomplishment. Time becomes the battle cry for the individual, rather than the individual being the one who purloins the structure of time.

The interior construction of reality involves a superimposition of two primary motives: the motive of space, which organizes, synchronizes, and refines the free-moving curve of reality, and that of time, which creates the structure or window whereby event sequences can be constructed. When space and time coincide, there is a rapid speed-up in the curve or distance that defines reality. Space and time work in rapid succession, organizing the refined momentum that makes up the core of unified reality. Space and time are frequency-related in that they exist independently of the reality spread that feeds them. They must synchronize rapidly or they break up prior to the formation of the binding event modules.

Space derives its principal orchestration from two parameters: (1) there is an underlying motive or sense of direction for every event curve, and (2) space, being the symbolic union or drawstring for curved reality, must function independently of time in order for an event curve to retain its true meaning. Therefore, the synchronization of time only occurs when there is a smooth break in the event sequence; otherwise time and space exist as codependent but equal variables with the same rate of flux for any appointed jurisdiction.

Unzipping Time

In the relationship of time and space, refraction, which is the best mechanism for shattering the fluidity that is natural to real organization, exists at all given points of reference. Refraction provides the vehicle for time to break off, creating the conditions that define the preexistence of variables as they arise. For example, in the context of time as an applied source, the standardization of time as a fixed medium in which event structures can be zipped or unzipped is illustrated through the principle of refraction. Time holds its place in the continuum, and as the variables are unzipped or unlocked, they take their place in the queue.

In order to understand the rate of flow that time must exhibit in order to create its response to preexistent conditions, a set of parameters must be established that defines that rate of flow for each variable. This standardization is created by determining two constellated points of reference. The first point describes the underlying chain of influence that defines the flow of time. The second is the point of departure for that rate of influence, signifying the rate of climb. Since both of these points occur at random intervals, they do not function as heirs apparent upon which any of the prior sequences can pin themselves.

The space/time vault holds these values until such time as they may be shattered by a new, seemingly adversarial flow of variables. The new set of time parameters is fed to that which lies within the vault and is spread sometimes evenly, sometimes at different frequencies or surge points, directly to the waiting set. This process is presided over by the flow of divine intelligence that wades through all of the information as it enters each new sector. The parliamentary procedure for time is that it must follow the rules of conduct delineated by the variables that it has chosen to conduct. Outside of these parameters it is forced to obey the commands that have been given to it prior to its investment in any one particular sequence of events. Therefore, event streams are limited not by their response to the mathematics of time but by their very nature as composites of temporal material caught up in a rapid and fluid stream of coexistence.

The Spatial Stampede

Space is in a rush to catch time. Space creates the seed out of which time can coalesce. Space is not empty. It is filled with a type of corelational light that creates the mechanism whereby matter and substance are formed. This lively aspect of space makes it capable of bunching up and creating an optimal rhythm for time to turn. Space and time revolve around each other in order to bring reality in tune with itself.

The space/time spread that is void is different from the lively flow of space. The active value of space is christened by this effulgent non-light waiting to become reality. It holds its own for a significant rate of time before it coalesces into the matter/time relationship out of which event sequences are constructed. Space is the antecedent of material reality. The causation is divine intelligence itself.

Time and space wrap around each other in a type of cushion that holds all of the variables out of which reality can be made. This cushion or pillow makes time more comfortable and creates the fluidity out of which all matter can be constructed. The underlying motive of time is to create event sequences that are randomly spaced in the continuum and then brought forward in an apparently organized sequencing that defines reality. The underlying motive of space is to create the vacuum or void state that will return time back to its previously luminescent and singular state. Space gives time energy. Time gives matter volume. Space and time together create the room for creation to manifest.

The union of space and time is necessary for the unfoldment of the infinite. Space and time rearrange their parameters to support the infinite structure of reality. The character of reality is subjective in that it is interdependent with consciousness as a means for constructing motive and conduct. Space provides the team effort that gives time its ability to change. Space exists in a free-standing state that locks time in and holds it there for all to see. There is no relationship between space and time that does not lock reality into place. It is the nature of space and time to make fixed events, even though they may appear haphazard or random from the surface level.

Conscious Dependence

The significance of event sequences from a psychological sense is dependent on time and place. Psychological events arise because the doer makes reality known and then causes reality to be shaped by the flow of his or her consciousness. No events happen that are not influenced by the doer. On the other hand, the apparent paradox is that no one individual is the doer of his or her life events. It is time itself which is the doer, the creator of the infinite spread that makes room for matter. Time and space wed each other, and out of this union the psychological mandate for reality forms around them. There is a pull or push towards event sequences that impart knowledge to their maker.

Those individuals who are more conscious or aware of their own process of creation hold a greater sway in the creation mechanics around them. They provide the impetus for events to happen through their own handiwork. However, since the event sequences themselves are actually shaped by time, time is the master shaper of all that is. Time and space give the individual psychology the room to construct a space/time reality that matches the subjective climate of the individual doer's inner state. Since the doer is really infinite intelligence itself, those that act must be willing to share the glory of composition with that which is.

Walking on the Side of the Infinite

Out of the house of the infinite comes the ruling value of space. Space gives the individual doer the opportunity to change gears, to go in a different direction from that which he or she originally planned. Antecedent to every event sequence is a seed, a particular flow of time that leaves the doer open to decision-making. This is the reason for free will, and is the parcel that determines the character of a different event sequence. Since space occupies

135

the flow of determination for reality, the doer must share the responsibility for construction with the point of determination that has been laid down by the flow of space.

Space is like a sidewalk on which the infinite may walk. However, like any path, there are others that may be taken. The particular flow or rhythm of an entity's life is interdependent with this flow of space/time. The language of the infinite is in signs and symbols. These road markings impart the shape, color, and size of an individual's surroundings and hint at the meaning that the artist, who is infinite intelligence itself, intended for the canvas of reality.

All artistic formation is based upon this relational knowledge. However, in the course of constructing his or her divine play, the individual loses sight of these markings or hints, which define the chorus of reality. He or she gets lost in the moment, unable to see the larger picture. When this occurs there is a bunching up of the time variables that causes the bigger picture to hide from view. The individual is caught up in a type of self-constructed, subjective event-web that cannot be mastered by any array of activity. This type of bunching up causes one to feel lost and unfree. One must recognize that in every event stream there is an out, a way to exit the labyrinth that is constructed when space meets time. Although every event sequence has a relational, internal balance that defines the time spread, it is often not easy to see.

Holy Visionaries

The purpose of true seership is to define and lay down the underlying meaning for reality. The seer offers a relational map, which shows the individual how causality is defined. Because all time/space enterprises are bi-relational in that they are made up of sequences of matter/time that compose holes in the fundamental construction of reality, the seer must learn to interpret these holes or windows properly. At first it appears that that which is empty is indeed full. But soon, the seer learns that it is really the other way around. The seer enters a world in which the gaps or surfaces of event cusps are modularly constructed. He or she enters these rooms or houses in which the infinite spread is mapped out and made available for view. Because the infinite is infinitely unpredictable, the map that is laid down is made anew at every moment. The seer must reach into the underlying seed of reality and pull up the event spread that seems apparent from the flow of information. The art of event prediction therefore is really the art of mastering the tricky patterns of event flow that make up the subjective sequence of reality for that individual.

All event sequences are created out of fixed laws of possibility. Although the sequences themselves appear random and infinite, they actually have mechanisms that govern them and give them pause to birth. Random event sequences are mapped from the logic of internal flow. The seer perceives this mapping from within his or her consciousness and delineates a possible sequence or spread, out of which an event sequence can be created. The seer reads the innermost secrets of an individual's desires and needs, and then stalks the variables that will pull these needs into the flow of events.

We could say that the seer is an event monger, a preacher of the flow of events. He or she delineates the pattern of the curve just as the individual him- or herself would do. The ability to do this with some success creates the vehicle for the seer to actually play a role in the shaping of a person's internal reality. The job of the seer is not just to see space/time coming but to help in its shaping. The seer redefines the flow of time for that individual and conducts it into a sequence that will ideally be most beneficial for the person concerned.

If the seer allows his or her own judgmental flow of energy to be caught in this sequencing loop, he or she can interrupt or impair the flow of subjective experience, but it is unlikely that he or she will alter the abrupt flow very substantially. There is a wave or movement of the time flow that stands independent of any particular gaze. It empties into the event sequences with a type of striping that causes the event sequences to randomly implode. As a result, all seership has an underlying safety valve that makes it possible to influence reality only to a point.

Shaping Destiny

For reality to behave properly, the individual must intelligently become involved with the shaping and relationship of life decisions. These decisions have precise markers whereby they can appear out of the life course and delineate their speed of departure. Because event sequences are the language that the infinite provides as a maker of its own intelligence, they must be spread through a system of unified understanding that is likely to be formed in each individual sentient chord. The possibility that the language of the infinite is made up of time fields or sequences of event pockets is not something that most individuals understand. Therefore, these event sequences play out on their own, unbeknownst to the individual.

However, when the individual begins to become a conscious player in his or her event map, understanding dawns. The construction of reality becomes a joy, a type of pleasure that is made up of the relationship between subjective consciousness and the flow of time. The patterns that make up the core reality are synthesized or wedded to the flow of time, and the individual takes pleasure in coasting through one event stream to the other, mapping the course of reality. Then the individual becomes not the doer, but the purveyor of the time spreads. He or she can fertilize reality through the subjective patterns that make up unified existence.

As the individual consciousness draws further into the symbolic landscape that makes up his or her subjective world, there is a flow of realization that allows the individual to paint a time/space canvas that keeps the infinite value of life more fully intact. The more realization is manifest, the more pure mastery is established. At the same time, the individual recognizes the underlying flow in all creation and surrenders his or her subjective viewpoint to that all-powerful flow or divine serpent.

In Service to God

The desire of the individual to know God allows him or her to be captivated by the flow of time. The individual learns that his or her subjective reality base is made up of God's wishes and is not simply an outgrowth of his or her own span of awareness. Out of service to God, the individual shirks the opportunity to go his or her own way and becomes responsible for leaning towards the flow of time that he or she perceives is valuable to the infinite itself.

From this knowing of the way, all of reality becomes more uniform, and in a sense the individual retards the course of his or her individuality in favor of a less subjective and more objective point of view. This ultimately brings a great deal of pleasure, but in the learning of it there can be much fear, pain, or distress. The surface of the personality, out of which the ego structure is formed, does not like to give way to the flow of time. Seeking to capture time and to hold it at bay, it does not give way very easily. It is up to the seer/healer to return the event sequences to their proper mapping, which can only be done with the cooperation of those participants who are engaged in the process.

When the seer breaks up the time values and ultimately helps in their restoration, he or she acts as a type of god-intelligence for the flow of matter and time. Then the space/time seal is broken and the whole array of possibilities is shaken down and returned to the infinite causation from which it springs. The infinite forms the backdrop for material causation.

2.1.2
the development of
nonreferential mind

The Interior of Bliss

the mirroring of event streams in one's personal reality is based on the felt sense that the knower, prior to any known sequence of temporal reality, can dive into the fundamental objective reference point without having to understand it. Once the knower is freed from the object of knowing, all reference points become continuous. In objective unification, the knower is freed to continuously ease into the referential object without digression. The catapulting of consciousness into the immediate frame of reference provides a feeling of thrill or inner bliss that eventually leads to full unification.

The interior of the mind stream creates referential objects as a means of fundamental expression. Because the mind creates points of reference, there is always a sense on the basis of psychological draw that these points of reference will have some known context. This is the mistake that the human mind makes. The human mind confuses obtainment of the personal reference point with objective unification itself. Because the human mind must cling to a reference point, seeing it as the point of knowing, it misses the process of knowing, which is the basis of human interaction. The root of ignorance is in clinging to this referential banner rather than relishing the relationship itself.

The Process of Knowing

Once the knower recognizes the process of knowing as the fundamental life process, there is a shift in awareness. This causes the knower to identify with the process of knowing as the source of being and delays the need to cling to any objective point of reference. As the need to cling to this point of reference subsides, the mind bites the intellect from the interior region of its own point of knowing. Then the intellect becomes a vehicle for instantaneous and immediate revelation, rather than having to ascertain the meaning or significance of the object in and of itself.

Because each individual has the capability of creating his or her own breakpoint with the central character of any known object, an immediate shift takes place. He or she is able to identify the source of being with the source of knowing. There is a change in the adaptable surface of the mind. The nonreferential mind, free from the process of having to ascertain meaning or significance through comparative reference, becomes essentially free and independent. This allows the mind to enter a free-fall in which it is able to see time completely as it is.

In order to stretch into the continuum of time, there must be an advantageous position for the mind. The mind must learn to rely on its own inner moorings, free from objective reference, and then dive into the time curve independent of any felt sense. This recognition of the now, the only reference point in the time curve, gives the mind a raw edge. It is a point of reference that allows the mind to free itself from the claws of psychological reference.

The need of the mind to return to the event stream to reference its known causality is essentially a physiological process, rather than a spiritual one. The physiology requires this form of psychological repetition as a means to ascertain the blood/chemical relationship between timebound consciousness and uniform consciousness. Once consciousness expands to change the means of relationship between the physiological reference point and the sociological time curve, time shifts within the field of awareness. This allows the individual the possibility to float freely in between the objective reference points and store time directly.

The Nonreferential Heart

Once time is stored without markers, there is a sense of exhilaration that carries over into everyday life. The individual who is able to live freely without referential markers enjoys a playground for the soul where it is not bound by any sets in the event stream. This expansion of the mind is continuous, without any possibility of stopping. This strong wave of expansion also returns to the heart. The heart, though it understands expansion from a different point of view, has heretofore also been explicated through historical reference and interlay. Once the mind is freed the heart usually follows. Since the heart no longer has to play the referential game, it enters a dialogue with the absolute that is pure and indistinguishable. There is no pain, no understanding of the nature of suffering, because the heart has been freed from the backwards-and-forwards interplay of the mind. There is no sense of jurisdiction, nor any sense that the time/psychological markers should be restored. Once the heart recognizes its own divinity, it becomes a highly creative source of individual union and understanding.

The essential development of man/woman from the vantage point of historical interlay is left behind. The person who is able to travel in time does not view his or her world from any historical vantage point. He or she is freed from the feeling that this event, this known object, is referential or time bound. The person experiences a free, open, and noncontiguous union with all points of reference. Each point along the sphere of unification is uniquely singular and completely absolute. Each dot in the chain references unto itself and for itself. As one dives into each and every marker, there is an acknowledgment of true and complete existence. One relinquishes the essential story of life, thus calling the bluff of the absolute. There is no change in any apparent direction. There is simply a heartfelt recognition of truth in and for itself.

Death Breaks the Circuit

The vantage point of time is that of an ahistorical circuit breaker which defies life and death at once. There is no need to make sense out of the event streams because they are seen to bounce back one over the other in a kind of loop-de-loop that leaves nothing spared. Because time has the capability of creating event streams ad infinitum, the mind feels that it must interpret these events completely and understand their inner meaning. This is the essential playground of the mind. However, once the inner meaning of events has been understood, they are like nuts in which the meats have all been chewed out; there is no longer any interest nor any substance there. In order for time to be freed, the inner self must divest itself of the interest in particular vantage points in the event stream and come clean from the mind. What follows is a type of trick imagery, in which the mind tries to wrest itself from this inner knowing or inner self-imposed emptiness.

The mind, once it recognizes the spacious nature of the absolute in its full value, is often intensely frightened. It does not want to lie in the bleak interior of emptiness. Since it constantly seeks the goal of unification, it does however eventually reconcile itself to the fate of continuous perception. This new style of functioning provides the mind with some activity. It can recognize new event streams as they pop up, but it does not identify itself with these event streams as a source of identification. In this way, the mind can organize, process, and even get involved with an event stream, while simultaneously recognizing that the time curve on which it finds itself is simply the meeting of time with the mind. Once the mind enters the simple pursuit of learning about time from the inside out, it can enter into the final stages of consciousness unification.

Unleashing Symbology

The symbols that the mind derives from the individual event stream are always subjective. They are relegated to the back of the mental field, a playground for the unconscious. The symbols that the mind generates are always interesting to that subjective awareness and can be recounted again and again. These symbols have a value physiologically because they represent the means whereby the mind recognizes objects and creates unification with them. When an individual sets his or her sight on an object, there is a stored bit of truth within it. The individual can see the object, see its method of recognition, and understand why the object has come into the field of reference.

The individual can unleash any event stream he or she wishes from the point of reference of the object, and thereby create multiple, heterogeneous timelines of infinite capacity. Since the individual is no longer afraid of wresting him- or herself from the point of reference, there is no psychological longing or need to complete any individual timeline. There is simply a grasping for the next straw, a break in the wave that allows the person to restore the perceptual links in the chain. Individuals who are living in the breath of this silent, continuous event of time find that they are no longer capable of holding to any individual event stream. They are just constantly leaping into the now like a child would do who has no a priori sense of now. The individual living in this infinite experience leaves behind the entire conception of a separate or individuated life experience. One recognizes oneself not only as part of the groove of time, but as the actual fabric out of which the particular life occurrences have been based.

The process of arriving at this spectacular—and, really, natural—point of reference is the true sign of spiritual maturity. Until that time, the individual is caught on the wheel of life and death and remains suspended there for many planes of existence. Once the individual catches onto the fire of uniform dimensionality, there is no longer any need to incarnate. This usually happens gradually, however, as often there is a clean-up incarnation in which the karmas or life sequences that have held the individual captive to incarnation must be completed or rearranged. It is like cleaning house after the guests leave. There is a sense of satisfaction that all of the rooms of the psyche have been gone through and returned to their original pristine condition.

No "Me" to Stop the Flow

Once the individual leaves behind the need to catalyze his or her own existence and identify it as something special or different, then he or she can truly come into the realm of infinite being. There is a great satisfaction in this, and not nearly the sense of loss that one might expect. Actually, the clinging to individuated event streams creates more of a sense of obliqueness or loss, because the individual is trying to hold on to the balance of time when time will not let itself be kept in any individual's grasp. The nature of time is to be free. Once the individual can maintain with certainty his or her flow in the stream of life events, without having to wrap around any one particular event center, there is a change in the psychological understanding of "me-ness" that is extremely pleasant. The former me is left free and the new me is that which is known as Self. It is the expression of the "here and nowness" of life itself and is essentially retrograde, interior, and known only by the individual seer.

All of the attributes of time reference must proceed from this point. The interdimensional intelligence of advanced civilizations is independent of any cosmic reference point. Once one stops viewing oneself as the doer, there is a shift in the macrocosmic reference point as well as the microcosmic. The individual joins the universal continuum and can become capable of shifting the interior historical time posts that keep in place one's hold on time. Since all of these reference points are psychological, and since the individual has graduated from the need to create such markers, he or she becomes completely free. Out of this circuitry, a new and outstanding relationship of mind to matter is established. The individual can govern the reality of time and also of matter. He or she can create, individuate, and respond to the realities of time/matter arrangement in a godlike manner.

Essentially, the "gods" step out of the boundaries of time because they no longer view themselves as having an individuated landmark within it. In order to be a creator of uniform reality, one must no longer impose one's own sense of territory upon the pristine attributes of the Godhead. The essential nature of divine intelligence is not logical by human standards. Once one ceases to impose one's own psychological reference points upon the substructure, the inner mechanics of objective creation bring themselves into view. One sees how Nature creates life as well as how it destroys it. One no longer wishes to interfere with this process, but by understanding how it has come about one finds a sense of renewed peace.

The Soul's Encounter with Divine Mind

The fabric of the mind is one of interior dialogue, and a kind of subjective postmortem that robs the individual of any innate sense of freedom. To change this state, the individual must cut the moorings of the mind. To do so demands a great deal of courage. However, once this is accomplished, time can be gardened from the inner templates of the psyche. There is no longer a sense of time as something that has been wrested from the soul. Time has become a product of the soul, a free, open, continuous feed from the soul's own consciousness which has been, and always is, essentially free. The soul does not need to strip the mind of its moorings; it is the mind itself that does that. What the soul seeks is to redefine the nature of independent living. The soul wishes to unite completely with all of its aspects from the many time streams of its existence. Because the soul is naturally multidimensional, parallel, and infinite, it does not need any individual mindstream for solace or achievement.

The soul seeks to encounter the divine mind, not the individual unit to which it has been attached. Once the soul is free to recognize that it no longer must be bound to the individual mind, there is a great sigh of cosmic relief. The soul enters a state of unification with all of its essential selves. It folds together, in an accordion-like referential sandwich, which allows the individual consciousness to collapse upon itself. Once the soul is able to enter this state of inner unfoldment, there is a return to the divinity from which it has sprung. All of the god references, which heretofore were excluded from the mind, come to the foreground. The soul knows how God made the world and how the soul came to be. There is a sense of return to the extraordinary underpinnings of the individual consciousness that brought the soul to the point of incarnational perfection. Since the soul no longer has to run up the mountain of evolutionary development, it can hang free and unencumbered, enjoying the big view of its own makeup. This is the nature of an interdimensional consciousness that has never sought referential unification. This is not, of course, the present state of Man, but is the state of Man to come.

2.1.3
the time/matter interface

Sensitivity Training

the organization of time into predetermined subsets is controlled by beings that are capable of both random and sequential organization. They exist as stationary visitors who, when viewing the range or amplitude of temporal mechanics, can identify the strata that a particular sequence must embody. The complexity of this process is due to the tabulation that must occur as each system of opposites comes off the assembly line of the absolute and must be processed. These beings are sensitive to the binary wave or curl of the data as it is being addressed. They derive pleasure from developing a standardization of relative meaning that they can attach to the data as it streams forward. Translation is inherent in the state of consciousness itself. Since time-empowered beings are vested with a direct experience of the pure consciousness value of time, they can live within the thickly enveloped launch pads that bring each cluster of space/time into being.

Matter, being a direct offshoot of the individual timespreads, must also be made available. Matter flies off the face of the timespreads directly. Due to the complexities of randomized event chains, matter must be routed or mastered in such a way as to comprehensively entertain the vast range of data at its disposal. Matter is like the dust out of which mountains are made. Matter forms composites which represent different spectral cues of celestial light/time. Here matter is opulent, presenting an entire range of encoded information that can come serially into view. Since matter is the carrier wave for creation, matter must learn how to communicate directly with time. Matter learns from time continuously, incorporating all of the variable instincts that time comes to offer.

Beings that work with the time/matter interface do so extemporaneously but cautiously. They must utilize their own intelligence to assimilate the data streams, bring them into view, and then analyze their temporal uniformity. Matter develops its opulence through throwing off event streams that are not mandatory for uniform transformation. Each set of event streams has a processor whereby possibilities can be signaled and rerouted if need be. This is why every event stream, though singular, retains its possible fluid constitutionality.

The Language of Events

Event streams control the rate of destiny but not the flow of it. It is through the casting off of paired opposites that the event streams arrive at a type of temporal uniformity that appears destined or fixed. The historical language of event formation is governed by the rate of fluidity of these event streams as they appear in relative formation. Matter itself is a composite of these event buffers and is the tool whereby creation can take shape.

The splendor of creation is its diversity. This diversity, which is unparalleled and unrivaled by any attempt to curtail it, forms the backdrop for all life. Matter, whether bio-organic or physico-chemical, is routed in the attempt of time to calibrate its own birth. Matter derives its pleasure from the field of diversity, but eventually moves everything to a wholly uniform state. Since matter is strangely opaque, even when it is virtually transparent, the opulence that material radiance projects is produced by the embodiment of time. The time-controlled event sequences pool their way through the annals of creation and are recorded as possible outcomes. They are imprinted directly in matter like prehistoric fossils. Matter records its history directly. Every object acts as a seed precursor for that which will come after or that which has come before.

The optimizing of time is done through dissolution of event sequences. As the event sequences wrap around the time/matter chain, they are downloaded into the subsets that make the time parameters come about. When we view an event sequence from the outside in, it is not usually apparent how that event sequence has optimized itself. In our dimensional context, optimization is principally of a psychological nature. It is a felt sense rather than a mathematical correlation.

The matter/time sequences that swirl and spin to form the backdrop of our racial memories are not subject to psychological investigation until they appear as documentable events. Then it is human beings that interpret them, giving them meaning to our previously naked eye. Those beings who map time directly are not given to such interpretation. They exist strictly by the law, seeking objectivity and operating from a stringent, though oddly flexible, means of organization. This flexibility is necessary because time must always have room to spin off and make new parameters available.

We are tied to event streams through our need to give them meaning. Since the code of uniformity is not bound by any one particular subtext, the event streams become linear or translinear depending on the rate or flow of the data that binds them. The anomalies that occur, which create breaks in the flow of time, offer the advantage of presenting new possibilities for optimization to encounter. Order is maintained through the standards that have been imposed on the organization of the time fields, which are always arranged so that they can be split at the ends or at the middle. They are not broken off or fragmented too tightly. They must be whole or complete in their mathematical documentation before they can split off to form new pairs or arrays.

The Romance of Learning

Learning to love time must be done slowly and with due care. Since time is an inherently interwoven activity with the motion of consciousness itself, one cannot seek to control or dominate its self-investigation. The random sequencing of data forms the event streams, and then spills them out so that they can be paged or catalogued later. All of the event streams manifest as a type of rapid language of opposites that can be stored in the nervous system of the operator. Those races which develop this type of entrainment are referred to mythically as time lords or beings who actually can ingest or regulate the flow of time.

The relationship of beings who are involved in language structures which have to do with time is intense and in a sense very romantic. This might seem strange, as we have said that there is no actual feeling in the way we might feel it to be, but there is a type of wedding of opposites, a uniting of the poles of origin of different time-related species. This creates a union that makes it possible for the time codes to be shared one to the other. In a sense, all of the emotional content that is involved in human interaction involves an exchange of time-based language. This is why, when a human being feels an emotional charge with relation to a particular event sequence, he or she feels out of synch with the time relationship.

The meaning or sequentiation of time-based reality is interpretational rather than absolute. In other words, human beings create language structures to describe the meaning or relationship of their life events. These events are pooled or sequentiated so that as they spring forth they are organized as opposites of one another. Their expression of one quality or another is angled in such a way as to imply different shades of meaning even within the dualistic nature of the opposing sequence. Thus there are truly shades of gray in the human condition.

The curves in the human process of relational sequentiation are mathematically derived directly from the impulses that precede language. Language sprouts up from the waves of intuitive and cognitive function that form the underbelly of a person's comprehension of reality. We store the tiny bits of event-matter liberally, giving voice to the smallest nuances of perception and are fed these bits in anecdotal streams. We become inured to our own process of comprehension, and as a result the events that are brought forward are patterned on the basis of how we think and feel as well as how we might choose to behave. We become subject not only to how we relate to the organization of significant occurrences in our life, but also to the way in which such events are fused with the patterning of habitual perception.

This is why we say that the human being's event language is entirely personal. Each person develops his or her own event streams, and incorporates them into the mother tongue of his/her life unfoldment. Each event stream sprouts others that arise again and again. This forms the patterning that symbolizes the structure of a lifetime.

The linguistic overtones find their way into the human brain and central nervous system, and control speech, thought, and range of motion. The emotional content—warmth or love, tenderness or compassion, anger or greed—is connected to the event sequence that interlays the mapping. Human beings derive their entire expression of language from the mother tongue of their own emotional makeup. Absolutely nothing is objective or opaque. Everything has a subjective stroke to it.

God's Resources

The life of a human being is a self-developed, random painting of event sequences expressed on the canvas of developing form. There is no break in these sequences, even if the language structures break down due to illness, stroke, or some form of incapacitation. These event streams play themselves out infinitely. However, the difference between a time-original being and a human being is that the human being cannot originate time. He or she cannot develop a means of mapping time because he or she is locked within it. This is why sages refer to the reality that has been constructed on this plane as "maya." It is filled with the emotional correlative material of millions of lifeforms and only has meaning with and for them. There is no objective time stream.

This is the value of a being who is a time creator, who can actually map time. The disadvantage is that it is like living in a world of emotional color-blindness. This type of being can regulate the flow of time, but not the meaning inherent within it. This is the paradox! It is one of the mysteries of God's infinite compassion and creative "resourcery" that He/She can create time and the understanding of how to map it, but not always give the entities involved the wisdom to know what to do or how to function with its expression. The future, however, of the human being is to become a functionary of the time continuum and to retain the unique psychoemotional character of his/her language streams. This is a wondrous destiny and unique intergalactically.

The time loops that are created in human awareness are always diplanar. They cannot be anything other than that because human beings view the world in a dual fashion. This expression allows the human being to control the random elocution of his/her personal universe. It is similar to the idea of the creation of a time/matter city-state without the creative maneuvers that signify the range of interlocutional language inherent within them.

The time frames that are created in each documented sequence are naturally opaque and inherently random. In order for the language streams to derive meaning from their incorporated subsets, there is a prismatic interlay that gives meaning to each random set. This is how prehistory wraps itself around an event stream and eventually allows it to branch out to form the continuum that has yet to appear. It is an anomaly that, as each event stream curves back on itself, the figure eight that is represented forms the basis for the next stage of the continuum. It is a type of time curl or loop, which can be documented from the outside in. It is as if the type of programming that makes up time also makes up space.

The human being cannot control his or her own destiny without beings who actually map the way. This is the humorous part of it all. The human being is a puppet for the time-mapping vehicles, but he or she is also an intelligent player within that field. The human being paves the way for other life forms that are inherently more emotionally driven as well. These other life forms, such as the animal or insect realms, are even less in control. They must learn to divest themselves of all of their linguistic time feeds and become part of the time spiral that humans present.

Humans are essentially masters over the animals, but it is the animals that actually give human beings the necessary linguistic impulses that create the time feeds they employ. This is the secret to the inter-expression of all life. All lesser lifeforms are inherently greater because they are less attached to the outcomes that they help to generate. They are expressions of a more or less direct nature from the interdimensional helpers who direct their every move.

Only those time dimensional beings who live in a particular event spiral can relate to it. The time dimensional beings who live in our world are essentially multidimensional in purpose but unidimensional in form. This is hard to comprehend, but it is true. The beings that we relate to on a daily basis are inherently the surface value of their own counterparts. For every being that we encounter, there are interloping entities that form the basis for their unification. We are looking at the seedlings, while the time-dimensional beings are looking at the crop.

The time-dimensional beings work with, expedite, and reroute time in such a manner as humans can actually see the workings of their own mind. The mind is essentially a research center for time to work itself out. One does not really have a mind of one's own. The human mind is an incorporation of all of the time feeds that are available in that region of the space/time continuum. There is no originality here, only a complex system of patterning that makes the presupposed event streams possible.

One could say that the human being is essentially a puppet for time. However, inside this seemingly limited scope, there is a richness, a documentation of values that is incredible in its intensity and meaning. This is the paradox: that there can be so much freedom in a state that seems very limiting. One can open wide to the apparent depth of the freedom and climb within it to explore the inner regions of the psyche.

2.1.4
the stretch of time

Fluid Mechanics

he fluid definition of time is what makes it possible for one to travel within it. Time speeds up or slows down both from a psychological and also an historical point of view. As event sets are introduced into the subswing of time, each set is put in the breeze, developing its own avenues or parameters through which it will be strung to create the particular interlocator that one wishes to express. Matter hangs on the eaves of time, and, as it incorporates each set of variables, these variables are expressed as event sets or twins. Matter/time creates the vehicle for event sets to springboard themselves into full awakening or power in the life cycle of individuals or nations.

For individuals to develop the conceptual and technical mechanics to travel in time, they must be willing to "lose their shirt" to the falling range of the absolute. They must become intensely interested in being shaken loose from all of the notions that they have of fixity or uniformity. Individuals who travel in time leave behind all of these notions in favor of a set of interior sensibilities that makes them sensitive, open, and keenly able to identify that which is right in front of them. They become boomeranged into the reality of the all-now.

Time becomes unitemporal simultaneously as it becomes unispatial. The quest to enter the dark, empty regions of space, affords time the opportunity to create the fluid, binary motion that causes planets to spin and nations to lose their hold on temporal power. As individuals and civilizations are dependent on time stretching itself to accommodate the psychological movement of human beings, time is dependent on the climate or mood of its own mechanics.

The weather balloon for time is space. Space governs the flow or movement of time, creating the ballast for time to take off, move left to right, or swing to center. Time travelers utilize this movement of time, literally shaking from one end of the spectrum to the other, shedding values like a dog would shake off water. Time travelers speed up or slow down in the continuum through their relationship, first, to their own psychological constructs, and secondly, to their own rate of speed.

Traveling from One Dimension to Another

In a sense, every individual is a time traveler because each person gobbles up the variables presented and develops a strategy for utilizing them to his or her best advantage. The traveling part comes in when one identifies or brings forward the field of motion. Now one is traveling, picking up speed, moving from one dimensional surface to the other. It is much like two trains passing each other, each with a particular rate of speed, a trajectory that has been calculated, but now, due to the interior configuration of consciousness itself, the angles of refraction have been changed or altered.

Time travelers travel for the purpose of investigation. Like any being who is intelligent and placed in living form, beings develop through an intense curiosity about the nature of existence. They learn to swim, fish, play hockey, or go outdoors in the summer air in order to understand the nature of their surroundings. Time travelers are seeking to understand the parameters of dimensional configuration. They want to understand what is fixed, what is uniform, and what is fluid. They want to play with all of the variables that make a reality come to life.

An experienced traveler is one who can see the conceptual basis behind an object but also maintain objectivity about it. One can then view significance in the field of form without becoming attached to it. This ability to play with the field of form, twirl it around to its best advantage, and understand how it is to be shaped, is reserved for beings who have learned to be conscious in the field of time. The stretch of time is the conceptual basis for all of the time travel technology available. To understand the rate or flow of stretch makes it possible for us to achieve a more steady relationship to time travel technology.

Time becomes a conduit for consciousness. It is never the other way around. In other words, time must stretch in order to accommodate the flow or speed of consciousness as it enters into this plane of awareness. Time is not a variable component in and of itself. It is consciousness that causes time to be permeable.

The effect of consciousness is to create a chain of event structures that allows time to be independent of any other variable. When time is left alone, stripped of its ability to interact with anything or anybody, then it starts to develop strategies of its own. It leans into the field of matter, and in so doing, recognizes certain patterns or shapes that will be efficacious to the beginnings of awakened life. Time is like a kaleidoscope, seeking out fresh variables for orientation and leaning into their patterning for the sake of both beauty and speed.

Out of the Time Trap

Time likes to encounter obstacles because through setbacks or hurdles it learns to program new vistas of opportunity. It learns to stretch or recede into its own flow or subset of understanding. Time is not to be reckoned by any set parameters. Any attempt to trap time into a set of locked parameters will only cause it to set itself free. This is why when you engage in an event there always seems to be a pull or stretch of time in which the time parameters fill themselves up and expand to meet the need of the event. This phenomenon is both physical and psychological.

In order for time to become a free and independent variable, one must escape any concepts of time that lock it into a fixed state. For this to happen, the participant must be open to looking at time from every angle. Once there is recognition that time is opaque and ideally independent of any preconceived variables, then a window of variability opens up that makes it possible for one to switch into a different view or subswing of time.

Time is a component of equidistant travel through the space/time continuum by way of the application of an internal and external technology. This understanding will have to increase substantially in order to make time travel available. As long as machines exist as independent mechanical beings that are separate from the life within, then there can be no technology that dismantles the fixed state of time.

The time traveler must learn first of all to discipline his or her mind. This is the key ingredient. This does not mean that there should be no thoughts in the mind or any emotions that follow from them. There should be a sense of peace, however, and a feeling that the mind is not the plaything of consciousness but exists independently as a stream or flow of feeling. The mind is not to be controlled but to be recognized for what it is and how it functions independently of the pure consciousness stream. Once there is a clear recognition of the mind, then there can be a clear understanding of how time flows in the context of the mind.

For example, if an event stream arises and there are certain applied variables that are part of that event stream, then time makes a place for itself within that event stream. It ripples or churns the flow of the event stream so that it is softened. In this way, time slips in and turns the flow of the event in any given direction. This is what is meant by the term "possible future." Once time has "sprung a leak" and is able to return back to its original source through the context of the event stream, such an event is no longer fixed. It becomes fluid and is able to trip over itself and return back to its origins. In order to become capable of leaning into time this way, the participant must journey into the fabric of time from the level of his or her own awareness.

This means that time travelers are not really travelers in a physical sense. They are travelers in a time sense. They leave the realm that they are living in from a contextual perspective and enter a dreamtime basis in which they are in the event stream but not of the event stream. It is possible, of course, to take the body with one on such a journey, but it actually is not imperative. Therefore, when you meet a time traveler, even such as those who have an external vehicle of some sort, a "ship," it does not mean that that being is actually rooted to that very spot in time. He or she can appear simultaneously in your world and many others at the same time. There is no limit to this in actuality. This is the nature of time travel. One can slip into many pockets of time and turn around in them, then slip back out again unnoticed. Or one can be recognized for purposes that are known only to the traveler.

To be able to slip into time in this way, the traveler does not need to leave the location in which he or she resides. Essentially, the traveler enters a fluid, noncontinuous, open space in which he or she rests in the subswing of time, neither here nor there, so to speak. This allows the traveler to become superfluid and enter the dreamtime. There, he or she can become sensitive to every nuance of the time matrix. He or she can understand the time flow and become one with it. Then he or she is capable of leaping over the back of time and becoming an interplay unit with its continuing unfoldment.

Those beings who travel through time this way use a vehicle not as a resting place for their weary heads, but as an avenue of change or variability. Since time travel has fixed parameters, due to the shift in the waves as they circumvent the event stream, the time traveler employs a vehicle to move time here and there and extend it in every direction. This is the concept of stretch. The more that the traveler can extend the variability of time through motion, the longer the traveler can extend his or her visit.

Objective Memory

How does time interplay with an object? This is the question. Take any object, big or small. When an object appears, it is in the event stream of your awareness. You note the object as being real or within the span of your awareness. It is not kept at a distance but actually becomes imprinted within the context of your mind. You register the object and catalogue its identity within your awareness. Now once the time stream is closed or has shifted in some manner, you might not experience the object in your awareness. For you, it does not exist; it has essentially disappeared. In order to understand this phenomenon, remember that everything that you see or hear is made of the context out of which it exists in your memory.

You do not have anything in your awareness that your memory cannot identify. If there is a new object, situation, or person, your ability to identify its existence is based solely on your past experience. If you cannot identify the nature of an object, then your brain simply switches off and returns the unidentifiable object back to Source. This is the key to understanding how time travelers can actually appear in your room and you do not know they are there. They are there in the window of their own continuum, but because you cannot register their whereabouts, their identity remains a mystery to you. It is not that they are not there; it is that you have no context to understand their location. They have slipped into an area that your brain and central nervous system do not yet know how to catalogue.

The Beauty of Childhood Discovery

When we work with other people in reference to light frequencies, we begin to bring these frequencies on to this plane. We invite other entities for the ride. This is true because such entities are attracted to the work that we are doing. They exist in our time reality but we cannot actually see them because they are not available for our nervous system to reference. Perhaps we do not want to see them because they would look strange or unusual to us. Our species is not very courageous in taking in the identity of other travelers because they do not look the part. They do not behave or live in a physical vehicle that is familiar to us. So they do not exist. We block them out.

This is what happens when we travel as well. At night, when we are asleep, we slip out of our time stream and move in different layers of sleep to have adventures on other planes of awareness. We have been doing this since childhood. However, we rarely ask ourselves where we have actually been, since our psychological experience covers the actual travel. We are aware only of the psychological parameters of our dreams and not of the change in dimension that they accompany. It is as if we are not willing to look at such changes because they would disorient our sense of reality.

However, when experienced time travelers enter our domain, they do not relate to the experience as a dream. It exists in their own time frame and is coherent for them. They see us as we see ourselves; however, we cannot see them. This is the beauty of the experience. In order to change this, we must be willing to see the entities that exist all around us. We feel that we are the only inhabitants of our domain, but this is not true.

The beings that coinhabit our time sector exist for many reasons. Some are available to offer assistance in particular situations. Others are there only to observe and would never interfere. Those beings that require an external vehicle to move in our sphere rarely come to join us unless they are invited. This is because it takes a certain amount of energy for them to leave their vehicle and enter our domain. Therefore, we must ask them to do so for a particular reason.

Recognizing Asymmetrical Parameters

In order to communicate with travelers in our sphere, it is important that we recognize that time, being asymmetrical, is not subject to our particular whims. Therefore, we need not think of time in terms of day or night or any such limited parameters. The internal mechanism of time enters the brain and central nervous system and essentially downloads the programming of the time variables that we wish to explore. We are not limited to some notion of present or past, because such things are only psychological constructs and do not really exist.

Remember that everything that we see on this plane is a registration of the brain and central nervous system and is no more real than the dream images that we see in our awareness in sleep. The difference is that they are more concrete; they are touchable. Why is this so? This is because we are congruent with them time-wise and spatially. It is this congruence that renders them solid and opaque. They have no solidity in and of themselves. We give this to them through the appearance of uniformity.

This is what is meant by the term "uniform dimensionality." The dimensions become uniform when consciousness is able to see them as terminal, definable states. This allows consciousness to be able to have a permanent window on time. It leads to the concept of simple mathematical time variance from a human perspective. However, multidimensional time variance does not rely on psychological constructs. It surpasses this level. One has to enter a place of unconstructed time functioning in order to travel through time with the random partners of mind or matter. Time appears uniform due to the wave formations of consciousness. The time traveler has to be able to transcend his or her own patterning, or better, be free of such patterning altogether. To do this, the traveler must be free of the limitations of his or her own mind.

The accomplishment of time travel involves the willingness to leave behind the dimensional cues that offer a type of temporal sanity to our species. This is why it is rarely accomplished. Our species relies very much on being able to dive into the moment and thrives on spectacular emotional events for its very survival. The species is not very patient or able to step into a framework in which nothing is happening for long intervals of space/time. There is a tremendous need not to be bored. When we enter the no-time, the stretch of time is so great that there are long intervals of emptiness or nothingness in which one just resides, patiently and without protocol. This is necessary. The human species is so impatient for its next round of experience, it is very difficult for it to suspend its physical and emotional parameters in order to "hang out" in space/time. The first step is to loosen up these moorings.

Imagining a Stretch

The exercises involved in opening into space/time in a more fluid manner involve tricking the mind to think that only a fraction of time has passed when it has been hours. This is the first step in stretching the time variables to fit the encounter. To do this, imagine that you are in a room and there is nothing but you and bare walls. There are no objects, pictures, colors or points of reference. Place yourself in this environment in your awareness and begin to count backwards from ten to one. Once you have reached the zero point, see if you can coast into the time variables independent of your mind. Let the mind go completely. Do not attempt to build back any references. Then wait. Let the time sequences open up on their own. Do not force the shift. Let it take place on its own. Once this happens, you will feel that you are suspended, out of time as it were. When you can do this at will, you will be ready to enter into an internal flow with all manner of time variable sequences that could be advantageous to your understanding.

The relationship of time and distance plays itself out in physical as well as psychological travel. The distance that time takes to go from point A to point B is not a matter of width or breadth. It is a matter of the inner vantage point shifting to accommodate the flow of time in a new direction. This is the way that you build time constructs in every moment. This is how you can interact with your environment and maintain a context. The fear of insanity is the fear that time context will be lost. It is that simple. A person whose mind is not in the flow of time enters a free-fall in which time references can be scrambled, lost, or interfered with.

The person who resides in a no-time context at all stages is comfortable with not having any sense of down or up, in or out, or any need to find a context for his or her mental aspirations. This is how one becomes free. It is not a frame of mind: it is a continuous, ever-expanding state of simple awareness in which the mind becomes free of the time constraints. In our vocabulary, the person then becomes ripe for interdimensional travel by virtue of the attainment of spiritual liberation.

2.1.5
the   random   organization   of   time

Random Avenues of Realization

randomization, which is the key to understanding how event streams picture or package themselves psychologically, involves the curving or twisting of time to create a form of prehistory which presages the formation of event sequences. The formation of time occurs in a rhythmic fashion that is governed by the sequestering of algorithms. These algorithms form locks or bracelets which, when interpreted by the individual psychological matrix, determine how the underlying establishment of personal reality will be performed. Reality is set up through the development of reason, which imparts a solidity or uniformity to individualized perception. Randomization presents the curve or circuitous avenue of realization whereby the individual will perceive his or her perceptual environment.

Randomization flowers through perception. First an event appears, unaccosted, clear, open-ended, and inherently circular. Then the event is greeted by a type of psychological clutter that inhibits the natural flow of the event in the stream. The event circumambulates around the flow of time inherent within it, picking up traces of the psychological entrapment that seeks to bind it. Once the event stream reaches a perceptual climax, the randomized values inherent underneath it are out of the box. They curve around the jetstream of the event, forming a wave or circuit that gradually maximizes all of the possibilities inherent within that subgroup. The curve or slope of time bunches up and all of the little grooves that cause time to be randomized, or made as opposite-seeking bundles, are arranged.

History Says It's Not the Case

One assumes that history is made up of events that are permanently established or stored, just as one would also assume that individual history is likewise documented. However, this is not the case. History, like individual perceptual reality, is formative, fluid, languishing in the eaves of perception just like individual language and reason. History accumulates a wrapper or codification around its event sequences that makes it subject to interpretation and internal development. Quite simply, the way one views history makes what we see historically relevant.

From the standpoint of history, psychological event sequences form the backdrop of the standardization that we call civilization. That objective reality is far more subject to interpretation than we might like to believe. This is not to say that there is no real basis for this standardization, but it is far more given to interpretation than we would like to believe. Since the event sequences are randomized gradually and given meaning immediately, there is a gap between meaning and synchronization. Each standard that is metered out by the event stream is entrapped within the subtext of the underlying psychological structure. Time imprints itself into the subtext of what has occurred before that subtext has even written its own script.

Randomized time is inherently circular because each system that breaks apart time into its curly subgroups develops a means of echoing or refining the themes or reference points which have been delineated. The random aspect comes in introspective rationalization of how an individual psychological backdrop will be imposed. Time and consciousness flavor or enhance an event stream and then this sequence is made "hot" by the adequacies or inadequacies of form and/or structure.

Algorithmic Templates

Algorithms provide the principal mathematical language structures that give time its shape. Without this algorithmic template, time would be amorphous, infinite, and inherently fluid. With the algorithmic section of time in place, time becomes permeable, mappable, and coherent. The individual psychology develops grooves or shields in its structure that interweave with the algorithmic fluidity of time. Time and matter are wrapped around the individual blanket of psychology, and the algorithms provide the stretcher, the seer that makes the dreams or ambitions of a given individual come more fully to life.

Algorithms live like angels, striking the flame of the absolute without quickening it. They flash their uncanny tracks directly in the face of form and give it meaning and altruism. Without the algorithmic component, time would have no face, no charm, and no means of sequentiation. With the algorithms in place, the mathematical candle of time is lit.

The striking similarity between time and consciousness is that both are given to recede when they interweave with the formation of matter. Matter trumps them, developing the concrete similarities that give third dimensional reality a sense of meaning and purpose. To understand the base-ten value of time, one must understand that when time, which is inherently binary, looks in the face of all of the mathematical constructs which could potentially define it, the sequences are categorized on a wholistic basis. Base ten provides a hologram of simulated light refractive consciousness that weaves its way into the event stream and prevents too many inadequacies. Time arranges itself in a pulse, a geometric circuit of light and form, which presupposes the event sequences as they are called up. Time is like an army marching, the soldiers line up on the battle field two by four, and time arranges them so that they will all be squared up in a sequence of one through nine. Time arranges them in a row so that they will have the opportunity to intermingle, to substantiate their temporal point of view. Referenced sequentially, the off/on binary thrust of time, which lends itself to twos and fours, is now stretched out of sequence into sevens, eights, and nines. This involves the change from a series of values squared to a series of values cubed. Now time has room to grow.

This is why modern decimal languages have given the number ten such power. Time quantifies, breaks apart, and ignites through the mathematical allowance that a base ten energetic framework makes possible. Decimal language, which gives time its metric equivalent, is not therefore simply coincidental, it is the raison d'être for time to mimic its manifestation in a concrete yet eloquent way.

The Magical Packaging of Time

Time is stored in packages. These packages are like strips or ribbons that give time the capability to be memory-sensitive to all of the events that are intertwined within it. When one opens a temporal package, light and consciousness are the cookies that are stored inside. Once the envelope is broken, light waves fractionizate in every direction, and time is sealed in for a particular ride. Time manufactures the direct outgrowth of consciousness in the form of movement. Here, temporal packages slither or move out onto the surface of concrete reality and form the interior windows that make up an event sequence. These windows offer a "room with a view" for each set of language structures to present itself.

Time is magical because it is concave. It purses itself like cool, smooth lips and shrieks when it is given cover. Time amplifies the cold, hard, clear reality of matter and gives it maximum coverage. It radiates its beam of spectral light on each antithetical docket and creates the means whereby matter will become sparkling, radiant, and uniform. Standards of deviation aside, matter and time trade their respective information circularly, but it is through the perception of time that it gains the vast appeal that forms nations and builds civilized sensibilities.

The tricks that matter performs are not documented instantaneously by time. They are tricks that prevent time from acclimating itself too much to the demands of space. Time fools space into believing that it can radiate out gradually while entrapping space into the folds or covertures that make reality live within its reach. The standards that space utilizes to entrap time are a subject for further discussion, but it is in the amplitudes whereby space and time are maintained and destroyed that reality comes in for its roughest, most popular ride.

The adventure of time is to find the absolute the most quickly, and with the least amount of advance notice. Time rectifies itself almost immediately with the absolute value, but trickles down onto the surface of creation in a much more lumbering and lazy fashion. The laws that govern time are not dependent on the artifices of human engagement. They are based solely on time becoming capable of developing the means for temporal engagement, much like a general grooms his or her troops for the charge without knowing exactly what the actual battle will entail. Time and matter strike out on their own, and then time must make up for the situation on the strength of the human will and intellect.

Time and consciousness are instilled in the constructs of history by the willy-nilly incorporation of terminal means or interests on the part of those who wish to seal the fate of their contemporaries. Systems of enterprise cannot be based purely on time because they would become fake operators, unable to develop perceptual strategies that would breed the formation of nation-states. The union of time must simply be born directly from the psychology of the absolute, stripped of all its armor and left bare to confront the pure temporal protagonists that give it reason and shape.

The Formation of Prehistory

Prehistory is the formative inspiration for event sequences. Each storage unit of presupposed time is packaged in a calendar box. These boxes are wrapped with the conceptions of civilization. When time arranges itself into the neatly folded envelope of unitary perception, the backfolds or conduits that present themselves are clipped by the randomization value. Time enters the sea of randomization and, once engaged there, encounters the precise system of envelopment that will give matter a standard of direction.

The calendar box is a random set of implied parameters which forms the bulk of the time material available for that time spread or data sequence. Time sweeps clean both the inside and outside of the event structures it encounters. The forward and backward movement of time calls into question all of the attributes that have given it its shape heretofore. Reality swings about, offering different points of view from every conceivable angle.

Time lashes out onto the surface of matter, creating the environment that will cause matter to spin around and take notice. Though at first quite shy when seeking to respond to the demand of time, eventually matter responds firmly, ever keeping the formation of the event sequences it is seeking to represent within grasp. All of the time parameters are thereby identified, presenting a sweep in the calendar box.

This is how the possibilities of presupposed time are presented: singularly, sharply, indefinably, and without hesitation. The law of opposites enters and imposes the optimization of duality upon the world of form. Time, honored by the curve of randomization, leaves behind its impetuous nature and follows suit, giving rise to the on/off universe to which we have grown accustomed.

In order for one set of parameters to push out or overweigh the others, there are laws that govern the formation of time from the absolute value. These laws govern the range or frequency of time from its individual subswing to its full expression. The absolute is like the fundamental chorus that maintains its full integrity even when stripped of the bars of reason. The absolute gives time and consciousness room to grow, but does not deprive them of their full originality. For time to be embedded in the halls of reality, it is matter that must give it the baseline of solidity. Only matter knows the laws of consciousness completely because it is matter that is most capable of expressing them.

Jaws That Free Us

Algorithms are the jaws of time. They form the laws that govern the mathematics of pure reason. These algorithms set up the basic lifelines out of which the governing order of time can quickly emerge. Once an algorithm is stricken with the light of developing matter, it breaks open, and the words, the sequences, the uniform codes that will create the event structures are ripped apart. Matter intercedes, and light and consciousness create a fluid rhythm, a type of categorical hum that causes the event sequences to develop their internal means for unification.

Events are manifested not only by the breaks in sequence, but by the hum of the absolute that surcharges or refines the event and makes it capable of encapsulization. Event sequences display themselves randomly, are encoded, and then captured to reflect the available slots that are incorporated within their subgroup. Once an event sequence comes online, it is like a soldier at attention. It loop-de-loops through each means of strategy, and, circumventing all of the avenues that would have at one time been available to it, comes up with just the right sequence that will satisfy the chain of command. This type of leapfrog or loop-de-loop sequencing of time is the characteristic that most easily rectifies the procedural mechanics of time and explains why certain event sequences pop up at inexplicable moments.

The random organization of time seems like a paradox when it appears that the psychological organization of events is so neatly ordered. In order for the psychological parameters to present themselves logically, there is a parametric shift that takes place each time the data sequences are presented. This data, which presents itself as a binary stream, is recalibrated to reflect the complexities that a decimalized series would offer. Through randomization, the mechanics of time are interwoven with the pop-up series of event mechanics that stores all of the data and eventually bring it back out for serial use.

The Elegance of Checks and Balances

Although programmed through the beauty and power of a binary stream, events then are captured in muse-like sequences of one to ten. They develop characterization here, and are likely to strike out on their own, creating the rhythmic impulses that make matter sing. Matter is created through the underlying values that are simultaneously captured as sequences of data flow through the congregation of opposites. Each flow of data has its concomitant stream that provides a check and balance system for information to move into this plane of dimensional awareness. The eventualities that are created as each set of data interweaves with the event sequences that have already been established are set long in advance of that which we actually encounter on our plane. Event streams trickle down from one plane of awareness to another, much like a waterfall leaves traces of itself in the rocks. These silent streams become powerful forces of reckoning when blended with the tributaries of consciousness that have already been established.

The data accrues through a temporal echo which acts as a buffer while the time values are reorganizing themselves. It is through this echo that time speaks back to itself, arranging the mechanics that simplify and refine the contexts of matter and motion. Time bounces back, across the surfaces which have been arranged, and, unlocking its teeth, opens up the "curly cues" and cross-weaves that magnify the impulses that have been represented heretofore. Time cuts its teeth on the absolute, but it gains its strength through the boundless influence of extraordinary means that consciousness represents. Without the throwback to the absolute that occurs when time bounces back onto the surface of the event stream, there would not be the possibility for randomization or the eligibility of data that wish to enter the stream. All would be lost in the quick range of signals that must encounter the entropy of maximization, and nothing would be gained in the full spectrum of temporal activity itself.

Round the Corner to God

The avenues of perception are inherently circular, but the event streams are always susceptible to being struck loose from the interior of the whole. There, unbroken and unwithered, they can and do develop on their own, and make systems of language and movement that are of their own type or region. When individuals attempt to strangle event streams in the rush of their own perception, they leave out valuable material which would otherwise come to be. Once one learns to relax with the flow of time, it responds in kind, stretching all of the possibilities and making everything appear homogenous.

Nothing can move when paralyzed by the precision of temporal advancement. This is why subranges of data are accrued through a type of echo effect, which, when working correctly, bounces back time signals at precise intervals while still maintaining the loop-de-loop or cross-sequencing that each situation indicates. This is why it appears that there is both a random sequencing to the event calendar as well as a wedding or weaving of opposites.

Time is rounded through the incorporation of strategic event sequences that give shape or meaning to reality as we know it. These event sequences provide buffer zones or intervals of light and dark that incorporate an event stream and eventually give it psychological structure. Time is rounded to prevent too precise a means of advancement, which would rob it of its individuality and give everyone the exact flavor of movement. This would constitute a theft of our individual will or a suspension of the laws of order when it is not in the mind of God to be so.

There are many types of rounding values that are incorporated into the time parameters. These rounding values are the curves through which the event sequences express themselves. There is an order to these curves, just as there is an order to any set of linguistic sequences. The order is based on an algorithmic language that stores presupposed data that form alternate sequences of time that spill out again at random intervals. This on/off, bipolar routing of time sequences keeps the heart of time jumping. Through this dance, the most intimate and precise movements of time are expressed. As each event sequence expresses itself as a stored parametric language, there is a christening, an awakening to the precise point of reference that will later correlate with the psychological meaning that one is attempting to create.

In order for time to synchronize simultaneously with events, it must create pools or openings in which the event streams will be squeezed together and wrung out for further use. Here, the pools become storage closets for the precise mechanisms of temporal mechanics. Each arrangement that is made works in lockstep with the other, so that temporal pools form arrangements that give the structure of time an aura of completeness. Once time makes arrangements for the formation of language that will express its mechanics in material form, then the union of opposites comes into play. Until then, this binary, dualistic cartoon of time is not drawn.

We are the orchestrators of reality, but time, the great organizer, is the determining factor that makes our world concert possible. Time enters the two-step of a binary world and returns with the complexities of ten. This is why the arrangement of time eventually must be operated by intelligent lifestreams that utilize the ten to incorporate the one. Time enters the base ten signification and then gradually, through incipient mapping, returns to the principal unitary thread. This God-weave, which is the significator for time, is the envelope out of which event sequences will be spread.

Towards a More Perfect Union

The union of time will eventually be based on the system of one rather than two. Yet it is structured first into the base-ten randomization method as a means of bringing about the greatest possibility of interweaving. The pools are the place where time becomes first two, then one, then back to two again. The pools reflect the language that must be constructed to express reality as a point of reason rather than as a simply chaotic and refractive string of circumstance. It is out of a time pool that one can gain access to the fruits of realization. Since time and consciousness live in the time pool together, they go past the usually disadvantageous construction of opposite means and develop a taste for uniformity. Then the two can become one and there is a cause for rejoicing.

Matter and time always seek to rectify themselves. This is why, when time is arranged sequentially, there is always a little kick that remains that will cause the temporal sequences to unlock from each other. As the temporal sequences unlock, the bipolar or opposite strategy comes into view. The temporal stream then has the opportunity to attract or repulse this opposite value as it wishes. When time is repulsed continuously by the strips of time/matter that have been accumulated, it is because the temporal streams themselves have formed a flashy veneer over the surface of the time stream. The perceptual curve is stretched out, and then the individual is capable of returning to the place of origination of his or her system or standard of ethical conduct.

Union is not imposed. It is based solely on the will of the individual to determine his or her destiny free from constraint. Union is built upon the dance of opposites, but luckily this is not where it finally lands. Once the individual is capable of original thinking, free from the constraints of any consensual obligation, the mindstream is set free. Then the moment-to-moment elucidation of temporal reality comes strikingly and permanently into view. This is not just a change in mood but a structural and behavioral shift of tremendous implication. The enlightened mind is like a wagon train where all of the horses that once pulled the cart have been entirely set loose. Then the train of mind can function unto its own, and the frequency of origination speeds up magnificently. The framework of perception builds and builds on itself, striking out bravely in every conceivable direction. Now there is pure randomization, and it is not necessary for any characterization of this temporal field to occur. The psychology, shorn of its moorings, is not limited by any categorical interpretation. It is only then that the mind can be freed from the constraints of time.

2.2
personal reality

2.2.1
love, fluidity, and time

Lovers in Time

ime leads while information follows. This is the law of the universe. Time gestures while the players of reality, which are purely material, score their advantage. Time provides the array of possibilities for reality to formulate its creative schemes, and shatters the mandible of fixed perception. For time to do its job, it must have a fluid canvas on which to work. This is why the vibrational level of material reality on our plane is advancing and the uniformity of dimensional perception is increasing.

In this interplay, the fountainhead of love and tolerance promotes creative advancement. How are time and love interrelated? When time encounters the flow of love, it is actually physically and dynamically affected. Are not beings who are in love more easily swayed, more easily malleable? Is not the being who is out of love, out of favor, isolated, and removed from others more easily left in a state of despondency and fear? Time and love work together to promote change in the lives of those who live within their bounds. Thus, when time encounters love it also immediately encounters a greater share of the universal intelligence and a greater perception of power. Time calls its own shots. It makes the mechanics of opposites more complementary and promotes the field of universal love.

Since love is a universal feeling, a universal state, and time is the backdrop for all universal expressions, time and love are natural friends. Love destroys the need to fix time and create bound expressions of isolation and despair. Love fills the need for time to become an expression of creative intelligence. Love makes time accountable. Without love, time would activate change without moral feeling or sensibility. Time would randomize event systems from its limited point of view without consideration of universal or causal motives. It is love that gives time humanity, gives time a heart. With time and love held together through the glue of awakened consciousness, all possibilities become alive.

As one strengthens the field of love, one strengthens the field of time. These two qualities, though seemingly opposite, form the basis for the growth of a compassionate witness in the hearts and minds of individuals. Beings are able to synthesize time by witnessing the compassionate voice of their own minds. They are able to make room for the passing of eternal time through the knowledge that love will be in their hearts. Without the juxtaposition of love with the fluidity of time, there can be no creative advancement that would support the development of morality or the wisdom of the soul.

As time and love become more interdependent, so does the type of fluid, immortal reckoning that is the most creative for individuals to achieve. This is not an immortality built simply on the desire for more, but rather on the desire for less: a revitalization of the demands of the soul in favor of a precise assessment of what is truly important and useful for universal evolution. This is the inspiration that love gives to time and time receives from love.

A Wrinkle in Time

Time is composed of a series of opposite or opposing values which create the smooth juxtaposition of dimensions from one sphere of influence to the other. The system of opposites is characterized both by a concrete or fluid mechanics of coefficients, and a binary, more abstract array of parameters. This fluidity and uniformity paired with the binary appearance of opposites is what causes time to appear either as paradimensional or as an indistinct backdrop to causal reality.

The appearance of time as a wave relies on the singular movement of time as a shapely, elegant configuration. The shaping of time is based on the programmable singularity of consciousness that is stretched, pleated, or remade in the face of the different qualities that time represents. Since time is infinitely shapeable, it can be smoothed, pulled taut, or left wrinkled, depending on the category it defines.

The smoothest aspect of time occurs when it is nonrepresentative, a nonqualifiable entity underlying the spatial configuration but not serving as any particular part. Here, time remains stationary, motionless, free falling, and smooth. It is like the undercoat of a textured landscape. Once this smooth surface is maintained, the colorations, stripes, ribboning, or pulls in the fabric of time can be addressed. Time self-colors or self-binds in order to create the algorithmic curls necessary to promote temporal definition.

Time's definition is based on three categories. First is the category of *definable speed*. Here, time must be sped up and offered like lightning to the first available shaper of time, which is motion.

The second category is *light*, which could be seen as the arbitrator of time, binding it to form and making it comprehensible to the field of matter, both light and dark. This array of matter/time causes time to become fluid, and eventually, through the effect of ribboning, to be completely opaque.

The third category of temporal properties is the *rate of change from matter to energy*. Energy is a coefficient of time and speed. It is the variable that makes movement become unifiable in a graphic sort of way. When energy is sped up along the field of matter, there is a grasping, quaking, leaning into the rhythmic pulse of the absolute that creates the pulsation that makes all light beings possible. This pulsation defines the scope of both relative and absolute life.

Over the Event Horizon

The principle of time as a fluid medium is based on the understanding that time is a wave. In other words, the wave of time is a graphable singularity with a curve that is programmable through the motion of consciousness. The temporal matrix is constructed via a system of parallel values that impart a curvature to time. When time flattens due to the rise and fall of the temporal underlining, the flat curve of time meets the singularity of space, effecting a temporal collapse. Time collapses due to the rate of change, which must present itself fluidly in order for there to be an elegant transit of perception. When the individual witnesses time in its collapsed formation, the fluid mechanics of time are sped up so furiously as to make one feel that there has in fact been no lapse of time. This would constitute the expression of flat or noncurved time.

When time rises to the point of the event horizon in which variables in perception become visible to the subtle awareness, time can then be described as opaque. In its more solid form, time ribbons or escapades around the event horizon, switching back and forth. The textures of time then become variable, moving from a thick, more striated surface to that of a smooth, less rigid form. The uncharted territory that exists as a function of space/time deleting or minimizing the rate of curve is due to the alteration in the progression of time as it moves from a thin, flat landscape to a fatter, more opulent zone. Temporal solidification is based on the mirroring that is produced when time moves from one state to another.

Flat time, when mirrored, is angular and driven by a transverse set of opposites that promotes a curve. The curve structures the wave function, transmuting the poles of time from their endpoints and producing the function of space/time mobility. The curve of time can be viewed from any point along the matrix and is frozen insofar as it is bent radically from one station to the other.

Fluid time is fixed time. One would think this would not be the case, but because the fluidity of time stacks up or parades itself as the host medium, the authenticity of time is based on its ability to compress or juxtapose time accordingly. Surprisingly, it is the binary function of time that produces the most fluidity, because there is a movement from one station to the other. Uniformity is a steady state function and therefore does not produce smooth or rapid courses of change except over eons of space/time regularity.

When judging the span of epochs or the rise and fall of planetary civilizations, the "clock" of fluid time is used because it is more capable of assessing such wide spans of movement in the field. But it is through binary time that change is calibrated in the lives of individuals and the rate of change is expanded within their interpersonal situations. This is why the on/off switch of linear time is necessary for the calibration of a personal existence, and also why time itself appears opaque to those who view it inside the context of their own lifespan.

Binary Influence

This opacity or darkness in the field of time gives it its shape, size, and distance. Relationships of opposites between the dark or encumbered weight of the time variables and their more translucent or fluid cousins create the signature of time that we presently enjoy in this plane of existence. Time, in its angularity, fluidity, and perceptual cohesiveness, meets the more jumpy, irregular, and banded expression of binary influence, causing a shift in the parameters of the matrix.

Fluid time meets binary time, invoking the representation of reality as a two- or three-dimensional object. Perceptual changes in the rate of influence of time are the result of either squared or cubed variables, which expand to meet the needs of the dimensional view. Each indigenously squared opposite meets up with its corresponding host variable, amassing a wave or pulse form that causes the standard package of variables to shift. The feed of time sliding from one field of opposites to the other creates the concept of coastalization or coastal variables where time is spread along a thin line or perimeter of the entire field. The stretch produced when these variables interlock with each other is responsible for the language of interchange between the Mother and Father principles of the universe.

Opposite values are like singular co-parents. Each has its set of responsibilities, objectives, and directions, but like any two parents, they often disagree on how these objectives are to be carried out. One set of variables, the dark or intransigent set, seeks to pull the quality of light or consciousness back to its resting point. The lighter, more buoyant set seeks to bring the time variables out onto the surface. The two are in a tug-of-war with each other, providing the stability of time that this dimension presently enjoys.

The Habit of Immortality

One should not romanticize a nonfixed standard of optimization. When time presents itself as completely linear it always has within it the more fluid and translucent state. Were there to be no juxtaposition, one would experience complete uniformity, but there would be no experience of progress, growth of movement, or of psychological structure. The eternal civilizations that feed completely on this fluid experience are therefore in a sense more fixed in that their habituations rigidify over the infinite structure of a lifetime. When beings have more confined lifecycles, they are more apt in theory to take risks, develop strategies for decision, and become death-players on a profound course of action. Eternal beings can become essentially lethargic and unable to make active, creative decisions. They are living on the wealth of time, the fat side of the creative lunge, and not on the more lean or productive side that produces the most intriguing advances. Immortality therefore is not always the most advantageous of positions.

Immortality becomes an asset only when the nonlinear structures of time are utilized as a type of jump-start for creative advantage. When the two types of temporal experiences merge together, we see a situation that is advantageous both for life to flourish as well as for creative advancement of civilizations. This is the ideal. Were it not true that fixed time motives were given to beings as a Divine gift, one would not see them in this sphere. Temporal opposites promote pleasure and seduction on the part of individual lives, but they also produce great strides in the advancement of culture, the relationship of science to universal order, and the understanding of God as a Divine purveyor of Truth. One therefore does not wish to end the paradimensional quotient of dark time, but rather to have both ends of the spectrum represented as fluidly as possible without intervention from forces that would seek to freeze time into a type of lunacy for their own advantage.

See No Evil, Hear No Evil

In the universe there are those who are time thieves or time robbers. What they wish is to steal the quality of time that a civilization merits through its own favor with God and use this temporal shield to their own advantage. These pirates are well known in the universal continuum and their activities well monitored. Each civilization has its own pulse, its own rhythm, its own penultimate stroke that brings it to the point of success or collapse. The policy of nonintervention prevents more advanced cultures from stepping in and tampering with what has been wrought through the creative intelligence of any given planetary civilization. But when such tampering has already been forged, as is the case with our present situation on Earth, then the universal forces have license to step in and make corrections which will restore freedom and equilibrium to the matrix.

In the universe there are truly forces of good and evil. But there is no real value judgment placed upon them. They could be described as universal balancers or continuum breakers. They are like the circuit breakers found in any electrical system. The off and on nature of progress and pain produces a type of universal synthesis that creates maximum learning and efficacy. It is not the plan for humanity to be released from suffering, but rather to understand the nature of its own suffering and reduce what is unnecessary or unjust. This wisdom comes from long association with history, with the time variables that create situational paradoxes. As humanity learns from its mistakes, it corrects them and causes the planetary civilization to rise to new vistas of perception.

One therefore does not wish to eliminate that which appears to be painful, but rather to destroy that which interferes with the natural progression of knowledge. This is the tack that the Universal Intelligence has presently taken with respect to the evolution of planet Earth and its inhabitants.

Since matter and time are arrayed simultaneously on the field of planetary influence, the nature of matter itself must be changed as time progresses. In other words, matter must become more fluid, less fixed, and more capable of celestial integration for planetary progress to grow beyond simply material investigation. As the vibration of matter is speeded up, there is a type of internal fluidity that is both open and clean and which promotes the uniformity of time in this sphere. Matter is subject to the confines of its time projections, and with time arrayed bilaterally without fluid interposition, matter remains fixed. With time splayed open, matter shifts to a type of gaseous or less solid state, which causes integration of opposites to occur more easily.

Living in the No-Time

Human beings fear that they will not be able to exist unless their personal histories remain perfectly intact. By the same token they fear the psychological confusion caused by the transition to matter that is nonfixed and fluctuating. Human beings must unhinge the grooves of their minds and recognize their existence to be wholly dependent on the fluctuations of universal mind before they will accept a reality where a cow can become a dog and there is no particular fixed sense of response of materiality. Human beings are for the most part identified with the objects that surround them and form their psychological framework from these environmental factors.

When human beings awaken to the nonfixity of material form, they experience a core shakeup in their fundamental condition of aliveness. Their sense of presence shattered, they are unable to place themselves squarely in any type of reality out of which they can make sense. To live in a no-time, nonmaterially structured reality is difficult for human beings, but not impossible. This reality will not destroy the field of opposites—it will enliven it. Human beings will be able to create more variety, more distinctiveness, and more singularity all at once through such a shift in the notion of time.

2.2.2
higher consciousness

The Inception of the Mindstream

as time enters the nervous system at more fluid states, the random interiorization of time speeds up and is calibrated differently. Time must be digested directly by the nervous system. As consciousness elevates its vibrational field, the flow or pull into the mindstream becomes limited. The mindstream is dependent on the flow of time within it. As the mind recedes and is no longer the propelling energy behind the flow of consciousness, its relationship to time changes. The gait or pace of time begins to increase while the flow of mind decreases. In this state, the mind becomes capable of relating to time from its pure, inceptionary state. Time encapsulates the flow of thought, but as time becomes more recessional, clear, and nonbinary, it trips past the chemical switches that relay thought to the brain, psychochemically altering the flow of time therein.

Time and consciousness rely on a materio-chemical stream of data from the nervous system. Once this system of data is altered, the fragmentation which is normally seen in the functioning of the brain is altered. In its place there is a full expansion of nonlinear activity which trips chemical switches necessary for a whole-brained panorama. The synchronicity that ensues is predicated on the speed of data that is now able to flow into the brain, as well as the degree of synchronous specificity that is now manageable. The brain becomes relational to the ground of pure being rather than to the flow of the mindstream. In this state, consciousness is elevated past the point of the mental flow of attention and sees its own light within itself. At this stage, time becomes secondary to being. The flow of time, however, continues to govern the pure singularity of inner awareness.

The development of an entirely different system of functioning begins to take place. Time becomes the governing influence for the unlocking of pure awareness rather than for the witness aspect of consciousness. The witness aspect recedes, reducing the flow of self-consciousness or ego-centered perception, and time enters a vaulted, inner domain of pure feeling in which activity is registered entirely as a subtle sensory perception. In this state, the witness aspect returns to its source, observing the source intelligence itself, and the intellect, driven by the new flow of temporal mechanics, begins to register a type of originality or independence from societal statements of belief. The intellect becomes capable of flowing from the level of pure being

175

directly, bypassing the conditioning of the mind. The individual finds that the temporal mechanics are no longer capable of producing a binary flow of movement, but rather create a carnal, internal pulse that regulates the flow of the breath with the movement of the intelligence.

The subtlety of language then manifests as a relationship of time, pure intelligence, and movement. Herein lie the infinite chasms in which reason lives separate from the mind. The mechanics of perception become magnified, and the force of peace, tranquility, and smoothness of the apparatus of pure being become apparent. The witness state can evaporate slowly or can be outlawed in an instant. The determination of this shift is brought about by the buildup of pure consciousness streaming directly into the glandular system. The intensity of this experience occurs at such a fast rate that it trips the chemical switches necessary for the determination of pure reason. Identity is essentially an interloper in the development of unidimensional perception. Once the consciousness has lifted free into its primary or wholistic state, the derivatives that define that freedom are then set in motion.

Without Reflection to an Object

Time cannot define the rate or flow of objects within its grasp. Time stands free of perception and enters the nervous system directly in the function of nonduality. The momentous shift to temporal singularity is fabricated on the basis that time will now know no one object upon which it must reflect. Time is absorbed directly into the body without mental apprehension and waves of subtle influence are generated that describe personal destiny.

Time becomes lucid, standoffish, and at the same time packed with the power of internal reason. Swiftly, the temporal mechanics develop a dominant position with the absolute, maintaining the standardization of reason without self-consciousness or fear. Freed of the self-negating aspect of the mind field, consciousness develops independently, regaining the crystalline clarity of a child. Children romp directly in the playground of the absolute. Time is childlike in its purity of being. It interacts with the higher mind to propel a twinning encounter between the absolute and relative curves of perception. The two meet like school pals in the park, exchanging a greeting, but being absorbed directly in their own field of play. They are temporal designates for the flow of reason, but are unlike each other in their attempts at disguising truth without coloration.

The play of duality freezes when the temporal mechanics are grounded in the absolute. Attention radiates around, through, and in-between the scope of reason, freed from the temporal moorings to which it has been bound. Time shatters the mind and instills pleasure in the heart. Time transfers pure being directly to the mind and installs the mental field in a radiant, unadulterated happiness. The mind is freed of the impediments that block the flow of singularity, thus perceiving itself as independent of any self-investigation. The will to perceive the egoic makeup is altered and any attempts to reaccount for the "I" are evaporated. When the temporal structures are shattered, new inner dynamics occur. The individual is infused with a type of internal vision that occurs separately from the elements of standardization that had been in its field of influence. The transfer of intelligence becomes dominant and the right and left hemispheres of the brain are permanently entrained. Dopamine levels are greatly enhanced and the flow of happiness is a result.

Matter and time retain a flow of synchronicity between them. The individual who is established in being is able to affect the flow of matter as it engages itself with the realm of consciousness. Time and matter intertwine in one nonradicalized movement that functions as a temporal magnetizer for the flow of God-being. The Godforce, preeminent now, distributes the range of being to every cognizant object that has been attracted to the temporal field. The flow of dimensionality diminishes for an instant as the range of temporal understanding is expanded. The individual calls out for the synchronous, randomized perception to interweave with the scope of power that he or she has accumulated over a lifetime. The elemental requirements of discipline, honor, and courage present themselves effortlessly in the field of character.

Accepting the High Jump

The shockwave produced by the flow of temporal mechanics directly to the autonomic nervous system can actually cause convulsion-like jumps or breaks in the autonomic wreath of the body/mind. These jumps signify changes in the rate or flow of breath, consciousness, and temporal imagery into the nervous system. In the system of kriya yoga, the impulses that create consciousness-temporal imagery are inherently shattered and break apart to create the flow of apparent or singular time in the individual. The nervous system adapts by creating new bridges of temporal expansion that redefine the pathways that nerve impulses must travel to relay information. In the transition from a subjectively defined nervous system to one that is more objective in its scope, the nervous system must learn to recognize information that is garnered from a cosmic or impersonal source.

The change from a mostly self-conscious orientation to one that perceives reality from a wider, more elevated framework involves a greater range of movement of the autonomic nervous system. The conscious mind, which now runs the functioning of the body/mind, must be replaced by an original mechanics of mind that is based on the free, independent stationing of impulses as they fly from one "masking point" to another. The nerve impulses are hidden by the dominant sensations of carrier waves that are split apart from one neuronal sequence to another, no longer freely displayed to the mind. As a result, the mind, unable to process the data at the frequency at which it is deliverable, must switch to its more autonomic capabilities. The mental and emotional state of the individual becomes unencumbered by the process of ascertaining what appears to be correct.

A common misinterpretation of this state is that the individual is outside the power of ethical structure or is separated from the norms of conventional behavior or understanding. This may be true to some extent, but this does not mean that there is not now a much stronger, more inherently knowledgeable governing influence that takes over the bulk of functioning. The individual transitions to a more intelligent style of internal leadership. The ability to assimilate and translate vast amounts of random information at incredible speed incurs the necessity to be unusually patient as one learns to redefine the map of reason. It may appear that the individual is now careless in his or her flow of speech or action but this is only because the transition is not complete.

The change goes deep into the fabric of how the individual perceives his or her physical form. The curved pulsation of infinite time draws itself magnanimously and completely into the range of intelligence, and the individual is able to speak much more closely to the mind of God. An intelligence is born that is capable of perfect self-reflection without a subjective self to censor or capture time. A dancing, floating sensation of the body unpinned by the flow of mind predominates. The body has to overcome the accident of internal illumination.

The Race to Sample Time

To circumvent any decisions that the nervous system might create as the body must adjust to its new condition, the mind "stays" itself. Silence, which may have been simply a backdrop to the awakening, becomes the foreground. Silence sweeps over the mind, moderating the attempt to reason or demand. The pervasive unification of the breath with that silence creates a frontier for the evolutionary juxtaposition of time and mind. The light, curving refrain of consciousness eludes the mind, dominating the temporal occasion where reason prevails. Then the fluidity of pure Self can enter.

The rapidity of this process depends entirely upon the predominant motivation of the seeker. One cannot seek this type of change without affecting the preeminent consequences. However, one cannot produce this change simply from the level of the mind. Since the mind must suspend its functioning unilaterally to prevent the interruption of pure perception, the mind must be taught to suspend itself for periods of time to create the shift. The mind must grow accustomed to the flow and predominance of infinite silence while at the same time developing a taste for its own demise. The breakfront here is in the sampling of the time derivatives directly from the heart/mind field. The heart develops a new flow of attention, a picture book of the perceptual field that is separate from pure mental creation. The heart amplitude magnifies, directly spilling onto the forefront of the brain.

The heart creates the passion for the shift. It desires the brain and central nervous system to overcome the power of percipient domination and enter the territory of source information unscathed. The determinant impulse is survival. The mind wants to survive and the heart wants to flourish separate from any internal object. To rid itself of the castigation of mind, the stem of the heart chakra breaks in two, shattering the subtle areas of the tonal field. The heart enters a collaboration with the body that restores it to a flow of direct feeling that is precipitated directly by desire. Desire becomes the obstacle of the heart only when it is dominated by mind. When desire becomes the constitutional requirement of the heart, then it is favorable, efficacious, and perceptually elegant.

The Voice of the Precise Heart

Precision in the voice of the heart can only be gained when the mental field is dissolved. Intelligence cracks open the steely chambers of the mind, and the self-conscious, reposing identity, which had clamored for every moment of attention, is stilled. The impulse to gain internal devotion, clarity of the flow of awareness, and the development of temporal restoration are the sure result. The limits of intelligence have been broken and the pure mental envelope, which descends only when the heart center has reached this level of maturity, can then flourish.

Systems of pulsation that register the mind in the field of the heart are the predominant influence. Perception, abraded by the strain of ego-gathered organization, cannot precipitate the caliber of pure reason that intelligence demands. Once elevated to the status of clarity that temporal liberation produces, the mind gains a momentum that causes it to feel unstoppable. However, because the ego-structure has been completely shattered, it gains no pleasure in its intelligence, but simply clambers forward and interrupts all of the other functions of the body. The body is a stand-alone player until such time as full integration comes to pass.

The shattering of the temporal field in the banner of the ego is the significator for the development of higher states. Reason pokes through the holes that the ego-nest has determined, and there is a searing clarity to perception. As the ego-nest finally falls from the tree, there is no feeling of loss, because the self-conscious aspect of mental circumspection cannot be brought to bear. The significance of this shift is great, but it is simply the beginning of the organizational flow of language as it regroups to codify the self-determination of the mental stream.

The right to play in the field of language is now enveloped by silence. Silence, indigenous to pure intelligence, becomes the mark of excellence for the mind. The mind loosens up, curls back over the compartments that have previously been set, and entertains silence as its principal attribute. Time enters quietly, luminous in its magnitude, destroying the last dimensional hold that the mind has had on its orientation.

Cutting the Heart Free

For a period, mind and body are split, as the system of rectification has not been completed. Then, radically, the mind pulls back and the body enters a fluid, refractory state of non-impinged physical acuity. The unfractionizated temporal corridor opens. The contact points of the jaw, or mandible, awaken. The shift to pure hemispheric dominance produces a rush of endorphins that cluster in the ring about the heart. The heart ceases to be limited by the confines of its own internal state. It is mercilessly cut free and made to function as an independent operator in the realm of pure being.

The heart cut free does not immediately understand the profundity of what it has accomplished and may not be entirely adept at such freedom. The fears, anxieties, and accomplishments of a lifetime may be reviewed by the elemental mind. As the heart regains solidity, it may alter its operational mechanics, with silence restored to its elemental pose. The heart is delimited by the silent encounter of intelligence and is structured therein.

Infused by the character of silent nonwitnessing, nonlocatable being, the heart is dampened temporarily. But eventually, the emotional state of young laughter and open-heartedness prevails. The heart, now shattered by the realm of unimpeachable silence, cannot last in a state of estrangement or melancholia. It is a preamble for the infinite state of happiness that magnifies as pure consciousness traverses the range of the body. The heart is free from both the stagnation of temporary mental distortion and the parameters of reason. It is independent of the *via longa*.

The heart is stripped down to the barest perception of love. It encounters the primary emotional responsibility of the human being to live in a state in which care for all objects of awareness is automatic and mandatory. There can be no other option. The coining of compassion is obvious because there can be no skin on the heart to impair the flow of love from the absolute. No strategy can undermine this nakedness. A mind without heart is tragic, but the heart without mind is authentically radiant. It overtakes all of the mental processes and begins to develop a new skin in which the sandwich of time and mind is arranged.

The systematic observation of the mind, which no longer encounters itself as a random collection of opposites, develops a repose that can only be described as absolute. In a field of random, enveloping impermanence, the mind creates a well of temporal domination that alleviates the need for stillness. It becomes fully creative and alive with the sting of perception. It is no longer weighed down by stagnant reason, nor is it engaged in self-examination. Awake to itself for itself, it is the internal lamppost of the radial dominance of the unificatory intelligence. All manner of activities, both of the intellect and of the body, are then fully possible.

2.2.3
consciousness and breath

The Respiration of Mind

he recognition of the breath as the key mechanism for the awakening of consciousness forms the backdrop for physical and emotional health. The health of the mind depends upon the intake of the subtle breath. Thought is a mirror reflection of the intricacies of the breath which, when introduced through the translation mechanics of the mind, are understood as conceptual material. The brain uses the breath as a repository for the energy dynamics that will eventually crystallize as intelligence. The breath is the field of intelligence made physical. Therefore, the organization of the breath into particular categories of respirational response in the body/mind regulates health for each physical organ or system.

Consciousness defines the soul of time. Since consciousness correlates the momentum of time through the development of the subtle level of breath, those beings who have mastered the reality of breath can keep themselves in an optimal state of health and refinement. The breath governs the process of aging on a cellular level. The cells learn to breathe through accessing the universal value of time. When a being is born to this dimension, the soul is infused with a calendar in which is written the approximate time period that this soul will be incarnated on the Earth plane. This incarnational period is also mapped out in terms of the system of breath that will be used to keep this being embodied.

Since the breathing patterns of beings are deeply influenced by their mastery of the breath, it is through the awareness of how to utilize breath that an individual maintains his or her fluidity of mental awareness. Mental alertness drops off with aging because the individual is not centered in the proper breathing patterns to promote cellular restoration. In order to master these patterns, psychic centers are established throughout the body. These centers function as control areas for the different types of breath attributes to be established.

The Six Types of Breath

There are essentially six types of breath that are identifiable in the human body. The first breath we will call the *breath of singularity* because it insures that individuals will maintain their discrete identity. This is the breath that makes individuals unique, not only in their personalities, but also in their physical and emotional actions and reactions. For example, a person whose breath of singularity is impaired will notice difficulties in the area of movement, speech, and, in the case of a woman, the ability to give birth. The breath of singularity therefore governs the process of speech and communication, which is so important in one's personal effectiveness.

The second type of breath we will call the *breath of unification*. This breath is the primary restorative breath. It is utilized in sleep and meditative states and can also be termed the yogic breath. This is the breath that is mastered in higher states of consciousness and promotes the understanding of higher dimensional aspects of perception. The breath of unification occurs through the coordination of the pituitary gland and the nerve ganglia near the base of the throat. This breath causes a temporal pulse that keeps the nervous system responding to stimuli from the environment without overwhelming the system.

The nerve impulses that penetrate the upper region of the throat and are retrieved through the mastoid process develop an anterior and posterior thrust that creates a vibratory imprint in the facial nerves. This imprint delivers the message of integration between the parasympathetic and autonomic nerve wreaths. Each wrap or cross-section of nerves going between the autonomic nerve wreaths creates a portion of fiber-optics that satisfies the coordination of the breath through the various subtle passageways. These impulses create a surge of wind in the system that makes the auditory and visual conductivity available on both gross and subtle levels.

The unification breath acts as a repository for the pure intelligence that is stored in the context of the parasympathetic nervous system, and makes it possible for autonomic impulses that are uncontrolled and unconscious to be recognized and restructured. This is what makes it possible for a yogic or dilatory breath to be achieved on a consistent, rhythmic basis. In this manner, higher intelligence can sweep into the cranial area and create optimal unification in the ganglial sheaths that are responsible for coordination, movement, and the breath of motion or sound.

The third type of breath is that of *random pulsation*. This breath is the randomized value of time as it appears in this dimension. It courses through the body/mind complex and is responsible for the digestion of food and/or information. The ability to assimilate the complexities of daily life from a psychological level is governed by this type of breath. It allows the individual to utilize all of the opportunities and adventures given to him or her. One becomes adaptable and is able to coast through life's encounters with a sense of ease. When this type of breath is held in the body, one experiences a sense of crisis when new physical or emotional demands are made.

The fourth type of breath is that of *quickening*, or rising, which causes the chest to expand and governs the circulatory system and physical breathing patterns. This may be impaired due to asthmatic conditions or problems with the circulatory system in general. The time differential here reflects how time is monitored in the heart. This differential governs the emotional variances of an individual with respect to his or her primary relationships.

The fifth type of breath is one of *motor response*, which is the governing force behind the autonomic nervous system. This breath governs the functioning of all of the organs and systems of the body and keeps them in harmony and regulation with one another. This breath is impaired during any sort of physical illness and may also be marred by colorations in the breathing pattern due to physical anomalies such as trauma or difficulties during physical birth.

The sixth type of breath is the most difficult to describe because it is the most refined. It is the breath that is generated when a person moves from a third-dimensional consciousness to a fifth-dimensional consciousness. In this time frame, the individual is actually witnessing the other areas of breath, and then, having viewed them all accurately and clearly, moves past this point so that the universal energy itself becomes the modus operandi for the body. This breath is what allows a spiritual master to transcend physical death completely and to begin to manifest physical reality on this plane. We will term this breath therefore the *breath of immortality* or the *breath of divinity*.

These categories of breath form the backdrop for the development of a complex set of time variances that allow the body to utilize time for different functions. Time changes depending on the laws of consciousness that are laid down before it. Time balances itself on the wings of the breath. As the different breath patterns are laid down in the individual, all of the other situational aspects influencing that individual's soul patterning or karma are alleviated. The individual learns to work with each breath and then to seamlessly intertwine these pathways in order to restage the formulation of knowledge in that area of life.

The Imaginative Breath

When there is a weakness in one of the types of breath, the individual naturally compensates by drawing on the type of breath/consciousness pattern that he or she is familiar with and that has become strong within. This is why it is possible to lose a system of operation, whether it be emotional or physical, and maintain the life of the body.

The person who has coordinated all of the systems of breath becomes capable of literally creating the temporal realities behind the flow of consciousness. It then becomes possible to lift free of time constraints and move backwards or forwards in the temporal fields. This situation allows one to survey past choices or optimal future scenarios easily and to make decisions that are better suited for the evolutionary patterning at work. These decisions are literally made on the basis of whether the individual assesses that he or she can breathe easily in a given psychological or physical environment. Such assessment is made by actually throwing the consciousness into a state where he or she can assess the functioning of the body in that set of circumstances. This is more than imagination; it is actually a living experience of prescience that cannot be defined simply from a mental or emotional standpoint.

The temporal reality of the breath then creates the passageways for consciousness to flow out into the environment and produces an atmosphere conducive to the governing of time. Civilizations that have mastered these governing movements can create enclaves of intelligent life in any situation. They are freed from the limitations of weather, heat or cold, or from any system that would inherently limit their capabilities of expansion. To engage in this type of system, the individuals literally synchronize their breathing patterns. They are able to breathe together, coordinate their consciousness, and create exercises in fluidity of a grand scale. Whole empires or star civilizations are based on this conceptual knowledge. Those civilizations that have mastered the breath of primary unification, therefore, can live independently of even a planetary system or civilization. Often, however, these enclaves of consciousness interweave with others to form complex systems that are asked to govern major shifts in galactic time.

Since the individual who learns to work with the breath must also be willing to change the circumstances of his or her physical reality, there is often a resistance to engaging in more subtle areas of such mastery. There needs to be a differentiation between yogic practices that are done for the purpose of personal glorification or power and those that are truly engaged in for the purpose of changing the core mechanics of a civilization. To engage in a spiritual enclave for the purpose of coordinating, synthesizing, and developing a collective life force is seen as a very high form of spiritual understanding and achievement. The individual's priority expands from simply being engaged in his or her own welfare to include that of friends or family, and finally to encompass the welfare of whole provinces or regions.

This type of ability is not practiced through a political or social framework but comes from full mastery of the breath, such that the environment itself is regulated and governed by the control of consciousness.

Meditation on the Indrawing Breath

The subtle awakening of perception that allows the individual to actually see the mechanics of group interaction from the level of breath/consciousness/time opens the doorway for the clarification of the individual's relationship to divinity. Since divine time is governed by the divine breath, it is only through awakening to the mechanism whereby the Godforce organizes, regulates, and controls civilization that an individual can begin to operate in such a realm. Each individual sees God in his or her own way. This sight is a construct of the ego, but the sight of the body/mind goes beyond this status. The sight of the body/mind sees into the domain of pure consciousness itself so that the birth of the subtle breath as an all-time experience can be felt behind every action.

The practice of refined aspects of meditation makes this experience possible, but it is also through indrawing the breath of God that such a state is reached. One has to draw the breath of God into the body through developing a relationship with that divinity directly. This usually occurs through entering into an activity that elicits the help of divinity. Through charitable service, the individual asks to become bigger in his or her influence, and in this asking, the will of God increases to make it possible for such service to be granted. In this process the temporal mechanics of the breath accommodate to make this vibrational change possible. The divine breath is the fuel for the individual consciousness to more fully recognize how to help and honor higher intelligence.

Since the individual cannot ask for assistance through the mind alone, it is the body/breath/consciousness that actually draws upon the divine. The individual establishes a sense of yearning for such an actualization to take place, but it is ultimately granted through the body and the body alone. This is why it is important to maintain the health of the body through regular practices and habits. Once the body is toned muscularly and energetically, it becomes a better repository for the divine energy to establish itself. This energy locks itself into the structure of the body through practices that establish the breath through all of its functions.

2.2.4
the development of
internal time perception

Children Without Scars

the ability of the human soul to communicate directly with its personality counterpart is a key determinant in evolutionary development. The information that the soul holds with regard to the voluntary mission of the individual must be unlocked through the physiological translation of the body. Beings who are raised in the company of individuals blessed with a high degree of spiritual evolution are given the benefit of an objective vision, which offers the soul the most freedom. Children must be weaned spiritually as well as physically from their mothers so that they can learn who they really are. Although love is an important ingredient in the raising of young people, the ability to see into the heart of a child, understand his or her essential nature, and encourage truth is often scarred by the traumas endured by the parents in their own upbringing. The human physiology is a complex bank of information. When fed by the genetic blueprint, it offers almost unlimited potential for the development of humanity as a whole.

The soul creates a prebirth process that maps the time breaks that an individual will encounter in his or her time/matter interface. The soul decides on a designated blueprint for the time differential. The matrix is imprinted onto the fetal structure through a rapid interplay of event sequences that are fed directly into the information highway of the RNA. The rapid intake of data through the cerebral cortex is made available to the body through the interface with the menningeal sheaths. As data streams through the cerebrospinal fluid, it is stored in layered compartments through the subtle levels of the central nervous system. Individuals who have through past existences been capable of sustaining a higher frequency orientation are more able to create life scenarios that incorporate this information into their everyday patterning. This supports an elongation of the internal perception of space/time that affords the individual a subjective vantage point that provides for greater comprehension of the soul's purpose.

The human brain offers a system of chambers or openings for the uptake of information from the pure level of awareness. These chambers do not immediately correspond to the architecture of the physical brain as it is presently known. The chambers or windows of the brain are more subtle in nature and represent arced, three-dimensional portals through which information can travel and be sustained. The storage of information and its syntactical translation are also key functions of the subtle neurological system. Thus, travel into and out of the subtle brain and central nervous system, the storage of information within it, and its subsequent translation and retrieval are the key formative markers for human intelligence and comprehension.

In this space/time dimension individuals respond to their blueprint through calibration with the physiological and spiritual orientation of the birth mother. The simple love and care of the mother towards her offspring combines with the parallel sequencing of information between mother and child. The consciousness of the birth mother functions as an apportionment manager for the fundamental intelligence of the child. Her job is to act as a foster parent for the soul until it can create an actual birth date in the subtle physiology that acts as a springboard for recalibration of soul information in an intentional manner.

Those individuals who do not grow up spiritually and become capable of taking charge of their lifetime do not form a birth grid that unifies with the central nervous system. The soul matrix does not reconstitute in an efficacious manner. During the twentieth century, most individuals did not create a fully developed soul imprint. The souls took on a less progressive character based on a standardized or pooled matrix. This was not a function of a lack of subtle physiological functioning but was based on the limitations set in place on a social and political level. These criteria were based upon a consensus of the shared consciousness of the individuals involved. This created a downward shift in the evolutionary matrix. The twentieth century was marked by a pause in development for the race as a whole, even as it appeared that technological innovation was rapid and productive. Consciousness and technology are not inherently at odds with one another, but when technology divorces itself from the moorings of consciousness it becomes hollow or separate from its cosmic intent.

Information Retrieval

The present state of affairs in the twenty-first century will involve a rapid shift in the calibration of many individuals to a more pure uptake of soul data and retrieval of information from other preexistences or future parallel universe information. Therefore, the present generation will uptake information much more rapidly and will not be strapped with the personality characteristics that formulated the previous modules. This will allow individuals to become more superfluid in their style of functioning and able to assist others in reaching their full universal potentialities.

The grid system set in place by the soul involves two functions. The first is the central grid where all of the data about preexistence lies. This data central matrix revolves around the core beliefs or essential value structure of the soul during many preexistence modules. The soul calibrates its future realities directly from this grid and constructs possible future scenarios one after the other, which are randomized and fed into the nervous system at birth. The individual then chooses from these sets of parameters as he or she moves along, recalibrating the matrix as it is necessary and restoring primary functions simultaneously. One is never far from the essential birth stream, however.

In the second model of functioning, the individual actually taps directly into the "God matrix" or patterning that is outside of the subset of consensus belief for that pyramidal structure. Then he or she is living outside of the norms and is less likely to conform to the behavior of others. In this scenario, the individual becomes able to download directly the rapidly visualized core intelligence of the Godhead and is fed information from this source. One then becomes capable of unifying with this source both intellectually and emotionally, and the core beliefs that were once part of the soul stream are no longer relevant. In a sense, the preexistence formations, though still established physiologically and energetically, are not influential in the underpinnings of the child's life. He or she is free to move outside of existing parameters, and all of the considerable intelligence that is developmental in orientation and filled with the direct transmission of the Godforce is now available.

The Primary Intelligence of Our Ancestors

Most individuals in the twenty-first century and beyond will formulate their core matrix from the latter continuum. Therefore, their birth mother's knowledge or that of the parent's ancestral makeup will essentially just be a standard feature in the function of the biological constructs rather than an essential predictor of the functioning of that individual in the present dimensional flow. The individual will be capable of lifting free from these limitations in a unilateral fashion. One will therefore become capable of raising the kundalini or life-force vibration directly and drawing upon the infinite and sometimes extraordinary intelligence of the Godforce itself.

The primary intelligence matrix for boys and girls in their formative years is essentially the same but in some ways completely unique. Boys are imprinted from an early age with the capacity to respond in a rapidly firing event-sequence orientation. Girls are more likely to be encumbered with the ancestral markings and less likely to be able to break free of them. This is true because at the present time girls are apt to be tied to the genetic apron strings of the mother. The mother is a more causative influence for a girl than for a boy, and the mother's indecision or lack of continuity with her own soul flow can cause a girl to recede in her orientation at a very early age. The correction for this will have to lie in actually taking girl children away from the mother at an earlier age and allowing them to live independently for a period of time. This is the best and most rapid manner of ending the present predicament that girls presently encounter.

Boys have another unique attribute in that they are more capable of external calibration with the environment than girls and tend to carry fewer fears. This causes boys to go ahead when it comes to activities that are in unification with consensual parameters, making them more likely to succeed. Girls, however, carry unique genetic markers for creative perception and an underlying ability to restructure the internal understanding of the mother and to rise to new heights in terms of emotional sensitivity and understanding. The combination of intelligence between the two sexes must be interlaid into the central nervous system at an early age and fostered independently of the parents. This is why it is difficult for both girls and boys to rise past their genetic predispositions at the present time. The environment continues to pattern the individual throughout childhood, which leaves the person with the task of redoing this essential influence throughout a lifetime. This is a frustrating and somewhat tedious job.

In order to change this situation, girls and boys would do best to be raised separately from the parents after the age of five. This might seem cruel or even inhuman, but in most extraterrestrial societies this is the case. Birth parents are really a control mechanism for the child, and are not seen to be evolutionary in most respects. Once the children are separated from the parents, intelligence can be recalibrated through a trigger mechanism in the central nervous system that will catalyze the development of original thinking and fluid ingenuity. The distinguishing characteristics of children brought up in situations where the genetic markers have been broken are universal. However, what is significant here is that children do better in an environment of love. The question becomes: what is a loving environment for children, and how does this interlink with the development of the core value structures in the individual?

Parents, Sovereignty, and Self-examination

The time references that are built in at the preexistence levels can flourish only when nurtured by loving influences that have no selfish or internalized agendas of their own. This is why children raised in such a loving and close environment flourish when freed from parental constraint due to habituation. However, for human parents to consider such a sacrifice they would have to change their core influences substantially. Human parents believe that they have a birthright towards their children and that it must be the same throughout the multiverse. This could not be further from the truth. Human parents have developed ownership rights with their children instead of a free-flowing matrix of parental sovereignty that is nonbinding in its intent. The child's desire for essential freedom is thus impaired.

For children to change their core patterning, they must go through an early period of self-examination which includes a very complex understanding of how the parental structure might rule them and how they could be free from it. This is obviously an impossible task when parents are bound to raise their children as themselves. Human parents wish to control their children rather than free them from past constraints. The child's heart and soul is bound up in pleasing the parents rather than in developing the core soul matrices that are linked to the "time bites" in his or her own awareness. These are the true control mechanisms that cause the time release of important soul information that allow one to contemplate, shift, and construct personal reality from a complex and infinite set of variables. The individuals raised in this manner become Godbeings from a very early age and maintain a standard of independence thought impossible at the present time for human children.

This change in the structure of belief is developed through an interface with the DNA streams as they are catapulted through the central nervous system during the birth canal process. The birth canal is actually an information passageway in which data from the mother is fed directly into the child. It creates the biometric calibration for personal reality. This is why the birthing process is central to the development of consciousness. The birth mother plays a role in this, not consciously of course, since human birth mothers are really not capable of such understanding at the present. The individual is fed the soul and ancestral blueprints of the lifestream during a rapid downloading process at the moment of conception and during the entire gestational process. At birth, this information is rapidly catalogued by the individual and fed into a storage center in the hypothalamus, the pituitary, and the thymus glands simultaneously. It is catalogued there for future developmental use.

191

However, since most human children emulate the past ancestral matrices due to the conditioning of the parents, this information never really develops. It lies dormant and is fed back into the central nervous system when the "silver cord" is severed during the death process. So, in a sense, from birth to death the individual never individuates and is never free to blossom in his or her own right. It is easy to see how tragic this has been for the human condition as a whole and frustrating for the individual souls who have accepted the drawbacks of such limitation.

Personal Effort and the Lightbody

Any essential freedom the individual now gains is based upon personal effort to break free from these time constraints and is not based on the willingness to utilize the information that is his or her birthright. The glandular system now functions as a kind of boarding house for this information, where it lies dormant until the individual actually leaves the earth plane. Once the individual turns on the light of spiritual development, he or she begins to work with the lightbody directly. The system of information that has been lying dormant in the nervous system can then be utilized.

The light readers in the cerebral cortex are awakened and the essential blueprints may be interpreted directly through the glandular system, the central nervous system, and the spleen. It is in the spleen that the uptake of information is the most advanced, because it is here that the documentation of the blood is done. The blood is the encoding mechanism for all of the encrypted information that the soul provides. The job of the spleen is to translate this information and feed it back into the glandular system for processing. The bloodstream is the carrier wave for all of the individual soul's potential knowledge and future attributes. If the soul is depleted of life force due to accident or trauma, this essential mechanism is lost.

Individuals who rely on the accumulation of data directly from the central nervous system are sometimes at a loss to understand why it is so difficult for them to recalibrate their lifestream. The reason is that the blood patterning has not been changed. This change can only happen when the blood is reoxygenated directly by the flow of data from the heart, the core processing center for the nervous system and the body/mind complex. When the heart is enlivened by the soul knowledge, it downloads information to the cerebrospinal cortex directly and the flow of soul knowledge can enter the individual nervous system at a rapid and fluid rate. All those with a "strong heart" use it as their primary center for organization. The core value structures are formulated directly from the subtle chemical matrices of the heart complex. Individuals who have attained the highest states of human development are always those who have mastered the workings of the spiritual heart and thus retain a certain fluidity. Here lies the reason why monastic traditions always took children away from the birth parents at an early age.

For parents to exhibit the proper influence on children, they must be extensively educated as to the uniqueness of their children, and have an understanding of their children's potentialities separate from their genetic markers. Children are forced to acquiesce to the needs and demands of their parents. This stops the flow of soul data and diminishes the potential for dimensional uniformity, which is essential for the development of full growth potential. Parents would have to mature as guardians and assume a more balanced place in the role of childraising.

2.2.5
the origination of time

Children Who Are Free at Birth

the point of origination of time is in the lens of perception itself. Human beings view time as a series of event streams or structures in which psychological attributes of consciousness paint themselves onto the screen of delivery. Since time is essentially fluid and rarely remains completely opaque for long intervals, human beings are able to stretch time so that it correlates to their individualized stream of unified perception. Time manufactures event streams through a steady flow of comprehensible attributes that shape or formulate the personal reality of the individual. As time accumulates, each event spread presents a type of psychological curtain that acts as a backdrop for the sequences of matter/time that the individual accrues.

There is a difference between psychological perception and the manner in which time fabricates reality. Time accumulates between advancing event streams, acting as a circuit breaker for each impending wave. As time dances on the instep of the coming event or circumstance, the individual picks up on his or her fundamental place in the curve and foresees or recognizes the sole advance of time at that given break. There is a recognition that at that moment time and consciousness are about to meet and create the curvature that will be the signature for that space/time event. Perception limits or frees time accordingly. It either freezes the event into a psychological construct in which the individual perceives him- or herself as essentially unfree, or it masks the event so that the referential point of judgment will be unsurpassed. The turbulence that occurs when event structures collide or are swept aside by psychological circumstance forms the backdrop for all of the manifest perception that has reasonably accumulated.

Perception does not register distance. In other words, when an event structure appears on the horizon, perception does not know when the event is near or far. It only sees the event as something that is directly in front of itself, and it enters into contact with that event as if it were in the present. This is why perception does not recognize the past or future, but is actually locked into an eternal now in which all event structures appear as though they are occurring at one omnipresent moment. Since perception is essentially locked into the now, event structures that precede or are postdated past their actual point of inception are always interpreted as "now" events.

Sensitization to the Matrix

Time does not create the past or future. It is perception, in its request to return to the now, that catalogues timely events as distant from itself in order to not be overloaded by the many event streams that are flooding its point of reference. Since perception is governed by time, time must maintain an even flow of randomization that circulates around and through perception and stretches the flow of information so that the nervous system can interpret and respond. Since time is essentially neutral, and is derived through perception, it offers event structures at random intervals that are perceived as present or past.

The majority of event structures are sensitized to time as soon as they emerge. In other words, when an event structure enters perception, it is already coded with a type of temporal sensitivity that makes it subject to being viewed in a given way. Time accumulates, forming the event structure, which acts as a mirror for the psychology. As time walks around and through the actual sequence of events, there are places in which time will not go. It actually stays clear of certain avenues of wakefulness so as not to disturb the sleeping memories that have accumulated throughout the lifetime of the individual. As time opens itself into the now, it skips past most of the difficult or traumatic past material and opens itself into the present moment. If this were not the case, the burden of time would be too great.

The psychological curvature of time is formed because the brain and central nervous system act as "coasters" for the expanding time frames that arrive. The nervous system scoots or captures the time wave, impressing it into the musculature of the body. This is why the body is essentially a memory cabinet for the mind. The body retains its shape, size, and elasticity through the curvature of consciousness. It is the retaining wall for all of the perceptions and impressions that have accumulated. The multiplication of time as a point of reference for consciousness provides the room, the space for event structures to categorize themselves.

Sharpening the Teeth of Consciousness

Time is dependent on the shape, reference points, and stature of internal data. Perception rearranges this internal data, giving it the coloration that makes for the array of knowledge that human beings possess. Since time is cumulative, it stacks up one set of circumstances and event sequences over the other, parading them through the neck or opening in consciousness. The demands of time are such that perception must keep up with the accumulation of event sequences and not be blinded by the alacrity by which they climb through the holes in unified understanding. The sharpness of time as a prod to consciousness is little understood.

Time sharpens itself on the teeth of consciousness by providing blades or tears in the fabric of reality through which it can pass. Time enters the doorway of the awakened moment and breaks open all of the possible futures lying within it. Time cracks the mundane trenches of consciousness, cascading through the rapidity of individual certainty and maintaining novel perception as it goes. Since the hope of consciousness is that time will arrive swiftly enough to maintain coherence, time must try to optimize its given range of choices as easily as possible.

The climb of consciousness to the door of matter is slow and deep. Consciousness touches into the full range of perception and anchors itself so that the individual will be able to collapse time as need be. Time collapses because it must destroy and rebuild itself fluidly in order for repair in the matrix to be maintained. Time develops synchronized flow through energizing the matrix with the power of variability and makes it possible therefore for uniformity to eventually take hold. The collaboration of time with consciousness allows matter to develop harmoniously in all of its many guises.

Matter and Synchronicity

The disruption of time flows does not impede the relationship of consciousness with matter. It actually prods it along so that all of the ratios of possibility can be fully absorbed. Matter thrives on the digestion of time but does not suffer greatly from indigestion. It utilizes every opportunity that time presents, and therefore crystallizes the state of consciousness out of which it springs. Matter develops a synchronicity with time in such a way as event structures are no longer strung together from disparate points but can wiggle together all on the same thread.

Perception governs reality by signaling to time how to dress and undress itself on the field of consciousness. Time is dressed in the style of the events it seeks to mirror. Each event has a precise entry point and exit point. Time seeks to identify this random, cyclical movement and restores order to all of the points of origination. Time translates the field of consciousness into event sequences that are then invested with the power of manifestation.

The secret to understanding time is to recognize the event sequences as they pop out of the hood of consciousness and before they are warmed by the clouding of perception. In the initial clarity that emerges when one sees an event sequence and recognizes its shapeliness, there is a dynamic, inherent energy that is apparent and circular. In this accumulation, all of the initial impulses that made up the point of origination for time to occur are calculated.

The standards that are set for time are randomly imposed. But the ability to work with time is always well organized. Perception catalogues time in the rooms of the soul. It works with time as a type of Geiger counter for the impulses and sensations that have been built up over the lifetime of the individual. When the event sequences heave themselves on to the imprint of selective awakening, a curve results that dilutes perception for a moment, allowing time to directly imprint itself. In this state of pure awakening or perception, the event sequences are randomly but thoroughly strung together, and form the backdrop for all of the accumulated futures which that individual could attain to in that moment. Then these futures spill out onto the ground of consciousness, essentially fertilizing the area for the flow of events.

The Ceaseless Movement of the Mind

The strategy of the mind is to recognize how event sequences are accumulated and create the vehicle for consciousness to refine and actuate itself. Since the mind is dependent on the past perceptions of the individual, it is rarely in a pure, untouched, or locatable state. The mind is traveling, unfolding itself into the cracks where pure consciousness has not placed itself. The mind travels constantly, checking on the mechanics of perception, but also interfering with the pure randomization of time variables that would accumulate without mental parity.

Time seeks to end the ceaseless movement of the mind by inserting a type of unifying mental presence that locks consciousness into the present moment without disturbing the advent of unified future documentation. The curve that consciousness inherently brings, which causes matter/time to recognize all the apparent means of creation, is brought to the forefront when time unifies with itself. There is a synchronized statement of time as matter and matter as time. There is no gap.

Since time and consciousness, when unified, have no need for individuated perception, perception then becomes free to travel through other dimensions of reality. Perception, once it is not bound by the judgmental attitudes of organization, will travel to many roundabout points to accumulate matter. It will leap into the unknown easily and develop strategies for future maturity.

Perception belies its own point of origination by determining how and why an event spread will accumulate and by leaving behind any false discord that has occurred due to errors in past advancement. Perception sends the awakening time/matter spread a retrievable document of variability, through which all of the events that could possibly be accumulated are verified. The circuits or streams of matter that arrive following the cumulative act of verification form the impulses of time that make up the continuum. The trademark for verification is the point of entry into the time spread itself.

Temporal Origination

The shock that occurs when an event spread is not fed full randomization is due to the fact that each event spread is self-reliant, but needs a particular field of documentation to give it the impetus for creation. An event spread needs a companion, randomized point of entry that will allow it to recognize where it is to begin and end. Time cannot do this because, as we have stated, it is locked into the present and does not know how to address the needs of a possible future or past. Therefore, the event spread looks towards perception to give it this orientation.

When the event spread is hit by a point of trauma, the event streams seem to lock up or back off from themselves. They lose their past style of functioning and appear irretrievable. This is the nature of perceptual shock. However, when the event spreads recognize the rate of flow that has been occurring all along, and see in it the patterns that will make the new future avenues break, they snap out of their frozen formations and reinvest in the flow of awareness.

Perception relies on the flow of temporal origination. Without this, insanity ensues. Insanity occurs because event structures, which as we have stated are highly randomized, build up a charge which causes them to repel other more advantageous points of view. The human being is always accumulating negative perceptions of his or her reality, but the insane human person is unable to avoid colliding with these negative perceptions and getting lost in them. When this occurs, the mind essentially snaps and is unable to retrieve original information that will offer the synchronicity necessary for a stable point of reference. Without a point of reference, the mind reverts to its initial, primitive instinctual behavior. It is unable to see how to retrieve the necessary data that would cause more flow of time/matter/consciousness and thereby a greater degree of coherence.

Time stretches past all of the outbreaks of patterning that emerge. Each signification of time lends itself to a past and future distancing of perception. This factor of distancing is the determinant for all of the psychological challenges that human beings face. Since they are unable to see that everything is actually accumulating in the moment that is being derived, they seem to have to fall back on a psychological determination to qualify their own existence. They cannot see themselves as inherently time-dependent but qualitatively free. They do not recognize that time itself will draw back the curtain for them and lead them into a positive and reconcilable form of presence whenever they choose.

Speed, Rate, and Flow

Since time and matter develop motion synchronistically, they spin towards the center of awareness rather than at the periphery. They pull into the center at a very fast rate of speed, taking on no apparent detractors. Once there, time and matter spin towards the point of origin, bringing each moment back to its independent and intransigent state.

In this race for the point of origination, perception can either enter the game or retreat to developing altered strategies that will color or multiply that which is to be viewed. Since perception is graded by the rate of origination that it can successfully alter, it is unable to recognize the perfectly stable mechanics of a mind that has been placed in a steady, flat continuum. The landscape of the mind is more likely to bend and curve in every direction than to stay fixed at the point of origination. Therefore, when time meets the mind it has to curve around all of the sub-routes that the mind has created. Pure perception is rarely experienced.

In the development of time, consciousness always presents the flow of opposites and causes the derivation of perception at its outset. When consciousness recognizes that both time and matter are derivatives of the circuit of events that have been presupposed, it can step out of the flow of individuality and create the type of uniform perception we see in those that have mastered the mind. Individuals who are free from the limitation of mental cogitation are also free from having to absorb time unconsciously, without reference to the Divine Plan or point of origination. To be truly original, the mind must rest on one principle, the fluid organization of time.

2.2.6
motion, emotion, and
cosmic intelligence

The Boundaries of the Physiology

time develops through the risking of psychological boundaries which cause adherence to different aspects of the interior psyche. The experience of motion quickens or reflects the value structure of a given individual. A person constructs interior reference points that delineate alterations in the movement of intelligence from one abstract field to another.

The energy field, with apparent fluidity, reconstructs itself to fit around the mental belief systems that an individual develops. These belief structures are frozen or mentally rigid due to the inability of the field to reflect a proper synchronicity between motion and consciousness.

In the human physiology, there is a synchronous order of movement that interplays with the central nervous system and underlies freedom of movement both mentally and physically. Fluctuations in the energy field give rise to this more fluid condition. The energy field wraps around the musculoskeletal structure, the joints, ligaments, and other areas of the soft skeleton. The configuring of the body is interdependent with this "body of motion," which calibrates the movements of the physical structure and gives it weight, form, and sustenance. When the energy body "breaks" due to amplitude of stress or mental indecision, the containment field around the body is no longer able to uphold the strength or character of the musculoskeletal vibrational field. Then the energy field exhibits cracks that can appear as breaks in the physical structure.

The Mechanics of the Energy Body

The relationship of motion to the energy body is not well studied because motion seems to be the obvious result of the mechanics of human mobility. Modern science does not acknowledge that there is a subtle aspect to the human anatomy. Therefore, the idea has been lost that there are even finer gradations of this energy body that govern specific functions of consciousness. The motion aspect of the energy structure is a system unto itself, which formulates the angle of refraction for each gestational impulse, albeit physical or mental/emotional. When the individual is unable to alert him- or herself to the signals that cause the emotional body to switch from bio-emotional to musculoskeletal impulses, adhesions form on an etheric level, binding the subtle bodies and eventually marrying themselves to the physical.

The human response to motion is not absolute. It is dependent on the flow of nerve relays from the joints, muscles, and bones to the central nervous system. This system of response can be impaired through a variety of factors. Emotional material can cause stiffness or rigidity in the musculoskeletal structure. In spiritually aligned individuals, such stiffness or even paralysis may be caused by a lack of adaptation between the multidimensional framework of the soul and the gross physical body. Essentially, the body is unable to understand the framework of motion due to a lack of signaling output from the causal body. The body stops, waiting, like a computer that is frozen, unable to express the impulses of awareness that are being downloaded from the causal or intercausal levels. The body is replete with its own messaging system, but it cannot dial up these frequencies without the assistance of the emotional body.

Motion is derived because the emotions are manifest. This is the key to understanding the human energy system. Emotions are the lubricants which actually drive the physical body. When the system is receiving a high quantity of cerebral input, the energy system can overload and shut down the physical structure. Ideally, function can be restored through lessening the output, but sometimes the frozen surface of the musculature cannot regain its ancestral memories and is left immobile.

Other types of paralysis do not necessarily involve impingement on the emotional body. There can also be structural damage due to accident or trauma or simply genetic weakness, which can slow or completely impair the range of motion. However, emotion always plays a significant part in the understanding of how the human being is able to fluidly go about everyday tasks.

Shock Absorbers

The emotions that a human nervous system experiences are stored intramuscularly. They are coded or catalogued by the muscles as a type of empathic relay system that allows the individual to have a lesser or greater sensitivity to the impact from the environment. Individuals who by nature are more sensitive to emotional stimuli are more caught up in what is happening around them and more apt to be overstimulated by sensory output.

To shelter or encapsulize these shocks from the environment, the body forms myelinic structures which act as tissue shock absorbers, altering the flow of impulse from the brain to the central nervous system and from the nervous system to the muscles. This myelin tissue is bio-refractive in that it represents the interior skin of the energy matrix. It is essentially a form of the subtle structure that appears on the physical. Since it is so close to the bio-light substance that forms the backdrop for the emotional body, its crystalline structure resembles that of glass. Glass is a very good conductor but it is also brittle and can break easily when shattered. The myelin sheaths are like glass fiber-optic cables that relay biomechanical information to the body in streamers or glazed outputs.

The body, because it is mostly a fluid medium, is not capable of creating solid matter without the bio-electrical output that it receives from relational energy sources outside of this domain of consciousness. The body splits the signals that it receives, storing them in the musculature, the brain, and the cerebrospinal cortex. Human beings are simply biological receivers for nervous impulses that are set up from the causal level. They are not intelligent in their own right. It is therefore not the fault of the brain or central nervous system when human intelligence does not function properly. It is the responsibility of that which is transmitting data to do so correctly so that the body, in whatever condition or circumstances it may find itself, can utilize the imprints that it is being fed. There are therefore no imperfect bodies in one sense, just like there are no imperfect students. There are only teachers on other planes of existence who cannot figure out how to feed that particular body the messages that will cause fluidity of consciousness.

The understanding that the body is nothing without the flawless intervention of outside intelligence is a bit difficult for modern minds to comprehend. There is a perspective that the individual exists as an isolated and independent vehicle and that divine intelligence plays some ineffable and unidentifiable role. This could not be further from the truth. The body is nothing but clay without the divine intelligence permeating it. Divine intelligence is not only the source of life it is the reason for it. It opens up the previously dormant channels of the body and sends information through the system that will be relevant for the systematic growth and refinement of that individual.

Light and Psychological Balance

The degree of motion that the body exhibits is in direct correlation to the information retrieved from the causal level. The inhabitant of the body is responsible for receiving such information in as clear and coherent a manner as possible. Therefore, the owner of the body must take care of the body. The most important ingredient in this care is actually the quality of light that the body receives. This is not just physical light, but cosmic light. This light is retrieved through the cerebrospinal cortex and the radiant aspect of the human heart. Light is received not simply as a psychological balancer but actually as the ingredient that defines and gives motion to the physical form. The human nervous system is structured through light, and then these impulses are translated into sound, motion, and bio-rhythmic synchronization, which is responsible for the different pulses of the body.

Since light is the conduit of intelligence, its sourcing may be increased through practice of bio-light resonance. This spiritual practice, which awakens the light centers in the cranial field and imparts fluidity to the system, must be undertaken under the direction of practitioners or masters who are familiar with this framework of knowledge. The practice of ingesting or releasing flows of cosmic light through the upper energy system causes motion to increase naturally, since the light or shakti has the capability of increasing the fluidity of the full range of emotional, physical, and cosmic intelligence.

Since matter is principally composed of the fractionization of time as it is rapidly brought forward in this dimension, bio-matter is also a by-product of temporal fractionization. As time bio-synchronizes on the level of the body, it splits or refracts intelligence to all surfaces of the body. The intelligence withstands shock or discouragement and creates waves of time/matter that form the epistructure of the human physical form. Time dilates or crystallizes much more rapidly when it is fed direct knowledge from an independent source of light. The central intelligence of the body is composed of time-dependent participatory reflexes of the central nervous system and other related structures. Signals from the central nervous system can be impaired through physical or emotional trauma or simply a lack of education on the part of the body/mind to interpret the intelligence that is being represented.

Individuals who have developed the capability to translate light impulses directly gradually become conscious of how to store, alter, and translate light for the use of their own mental capacities. Such individuals develop a much more synchronized reception for the light/flow information that is constantly available. Human intelligence, even at its lower amplitudes, relies exclusively on the downloading of such light intelligence. As we have said, there is no independent flow of intelligence. The basic definition of Self is that which utilizes the nonphysical for the purpose of physicalization. However, that which is Self is a much larger domain. The human individual is composed of many selves, or regions of intuitive/perceptual relationship that form a "cosmic wafer" for the smooth flow of cosmic intelligence into the nervous system. The human individual is a byproduct of the flow of cosmic intelligence. The degree to which he or she is able to contact the multidimensional or wafer-like formation of selves governs his or her placement in the constellation of abstract time.

The Continuity of the Body

The field of motion synchronizes the field of intelligence in direct continuity with the body. Through this field, the body experiences a push of cosmic intelligence expressed as a wave-like blanket. Intelligence is rerouted through the spine, causing switches that are purely biochemical in origin to be tripped. Thus, the body recognizes these streams of intelligence as synchronous with its own pathways and wakes up the nerves, muscles and skeletal organs. Smooth and striated muscle are equally affected by these changes in intelligence, thus promoting different mechanics of synchronization. The subtle energetic sheathes recognize the signals that are passed to them and cause the musculature to respond in a highly coordinated manner.

The body, when in good working order, is a perfect conduit for the medium of intelligence and truth. It recognizes motion and understands how to synchronize it with the flow of intelligence, randomization of time, and the development of matter. It is a biomechanical marvel. However, when the body is toughened or withered by stress, it shuts down the mental and emotional nature. Stress demands the attribute of randomization, but the desire to minimize stress emotionally often causes a premature experience of uniformity. In other words, the body seeks to synchronize information at a much lower level of vibrational amplitude, effectively stalling cosmic intelligence from unifying dynamically and fluidly through the form. The body tries to effect this unification from its own stultifying and exceedingly primitive level of instinctive impulse, rather than receiving directions from a higher source. Thus, it is cut off from the field of intelligence that it must rely upon for sustenance.

Physical paralysis is thus an outgrowth of two distinctive factors. First, the body is no longer properly logged in to the primary intelligence matrix with a fully synchronized field of motion intact. The other possibility is that the body has withered or stultified so as to become unresponsive to the messaging that is entering its reach. In such a case, there are usually dormant energy pathways that can be reconstructed. This requires a great understanding of the flow of energy into the musculature to reroute systems that are best addressed from a random and automatic response level.

In a sense, all human beings on this dimension are experiencing a form of paralysis. This being said, it is possible to realign the energy body by restoring the light information to the musculature. This science can develop new reference points for the operation of temporal memory and can create more evolutionary attitudinal frameworks. This type of work will generate much interest in coming years, but only after modern science recognizes the interdependence of the human intelligence field with the cosmic light matrix which forms the backdrop for all that is.

2.2.7
Light and shadow:
the formation of reality

Awesome Cognition

in the first stages of absolute cognition, one experiences time as purely a subjective byproduct of perception. Once time peels back and begins to reveal the fabric that forms the heart of its nature, consciousness attempts to recognize or describe the fields that time is given to tread. Since time and matter recognize each other first through the extension of opposites, it is always through becoming aware of what is not rather than seeing what is that extends the field of reason. Thought registers a sense of wonder or awe that, when met with the next stage of cognition, forms the backdrop for the development of what seems to be the opposite point of view. Although that which appears may seem to be as close as the tip of the nose, recognizing what is truly right or important is not always so distinctly obvious.

Once time awakens to itself, the hum or rhythm of time is heard directly in the chorus of consciousness. This hum corresponds to the glue that binds reality together. The fabric of reality builds up a kind of sticky internal coagulate structure that holds all of the event sequences together. These event sequences are in precise frequency resonance with one another. When these event sequences have learned to dial up the vibrational frequency of their neighbors, a totality of motion occurs which signals to time that it can now enter the field of awareness undisturbed.

Time is the glue that builds reality. Time curves around the opposing views that reality creates, attempting to bind each point of reference to itself. As reality spreads itself over the field of perception, time creates a backdrop that allows each event sequence to find its corresponding resonance. As the event sequence sprouts or weaves its way through the specific time formation, time enters and radiates its orientation into the field. Time adheres to the surface of reality through a type of interdependent weaving of opposites. Time moves back and forth through the different possibilities, creating a marker point for each possibility as it might appear. As each possibility presents itself, time creates a knot or break in the matrix, which signals how that particular category of reality will project itself onto a waking plane.

Joining Time at the Apex

Though time is essentially even-handed and smooth in its fabrication of reality, it becomes necessary to vent or tear reality as it breaks onto the plane of awareness. Reality becomes the fabric through which the smooth surface of time can present itself. At first, this surface is filled with the temporal anomalies that form the categorization of time in the relative. Then, gradually, the value structures that time is presenting appear on the surface of each gradually joining apex, and the texture of reality is the result. The imperfections that are seen are inherent within the fractionization process of time itself.

Time breaks are created as a result of pauses or windows in the perceptual framework. Each time break corresponds to an instant, a moment in the shift from causal reality to a relative circumstance. When time enters the field of reality, it must pause, make space, and give room to the essential nature of the absolute. Then, as this level of pure consciousness reveals itself, time picks up the pace, creating the marker points that will make individual or collective circumstances jump to attention. Time is circular, opening itself gradually to the different possibilities and revealing them in a type of open-ended sequence that makes all the different swings from relative to absolute appear in randomized combinations. Once this information meets with the uniform reality, it is stored there, entering a type of temporal repository where the sandwiching of reality formations can come about.

Time is banked, slated, and designated through the impulses of collective perception. Perception opens the envelope of reason, laying bare the possibilities of confirmation, and there, unbeknownst to the innocent character of time, all the avenues of choice are made available. Time knows no contest in its quest for dissolving all of the parameters that are no longer valuable and is constantly refurbishing the reality stream with new ones. Within the context of our dimension, we experience events as coming or going, often in sets or sequences but sometimes as singular outcomes. Time infuses each event sequence with a type of punch or jump-start that causes the event sequence to open up and change character, shape, or size. As the event sequence opens, the light of illumination reveals itself on the surface of the absolute, and the perceptual shift that causes a sequence to become knotted or curved begins. The event sequence takes on the character of the perceiver, entering the wishing well of subjective sensibility.

Since time dances on the surface of each event sequence, it maintains an independent wave-like formation which creates the subjective reality that each perceiver believes to be solely his or hers. This is the mechanism of pure reason. It does not stop to think of the solidity of an outcome, whether it is a psychological situation or one that requires a more manifest solution. Instead, the instinctive and delicate quality of pure reason fans out in every direction and slyly awaits the instructions that a unified time value offers. This is how time binds reality to itself. Time calls forth the possibilities that reason has to offer, and, looking them over in the context of their sequentiation, breathes life into all that seem competent. This subtext of time, this ability of time to generate the unfathomable underpinnings of life, is what makes time the great giver of hopes and dreams, as well as plunging many an individual into the hopelessness of that which has not turned in his or her favor.

The Restoration of Order

To recognize the drive of time to restore order to each set of possibilities, one must recognize that time is the driver of action. Action does not occur separately from time, but exists simultaneously with it, moving along like a horse that is free to rest its gait on the merits of its rider. Time is controlled not by the field of action but by the individual's own perceptual curve. Concrete reality is not composed of anything more solid than what we would think of as subjective reality. It is composed of the thought streams of many individual consciousness units, which when assembled are like a beautifully designed building. The celestial architecture that governs the formation of contextual reality is vividly apparent through the lens of time itself. One sees the formation of personal reality, views it subjectively, but notices that it changes color, shape, or size depending on who is viewing it. Therefore, the construction of reality is based not only on the curved point of view of the seer, but on that of time itself, a pure witness for that which is unfolding. Time makes room for the solidity of objects and makes space for the transparency of emotion.

Emotion is formed through the experience of time as a voice of the heart. Time hears the call of the heart and plants seeds of awakening in the heart that assist it in digesting experience. The heart is a playing field onto which the pure aspects of experience can display themselves. The heart is freed by the rhythm, the pulse of time, which pictures itself through the beat of the physical organ. Time tries to break free from its encapsulation in the heart because it is always seeking to strike out on its own. Time is an adventurer, an escape artist. It wants constantly to be free of anything that would try to bind or contain it.

The Eyes Light the Way

Time enters the body through many different passageways. One of these passageways is the eyes. The eyes utilize time through the mechanism of light. Light curves or bends through the cornea and is split apart prismatically in a wave or particle beam that circulates throughout the physical structure of the eye, finally emerging on the screen of the retina. The eye creates a picture window for the temptations of the soul. It orchestrates the construction of perceptual reality without really understanding what it sees. All of the appearance of random significance is constructed through the nervous system. The eye, in its innocence, remains blind to its own construction.

Since the eye does not actually see in a linear fashion but prismatically, it must be trained to see in the limited field of this dimension. The eye is trained to do this by time. Time creates the internal programming that allows the eye to view this dimension of reality as its true or just cause. It gives the eye permission to limit its own field of reference. Since time captures the attention of reality through the physical eye, it must balance this encapsulation through the delicate chemistry of the heart. The heart gives the eye a sense of feeling, causing the emotional majesty that each set of circumstances is attempting to address. Although the eyes are safe, cozy containers for the limitations of pure consciousness, they are also the place where eventually all of these limitations are permanently erased.

The reason that time appears opaque is because the lens of the human eye is quick to respond to the light codes or fractionizations of time/matter. The illusion of solidity of our dimension is directly dependent on the eye's ability to reach into the substructure of time and interpret these codes so as to reveal the nature of a visual impulse to the brain and central nervous system. Solid objects seek to possess time. They seek to make time accountable, leaving tracks or footprints that echo all of the possibilities that have gone before. Solidity is a temporal reflex, a kind of break in the endlessly fluid, perfectly hollow vestibule that constitutes time before it has been framed by the enclave of perception.

Time mounts up, leaving tracks in the snow. It creates a system of identity markers whose destiny it is to be the systemization of memory. Human memory must be approached delicately because its internal structure is filled with intelligent ghosts, afterburns of experience, contemplation, and reason. Since human beings are filled with many temporal tracks that have been garnered through lifetimes of wear and tear, it is up to the systemic organization of pure memory to keep everything centralized and available.

The track that time leaves is what allows the human nervous system to proceed with the process of memory. Every instance in which time tracks itself is filed in the brain and central nervous system. Time is fractionized through the chemical switches inherent in the brain. The acetylcholine ribbons which bind proteins and make it possible for pure time digestion to occur are not attached at any one point but exist throughout the matrix. Once time trips over itself, these switches are tripped and the individual is arrayed in beams of light that appear as organized reality. There really is no pure organization to reality. It is the human nervous system that organizes reality so that it can be perceived by the eye.

Learning to Function Independently

To understand time, one must recognize that time provides no interpretation for reality. This is done through the net that is encoded in the individual nervous system. Time is interdependent within itself and exists as a covariable within the human structure, but it has no life of its own without the function of interpretive psychological understanding. The moment that time links with the human nervous system, a system of data is created that functions independently of time. This is why our species is so time-derivative: in order to exist outside the matrix of time, the body must be able to assimilate a much wider and faster range of apparent data. The need to interpret the time variables and make them into a coherent substructure limits human consciousness greatly, but it creates the illusion of reality in such a way that it is possible to feel a sense of stability.

Interdimensional species do not have an interpreting mechanism that encodes data in the same manner. Interdimensional species rely on the width of the time variables rather than their length. This is why we say that time is longitudinal in frequency but latitudinal in momentum. Interdimensional species rely on subfrequencies that are beyond the range of the human eye or ear. This is why the firefly fractionizates light in prismatic fashion. One cannot recognize the data unless it appears in a brightly lit coherent form. Otherwise, to the human eye it is all shadows and no shade.

The elevation of consciousness involves a different system of data interpretation. As long as one must see things as opaque and invariable, there cannot be an accurate assessment of dark and light. All of the time streams must wrap around each other forming a net. This bunches up the variables and keeps them dependent on each other. In this way, time becomes limited, finite, and reachable. However, the inherent beauty of the interdependent web is lost to infinity. There is no possibility of extending reality past the thread that is presented. This is the crushing blow to the tide of humanity. Once human beings are linked to a finite thread of time, they must circle back on themselves again and again, creating what one would call karma. The tide of time recedes and advances naturally when it is caught in the fixed motion universe that our civilization has created. There is no karma if there is no system of recognized repetition for the time variables to repeat within. The first step to an interdimensional consciousness is to break these variables and this has to take place within the individual psychological makeup itself.

Time is a freer of races and a destroyer of differences. Once time is covariant with itself, races are able to leap past any differences of custom or strength and rely entirely on time to boost them to different strata of perfection. There is no need to rely on time as a booster if you already know how to do the work yourself. In order for our civilization to be truly free, the individual must become free of the cloak that wraps time around the individual consciousness and keeps it from knowing the source. This significant factor is the reason why it is impossible for us to understand the true nature of reality.

Imprints from Universal Intelligence

Time is the imprinting mechanism whereby the Universal Intelligence can encode itself. The Universal Intelligence uses time as a kind of barometer to feel into its creative matrix and make it anew. The Universal Intelligence knows that it must actually count the threads of time. It must proceed in such a way that time can weave itself through the fabric of creation and restore motion to objects. If objects do not have a time wraparound value they cannot appear solid, and the Universal Intelligence understands the difficulties in relying on translucent variables in a three-dimensional background. It is impossible to distinguish differences.

The first step in bringing time into the foreground is to dip into the background of the Universal Intelligence. All manner of creation is possible once one recognizes that time is the purveyor of intelligence rather than the source. Once one can enter into the time pool independent of any particular marker or locator point in the sphere, there is a possibility of receding past the original opening into time, and then there can be an original rendering of the nature of reality.

There is no reason to fear the breaking up of reality. This is of course what most humans fear most, the insanity created when the time variables have collapsed. It is true that there are psychological constructs that must be recreated to allow an individual to become free in time, but these constructs are necessary anyway. No one lives in our dimension without some conceptual framework upon which to hang his or her life. However, if one can take the time window in a different manner and learn to go into the slipstream where time remains an independent player, one can truly have a measure of freedom that is not usually available in our dimensional sphere.

Therefore, to know time is to know reality. This is really the issue. As time fractionizates, time spins back to reveal each and every breakpoint. These breakpoints are no longer invisible; they become highly visible and uniform in context. The time variables that are thus engaged form the imprint of civilization as we know it. There are many ways to incorporate such time variables into the fabric of reality, but the best is to break free of any inherent relationship to time that binds the individual into a dualistic notion of infinity.

2.3
social reality

2.3.1
transdimensional education

One-Dimensional Education

the present educational system is based on two factors. First, time is a fixed event matrix and therefore historical interlay can be documented from many different perspectives of space/time reference. Second, the corollary understanding of the relationship of free time, or uncalibrated time derivatives, can be understood through the study of philosophy or social interaction. These belief structures inhibit the knowledge of time as a nonabstract, concrete derivative in the historical perspective of advanced civilization. They also inhibit the flow of information from one dimensional reference to another.

The educational system presently educates human beings in a consensus format that causes children from an early age to agree with the thought repositories in relationship to the nature of time and human consciousness. Prior to birth, children have a deep and profound remembrance of dimensional time reference, which precedes the inclusion of clock time. Once children enter into this dimension they are invariably conditioned to function within the frame of reference that their society and parental obligations elicit. For example, they are fed "on time," given proper attention from a hygienic perspective when needed, and are essentially attended to much the same way farm animals or other domesticated beings of a lesser dimensional stature would be. This causes a type of conditioning whereby children are imprinted with the idea that they are essentially helpless and must rely on the parental structure for their needs and sustenance.

Avoiding Psychological Damage

In addition to creating psychological damage in this way, the society imprints upon the child the lessening of all possibilities with relationship to his or her framework of time. The child becomes limited to the scheduled happening of routine events and is unable to create new time references. From an early age, the child is imprinted with the understanding that life is a limited reality that must be accepted in order to be free from worry or difficulty. This causes the child to actually freeze the part of the central nervous system that relates to the development of original methodologies of time reference.

Left to his or her own devices, the individual develops an intimate time sense. Ideally, with proper training, one learns to move in the dimensional bandwidth that one is capable of rendering, and thereby is free to explore the personal domain of body/time/consciousness that destiny demands. Without such training, the individual must conform to the educational process, whether home-based or institutional in character.

Children experiencing "learning disorders" often have difficulty conforming to the strictures of a rigid dimensional time reference. They are actually seeing or hearing information from an interdimensional time source and are seeking to make sense out of such information from a third-dimensional reference point. Since they can find no corollaries for this backdrop of information within their psychology, they become despondent and are likely to develop a sense of amnesia that makes them incapable of remembering how to function in a consensus manner. These children are often very high-functioning interdimensional emissaries, but due to misunderstanding and improper identification of them on a soul level they are bound to encounter difficulties within the present educational system.

It would be beneficial to develop a course of study starting in elementary school about the nature of time and consciousness. This demands of course that the instructors be highly knowledgeable themselves. Children would be able to identify precise intervals of arrangement in their internal structure and thus be sensitive to the demands of their original soul blueprint.

Children Who Are Free at Birth

The time interval structures develop in early childhood through a system of checks and balances between the respiratory, circulatory, and digestive systems. Each system has its own internal time clock, which acts as a messenger to the rest of the body. In early childhood, time is constructed by the circulatory system, setting a beat for the individual. This gives way to the rhythms of the universe that are set in motion in an individual's lifetime. Essentially, each individual is a cosmic musician with tonalities and rhythms that have been put in place before birth. The individual utilizes this harmonic and rhythmic information to develop synchronous courses of action. From these arise the event sequences used to construct a personal reality framework. For example, when a child is about three or four years old there is a sense of brotherhood or sisterhood that is developed with members of society. This sense of trust or friendship allows the child to feel part of a given tribe. The tribal understanding includes a sense of fixed time reference in which events are sequenced in a linear manner and their significance is understood.

A child loses the immediate sense of random formation essential to comprehending the underlying freedom of response to the time continuum. When there is a choice to be made with regard to activity, study, or function, the decision is made in accordance with previously held preferences and beliefs rather than a sense of the now. This deprives the essential originality of the soul blueprint and causes the child to feel contracted and separate from the God source, which is essentially unified and available at any frequency of recognition. Once the child loses the sense of unification, the fragmentation of the individual psyche begins. In its natural state, each sequence of information would originate randomly and then be filed in a translinear formation in the nervous system. Instead, in the current system it is linearly arranged and compacted so as to support the sense of hidden or abstruse psychological meaning. In this way, the significance system is set in place.

In a freer, more translinear approach to inductive civilization, the individual would be shown the actual mechanics of the space/time formation from early childhood, from the time he or she could formulate thought. Thought, because it exists prior to the actual maturity of the brain and central nervous system, is independent of the development of the mind. Thought is an a priori event. Thought occurs through the electromechanical interaction of the brain stem or medulla with the cranial nerves and related fascia. Individuals therefore can think while they are in the womb even before the fetus is fully formed. Once there is the development of rudimentary circuitry in the fetus, thought becomes possible. Until then, the soul entity is living in the thought field of the mother, and in fact until well into the twentieth human year, individuals live off of the thought field of both biological parents. They are not truly independent of this field until they can physically function on their own.

This is why individuals often imprint with the psychological constructs of the parents and why children often are unhappy in childhood. They are in the position of having to be dependent on the thought constructs of their parents because this is mandatory until the nervous system fully develops. They are incapable of independence. On the other hand, if children were educated with more consciousness and precision, they could be taught to recognize the flow of time, the actual mechanics underlying the organization of reality, and would thereby become originators of that reality at an early age. If a child lives with a fully mature spiritual adult who is capable of interdimensional dialogue and is spiritually free, that child develops an extraordinary freedom of interlogue as well.

The time references are created through a balance of personal need and individual expression that must be gained through the advancement of the nervous system and its related corollaries. Children become receivers of information long before they can trans-receive or enter into the interdimensional gateways where time references are less distinct. Individuals accumulate a lifetime of sacred references that they use to make sense of their reality, rather than approaching each moment as a power point for the underlying psychological consideration that makes for uniform existence.

Children who live with advanced beings become capable of spiritual sight and vision from a very early age. They are not limited to sight in this dimension nor do they wish to bind themselves to it. They are freed from the gates of maya and can live in any dimensional wrap of their choosing. Such children exist transdimensionally, moving through the space/time continuum without the confines of the human body, transfiguring the body as they so desire. They are capable of becoming interdimensional "voyageurs" at any early age, even while they exist on the physical level. They grow up in a different manner entirely and are never bound to the space/time reality of their parents. They can then become adventurers in the great play that makes up human existence, and can enter into that play with a sense of purpose born out of self-knowledge and true personal power. They see the world as child's play and understand the limitations of the third dimension as one would understand the workings of a computer game or other sport. They remain free and retain their individuality permanently.

When children are deprived of this type of upbringing there is always a sense of loss or misrepresentation. This sense of loss in some individuals follows them throughout their earthly existence and can be the cause of physical or emotional challenges to their health. Individuals who are allowed the freedom to become creatures of independence at an early age can understand others who are bound but they cannot enter into such a state themselves. Because of this, those forces that wish to keep the society locked in these dimensional dockets will continue to limit the language, development, and psychological independence of children.

2.3.2
the inner mechanics of reality

Unilateral Perception

nner time is governed by the ability of the human nervous system to refine its impulses while being sensitive to the environment. In a unilateral act of perception, the individual imposes boundaries upon time, and is thus likely to be bound to the situational episode that is being presented. Prior to the experience of that moment, the individual perceives him- or herself as separate from the surroundings presented. The individual becomes bound to the event sequences that are springing up all around.

Think of the situation like a dog that has been forced to move back and forth in the same courtyard. After a while the animal adjusts to the boundaries of its surroundings and does not attempt to escape. He or she knows exactly what to do and how far to travel. It is the same with a human being: if one knows what the boundaries are in relationship to one's environment, one will adapt accordingly.

Were Time to Seize Up

When the individual gazes upon the surface of a given object or interacts with a life situation, an immediate feeling of numbness or paralysis of brain-wave function can arise. This is due to the nervous system attempting to adapt to the underlying avenues of perception that have become frozen as time no longer has room to play. With time seized up, the environment can impair the individual so that he or she is robbed of individuality and is left paralyzed to act autonomously.

This paralysis or laziness is a result of two factors. One, he or she has become too dependent on the previous event sequences. This will force the individual to realign the energy system through systematically breaking the time line to cause a cessation of movement and a change in the backdrop of psychological reality. Two, the individual has been cast about so forcefully by a previous event module that he or she is unable to break free, and therefore is lost to new modes of conduct. The individual finds him- or herself impaired by the limitations of the environment and must create a new set of parameters in order to bring about full individual entitlement.

217

The individual retains this sense of paralysis until new messaging systems are relayed to the brain and central nervous system. These systems create pathways that allow the individual to digest the biosyncratic understanding of time. Time occurs through a breakaway system of dots and dashes, a binary thrust of pure energy through the cerebrospinal cortex that moves through the gates of the hypothalamus at a very rapid rate. The brain is the gateway to multidimensional time. The brain, of course, is simply a reflector of divine intelligence in the human body, but as a perfect reflector it will mirror the sequences of time that are being pulled up onto the surface of consciousness and will suitably rearrange them. In the context of a particular present moment, the opaque lucidity of an individual event stroke will be limited only by the presence of stopped or interrupted time breaks. Since time usually moves at an infinite or fluid rate, it is necessary for it to be altered just for a moment until all of the new sequences can be lined up.

It is for this reason that, in some instances, the relationship of time becomes so lucid that one can actually intervene in the foundation of reality through the understanding of temporal awareness. This state of consciousness, which gives one access to the underlying values that create inceptionary awareness, is not limited to simply a select few. It is the birthright of all individuals. Once temporal consciousness has become completely luminescent and fluid, one is able to break apart the eaves, the humidity, the temporal stew of consciousness and reveal within it the full measure of possibility. Then all of the structures that have previously defined the event stream and given it life and substance are now forever dismissed. There is a ferocious intensity to this ability to realign the fibers of temporal alertness and this feeling is what is necessary in order to break the bonds of what had been permanent temporal restraints.

In the Direction of Sentience

Most human beings, when faced with the sequences of reality stretched before them, back away from the challenge of becoming free. They do not understand that psychological events are real, that they are not some abstract notion placed on the subject's background or foreground. In fact, psychological events and the host temporal sequences leading up to them form the core background for all of sentient life. Individuals who live by their ideals, dreams, and ambitions are in a state of evolution that is comparatively different from those living simply from event formations prepatterned from their ancestral past. Those who walk the line in the direction of true temporal compatibility learn to become one with the time lords who govern each and every perception that is brought forward in human awareness. It is difficult for human beings to comprehend that nothing that they feel or think is, on one level, actually theirs. Everything that is going on belongs to a higher intelligence. This is truly disconcerting, but is obvious fact. On the other hand, the rule of thumb for individuality is not limited to simply thinking that one is having original or novel ideas. Authenticity is based on what one is, rather than what one says one is.

The intellectual fabric of the mind is candy-coated with certain ideas that have been imprinted upon it for lifetimes of use. These imprints are there because they increase the ability to become a civilized or culturally imprinted person. Without these sugar coatings, which are quite literal because they are in fact glycogenically based, the individual would not have the memory to function in an orderly and fluid manner in society. Even those born into primitive societies have been highly socialized, with rules of conduct that would make any modern government proud.

Conformity and Grounded Responsibility

So how can one live authentically while adhering to society's rules? The answer lies solely in the individual's response to the waves of time coursing through him or her. The individual is subdominant when it comes to the imprinting that pure time provides. When time circulates correctly, one is able to simultaneously perceive the reality of time and the psychologically based governing forces that are imprinting it. There is a subconstruct underlying the meaning of everything that is, which has a purer, freer reality base within it. When sages state that this reality is a dream, they mean that the psychological formation of event streams is interdependent on the human beings who live them. There is a rockbed of reality underneath the dream. How can one understand this rockbed and gain access to it?

The fundamental life is lived through the gateway to creative temporal irrationality. This fundamental field, in which all of the time codes can be interrupted and jiggled around for the sake of uniformity, provides the individual with access to the temporal absolute. This field, which holds all of the formulations for time within it, forms the basis of reality and causes all of the event streams to be temporarily impaired while it searches out the perfect set of characteristics for a given psychological parameter.

Nonrigid Personality Formation

Fluid individuals are apt to fall down when reconciling their psychological and highly personal needs with the event structure as a whole. They are not capable of holding their own when a certain set of parameters presents itself. These individuals have a tendency to lose themselves in what is presented to them. However, because they are so malleable they are also able to see that what is presenting itself is the same thing in many different guises. This perceptual understanding gives them the ability to see behind event structures.

The more fixed or rigid personality has a difficult time seeing that what he or she is perceiving is purely a symbolic construct of his or her individual reality. He or she must see reality as a rigid, fixed form for the sake of security and individuality. By seeing oneself as drawn into a finite continuum of possible outcomes, one feels a sense of freedom in that there are limited possibilities for either success or failure. One has a secure foothold on life that creates a pure feeling of individuation free from contamination by outside influences.

Those beings freed from either stance, not dependent on the event streams confronting them, are unbound by temporal demands. They live through cognizing their own gravitational center at every moment. This condition, referred to as liberation, simply frees up the ground under which the individual walks. It is not a determination of worth or stature in God's eyes, nor does it make him or her exempt from the "taxes" exacted by karma. It simply allows the individual to stand in a place where the event structures no longer perfectly mirror the psychological consciousness.

This state of freedom provides the opportunity to determine what is real and what is not. This ability is not, however, one that is gained overnight. What happens is that gradually, through the intervention of divine grace, the individual becomes capable of lucidly viewing the "flipside" of what heretofore was a complex event stream puzzle. He or she can see down deep into the fabric of the absolute and essentially call into question what is to be born and what must die. In this sense, the individual returns to the responsibility of being a creator in his or her own right. However, this temporal solidity is still determined to great measure on what the individual holds valuable within his or her own heart.

The Beauty of Order

When one meets an individual who has been ostensibly freed from the confines of a limited temporal view, there is still a film there, a kind of opacity that limits the perception of the eternal. It is very seldom that an individual awakens so completely that he or she can see everything in a completely open and lucid way. Temporal reality is so difficult to work with because it is not based on anything that is actually real. It is based on the premise that when one is in free time one sees the world from the point of view of the Godhead, a state of reckless abandon and at the same time of perfect, unlimited order. Recklessness and superfluidity are necessary because the creative principle thrives on them. Limitless order is also necessary because to view what has been created the Godhead requires a standard of organization unsurpassed by anything any human individual could derive.

When an individual sees the beauty in order and the chaos in freedom, he or she has begun to live the psychological time matrix in a more evolutionary way. In this state one views three-dimensional time as containing breaks or curves, "scalawags" in the time performance ratios that cause time to break loose or curve back on itself, preventing event sequences from taking hold. This allows time to be random and sequentiated all at once. The individual who can see the possibility for change in the sequential unfoldment, and at the same time can obey the event sequences that appear to be governing his or her uniformity, is an advanced soul indeed.

To arrive at this state, it is necessary to become extremely patient. This is true because patience, in relationship to time, is the supreme virtue. If one is to live in a state of eternal time, one must trust that all of the patterns that are being worked out will eventually return to their source and be perfected. That means that all of the petty or large injustices that are played out in the field of living are all seen as part of the sequential unfoldment of time. In that larger context they have little meaning, but to the individual who is living them they are the building blocks for cultural and planetary art, the making or breaking of civilizations, and the random understanding of beauty.

The basis for time in the living brain is patience, because it is this quality that allows one to be able to stretch or retain the knowledge of truth even when the atmosphere does not justify it. It is more difficult to learn to love, plagued by the pangs for something different, on the basis of ego, than it is to live a life unbound by the curtain of the psychological mind. Those who gain the ability to love filled with the capacity for infinite patience are extremely rare.

Love and Time

Love patterns itself on time. Love and time are purely infinite, incapable of creating event sequences that are inherently dominant or destructive. They rise directly and absolutely above all the patterning presented to an individual, race, or society, and demand a type of perfection that is not bound by any notion of morality. The structure of love and time is based solely on the experience of the experiencer. The individual grows in his or her relationship to the performance of deeds or situations until he or she is left completely speechless when it comes to understanding the role of the Godforce in the stretching of eternity. In this state, a type of equanimity about the fundamental causality of individual event sequences magically and unutterably takes place. The individual is left simply holding the bag of love and is unable to break free from the awe, the wonder of simply viewing life from its raw simplicity and understatedness. The moment is simply left bare, untouched, and there is an unutterable peace that is created through this realization. This is the peace that surpasses understanding.

In order for there to be room for that peace, the individual must continuously unify with the possibilities of time. When the individual can see every raw moment as an opportunity to return to love, there is a breakthrough that occurs on the level of the heart. The individual understands that although it may appear that self-awakening has happened, it is actually an awakening to all that is. In that moment, the need for understanding, explanation, or platitude is no longer there. The individual can then see that the time constraints that have been placed on his or her life are not bound by any shift in awareness. They are bound by the absolute!

This understanding, that the Godhead itself must create constraints in order to create perfect order, frees one from the responsibility of having to reconcile all the apparent injustices and complaints that make up the bulk of human experience. The appearance of opposites makes everything that is human difficult. These opposites create the limitless expanse of event streams and possibilities throughout the omniverse. To realize this is to be set free from having to pull them apart and from understanding what makes them necessary. Then and only then can the knowledge of temporal complexity become self-evident. It is a very enviable and worthwhile state to aspire to.

2.3.3
the   language   of   time

Language and the Central Nervous System

ime appears as a formation of language due to the interior sweep of perception that forms a counterbalance in the webwork of the central nervous system (CNS). Language is a felt event in the emotional structure of the individual. Through a sweep of control within the context of the nervous system, the entirety of language is calibrated.

Language pictures itself in two major categories. One is physiological, having to do with the characteristics of the brain that syntactically dialogue with the CNS to produce the impulses or sensations of language. The second is the psychological apprehension of language that is essentially pictorial and is given to individual interpretation.

Language and time are related. Time is pictured in color-cued modules of perception translated into linguistic form. Language is a representation of the areas of pure consciousness that are transceivers for the formation of temporal cues in the CNS. The CNS utilizes language as a central programming or dialogue to represent the understanding of pictorial information. Once language has been created, it is fed directly to the arterial nerves for translation by the cerebral mechanics of the nervous system.

The felt language produced by psychological or linguistic dialogue is of a different subjective order than that produced by the objective, pure nervous centers. The language of the heart, of the interior organs, or that of any part of the human body is produced through an alchemical synthesis of felt information and purely chemical dialogue. Language is produced by the body as well as the brain for the purpose of communication between the different attributes of the CNS.

The Athletics of Communication

Time communicates through language. Through language, receptor sites of the nervous system translate information to be utilized for the purpose of organic timing and motion. The barriers to motion in the nervous system are many. There is a profound inertia to the human body that must be overcome through the development of objective reasoning. The human body wants to move but the psychology of the individual directly affects the development of athletic or artistic prowess. The development of a highly sophisticated timing in the body is the result of training and practice, created through an understanding of how the brain/mind/body communicates.

Individuals who utilize these pathways in a disciplined fashion create the linguistic/nervous/energetic pathways that promote the development of the musculature and high degrees of advancement in coordination. Ordinarily, these linguistic structures must be formulated in the body at a very young age, but they can be enhanced later through specific training and attention to their formation. After the age of thirty-five, it is difficult to enhance the linguistic/energetic pathways of the body and promote a high degree of functioning. The time codes of the human nervous system are not as easily calibrated after age-related deterioration has taken place. This is why it is so important to develop these pathways early.

The process of language and its development from an energetic perspective takes place early and develops during infancy. The infant, when faced with the prospect of learning to communicate with the mother, develops a set of infantile linguistic components, or baby language, which allows the individual to communicate directly with the mother. This type of preverbal simulation allows the infant to exercise certain facial muscles but also promotes the development of motion in the body.

The motile body is a little-understood factor in the development of reason in the young child, because at this point, physicians do not understand that motion, reason, and temporal perspectives are deeply interrelated. The process of awakening to the development of fine and gross motor coordination usually precedes the development of detailed language structures, but once these structures have been implemented they rapidly advance the development of the body.

Once the infant has learned to crawl, he or she is in a position to develop language. Language formulates itself out of the birth of the body. The body actually mirrors the temporal cues that bring language into the cerebrospinal cortex. The body becomes an information highway for language to be formulated and provides the actual timing for all of the nervous impulses that promote the advancement of unified intelligence.

Since the body is the transceiver for these impulses, it creates the ratiosynchronization of them. The body is not really an opaque transceiver, but actually brings all of the signals that it implants into a "body of light" that is then downloaded directly to the physical structure. The development of these temporal codes or markers in the CNS creates the uniformity necessary for optimal coherence and advanced stages of perception. Therefore, one could say that the coordination of the CNS is highlighted by the advancement of the body.

The Advancement in Perception

There are many instances in which the advancement of unified intelligence is stalled by the inability of the body to register the precise cues necessary for functioning. In cases of acute paralysis or instances in which the body is unable to register these light cues, a different system takes over. The autonomic nervous system supplants the physical body as the main conduit for light-based information. The individual is immediately signaled as one who will function more from the body of light than from the physical structure itself.

This decision on the part of the nervous system takes place very early and is based on the soul orientation of the individual. Some souls enter into the body with the linguistic centers on tap. They are immediately able to utilize the body for the purpose of language and the development of motor control. There are others who from a psychological and soul-level standpoint have an aversion to the use of the body. These individuals will opt to download directly to the subtle bodies rather than utilizing the gross body for optimal light-encoded information. They must learn to download vital information from a learned perspective.

There are those rare individuals who are able to utilize the body and mental intelligence fully and are thus able to function at their maximum capacity. They can continue to accumulate the temporal mechanics of higher intelligence throughout the lifetime with little impairment due to aging or disease.

Language presents itself to the central nervous system very early and is related to the feeling level that the mother presents to the child. One has to speak to the young child early and often for the child to develop a comprehensive understanding of language formation. Stimulation by the mother is the crucial factor, particularly the inclination of the mother to read to the child. Music is also an important mechanism of stimulation and can enhance motor skills and the development of reason. In some instances, children are not able to digest outer stimuli due to an impairment of their ability to hear. In these instances, motor and auditory stimulation must occur from a subtle vibrational standpoint. Situations in which children are not able to hear spoken language must therefore be supplanted by other sensory stimulation, but it is considered optimum that the stimulation be primarily auditory during the first five years of life.

The Chemicals of Reason

Time develops through reason. This occurs because the individual must learn to swallow time through the development of the salivary glands. The first swallow that the child is able to make actually stimulates certain centers in the CNS that develop the timing and elocution of language. The salivary glands produce a chemical that functions as a circuit breaker for the temporal mechanics of the body. Certain animals that produce sounds that are pleasing to the ear also produce these chemicals. Repetitive annunciation of tones, given in rapid succession to the young infant, produces the advancement of these salivary chemicals and promotes the health and well-being of the entire body.

The entry point for the temporal mechanics of the body is in the spleen. It is here that the codes or imprints of language are actually formulated. The spleen is also an organ that is rarely studied for its effects on intelligence because it is viewed principally as a mechanism for blood to be purified. It is in the spleen that language is actually downloaded and focalized, not only for the purpose of self-expression but also for the coordination of temporal cues in the body. The blood is a picture book for time. The body learns to reason through information being sped along the blood stream and documented in each available sensory organ.

The eyes hold the key for the development of language and the ability to relate in complex ways to the environment. Those individuals who do not utilize their eye muscles in a disciplined way during early childhood often develop a distinct aversion to certain linguistic clues that make it difficult for higher orders of intelligence to be formulated. The early childhood markers of intelligence therefore depend greatly on two factors: stimulation by the mother and stimulation by the environment. The environment must become conducive to the refinement of the nervous system. These cues occur very early and produce a significant scent or flavor in the salivary input of the body. The body becomes attuned to the scent of the environment, and it is through these aromas or flavors that the child becomes accustomed to accumulating the standards of reason that will govern his or her entire life.

Adults who have not been exposed to a refined perceptive stance in early childhood will often appear psychotic in their behavior. Individuals must have a sense of peace, contentment, and safety in early childhood in order for the temporal markers that signify nervous organization to develop properly. This is why it is so important to produce a quiet, peaceful, and orderly environment in the home of the infant. The early childhood memories should include those that provide a sense of attunement to the subtle aspects of the individual. The formation of language depends upon these cues

becoming synchronous at a very early age. Language is documented directly by the body and governs the formation of movement. Individuals given
stimulation of both an auditory and physical nature are more likely to
become fully coherent in their patterns of response.

Bio-organic Patterning

Very little attention is now paid to the education of the body in early
childhood. All movements could be precisely patterned to elicit muscular
coordination that would enhance the development of reason. The child
should be given every opportunity to expose the developing muscle groups
to the influence of sound. The muscles respond directly to the cooing nois-
es of the mother but also to any sonic stimulation that occurs in the environment. Certain instrumentation can be developed that directly simulates
the entry of the temporal cues or codes. This can be done through investigation into the precise markers for timing and intervention on the part of
the central nervous system.

Individuals who present highly developed linguistic structures are more
apt to be successful in adult life. It is essential that these markers be formulated early. The advancement of understanding of how time feeds the body
will one day be more fully understood. Time and motion act as reciprocal
entry points for the genetic programming of the body. Once time is understood as a precursor for motion, then the body can be seen as a "dream
machine" for the development of language.

It is through the unconscious that the mind develops a system of bio-
organic reasoning. This is reason not purely of the logical type but of a psy-
chocognitive nature that strengthens the core balance of perception in the
individual. One who is able to liquefy the strategies of perception through
the envelope of the body creates a symphonic interplay of auditory stimulation that promotes the health of the intelligence.

The dialogue between the temporal performance of the CNS and the
physical body occurs through a system of chemical markers that originate in
the spleen but translate throughout the circulatory system. These chemical
markers cause the organs to develop exquisite perception of timing that
allows them to function at optimal levels. The functioning of the body is
largely autonomic in scope. The autonomic nervous system is the main
component for advanced intelligence in the human being. However, we are
not accustomed to thinking that the autonomic nervous system has many
advanced stages of symbiotic development.

Yoga and the Inner Child

Through the development of subtle sonic technology, individuals can attune the autonomic responses and make them more pliable for the advancement of pure intelligence. Within the context of yogic practice, the body formulates a system of markers or codes for such intelligence to spring forth. In the practice of yogic sadhana, individuals can advance the system of perception even at advanced ages. Those who practice such systems of discipline can essentially retrain the body to function independently from the aging process.

The aging process is an organic function, similar to the breakdown of any organic material, but the process of unified intelligence can continue even as the body begins to deteriorate. This is why one could say that the body of a yogi is the body of a child. The yogi, whether of advanced or young age, creates a body of consciousness that is independent of the functioning of the physical structure. It is here that the subtle temporal markers are most evident.

The yogic structures develop a system of radiant language in order to translate themselves into the structure of the body and signal to the muscles, ligaments, and joints to do the dance of life. This yoga is not purely physical but is in fact mostly of an advanced mental nature. The practitioner learns to work with the higher aspects of the mental field to calibrate advanced perception. This knowledge of the workings of the precise timing of the body causes intelligence to rotate back to its essential and profound core. It is the predominant influence that instills in the individual the propensity for higher states of awareness.

The inner child and the yogi together create a state of awakened innocence in which the individual is able to recollect the information that has accumulated on a soul level and translate this information to the waking state. Since the soul intelligence is marked through a system of light-based frequencies in the body, it is through the soul that the individual develops an advanced matrix for unified perception. The soul develops language through visual and auditory cues that are naturally symbolic and are essentially pictorial.

The representation of soul language is downloaded through the hypothalamus and travels through the medulla to the portions of the brain that transceive pictorial information. Those individuals who have developed high degrees of mental reasoning utilize the felt sense of the body as a marker point for the development of consciousness. The transliteration of yogic formations in the regions of the brain that have to do with sight, hearing, and taste form the basis for higher degrees of temporo-linguistic develop-ment and the stages of reason that lead to enlightenment.

The perceptual structures of the highly advanced person shift to a state in which the awakened nervous system perceives language through the medium of consciousness itself. In other words, one looks upon the light impulses that accumulate through the felt structure of the body as sign-posts for the doorway of cognition. One skips over the elementary con-structs of the mental body as one would skip over the images that appear on the highway. One dials up directly with the avenues of perception that occur through the systematic intervention of time and consciousness, and feeds these cues directly to the heart and other organs for the purpose of refined temporal organization.

The Doorway to Cognition

As time accumulates, the doorway to cognition presents itself, and the platform for advanced auditory and mental refinement becomes available. In instances where this occurs, there is a very high degree of buildup of brain sugars which are the glycogenic variables that define the higher mental sta-tus of the individual. These glycogenic markers are actually the seed com-ponents for the interval equation of time derivatives in the development of unified cerebral intelligence.

Once the individual has become capable of calibrating time through the development of light, the temporal mechanics are now fully adult. This is the signal to the brain and central nervous system that a whole new style of functioning can develop. Until this time, the individual is held at bay by the infantile mechanics that originally took place in his or her childhood. Therefore, any impediments that occurred, whether emotional, auditory, or environmental, may limit the development of higher states of awareness. Once this chain has been broken through yogic practices that advance the range of perception of the nervous system, the individual can become psy-choacoustically aware. He or she can utilize the time/sound/sight compo-nents of the hypothalamus and the visual/sonic regions of the brain to crys-tallize higher states of awareness and become a literal sounding board for the development of intelligence.

Since language develops rapidly at these intense stages of yogic develop-ment, the individual transcends the birth language and opens into a system of light/relay input that makes him or her susceptible to input from higher realms. In this stage, the individual becomes an encoder and developer of original attributes of light language that are ingested directly into the central nervous system. These may picture themselves as visions or sensory cues in the nervous system that will, when properly organized, come to fruition as language. This ability to create language directly from the light centers in the cerebral cortex causes the spiritual energy or kundalini to ripen. Spiritual energy marches from a dormant position at the base of the spine to its final culmination as a permanent temporal marker in the upper regions of the brain. Through this, a set of spinal mechanics develops that will cause the individual to become a superfluid internal preceptor for awakened consciousness.

The germination of light-centered mechanics as a linguistic approach must be advanced early in the maturation of the individual. The development of these light centers must actually be encouraged through proper stimulation from the environment. In cases where this is impossible, the individual can transcend these impediments through disciplined practice. Once the stimulation of these centers has crystallized sufficiently, the language of the gods can present itself. In this stage, the individual no longer functions from a state of limited or individualistic reason, but enters a collective, awakened universe in which the conceptual material available from the higher centers of development is now instantaneously available. The individual essentially dies to the infantile identity and becomes capable of developing a temporal landscape that is at once original, uniform, and synchronous with the underlying capabilities of the body.

2.3.4
the pictorial imprint
of language

Stereoptic Language

anguage pictures itself as waves or curves on the imprint of temporal motion. Time and consciousness produce a singularity that by its nature is not temperate or reasonable in response to the core influence of human language. Language is required to reference itself universally and then proceed down the inferential slope of reason.

Language presents itself first as a stereoptically defined messaging ground for temporal consciousness. It grounds itself first in the hypothalamic ring and proceeds laterally through the awakened consciousness as a streamed influence of perception. Language is startling in its ability to garner selected mirrored impulses and repeat them in coherent phraseology that delineates the sequestered impulses of pure reason. Since language is delicate, it must constitute itself from the point of origin that time derives. Language is a temporal stream; its vantage points must be painted unilaterally rather than being an outlook that the individual defines.

Language delineates the stream of time. It opens into the corridor of reason and defines sense perception. It also denotes how the temporal derivatives will be spent or coagulated in response to each window of opportunity. Language must present itself first as a gradation of impulses that are not easily translatable from a mental point of view. The temporal imprints must arrange themselves prior to the influence of the language stream. These imprints form building blocks of linguistic structure which are the basis for human language. They are composed of strings or impulses of pure, radiant sound that emanate directly from the outer foundation of the nervous system and then enter through the cerebrospinal cortex.

Language forms the backdrop for the entire functioning of the nervous system. Every species has its own language, and within that context, each individual sets his or her language stream in motion. Whether audible or internal, the language that an individual uses is determined by the idiosyncrasies of his or her personality. Language therefore is primarily an intimate and personal matter. Though created through the mother tongue of an individual's collective influence, language is influenced by a person's own psychological sensibility.

Time incorporates itself into the language stream via a complex system of relays that manage and at times circumvent the actual array of linguistic structures. Time is a system of language in its own right. The linguistic pairs that time creates, pooling seemingly opposite values against one another, form the basis for human language. We think in terms of streams of opposites, opposing forces of logic that commend to us the various options of daily life. Time forms the backdrop for the unification of language in order to encompass all of the many variations that seek to describe the range of human life. In our affairs, we seek to understand the origins of our behavior through the use of clock-time, a system of contrived events and objects. Time, however, when fed directly to the linguistic centers of the brain, will make a language that has no such temporal marker points. Although considerably more free, it would appear childish, impractical, and strange to us.

Precise Speech

Time must create its own language and then feed this language to the cerebral centers. Human speech is therefore a tripartite process. First, the language streams must be relayed from the level of pure consciousness itself. Second, they must be calibrated through the temporal methodology of that species. Third, they must be translated into audible human voice. These three functions can actually exist independent of one another. It is not always easy to translate the temporal mechanics of pure awareness into spoken form. This is why some people are functionally more articulate or expressive.

Human language is by nature imprecise. The timing of linguistic impulse is preceded by a trip in the switch of perception that gives the individual the capacity to perceive how language streams are to be formulated. When an individual is unable to trip or catch this wave, it becomes difficult to wrap the event stream in the cloak or cocoon of time that would make the psychological construct manageable. The individual becomes accustomed to the event stream as it is without being able to distinguish a particular vocabulary to give it meaning or voice.

The formation of timing precedes the linguistic event and is tied directly to the individual's ability to grasp that particular portion of knowledge. The individual must unconsciously map out a gradient or underpinning of response to each temporal equation. This understanding of time as a mathematical imprint underlying the foundation of consciousness and speech is not known to human science at this time. However, it is the fundamental knowledge that allows one to formulate linguistic impulses that are expressive of the weaving of consciousness.

Interpretation Is the Key

The internal dialogue of time is meaningless without the seed form of collective interpretation. Time must become collectively recognized in order to gain significance. Time is essentially a chorus of these fundamental values that are downloaded repeatedly into the collective structure. If this were not the case, each individual would develop his or her own personal frame of reference and also his or her own language. There are individuals who actually do maintain such a particular imagistic unification but they are more than likely to be viewed as insane by present standards. In order to create an individual language structure and a collective language structure simultaneously, time must be present in both its unificatory value as well as its particular value. The two must create a satisfactory frame of reference so that the individual maintains the ability to speak to others while maintaining the ability to speak directly to time.

When one wakes up to the language of time, two things occur. The first is that, through being subject to the actual song or fabric of the impulses of time, the individual becomes inordinately sensitive to how they appear. The individual can actually hear these impulses directly, and becomes capable of managing their appearance as a fundamental backdrop for linguistic formation. Then, once this faculty awakens, consciousness creates its own linguistic structure to articulate or manage these impulses. One could say that all originality emanates from such a backdrop. In the opening to pure consciousness, time dances out onto the face of the individual plane of reference and reveals itself through the advent of language.

Although time normally precedes or intertwines with language formation, the temporal viscosity rapidly and advantageously reveals itself in a transducible form. Since language normally is a response to the thinking process, in the awakened individual such thinking is actually put aside in favor of a more rapid and intense version of linguistic formation that works directly with the impulses of time and consciousness.

Time betrays its meaning or rhythmic variations through waves. These waves could be loosely seen as the sentences of time, the phraseology that time develops to express itself over a chorus of infinity. Since time and matter must always retain a shape or dimensionality to be utilizable in a captured or limited sphere, language must also be made repeatable. The impulses of time present themselves to the nervous system, and the musculoskeletal functioning of the fascia are stimulated by these temporal cues and spill out into language. The system of rests or pauses in normal speech mirrors the temporal rests or relays that underwrite the manifestation of language.

Updating the Software

One could say that the software is the programming of temporal mechanics itself while the hardware is human speech. To translate from pure consciousness to a temporal framework requires that time divest itself of any notion of reason. This is why when people truly manifest insanity they are unable to stay within a given time frame. They are moving from temporal present to temporal past without any indication of difference.

Time also governs motion. As a result, the motion that forms systems of human language is related to how time is invested in them. The phonetic structures of syllabification are formed on the basis of how a given set of muscular responses will best decode or rectify the temporal impulses as they appear. The mouth, the tongue, and especially the vocal cords are focalizers for the methodology of temporal linguistic structures. Time interplays with the tongue. It enters through the hypothalamus, traveling through the brain stem and entering the language centers in a burst of radiant perception.

This pure perception or linguistic preplay is translated by the central nervous system, forming a system of learned response that is the collective expression of that matrical realization. Time is the balance beam on which consciousness places itself. It is up to language to correct the forward or backward movement that is naturally created when time impulses feed themselves directly into the nervous system. Sometimes this may be seen as a type of quivering in the articulation of the individual as the proper sequentiation lines up in the cerebrospinal cortex for germination and expression.

The spiritual energy or divine force is of course the prerequisite for any translinear germination of intelligence. The spiritual energy mixes with the time correlates that have been laid down. It forms the backdrop for the curls, waves, or other temporal formations to develop. The spiritual energy is translucent, and therefore for it to be captured by the vocal intelligence, it must be made spongy or permeable. This thickening of the temporal wave is created in the saturation of the medulla with clusters of time imprints that are then fed directly to the rest of the brain.

The spongy or porous nature of brain tissue is the physical outgrowth of this phenomenon. Time must array itself on porous surfaces. This is because the cheesy texture of these surfaces makes it possible for time to collect in the gaps or surface structures, ping-ponging back and forth through them to form a vessel for the accumulation of a temporal pool. There can be no accumulation of time in a solid or opaque form without such collection. Otherwise, time and consciousness just spill out into the motivational array that occurs naturally above the energy system and there is no organization or development of pure reason.

No Brain Strain

The capacity of the nervous system to stimulate temporal movement is determined directly by the fluidity of creative intelligence. Intelligence is not a determinant of reason but a backdrop for its accumulation. Intelligence, in its own right, does not tempt the analogues of reason. It takes a fully organized mind, equipped with common sense, the organization of language, and the ability to document perceptual changes, for an individual to be fluent in the ways of the world. When time and consciousness get together and influence language from the ground up, a seed of awakening is planted.

Those individuals who appear reasonable often are not. Reason is not the result of the accumulation of collective notions of reasonableness. Reason is not a system of mores or statutes visited on a civilization by a collective structure. Reason is the underlying impulse that formulates the temporal structures that develop the mind and make originality possible.

Time must saturate the brain for the mind to calibrate temporal responsibility. The human brain is completely holographic, in the sense that any part of the brain, when sectioned off from any other, will mimic or imitate the configurations that were presented when it was set in place with the whole. Thus any portion of the brain can be stimulated or programmed to endear itself to any other part. The relay points or matched sets that make this creativity possible can be affected adversely by traumatic injury or illness.

This is why, in the event that the brain is physically damaged, the nervous system will seek to mirror its initial imprinting and eventually recreate the pathways that will make the original field of intelligence flower. However, this will happen only if the original field of temporal intelligence was lively in the first place. In the case of mental retardation, it is often true that the language structures cannot portray themselves fluidly to permit the validation of reason. One could say that a severely retarded individual is "out of time" with the universal knowledge. It is solely the grace of divine intelligence itself that deposits the merit of language and the capacity of linguistic functioning to an individual.

Deposits in the Spiritual Account

Language development and the capacity to understand, articulate, and manifest human knowledge follow the law of random opposites. In other words, intelligence is random in whom it seeks to deposit itself, and opposite in that it develops dualistic notions of mind and perception to incorporate its movements. The spirit of excellence, gained through the union of both spiritual practice and its incipient grace, forms the lead-in to the pure organization that is fundamental to divine intelligence.

Civilization has become accustomed to excising individuals and cultures that do not ascribe to the type of linguistic mores that its situation demands. Since individuals are unable to develop their own highly specialized and unique forms of communication, the collective interpretation of reality has become the rule. This has produced a type of temporal tyranny, in which the individual is forced to adhere to the standards determined by the country or province. In smaller, tribal systems, language formation retains a more individualistic character. Its standardization, to the extent that is now apparent, is a relatively modern phenomenon that has its merits as well as its drawbacks.

Temporal originality is the basis for the advancement of civilizations. Thus, future civilizations will be inspired to return to a more individualistic notion of language. The collective flavor will be retained, but individuals will create their own stamp or imprint on language. This will magnify the individual's ability for inner expression as well as the degree of creative intelligence that will be able to flow out towards others.

2.3.5
the eternal present

The Present Comes Through

he eternal present is essentially a temporal composite of past and future parameters required to restore order to any given point. As the present comes about, it brings a taste or flavor of the past. This flavor is based on the need of the present to create a vantage point for its structure in reality. The present restores order through combing through the archives of the past and examining how the past needs to come through in order for that moment in time to crystallize in its full spectrum of possibility. The human mind borrows from the past continuously, inventing thought material from stories or anecdotes that infuse a sense of meaning into a particular event sequence.

The present is the temporal representative for the past in this dimension. It represents both the forward and backward climb of the event sequence into the absolute. Since the past always presents cues or temporal meanings that are useful, the present archives the past and utilizes bits and pieces of it to represent a particular point of view. Most human experience is subjective. Therefore, the present restores a sense of order or meaning by developing temporal strategies that are intensely personal and representational in nature. The human mind feeds off of such anecdotal material until such time as it becomes nonrepresentational or nonsymbolic in its functioning. For the human mind to work within the literal mechanics of time, it radiates and creates time through its own awareness. As this condition is rare, most human beings create their present circumstances through the underpinnings of their perception.

In order for the past to become the present it must be instilled with a sense of drama or meaning that corresponds to the time. This is how the present allots certain sequences of understanding. The present curtails the past sequences that are not fully randomized or developed, and attracts sequences that will document the point of view of the individual. As the present is brought fully into light, it pulls forward in order to bring in random sequences of information that the future dictates.

Human beings who are growing in awareness continue to be borrowers from both past and present. They look to the future for inspiration and hope, but also for a heightened sense of confirmation of their spiritual vision. This is why the future is accessed more and more as an individual regains his or her understanding of the mechanics of optimal individuation. The individual opens towards the future and borrows sequences of events, conceptual material, and a point of view in the field of consciousness that will yield the desired result. The individual who moves back and forth from future to past so consistently may not easily be able to determine where his or her identity structure really lies. He or she is essentially straddling two worlds and is neither in the past nor the future. Instead, he or she has the opportunity to develop a more fully enriched temporal present.

The Shape of the Future

The information gained from future activity is not put forward simply for the purpose of greater understanding. Future material is accessed for the purpose of literally creating different streams of event possibility. One could say that these event streams are places in the domain of consciousness for public use. This is why when an individual begins to awaken he or she must become more responsible for and conscious of how he or she uses mental or emotional activity. The words and actions of an individual in the present have a great deal to do with what event streams will become available in his or her future.

In order to understand the realm of event personalization, one must understand that each event sequence has a stamp or signature that makes it entirely intimate or personal for that individual. He or she stamps a point of recognition on the event sequence and gives it shape or character. When the event sequence is a composite, as it most often is, between the past and the future, it has a particular shape. This shape may be referred to as a sequence blocker or inhibitor.

As the event sequence fans out, there is a characteristic hold or pause that is placed on that sequence until such time as it picks up all of the material it needs from different points of randomization. It will gather all of the information that it needs from a myriad of domains before it actually occurs on this plane of existence. As a project or set of circumstances gains momentum, it may go through a period during which it appears to be stopped in its tracks. In light of the prerequisites of information management, event sequences might have to wait their turn in order for certain possible futures to be created. It is similar to the wait one has when certain data streams are lifted from a computer matrix and must be downloaded into the main drive.

When the present is laden with both event sequences from its temporal past and possible future, it creates tracks or breaker points in each of the event sequences it wishes to attain. These breaker points are like dams in a river. They create energy, momentum, and power for the event sequences, and like a dam they allow a certain amount of energy to flow out to each particular event stream when the point of origination calls for it. These event streams may be viewed as windows or portals—doorways for the combined mass of possible future and temporal past to be presented. The present in all its power is the activation point or mixing ground for the future to create itself.

One cannot truly create the future because the randomization and the counterpoint of opposites that create future scenarios are laid in through the movement of the event streams. One's character structure and likes or dislikes play only a small part in the picture. Much of the mechanics of future actualization goes on behind the scenes in the locker room of the unconscious, where not only the primordial impulses play but, fortunately, the more elevated awareness of the higher self is available.

The possible future outcomes of each individual are mapped out continuously in the present. In fact, there is never a moment in which the calculator of the unconscious is not spinning future realities, which are often masked to the conscious mind. When the individual becomes aware of the underpinnings of this process, there awakens an illumination of all of these streamers or curtains of reality. The individual awakens to that which he or she knows to be true and begins to be able to bring about the truth. This truth is not simply personal or subjective. It begins to take on the characteristics of Universal Truth, which are beyond that of anybody's own beliefs or theories of optimal existence.

The purpose of the present therefore is to be a magnetic clearinghouse for waves of the past and possibilities of the future. The present therefore is the most dynamic of all the temporal opposites, and is structured to bring about the most possibility for change. It is up to the individual to discover the power of the present and to begin to reach into the recesses of what was once unconscious to utilize the fruits of the moment.

The Limits of the Ego

Time and space, being subjectively intertwined in the minds and hearts of individuals, must be circumvented momentarily in order to bring about true change. The individual must stop for a moment and go through a self-clarification or examination of goals and divisions of spirit that might prevent him or her from actualizing the highest potential of the mind and heart. Each person finds that in wandering aimlessly from one event sequence to the other without a goal in mind, it is difficult to pursue a coherent set of events. However, the goal setting that must be done is not from the level of the mind. It is a synthesis of what the heart desires to be free, independent, and unfettered, and what the higher mind wants in order to accomplish the given set of possibilities. The individual's tendency is to set goals through the contracted lodgings of the mind. It is the job of the soul to set the individual on a course where he or she will actually collide with the desired evolutionary future.

The course setting for the future is created through a specific set of physiological and empathic processes. Access to these subsets is gained through inner recognition. The individual must become aware of the subverted tendencies of the psyche. He or she must understand how one set of circumstances might affect future outcomes and learn to control the underlying tendencies that color or flavor the choices of the life drama.

Each individual is his or her own player on the field of the absolute. God draws various circumstances to one for the purpose of learning and inner growth. The Divine does not make mistakes in this regard, but rather presents a teeming pool of different possibilities. Included are all of the sensate experiences of life, presented for the purpose of helping the individual to refine the field of choice. As one grows in the ability to identify those choices that will be most evolutionary in spirit or attribute, one becomes capable of a greater level of self-mastery and personal power.

This process must be distinguished from the quest of the personal ego to achieve some type of lasting success. The ego, in its quest for immortality, tries to vanquish the successful forays of the spirit into the territory of the future. The ego must be mastered not by force but by wisdom, love, and the quest for the truth. The ego is a very skillful player in the human endeavor and must be treated with respect. The ego wants power in and of its own right and will seek this power at every junction point. The individual has the capacity and divine injunction to free the ego from the quest for power without strangling its right towards full individuation and freedom. This is a very delicate situation for most human beings, and even for the Divine Spirit or Pneuma itself.

The individual must remain free while at the same time be brought to a state of full awakening. He or she cannot be forced to engage in the quest for self-improvement; it is up to each individual to undertake this journey. The individual pulls from the catalogue of opposites within the "hard drive" of his or her own psyche. One could say that the code for the human mind is indeed binary. There are really only two choices for the human mind: right or wrong, good or bad. The shades of gray that are discovered are based solely on subjective interpretation.

The reasoning power of the human nervous system is dualistic until such time as the thrust towards full unification becomes infinitely stronger than the tendency of the human mind to maintain this false sense of empowerment. As long as the human mind works on the basis of judgment or lack of understanding of the categorization of opposites, it pulls from the tracks of the absolute those portions of reason that justify its given position. The human mind must therefore learn to compassionately but emphatically step back from its own prejudices and become free to evaluate that which proceeds in its path.

When the human mind becomes ostensibly free from the colorations that create the off/on dualistic notions of what is true or false, a new type of truth emerges. This is a unified or collective participation in universal understanding that is brought about by synthesizing the temporal patterns of many civilizations or thought cultures. The person is really no longer thinking like a human being but has transcended its speciate identity. Then he or she becomes part of the collective pool of light-awakened individuals who are working on the part of the whole for a rapid and collective change.

Since the subjective ego structure is not inclined to go along for the ride, it must often be kicked into submission by the greater aspects of the person's character. This involves a core realization of the egoic patterns of the individual's makeup, and a deep and profound recognition and willingness on the part of the individual to turn such patterns around for the greater good of the whole. This must be an activity that is at once ruthless in its honesty and compassionate in its effectiveness. The individual must be willing to undergo in-depth scrutiny of his or her passions, beliefs, and expectations without becoming mired in a quandary of guilt, fear, or contraction.

The individual who is capable of such full scrutiny is gifted with the light of understanding. The possible choices that he or she is about to map out become available to create a new blueprint for subjective reality. One is uplifted to the level of the spirit and is reborn into a different type of being, one that is capable of perceiving truth while at the same time willing to forego certain conclusions of the intellect that mask the welcome softness of the heart. The individual who awakens the heart and mind enters a symphonic point of reference. One is able to build a direct understanding of the best future outcome and how to materialize it. Completely free from the fears and rigidities of the ego structure, one can enter the avenues of organization on a risk-free basis. There is a sense of triumph as the small vestiges of the mind are lifted free in the light of the reality of the now.

The power moment or crystallized attributes of the now are formulated and developed. The heart-mind undergoes a kind of revolutionary spin, capable of returning the individual to a state of grace, innocence, and an uncaptured demand from the innermost realms of spirit. There, the future and past are mixed, made ready, and brought forward without being entrapped by the dualistic demands of the ego-structure. Human beings are not destined to be completely trapped by the demands of the ego. One has a future form or cast that can help one attain a sense of clarity or poise in the face of obstacles. By calling on the future-present for optimum clarification, the human being is set free from the demands of the ego superstructure and becomes truly capable of independent or illumined thought. This must be the goal if an individual seeks to truly reclaim his or her individuality of spirit and sense of adventure.

3

Cosmic
Time

3.1
the structure of the cosmos

3.1.1
the living experience of time

Journey in the Subtext of Time

he living experience of time involves the relinquishment of reality as a known object. As time curves back on itself, the subjective experience of the knower is crystallized into a felt sense of eternal now or present that precludes any knowledge of future or past. This suspension in the reality of the present is a precursor of the dimensional expansion into a know-all-time reality, which is necessary for interdimensional travel and perception.

The experiencer of time as a dimensional expression recognizes this eternal present as the kernel for all subjective encounters with other realities or futures. He or she learns to journey in the subtext of time, relinquishing all temporal moorings. The mysteries of the inner temporal dialogue are borne up through the longing of the inner self to reveal the truth of reality from this felt sense. Since time has no trappings in this model, all of the event sequences that would stem from any one anterior present moment are stripped of their relationship and one is left with a naked bare presence.

The key to the experiencer's relationship to time is that time has no future or past. This means that when the experiencer dives into the analogue of his or her personal life expression, there is nothing enclosed there. This emptiness, this relinquishment of one's personal story or accoutrements, leaves one in the position of being turned inside out. One is left without a proper temporal envelope in which to gauge reality in a purely emotional or subjective sense. One becomes independent of any known truth other than what is placed directly in front of one.

This state of suspension, which is developmental, takes place slowly. It is not instantaneous. The individual gradually awakens to this no-time reality and is able to climb into the subjective skin of time without feeling fear or apprehension. This process allows one the freedom to explore reality without a referential time sense. It is a felt sense but it is not entirely fabricated by the human mind. Since the mind cannot comprehend time without an envelope, the mind will develop a new refractory sense of time involvement that is different than what was previously referenced. This state is a nonreferential, time-based reality. It is not based on psychological relationships between up or down, day or night, or any category of opposites, but on a direct link between the individual and the Godhead. It is at once simultaneous, immediate, and direct.

Therefore, once the individual has reached this state there is no turning back from the absolute. There is a sense of being completely riveted to the interior of the soul and a feeling that looking out onto the playing field of life is the only recourse. This process of witnessing is organic and spontaneous. When the individual awakens to this state, the fundamental requirement is that he or she become capable of realizing the interior assessment of truth from any angle. Truth in this sense is a priori; it is not based on anything other than what appears in front of one.

Things show up, appear, and disappear, and they are no longer judged as wrong or right. Since they simply exist as they are without any subjective angle, they are no longer time-based and no longer historical. They are made up of the memory of the time. They live for and of themselves and when they pass away they are simply gone. There is no yearning for completion, nor any sense of longing. Since power is the only element contained within them, they exist for and of themselves. However, since they are free from time, they exist in the extension of the absolute, which is also bound by the reality of love. Time becomes ever-loving, ever-spontaneous, and completely free. Nothing can contain such a consciousness and nothing can complete it.

Cracking Absolute Time

Time is the mechanism whereby the intellect realizes the absolute. When time appears on the surface of life, the individual at first feels that time is the purveyor of his or her own personal kingdom. However, once time has surpassed this reference point, then the individual metaphors that describe and create uniform life are stripped away. What is left is the pure time value, unimpaired and no longer elongated by the psychological needs of the individual. This pure experience of time has no a priori surface, nothing to cling to. It shines out in its own right and mirrors nothing but its own reflection.

Since most human beings are not living in such a state, it is difficult to convince them that it is possible. What is even more difficult is to recognize that this state signifies the beginning, not the end of something. Once the individual has popped out onto the field of uniform time, it is only then that he or she can crack the modified formations of reality that heretofore were the only areas of life that were known. To live as a truly multidimensional person, all of the avenues of response that relate to life as we know it must be doffed. There is no reason to suppose that an individual who has cracked this field of absolute time is human in a conventional sense any longer. This is because humanity itself is composed of its relationship to a fixed state of time reference. Once the individual pushes past what is conventionally thought of as human, then the range of possibility for evolution increases incrementally.

The mathematical expression of time with respect to this subjective reality can be described on the basis of algorithms. These patterns form the backdrop for the coming together of seemingly opposite variables, which when examined more closely have many points of similarity. The mathematical model illustrates clearly how diverse viewpoints in the temporal spiral can be delimited or entertained from seemingly opposite vantage points. This mirrors the documentation of time as a metaphorical union between individual consciousness and absolute awareness. It is a dot in the playing field of perception.

When one lives in the category of complete temporal recognition and leaves the field of opposites, there are no opposing points of view to block the spatial documentation of free space. Therefore, the algorithmic expression of time at this point involves the relationship of matter, motion, and distance. When time leaves the circle of accustomed reference, motion is speeded up. This is why we say that time and motion are relative to distance. Since motion is speeded up, time slows down and distance becomes nominal.

Noncategorical Time

Noncategorical time is viewable from any forward or backward reference point. This view of time is nonreferential in its essence but staged or referenced in accordance with the psychological state of the individual. Time is masked or occluded, creating the effect of feeling that one is awake to the senses rather than pulled back into the absolute. Algorithmic time, which describes time in terms of distance, speed, and motion, may be contrasted to the more fixed state in which we often live. The two cross, offering the viewer a dual perspective through which the witnessing or bridging of temporal reference comes about. Time is foreshortened through psychological response.

In the algorithmic view, distance, being an outgrowth of motion, is no longer seen as an obstacle to travel. The individual pushes past the range of distance and essentially trips over the quanta of light/time that make up conjectured space. One goes into a type of free-fall that hurtles one over the boundaries of the absolute. This state of mirrored time affords one the opportunity to become concurrent with the time bands as they express themselves directly. Personal relationship no longer becomes limited by the characteristics of relative time but expands so as to open up the range of possibility inherent in emotional currency. There is an incremental slip into a permanent experience of goodwill. The concurrent accumulation of time causes everyone associated with a particular space/time instance to feel safely caressed by the melody of free space. The tendency towards conflict in the face of opposites is greatly softened.

When time opens into its own framework, it becomes a categorical expression of opposites. Time works both doors at once, moving from referential to infinite continuously. This is what leads to the possibility of governing or gardening time. Races that utilize natural time gardens as an expression of their individual sovereignty do so because they are no longer bound by event streams as a psychological medium of response. They can actually grow the time intervals necessary for particular states of response, activity, or union. Such beings live in a type of ongoing interaction with the Godhead, which leads them to a synchronicity of being, beyond the recognition of any one particular set of circumstances. This means that all that appears to be opposite is brought into balance and dualism ceases. The mechanics of this psychological and physical state lead to a type of temporal immortality. The individual is not bound by any physical or chemical aging process, but leaps the bounds of such a dualistic interval and lives independently.

Although this may seem impossible to some, there are beings that have already achieved this possibility. They are living an immortal and nonreferential life because they have split the boundaries of time completely. Such beings exist in their own point of reference and encapsulate in physical form only as a means of getting around the universe. They do not have any real reason for incarnation, as their consciousness does not live in the plane of opposites. Having recognized the eternal truth of time, they can live freely for the purpose of self-exploration and union with God. Such union is not an immediate process as the Godhead has myriad forms and circumstances.

Playing in the Field of the Gods

To play in the field of the gods is to reach into a state of infinite possibilities and eventualities. The being that has reached such a state is fearless in his or her pursuit of these eventualities. These are not stories or false imprints of consciousness; they are actual intermechanical consciousness scenarios about the fabric of reality itself. The individual moves in the machine of reality rather than constructing personal motivational parables that he or she must draw out in order to create material form.

Once one is living in this pulsing, rhythmic dialogue with the absolute, the ability to come to terms with one's identity becomes commonplace. One can still understand personal identity but is no longer bound by any of its myriad traps. This interdimensional intelligence is not human nor is it non-human. Even the definition of such a state is no longer sufficient to describe the avenues that such a being can pursue. Of course, the gender differential is not maintained either, as this is simply an expression of the dualistic relationship between matter and time. Since the algorithmic expression of pure gender is really the interface between light and heat, the relationship of masculine to feminine is no longer relevant. Essentially, the masculine or feminine guise is created through the formation of sight, sound, taste, and smell, which are the senses that create subjective psychological language. These senses crystallize into what is thought of as sexual differentiation. However, as consciousness marries itself, these differences become less acute until they are in fact no longer apparent.

The possibility of becoming twins with the infinite exists here. One could say that the individual is really no longer just a one or a two or even a three or a four. The individual is able to cut itself apart and become simultaneously generated in many dimensional vehicles at once. Some of these may be opaque forms while others are more translucent or opulent in their splendor. This interdimensional intelligence is able to transmit packages of information to less developed life forms and to function as a type of message center for consciousness. Such lifeforms are not locatable, nor are they nonlocatable. They exist in a type of interdimensional ring-pass-not that allows them to function independently or collectively as needed.

The reality of a timeless existence, though it may seem out of the ordinary, is common throughout the multiverse. It is in fact more common than uncommon. Those species that are bound in form, such as those of the human kind, are less populous than those that are not. This is because the binding influence of human birth is actually a condition formulated so that interdimensional beings can experience a limited expanse of space/time. To live in a fixed state of time has its advantages. There are many things to be learned from this state. The greatest is compassion. This fixed condition is meant to increase understanding of how beings will relate to one another when there is no escape. They cannot leave, except through physical death, which by its nature is abhorrent to those beings that view themselves as bound by form.

This experiment in human encapsulation goes back many millions of years in Earth's history. It is now coming to a close. There will be many beings that in the years to come will be returning to their natural, immortal, and timeless state. Such incarnation as we see now will gradually become a thing of the past. This is not something that is being willed by the human beings themselves; it is the will of God.

When individuals are bound one to the other in a limited state they learn to understand their imprisonment and grow to recognize the beauty of all they behold. They come to reason that their circumstances are not unlike other beings and they become sympathetic to the causes that these beings express. However, once these beings recognize themselves as unified expressions of the same stuff, the same consciousness requirements, then a shift takes place. Time no longer matters and incarnation is in a sense complete. Many, many beings are now waking up to a more infinite state, bringing about a timeshift. This will be a true interdimensional gate through which the human race will not return.

3.1.2
time the unifier

Raising the Threshold of Change

ime is the unifying principle in relationship to consciousness. It retains its figurative uniformity throughout the constructs that manifest material reality. Time raises the threshold of change by breaking the patterns of relative existence. Time unites the capacitance of relative experience with the qualifying trends of the absolute. A change in capacitance implies a change in tempo, speed, or motion.

Capacitance is adjusted to the point where the directionality of the time wave becomes uniform. The capacitance stretches or breaks open over the wave, reflecting the absolute ability of time to return to its full measure of uniformity. This quality of time as a unifier is the essential component that supports the elasticity of the time/matter continuum. The mind of the Godhead brings about this unifying influence. The time breaks are given a forward pitch that heaves them directly out of the absolute. The time/matter interface comes in contact with this pure, forward-thrusting movement, coupled with the advancement of matter as it manifests.

The Forward Drive of Matter

Matter is a congealed aspect of the configuration of time. Time is the essential ingredient for matter to become dominant in the field of reality. The capacitance of time is the vehicle whereby the randomized values of consciousness are pulled or thrust into uniformity. This elasticity of time provides the backdrop for matter to manifest. Time couples with the advancement of matter.

Matter forms through the forward drive of the time breaks. As a congealed aspect of the time configuration, matter is capacitated through the breath or inhalation of the time/matter structures. The speed and rate of the time chords and their distance one to another is coherent, even if the relevant stationing of the time breaks is not always uniform.

Time and motion are figurative players in the realm of the absolute. Once time emerges from the realm of the Godhead in an initial unifying thrust, the lords who govern time randomize and polarize the essential components as they spring boldly out of the absolute. Time is then compartmentalized by these beings that have the power to maintain the internal sweep necessary for full domination and coherence.

The capacitance of time is governed by frequency ratios that are the "heirs apparent" of the time lords. These frequency ratios are the mathematical determinants of how time will be spread into each and every dimensional sphere. The qualitative movement of time into a dimensional sandwich, or layering, causes the different strata of reality to fold back on themselves to create the thrust for full dimensional experience. Since time is essentially uniform at the outset, how is it possible that the dimensional occurrence is so evenly spread?

The answer to this question lies in the power of creation itself. The absolute creates the drive that heaves the time/matter complex out of its underbelly and regulates how time functions in each dimensional zone. This process is governed by beings capable of understanding its merits. The relationship of the dimensional substructures is not random but highly synchronized. This is why it is not so easy to jump or hop from one dimensional apex to another. The feeling of being locked into the time/dimensional sphere to which one has been birthed is not a coincidence. It is maintained through the gauged capacitance of ordained beings that are responsible magistrates for this process.

The dimensional intelligences who serve these orders are all chosen prior to incarnation through the development of ranges of influence which can be called the realm of the gods. This is not a figurative or imaginative domain, but is essentially the impulse of consciousness as it arises directly from the Godhead that creates, destroys, and multiplies consciousness into its multifarious forms. The unifiers are the celestial beings who become the governors or charioteers of this influence. The time lords parry or fence their way through the dominant structures that are locatable, and develop systems of elocution that permit the carrier waves of consciousness to randomize themselves in the downsweep.

Flexibility of Time Travel

Time travel is made possible by the astonishing standardization of dimensional structures in all spheres of influence. Because the rate of polarization of the dimensional structures is so highly flexible, the dimensional ascertainment of where the structures are located is always provable and easily maintained. This allows the time traveler to leap or circumambulate around and through the gates or barriers that separate the different domains of reality from each other. The dimensional traveler is always one who is knowledgeable about the rate of flux through these domains, and maintains an eye for the sharp refinement of the time values as they appear fluidly to develop. It is not possible for the dimensional traveler to lose his or her way because the gates to these different dimensional outposts are mathematically verifiable.

The time lords prevent premature penetration or puncturing of the belts that surround the dimensional spheres, and cleanse the area around them so that the purity of consciousness is maintained. The synchronicity of events and their pure randomization is governed directly by this cleansing of the laws of possibility as they are grounded in each dimensional sphere. The fluid organization of these structures is uniformly maintained. In order for the guardians of each sphere to perform their tasks correctly, travelers who hasten to engage in interdimensional experience must first ask permission. They should not hastily enter into areas where they lack expertise.

All of the time breaks form a fluid chain of command from one set of event structures to another. In the organization of reality, one sees event structures coming and going in what seems to be a full sweep of randomization, even as the coincidental values of consciousness are maintained. The event structures thrust themselves onto the surface value of consciousness, creating an interwoven, light-bearing reality that gives rise to a myriad of projectable lifeforms. Lifeforms themselves have no real jurisdiction in the capacitance of time. They act more like rats in a maze governed by the celestial forces than like creators of these forces. It is only when one rises to the level where all of the dimensional transparencies are revealed that one is capable of actually creating a pathway through the maze.

Developing Ranges of Influence

Dimensional structures are playgrounds for the absolute. Beings that enter into these structures form event sequences governed by their divine intelligence. These playgrounds are full of the imaginative effort of these countless divine beings, who weave the substructure of time around the event sequences and manifest objects.

This does not make the matter of living less serious nor does it limit the matter of creating reality to simply a few celestial entities. Playing with the building blocks of time is the destiny of every sentient being. The fluidity of time is dependent on the uniformity of consciousness, and as beings strive for this uniformity there is a marriage between mortal and celestial influences.

The development of ranges of influence is categorized through the organization of dimensional structures. This defines material reality. Materialization is based both on the pure value of time as it reveals itself and the interplay of consciousness as it breaks open around and through the field of time. Consciousness derives meaning from the circumstances around it. This is why consciousness can maintain the fluidity of being.

Matter and consciousness are perfected through the influence of sentient concordance. The perfection of matter is the reason why dimensional influences are so important. Matter and consciousness develop as a team, causing sentient influences to develop the underlying perception of how reality is to be constructed. The ardent strategists of reality are the sentient manifestations of being. Sentient beings cause matter to become locatable in each parallel dimension. The dimensions are layered, structural influences in which many forms of sentient life come into play.

The Godhead does not view these dimensional formulations in a hierarchical way; rather, the Godhead searches out the purest refinement of its own mathematical reference points to develop the determination of how matter will be constructed. The Godhead does not see one form of life as superior over another. It offers each being its right to be organized within its own dimensional sphere. Creation brings about the influence of change, prohibiting one aspect of consciousness to be dominant over the other.

Then how is it that different forms of life become aggressively capable of interfering with this plan? The answer to this lies in the coalescence of the time variables themselves. Since the Godhead offers the free-will determination of how its own structures will be built or torn down, it is up to the sentient beings themselves to limit or define their boundaries. Since these beings become aggressive through a misunderstanding of how scarcity or abundance is to be delineated, they try to control or dominate their sphere of influence. Of course, this causes imbalance and puts the components of reality into a state of flux that limits the powers of creation from performing the magisterial tasks necessary for unification. This cannot be helped, however, because it is in this struggle for uniformity, which apparently is interfered with by these ranges of intelligence, that the pure time variables make their mark.

The Switch of Time into Sentience

Time becomes randomized through the development of sentience. Sentience is always capable of steering clear of any point of bias. However, in the end, unification is inevitable. The switch towards unification in each dimensional sphere happens when the sentient beings who are living in that sphere have a desire to be governed by the pure intelligence by which they were founded. Then a timeshift or change in the lesson plan is assured.

The foundation of dimensional memory always adheres to the initial forms that constructed it. The initial forms—the time lords or quadrants of information that have been given directly from the center of intelligence itself—will always randomize, synchronize, and then break open again. When one learns to actually travel through the dimensional corridors, one becomes perceptually sensitive to all of the waves or perturbations in the field mechanics of the atmosphere. One can actually smell, taste, and touch the fields of time. These fields are not abstract; they are fluid and not randomizable by any particular strain of influence that is not meritorious to the entire creation.

The time traveler does not operate outside of his or her dimensional experience. Instead, he or she becomes cognizant of how this dimensional experience is being defined and essentially organizes intelligence in such a way that all of the dimensional influences can now be lined up to cause a trip in the switch. The subjective unification of time is the precursor to the dimensional wrap in which the individual is able to define his or her time sense in relationship to a purely internal barometer. The mandate to know where one is in response to change in the interval management of time is bound not to the circumstance of the dimensional sphere, but ultimately to the individual's pure awareness alone.

3.1.3
universal time

The Celestial Laws that Govern Time

Universal time is the calibrator of multidimensional reality. It forms both a subjective and objective unit of measure for how reality is to be shaped. Time is reckoned on the basis of the internal perception of the species and not purely through an abstract sense of reason. Celestial objects form a window into the time requirements that they represent. These universal requirements are governed by celestial laws that occur simultaneously in all levels of existence. Time and consciousness appear in the environment of celestial objects for the purpose of clarifying the role these objects are apt to play in their spatial surroundings.

Celestial bodies configure their appearance on the basis of light, sound, and color. These variables are considered to be their "chronal mechanics," referring both to the synchronization of color and its effective role as a medium of universal signature. Planetary objects play in the field of color, creating representation for the space/time variables that will define their dimensional status. It is logical to assume therefore that each planetary player will develop its own synchrobiotic resonance, dancing in the field of time in the way that it sees fit for its own evolutionary role. This develops a very unique flavor or time signature that is translinear in its character, action, and perception.

In the study of harmonics we find that celestial objects develop a pitch or tone that is the significator not only for their orbital range but also the length, breadth, and speed of their trajectory in space/time. Celestial objects travel not only in linear terms but develop a type of cradled phenomenon in which they rock themselves into different strata of space/time through the essential causality of their motivation as spatial players. Space/time witnesses the birth of celestial objects, viewing their heaving and sighing actions. The breath of planets, galaxies, and stars is represented by a cataclysmic dance of collective physical momentum.

Space/time is a universal player in the dance of the astronomical world, and also plays a part in the characterization of this dance. The mannerisms that time exhibits are the avenue whereby celestial objects define and recognize their internal and external motion. These idiosyncratic movements of time are like flags in the wind progressing across the space/time field. They may be seen as banners that appear on the horizon of time as it breaks through the dimensional barriers. Celestial objects also appear on the horizon and develop synchronization with the time banners they represent. The constant change in the pulse or rhythm of celestial objects as they move through pure time develops a format that can be simultaneously solid or representational as well as subjectively symbolic. Thus one can experience the wrap that time projects as modeling a planetary body or simply as a forecast in consciousness of what will eventually develop from the realm of the absolute.

The Breath of Celestial Objects

Celestial objects breathe because this is the process whereby they achieve recognition of their place in the space/time map. They project both longitudinal and latitudinal awareness. They sense the state of those trajectories that map their influence, and they learn to sensitize themselves to the array of special objects that form within their reach. These include planetary-based asteroid belts and the formation of crystalline structures. These structures develop due to the web-like method of bonding that they acquire as they move in regions surrounding "cold space." This is space where cold does not refer to temperature but to the character of time as frozen within it.

The motion of celestial objects governs the flow of translinear consciousness. Objects in the space/time continuum retrieve information by analyzing the event sequences that are fed to them. They are able to synthesize the vast amount of data that is placed in their reach and formulate the strategies of evolutionary function that will form the basis for multitemporal civilizations. A cultural exchange is established on the basis of these information retrieval systems that exist in the collective consciousness of civilizations. This is how civilizations can communicate across vast galactic regions and develop synchronicities of facial characteristics, cultural mores, and universal holography.

On our own planet, one could use the example of ancient Rome and the city of New York. A space/time traveler, examining the cultural and temporal characteristics of the two cities, would be able to find similarities in patterns of existence and frames of reference that would speak to a type of transtemporal pollinization. One could invest buildings, styles of water storage, and statues or objects with a particular sentimental meaning that would register through both worlds simultaneously. This is how one time bed magically crosses over to another. The features of culture and history do not simply weave across a distance of linear space/time, but actually are homogenous, interlinking like fields of flowers within the given temporal landscape they are seeking to represent. Time waxes and wanes from one set of variables to another, making present and past fuse and collapse in a kaleidoscopic effort to make time completely simultaneous. The present becomes a vehicle whereby all that is meets all that was.

This is why, in the great imagination of poets and artists from different planetary constituencies, one sees that the array of understanding of what it means to be fully alive in the face of God does not really change shape over the millennia. The relationship of the particular species to the formation of time never changes and is completely eternal. What does change is the structural language whereby such time values are expressed and internalized by a given race or subculture.

The motion of celestial objects defines and in some cases deters the formation of particular civilizations or species. Not merely a spatial representation, this idea of motion or movement creates a picture of change that becomes apparent once the civilization becomes an expressed value. Celestial bodies do not merely create a stamp of uniformity upon their nearest spatial cousins, they actually zoom in on their range of motion, providing a lens or scope of vision whereby civilizations can concur or collapse. Each civilization is a tribute to the celestial body upon which it finds itself.

Sentient beings live and breathe through the development of specialized time sequences that define their sense of honor, conduct, and speed of development. When one sees a civilization that has not conducted itself in what we might think of as a civilized manner, it is simply expressing a lesser variation of the time seeds that were the nascent representation of its development. Civilizations are seeded through the vehicle of time and betray their characteristics accordingly. Sentient beings pose a challenge to the celestial bodies that govern them. Sentient beings do not like to be toyed with. They wish to create their own style of functioning through the category of free will, but in their desire for autonomy they often leave behind the essential blueprint that the Godforce has designed. They become subject to their own childish whims and leave the will of the Father/Mother at the door of creation. For a sentient being to become truly wise, he or she must learn to utilize the specialized temporal structures that have been made available through the universal mathematical symbology laid down by the Godhead. It is only through this quality of subtle interpretation that intelligence can be fostered.

Birthing through the Field of Opposites

Time emerges both from the realm of unitive symbology and from the understanding that creation is birthed through the field of opposites. Life poses challenges and creation meets them. Through the concept of fractionization, we recognize that time prismatically binds itself to different valuations of itself, stressing different breakfronts of cognition in its quest to establish reality. Time accomplishes a dialogue with the many intelligent species it governs through this prismatic interlay, which gives individuals the opportunity to develop their own point of view in relationship to their subjective reality. Although event structures appear randomly, they are locked in through objective reference points that act as a kind of point/counterpoint in the musical epilogue of existence. Series of events present themselves as ribboned surfaces of existence that form boundaries in the space/time continuum. Through these colored ribbons, light, shading, and points of reference are given breadth and freedom.

One can see this variegated shading in each step of creation as it forms the mountaintops, valleys, and estuaries that define and shape our world. Planetary features occur as signposts to the time lords, forming the "valhallas" whereby they percolate their ambitions and concerns. This is why many civilizations view planetary features as homes for the gods or angels that govern them.

Mankind is a multitemporal, multispatial race, built upon many seed races that have been stocked here over millennia. We are therefore neither fully human nor fully divine, but a kind of crossbred configuration of beings. Our divinity is seen in our finest qualities: our ability to focus, to define, to understand, to synthesize, and to love. Our humanity is also something we can be proud of, but it is not entirely based on any one particular set of human origins. We are an amalgam of temporal reference points that have been stacked so as to vibrationally resonate or synchronize with the frame of reference that God has laid down in our sphere. We are the product of time as well as the product of space.

Since we are thoroughly tied to the celestial colorations, we are also infinitely capable of utilizing them for the restoration of creation. We can utilize the light/temporal language that has been given us to restore the former beauty and efficacy of the planet. The bedrock of this understanding is that the celestial bodies of local origin—the moon, the stars, the sun—are forces in a type of interplanetary clockwork that govern our understanding of who we are and what it is possible to become.

The true clock of Man is essentially both lunar and solar. The lunar value creates the flow of the tides and makes man susceptible to consecrated emotional states developed by the planetary bodies as a type of smokescreen for the absolute awareness enveloping them. Man is a temporal host for lunar intelligence, alighting on the field of the one moon. The visible moon is such a strong celestial representation for mankind, functioning as a frame of reference for understanding where Man is in relationship to time and how he will accomplish his dance to uniformity. In addition, there are many spheres of influence unseen by Man that help him to recognize where he is in relationship to transtemporal space.

The Concepts of Male and Female

One cannot say how the concepts of male and female have been developed. This universal mystery, connected to celestial intelligence, appears to be essentially arbitrary. One encounters species that are both male and female and every gradation in between. Celestial objects also manifest the characteristics of male and female as god-bodies with both subjective and objective forms. They take on the guise of male or female, solar or lunar, for the express purpose of guiding civilizations into a framework of understanding about the push/pull of unified objective reality. The power of the feminine is that it encourages the propulsion of unified intelligence into the hub or core of matter, offering matter the possibility of uniform dimensionality without the differentiation that the pure masculine principle might produce.

The punctuality of celestial forms determines the timing whereby each creature will enter into embodiment, which influences the decision of sex. The flow of creation towards the feminine is a slower, more gracefully timed determination. The flow towards the masculine is quicker, more expedient, direct, and sharp. When celestial intelligence is in the process of determining the sex of a creature, a clearly delineated choice is not always made ahead of time. The individual soul will lean more steadily in one direction or another in the case of beings that are clearly sex-differentiated, but will be more of an amalgam in cases where they are not. The celestial or soul body always remains fairly fluid and predominates over the personality even during adulthood. When the individual returns to the identity of the soul, the extrapolation of the personal identity is no longer so pronounced.

Since individuals who are allied with the flow of time often synchronize themselves through the solar principle, the sun or suns that surround an inhabited planet offer the value of juxtaposition of opposites. They create the flow or meaning of a binary, dualistic civilization, which must increase its influence by developing synchrony and fully radiated harmonization. Things that are out of balance must seek their balance.

On the other hand, things that are balanced are sure to fall away from their celestial midpoint. The crises found in celestial civilizations always revolve around the pursuit of more or less masculine or feminine causes. The array of time values is constructed to prevent or enhance the formation of opposites. From the standpoint of coequal gender, it is a relationship that is universal and continuous. It actually forms the backdrop for the interplay of time and its relationship to human civilization.

How is it that time can become fatherly to one set of variables and motherly towards another? In the transmutation of meaning of celestial objects, there is a birthing of uniformity that precedes the development of either the mother or father principle. Time in its essence is neither, but instead is a system that develops synchronization of these apparent variables and gives them fluid transport onto the field of events and civilizations. Time ripens according to both the contribution of mother and father in the flow of destiny. Since time and the Mother and time and the Father are essentially one voice, then consciousness, which is the outgrowth of time, will also stand as one voice with respect to the field of sexuality.

Time crystallizes the knower, the seeker in the individual, and causes him or her to develop a sensitivity towards one gender spread or another. Since this is true, most individuals find themselves to be a fluid combination of the strokes of luck or chance that developed at the time of conception and later through their gestational cycle. They are color-coded, advanced sequences of information that are delineated through gender speciation but are by no means limited by them. It is only the cultural imposition of boundaries that makes the sexual differentiation more desirable or problematic.

The Genealogy of Time and Consciousness

Time and consciousness lend their synchronistic values to the sequencing of gestation. The mother, who is giving rise to the field of birth, is apt to feel that during her gestational period she is more partial to one sex or another for her child. This is perfectly natural, because, in fact, no human being is really just one sex. He or she is a system of sexual cues that determine the origination of certain temporal impulses and help to develop the nervous system in a manner that makes familiar the system of standardization of divine intelligence. There is no right or wrong when it comes to such development, but rather it is the preference of Mother/Father God for its own formation that creates a leaning towards one sexual expression or another. The timing of light, color, and sound in the fetal encounter plays a large role in this favorable attitude and makes the individual develop along one line or another.

Homobiotic species, or those that we would perceive in the family of the human, behave similarly in that they have characteristics of generosity, thoughtfulness, persuasiveness, and ingenuity that set them apart. They derive pleasure in social relationships and have a particular partiality to the use of the mind for the purpose of entertainment, adventure, and even dogmatism. The purpose of sexual differentiation in humans, from a psychosocial point of view, is to create an interplay of these characteristics that allows us to debate our faults, enhance our strengths, and develop a flexibility of spirit necessary for higher levels of spiritual advancement. It is a parry of the wills that leaves the soul available for more perfected levels of unification in its full maturity.

Species in all walks of existence display their plumage through the expansion of color-coded symbolic gestures that give rise to mating and the dispersion of genetic material through changes in atmospheric conditions over the course of earth's history. All species utilize color and sound for this purpose, and human beings are no exception. They do so not simply through clothing or outer adornment, but through "speeches" carried on through spectral luminosity in the auric bodies. Male and female consorts derive elaborate garments of color that signify their relationship to each other as well as the world of form surrounding them. These speeches or gestures form the backdrop for courtship, whether it be hourly in duration or throughout an entire lifetime. Individuals develop bonds of attraction that create the mechanics of auditory language and gestural attraction, which can be standardized and disseminated as a procreative tool in the perpetuation of human life.

The standardization of forces in the direction of time, consciousness, and gender speciation is governed through the language of the brain and central nervous system. Those individuals who possess significant arrays of one set of gender breakfronts over another become known as a boy or girl. However, this speciation is more dependent on the concept of time and awareness than it is on any cultural norm for behavior or adjunct operating mechanics. Men and women become gender speciated through their ingestion of particular sequences of time stored as data in the central nervous system. They spill out in the embryonic state to develop the "transistors" that make it possible for the embryo to communicate in the womb of the mother. Gender speciation is a result of the particular communications highway developed umbilically. Gender choice is not made on the basis of the soul's volition or jurisdiction in the field of incarnation. The soul does not choose its nature as to whether it is male or female, but rather its flow of temporal mechanics begins to lean in the direction of one or another matrix.

The array of thought in an embryo does not begin until approximately the eighth month of gestation. The gender speciation, from the perspective of internal intelligence, does not really come to pass until that time. The outer body or covering of the soul is not really a determinant of how he or she will feel on the inside. The feeling of gender is created through bonding of the soul to the body, imparting a sense of wonder and awe at its own magnificent form. The experience of witnessing the body is akin to visiting a beautiful woods or seacoast for the first time. One experiences the pleasure and wonder of the incarnation but retains a detached point of view that maintains a bridge between subject and object. The transverse flow of the soul through time from one set of speciate memories to another is governed by this sense of bliss. One returns to that which is comfortable, attainable, and familiar, but recognizes that the seed of change is ripened through an odyssey of fluid sexual parity.

3.1.4
the evolution of parallel interdimensional reality

The Rhythm of Time

time and consciousness compose the base of the field of reality, yet they can also exist independently from it. This causes our personal process to be multitiered and unlimited. The archetypes that we engender in the course of our psychological life are constructed from the interface between time and the choice points it presents. We become centered in a different stream or rhythm of time that awakens us to deeper and deeper levels of being. We are strengthened by our knowing and infused with the character of this realization.

Through the characterization of each given choice point, parallel tiers of information open up and we can peek through them to the other side. Each choice point is surrounded by a field of energy that could be termed biotechnological in nature, in that it is both organic and technically engineered to permit full temporal fluidity. The spatial dynamics of the time continuum lead to the flowering of alternate worlds or civilizations within the context of what we normally perceive. Alternate worlds are nested in the fabric of our everyday experience, arising directly from the elasticity of time. At each given point of arising, time shifts or alters the content of possibility. Streams of archetypal information present themselves, often poking at a particular theme or rhythm. We become part of the wave, the dance, the epicenter of time, and are struck by the synchronicity. As we have that moment of pure realization, time is altered, changed, brought to a different base. The parallels of determination have taken hold.

Time rules when it comes to the interloping of matter with consciousness. Time spins out mandates to the collective consciousness. These mandates restore or unwrap the particular time perspectives in which nature or pure organization plays a part. Time skips or curves around the inexact stations that present themselves, rather than interloping continuously through the many avenues of juxtaposition. The flow of matter through the time breaks creates waves or perturbations in the previously impervious or rock-solid foundation in which the time avenues have been based.

To upset the foundation of time, one must actually decrystallize the matrix in which time has played its origination. Since time and space are directly in opposition to one another when it comes to pure organization or foundational relationships, time and space must come of age together in order to create a parallel dimensional field or time break within a precise window of continuum. The tourniquet that is created when matter and time are squeezed through the doorway of a particular life event sequence is not easy to undo, nor should it be. The disposition of parallel gates of existence is purposely placed at equidistant intervals from each other in order to prevent purges of fluid time/matter from leaking from one continuum or energetic field to the other. This safeguard prevents the flow of identity from one archetypal stream to the other and prevents the confusion of identity and time/space unification that would be the result.

Seeding Dimensional Travel

Parallel dimensional travel involves the seeding of a consciousness with all of the necessary parameters that would shift the attention from the locus-centered to the all-encompassing now. There is a tendency for those interested in time-centered dialogue to break this ring-pass-not or seal. This is not to be recommended lightly because the parallel influx of time-dimensional material without the proper caution to understand and maintain its usage is very costly to those who enter into this domain.

The job of the time lords is to keep these seals in place so that those who wish to enter into parallel dimensional fields have the opportunity to view information in a more organized and safe fashion. The dominant theory that time is essentially made anew through the rapid introduction of parallel temporal data is incomplete. This is because the time traveler must recognize that it is through the portal of his or her own awareness that all of the understanding of personal or subjective time sequences will be addressed. There is no standing session of time, therefore, but rather a myriad of personal time bands stretched together sequentially to form the reality that is engendered by that framework of space/time and consciousness itself.

The study of parallel reality involves an understanding that all sentient beings exist simultaneously in various dimensions and were never limited except through their own imagination to think or feel otherwise. The perceived limitations are strictly psychological and biological in the sense that the degree of information necessary for the central processor of the brain to absorb and digest would be so overwhelming if there were not key limits placed on its usage and output.

As one's consciousness expands, the degree of uniformity between these dimensional gates is increased, and then, through the grace of purity of heart, one's consciousness can gain access to different avenues or parts of its own archetypal framework. This parallel perception enables the consciousness to leave the context of its limited or partially centered identity and come into a more cosmic or wholistic point of view. At this point in development, the evolution of a perspective of unity becomes self-evident. The individual no longer views the personality as the seat of reason, but instead becomes a merged identity, capable of altering the seat of reason through the correspondence of curved or parallel windows of pursuit that cause consciousness to be seeded directly from the absolute. Since the absolute level is never finite, but is constantly expanding its point of reference, the parallel statement of infinity is readily in view.

Parallel realities exist not as testing grounds for the psychology of the individual, but rather as frames of reference in which historical material relevant to the individual can be altered or retained, similar to the memory bank of a computer. These alternatives provide recognizable cues or signals that the individual's consciousness can utilize to give it a frame of reference through which it can create in its present context. These information bits are essential at all stages of life, down to the cellular or microcosmic levels. The parallel statements that are vested in the genetic superstructure of the individual give him or her the capacity to think. The whole process of thinking demands constant interplay between parallel archetypal chains.

The Biochemistry of Thought

Thinking is a biochemical process involving changes in the fluids that move nerve impulses from one part of the body to another. These liquid nerve impulses mix with the reservoir of blood proteins that move freely through the circulatory system. The brain, capturing both the liquidity of nerve movement and the propensity towards the creation of these blood aggregates, creates a complex communications highway with its own rhythm or pulse. These pulses of intelligence are communicated throughout the body, with particular attention paid to the chorus of the heart.

The brain and mind are synchronized through these parallel stations of information, which enter the nervous system and are rerouted through all of the "parallel ports" of the body. The body is a fluid retention field. It is based on memory, and must store information in great capacity to be able to function on a daily basis. This need of the body to ascertain parallel avenues of functioning at all times causes it to be a complex but very compact circuit with unlimited capacity for understanding or breathing new information into its tissue framework.

Parallel structures are derived through the interior balancing of the parts of the body with its whole. There are no coincidences when it comes to the routine maintenance of the body. Everything that happens is a result of the microcosmic planning committee at the basis of everything. The parallel shift from one stream of reference to the other maintains the shape, elasticity, and form of the body; otherwise it would simply collapse.

The standards that have been set to maintain the parallel reasoning of the brain and central nervous system do not allow for tampering in terms of breaking the seal on interdimensional identity matrices. This is because, were the individual to actually live simultaneous identity flows too rapidly, there would be a shattering of the avenues of perception that qualify and give amplitude to reason. Therefore, the parallel avenues are kept locked away until such time as the individual has the capacity to live in a more depersonalized or objective manner. Then, gradually, these doors are thrown open and the whole array of matter/time becomes more available and variegated.

In this situation, the individual can peek into the parallel reference points of his or her own situation and understand all of the implications and theoretical changes in vision that such choices would produce. The individual arrives at a state of awareness in which the choices or liquidities that are available in the awareness are capable of unifying completely. This state involves a complete change in the orientation of the individual from masking awareness to formulating awareness.

Temporal Cues to the Future

The God-recipient of clear, cogent, unified information forms a bridge with parallel perception in which he or she is able to cognize the form and shape of interrelated realities as they appear on the board of perception. In this new dialogue, the intelligence frames cues or reference points that give it an upcurve on the rate of synchronization between parallel points of view. This situation allows a dramatic increase in the degree of productivity and creative origination of the individual, as he or she is now capable of tapping what could be called the future or the wave of the new. After all, the future does not really exist from this fluid standpoint. The future is simply a derivation of the "now" or temporal cues from the moment of inception into the present. The future is an array of possibility that individuals execute within the context of their awareness.

All of the avenues of perception that are parallel to the play of language and artifact are now available. One is able to dialogue directly with the cues or imprints that exist in the dialectical avenues of the brain and central nervous system. In this situation, the stratification or interiorization of new ideas or information is left "ambular" so that all of the waves of information that arise are numerically opposite. When numbers stretch out over the flat surface of space/time, there is an ambulatory movement that allows these expressions to become randomized. With the advent of each successive curve or swing of consciousness, the value points or felt expressions of this dialogue become compellingly synchronized. The flux or rate of speed at which each of these expressions becomes intact is necessitated by the flow from one position in consciousness to the other.

Judgment of Right and Wrong

The encapsulated state creates movement, and out of this movement the rapid reflection of curved opposites is imposed. This is how reality maintains variety and objectivity, and eventually returns ably and willingly to its source. The function of parallel realities is to provide for the system whereby reality will be made real in light of the psychological state of its participants. Each possibility for solid reflection is an expression of the glory of its host. Without randomization and the adjunct system of curving, these ripened possibilities would never come alive. Reality without opposition would be static and void of creative spark.

The perceived effect of right and wrong, good or bad is based on the dialogue between paired opposites. This is formulated from the fundamental structure of seed appearances that underlies the entire strata of reality. When pairs interlock, they form a set of subcultures or formative dialogues which, when placed near each other, begin to form singular expressions that we would term good or bad. Judgment therefore is not simply based on psychological parameters but on the essence of reason. The placement of these pairs of opposites in the cultural or normative functioning of social structures creates the climate for philosophical or religious thought. However, from the perspective of consciousness, the explicit standard of logic is not directly assignable from the standpoint of reason.

Life fans out onto the field of opposites for the grand play rather than for any apparent psychological basis in feeling. When one systematically reengages the standard of opposition that is at the basis of thought, a new standard of reason emerges. This is based not on the creation of judgment but on felt opposition, and there is a sense of justice or rightness that emerges. The discussion of what to do and what options are available becomes completely unlimited. There is still an ethical structure, however, but it is based on the random identification of cloaked opposites from their packages in time and space and not on the beliefs or attributes of the awakened consciousness.

This situation causes the individual's intelligence to expand at an incredibly rapid rate. The individual sweeps the domain of his or her inner experience, recognizing cues or imprints along the way that will tap the expansion of consciousness from the outside in. The language structures decompress and there is an inner awakening of the mental centers that govern origination and psychospiritual development. The parallel portals of the mind are ripped open and one is able to express oneself telepathically with the capacity of a subtle auditory or imagistic light language.

This ability to express the information without verbal ideology allows the individual to intercede with the rapid impulse of intelligence as it is downloaded into the brain and central nervous system. When the individual no longer has to rely on the language centers for the fluid passage of relevant information, the archetypical or tribal origins of the life paths change. Then the ancestral documentation of information, which heretofore had been necessary for historical or archival organization, is no longer relevant.

The expansion of consciousness to the point in which the brain and central nervous system can act synchronously through their dimensional avenues is essential for the development of the species. But obviously this expansion cannot and should not be rushed. When the individual gradually awakens to this perception, the parameters for interpretation are also brought into play. One can witness the streams of information flooding the brain and become capable of interpreting that which is simultaneously being viewed. This interface between receptivity and translation must be developed gradually. The cues or imprints that cause one to derive sense or meaning out of the environment cannot be risked at the expense of parallel expansion. One directly orients oneself in the wave or continuum of information as it flows into the field of perception. One is then in the safe zone for the digestion of information via the nervous system.

The Parallel Ingestion of Information

Once the parallel ingestion of information is possible, all of the avenues that cause choice or gain in the wave are now in view. The individual locks in the given choices without concern for consequences, because the understanding of those consequences is built directly into the process of choice. There is no gap. All of the future curves or perceptions that make consciousness parallel are then capable of interlinking with the individual matrix.

When individuals are given the chance to become hookups for interdimensional wisdom, there is an expansion of the heart. The individual recognizes the potentialities of service and devotion that the heart brings to the randomization of fluid intermediary consciousness. The heart is the place where reason is softened and made pliable. The recognition of those impulses that will be most productive and enlivening to the individual is situated in the intelligence of the heart. The flow of language into the brain is a specialization of feeling that moves intelligence from one domain to another. The identification of where one goes in the arrangement of personal reality is influenced by the flow of event streams viewed as most precious. Reality is reconciled from two or three simultaneous event streams.

The individual does not really exist as a separate medium, but, through the heart, becomes "christed" in the spread of interdimensional relationship. He or she then can christen the arrival of strategic information and develop the parallel interest that will make choices more predictable and fruitful. Since the ensoulment of an individual into the body is done at many dimensional gates at once, the individual, as we have said, is always operating from many different points of reference simultaneously. However, in the more aware or conscious individual, the gates of memory have been stripped so that more of what is known to be essentially true or accurate in the context of that individual's soul stream can come online.

The process of awakening to the soul, or trans-strategic identity, is built into the fabric of the central nervous system when the individual has ripened to the fuller extent of the love- or heart-centered process. This is ideal. Unfortunately, there are those beings who awaken these centers without this ripening, and then the parallel gates of perception become simply another form of intellectual exercise. The devotional mindstream, from the Mother God, creates the linguistic pathways that allow the information to enter the central nervous system. As they become psychologically useful, they are sometimes interrupted or destroyed. There is then no moral or internal identification of "feeling truth" on the part of the individual.

This is in contrast to the ripening of devotion, which strengthens the qualities of poise, honor, and centrality of power that make it possible to realize God. With this felt truth in place, one is able to see that there is a God, a personal identity, and a fundamental angular perception that unites them in the centermost region of the spiritual heart.

3.1.5
the formation of universes

Creating a Time Continuum

the first concept to understand in the organization of a universe is that it is a time continuum. This means that all of the centrally located objects that form the backdrop for interior organization are pulled along a central axis or continuum that stretches the timebreaks to their maximum level. One could say that the universe is formed like taffy on a string, pulled or stretched almost to the breaking point of the continuum. Then all of the celestial objects are catapulted from the center of the time/mass curve so that that they will depict themselves randomly and coherently with respect to the mass point.

Since time and consciousness naturally create the advancement of star civilizations, each central star cluster is inherently magnanimous in developing the celestial objects within its grasp. The star cluster creates loop motions that throw the advancement of time from one region of galactic swirl to the other. The swirling, tugging, pulling formation of matter/time then hurls itself in the direction of greatest momentum or response.

Since time and consciousness develop simultaneously, celestial objects are like the children of the universe. They form objective reference points for the congealment of matter/time and are either "hot," which references them in the direction of maximum energetic development, or "cool," which means that they are older, more rigid forms given to possible breakup or streaking in the continuum. Since the celestial objects are themselves intelligent, they present light-encoded information to all of the balance points within the continuum that they serve. Celestial objects are inherently selfless in that they serve the intelligent civilizations in their influence without pause. On the other hand, they are selfish in the sense that they look towards their own development first and will throw off those civilizations or cultural influences that will directly retard their self-determination.

The manifestation of universal intelligence is based on the rapid adherence of celestial objects to a program of response that is built into the creation mechanics itself. When the energy/matter/time continuum begins to speed up, there are wave formations which essentially rocket the energy from one celestial curve to the other, much like the arms of a nuclear fusion reaction. In this curvature, the celestial matrix breaks off from its initial ground points and bends to fit the structure and function of the curve. The solidification of matter is based on the willingness of the celestial energies to coalesce around a true centerpoint. This mass centerpoint phenomenon holds true for all matter/time meeting points and forms the basis of past/future documentation as the energetic streams interpret incoming data.

The universes, which are multiple and in some cases infinite in scope, form the backdrop not only for sentience but for what we would term parasentience, or the elevated strata of intelligence that precedes the formation of life. The universes, whether singular or clustered together as banded radiative centers, are birthed on the basis of essential order or magnitude in the God formation. They are seeded by the God formation at different effervescent or saturated points of reference and are therefore aged based on the information they have been fed at their resting point.

Coparticipation with the Godforce

The Godforce is infinite in its ability to create and dominate the matrical platform of universal perception. It essentially births the universe into being all at once without attention to the effect that this birth will have on the Mother Intelligence surrounding it. As the universe matures, it is the Mother Intelligence that directs the formation of sentience and determines the degree to which it will become functionally participant in the intelligent life of that sector. This is why there are so many different types of paraintelligent lifeforms operating in the universal matrix and why, as they ripen, they come online gradually to enter into the transdimensional whirlpool that divests itself of its previous temporal markers and becomes accentuated as a new beginning.

The determination of how a universe will spring forth is based on how it is antecedently placed in the reaches of time. Time determines the degree of magnitude of the event streams and instructs them in their dimensional placement. The event streams appear as streaks or breaker points in the feed and they occur randomly. As the event streams are brought to the point of maturation due to the intercedence of the Mother Intelligence, they open themselves out to the internal environment and become capable of flowering into intelligent lifeforms.

The myriad sentient motivations of the universal intelligence are so hugely vast in scope that it is impossible to describe them, but the nature of intelligence is beyond anything the human mind could control or delimit. It is a matter of investigation for consciousness in its self-generating capacity to bring forward those lifeforms that are strategically capable of accomplishing the unified objective of the Godhead. This occurs essentially to bring about the rising of collective merit on the part of individuals and collective organisms to uplift the spiritual energies involved. Each parallel or concentric universe is a mirror of the other. They are crystallized investigations into the interior dynamics of consciousness from every conceivable point of view. There is no limit to the dimensional expression of intelligence and therefore no limit to the expansion of celestial awareness.

Universes spring up as backdrops for another aspect of celestial organization, which could be called celestial pools. These pools, which are not studied by present science, are actually time-centered backwaters for the universal intelligence to feed the formation of each parametrically aligned universe. They are the anchors whereby time formation can occur at the most rudimentary of levels. Time must incorporate these pools, forming the winds of time that create the environment out of which a universe forms. Rather than some explosion, as depicted by the theory of the Big Bang, these pools come together very gradually, forming the thrust or kick that produces the time current necessary for manifest creation.

As creation is both spiritual/etheric and physical/material, the celestial pools must function from both angles. When the arrays of light crystallize, the pools of time open up and create the proper currents for the formation of bright sheaths of universal light which then determine the size, shape, and formation of star clusters. The vast twinkling array of light formations that compose the stars as we know them are actually light-encoded star delivery systems for categorical information about the nature of the universe itself. Since the universe is a vast educational library of information about the nature of reality, it is the job of the stars to edit, delete, and magnify the light intelligence that forms the basis for both material and nonmaterial reality.

Concentric Universes

The universes are concentric in the sense that the dominant or windowless universe forms an opaque or "darklight" picture in the spectral mass. As this darklight formation spreads itself continuously and finely over the environmental radiance, there is a "dawn" that occurs, much like the dawn of a star formation. This dawn is the radiant accruement of light apportionment throughout the star cluster, which signifies that a universal force is about to appear. A universe is essentially a celestial intelligence in its own right with a thought process that is emanatively directed from the Godlight itself. A universe thinks, feels, and reasons from the continued appearance of the time/matter constituents that enter its grasp. The universe chews on the food of the Godlight and, like a newly birthed babe, enters the radiance of the Celestial Mother for the purpose of information-gathering and the harboring of new vestigial civilizations.

Universes are made and destroyed constantly. There is no end to the annihilation or the continuation of the time matrix. This is because the living, breathing Godforce is itself solely infinite and vested with the power of continuous eternal creation. There can be no end to a universal construction, only a saturation point when the Godlight has reached its optimum peak. At this point, a type of thrust or kick occurs which stretches the time/matter feed beyond its breaking point and throws the universe into a new dimensional spin. Universes move from the eternal, vastly centered origins of the light continuum through their own internal momentum.

The movement aspect of the universal balance point is brought about through the particular arrays of consciousness that have presented themselves at the basis of that formation. Each universe is essentially a parlor for uniformity based on the knowledge that messages related to the formation of a particular intelligence will be necessary for the objectives of the Godforce in that region. This is why all of the intelligent formations within a given universe are precisely related. When one visits randomly the "blocks" in a particular star system, one finds that all of the intelligent lifeforms appear related in some way. They are vestigial integers of each other, sometimes resembling themselves both in outer appearance and inner character. A universe is composed of civilizations of various degrees of conscious uniformity and order. There really are no lesser or greater lifeforms in the mind of God, only different arrays of message units which transmit information necessary to the central intelligence of the Godhead.

Equality in the Mind of God

Since all beings are equal in the mind of God, the competition and enmity that arises among lifeforms is due to an essential misunderstanding of the value of life in all of its myriad attributes. Those individuals who have not yet learned to value the importance of shared experience must learn through the trials and tribulations of the more self-centered ego nature. Surprisingly, there are many civilizations that are trapped in this level of interaction, and they often are seen as clusters or bright points in a particular region of universal order. The civilization of Man is one of these. It is related to many other civilizations of a similar order of maturity and intelligence and is considered to be in an adolescent period of development.

This means that although humanoid species are very predominant in this section of the Galaxy, they are by no means the only species that present themselves. Nonhumanoid species are more likely to be paradimensional and are therefore not incarnated in the same manner as those that are inherently body-centered. Nonhuman lifeforms generally take the form of star children who are not truly bio-organic life/matter structures. The imprinting of different star races is done prior to their origination and is based on the necessity of study that is generated as the Godforce brings Light into full crystallization.

The universes are rotating pools of mass light with time continuums stretched around them like bright bands of paper. These shredded, continuous, open-ended circuits of light drape themselves over star clusters and present the time/matter ribbons that make up the backdrop for creation. The universe is filled with these ribbons, which are the time wrappers for creation/matter to formulate. Although individual star clusters will encounter these ribbons and work around them in some cases, they must usually encounter them in their search for the proper configuration of time that will build the planetary attributes they desire. Light and time work as a kind of tandem, randomized computer disk, stretching the light codes around the perimeter of each time pool and vesting it with the ability to form a given galactic region. These time/cluster centers are mapped through the development of parasymmetric programming, formed on the basis of linguistic symbology originating directly through the calibration of the Mother Intelligence.

Since light and sound form the backdrop for the mapping of interstellar pools, the universes maintain their continuity despite interference from many other streams of influence. There are in the continuum structures that exist outside of what we would consider to be the universe. These structures are so nondeterministic in scope that one could say that they are right out of the lips of the eternal. They are so complex in their derivation that is difficult to express their scope in human language. These structures are the paradimensional expressions of the Godforce, related to Its breath, life, and expansion. They precede the formation of universal modules, but also develop the mechanics whereby such universes would be born. They are, in effect, the cradle or epicenter of such universes, and exist in their own separate continuum.

There are intelligences that actually work with the magnification of light centers for the purpose of celestial creation. These intelligences limit the scope, size, and parameters of universal investigation, and also bring about changes in the degree of amplitude necessary in case of celestial calamity. Universal intelligences are the central organizing system for all light formations and create the time/matter basis for sentience. Sentience is really a power of magnitude rather than an aspect of pure reason. Sentience is at the basis of awakening, and even the celestial must awaken directly to its own Source.

3.1.6
the relationship of
time and matter

Characteristics of the God Intelligence

t ime and matter are coequals, as determined both by their connection to the God Intelligence and their fundamental interrelationship. The event sequences that spring up are related to the flow or felt value of time. The God Intelligence feeds this flow, permitting the time/matter sequences to develop independently. Time can be sharp, pulsing, exclusionary, and forceful, all of which are characteristics of the God Intelligence in its need for creative dynamism. Time can also be acquiescent, patient, fluid, and manageable, a nature that permits creative expression.

Matter forms from the underlying threshold of unification between the God Intelligence and time. Matter underwrites the proportional character of events, giving them substance, breadth, and perceptual color. To incorporate the time values evenly, with the necessary consistent makeup, time and matter must coordinate their focus, holding to the God Intelligence while simultaneously bringing forward their own original functionality.

To move easily from time as abstract, undifferentiated, and multilineal to matter as concrete, dormant, and dimensionally lean requires the intervention of the divine. The atmosphere that is produced gives rise to the possibility of sentience. As thinking is sustained through the flow of intelligence into the field of time/matter, our thoughts are emanations of the finely coalesced status that brings time into relationship with our physical bodies and our environment.

Time, in its desire to become independent, reaches out to matter to give it life. The Mother intelligence, which looks after the formation of matter, works to refine and smooth the way for time to meet on matter's terms. Time, because it is opaque in the form of matter, can be visible to the naked eye. Matter holds the field of time within it, and as such is solid or opaque as visibility demands. When time is held in the infinite, it is left in its most pure form. It cannot return to matter until matter feeds it. Time is interdependent with matter and as such must wait for its Mother, matter, to give it nourishment, sustenance, and meaning for its existence.

When time is perfectly coherent in its substructure and exists as a flow or sequence of data unto itself, then time can create its own "phonebook" in the address sequence of its own essential nature. Time is not something that can be found at any address, however; time must become developed through the consciousness of living things. To be alive is to know time and to utilize time for one's own reality.

The Inception of Matter

The spectral continuum is ripe with the interplay of time, as it cools from the stream of its volatile center, and matter, as it waits for time to come around again and again. The lively flow of matter as it expels time, and the seasoned patience of time as it waits for matter to come forth, reliably instate the valuable environment out of which the God Intelligence can make all living things. The active, creative, inceptionary power of the God Intelligence can be found in the archetypal function of the Divine Mother.

Time incorporates the substructure of matter within it as a child incorporates the value structure of the Mother. Inherent in time are all the codes, the bylaws, the rules of conduct that give matter the possibility of inherent form. Once time rules matter through its own outlook, it is no longer the child. It becomes the friend of matter and looks out for its well-being. Time must exist interdependently with matter because as a vehicle for the assemblage of unified creation, it has a purpose, a reason for being.

Each step of the way is a means whereby matter and time can befriend one another. They exist side by side for a given stretch of eternity and then marry together for the express purpose of giving events their proper sequentiation. When events unify for the purpose of historical reference, there is usually a timing to this. Events do not occur in and of themselves. They are rolled on the board of time, shaped, given substance and merit, and then spilled out again, over and over. Their shape, timing, texture, and substance are always controlled by time, but not in an overbearing way. Time always consults its Mother before making any decisions. Time decides how to express itself to form an event sequence, and then twirls around, spinning its web into the interface between the event sequence and matter itself. Thereby, the time/matter interface becomes complete.

The flow of time from one event sequence to another is determined by two factors: first, the repetition of time as it develops interlocutory event sequences, and second, the relationship of time to events as they arise. Time is interdependent with the event sequences that it gives rise to, and does not develop event sequences that are separate from its own natal flow. The event sequence "sits on the belly of time," meaning that the sequence is maintained whether or not time feeds it adequately. Once the event sequence is sprung, the time apportionment is not crucial. If it were, time would simply arise, develop an event matrix, and then return to its Source, without ever impairing or developing the event matrix as such. However, since time is an interdependent medium, it relies on the event sequence to spread itself over an historical interface.

Time forms crystals or matrical interlays of time/matter that are at once translucent and opaque. The translucent aspect is based on the reality that time, unhinged from its source, skips lightly over the realm of the unmanifest and creates a "magic box" whereby its proportional amplitude can be dealt with directly. It spins, twirls, and maintains its fairy character fluently throughout the space/time vault. On the other hand, once time finds its stasis, its semi-permanence, it links with the field of matter and begins to form a sandwich of matter/time that leads eventually to its fully opaque character. This is why it is possible for an event sequence to jump-start right at the brink of this configuration. Matter leans into time, creating the event patterning that makes order out of the chaos of infinity.

The Subswings of Time

Without the chorus of time present in matter, each separate voice would go off on its own. There would be no means of repairing the event sequences as they are strung about. Time becomes capable of repairing itself by creating interlocutory subsets or subswings of time that reach back and forth, making their way through the matter/time continuum and creating unification wherever they go. Without the movement of time into the form of matter there would be no creation, but of course time could exist independently of matter and so it does in the unmanifest creation.

The ancillary spread of time depends on two functions: first, reason, which allows time to decide what it must become, and second, intuition, which allows time to feel into its character and shape itself according to need. Thus time is both reasonable and feeling-centered. Time returns to the birth of its own creation by identifying event sequences, following them out to their ends, and then returning to its Source. The rounded character of time, flowing from end to middle and from middle to end in its infinite capacity, spins a web that is tangible to the field of matter. Creation forms the spiral shapes of galaxies, star systems, and universes in the bright center of this web, reversing duality by spinning out towards the center and perpetrating the reality of union.

The process whereby time becomes unified is the same as that by which consciousness achieves unification. The ordinary temporal continuum leans heavily on the field of consciousness as its means of organization and drive. Unification is central to the need of creation for independence and a sense of purposeful direction and outlook.

The Independence of Consciousness

Consciousness exists independently of Man or of any of his forms of creation. Consciousness is a vehicle for Man to achieve something that God has already wrought. There is no need for Man to achieve a state of consciousness, in that the state of consciousness inherent in Man is fashioned directly after God. What Man must do is to come into the flow of consciousness, to develop a taste for matter/mind independence, which allows him to be in the field of matter and also in the flow of time. Time is the vehicle whereby Man becomes interdependent with God and develops a taste for His consciousness. God and Man are one in time, and time exists a priori to Man in every sense.

God and Man are unified at the basis of creation. Man is held in the hands of God through the process of the congealment of time. Time holds Man at bay, creating the circumstances in which life arrangements can be made. The insurgence of matter into the backdrop of nothingness that provides the canvas for creation is produced through time witnessing its birth at the Source. Since God trusts Man to guide the footsteps of Nature to its completion, He insists that Man live up to the trusteeship of Nature that he has been given. Man cannot justify his existence simply through the arduous employment of Nature as a means to his own ends. Man must work towards freeing Nature from Her dependence on any particular objective or motive, and must free himself from dependence on God to correct ethical misconduct.

The freedom to exist as an independent being is given to Man for the purpose of maximum satisfaction. God asks Man to justify his own existence rather than depending on any outside force to do so. Why must God exist independently of Man if Man is already an expression of Him?

One might assume that He is simply playing with Man. This is not entirely the case. God needs Man to express the boundaries of time and show him that he is not alone in the universe. With the advent of Man, God has been given a primary picture window into His own essential nature. The inherent beauty of God shows itself in every form of creation, and time makes this possible.

Out of the radiant creation, time and matter become twins and live on to dwell in the house of God. Each breath of God teaches one the mechanism of the other. They understand one another and are not slaves to that understanding. This friendship develops all of the stages of matter from the absolute to the finite.

The concept that time has a skin, a framework, through which the lens of unified perception peeks out and reveals itself, is inherent in its process. Time creates ribbons or spirals, each of which is encapsulated in a type of celestial envelope. When one of these ribbons spills open, inside are all of the new time values waiting for incorporation into the time/matter interface. Time sheds its skin repeatedly, not because it is bored or tired with the configurations that have so recently presented themselves, but rather because each new avenue of perception invites a consummate originality.

The avenues whereby time can be shed are myriad and cannot be understood by the mind of Man. Time develops itself, curls back on its own nature, and gives rise to all of the outpourings of understanding that Man has in his possession. Why does time need a friend at all? Because time needs an avenue for expression, and matter simply delivers it. But time must become a sanctuary for matter, or matter will not receive it.

The Boundaries of the Ancients

The ancient civilizations on this planet that knew time directly did not rely on matter to tell them where they were or how old they were. These civilizations drew on time directly and thereby could travel in any direction within it. They were therefore not confined to their historical reference point. They could walk the bridge over the river of time and matter and create their own universes, their own understanding of what it meant to be alive. To be a vehicle for time in this interdimensional sense does not rob time of its divinity. Time is divine because it is so malleable and fluid, as is the nature of God. Patterned after the divine mind itself, time knows no real boundaries, and thus everything that one sees as real is essentially manmade and psychologically referenced. This is what is meant by maya. But maya is not harmful; it is playful. When one learns to play in the field of maya, then one can control the outpouring of time and go within it to develop an interdimensional portal into the fundamental laws of nature.

The reason that interdimensional travel in this sphere is so limited at the present has to do with the belief that matter is essentially solid and therefore immovable. One cannot travel in time without ripping apart this false solidity in the matter/time conduit. The realization that matter is at once both translucent and opaque gives one the sequence of events that can allow one to rule time. Interdimensional civilizations do not live by a clock; they live by the correlates of presupposed time that their minds represent within them. They do not have any mechanism of boundary-making other than the subswing of time itself.

To carry on with the message-making aspect of time, one must be free of any constraints on the level of mind or consciousness. To do this, the time traveler sheds his or her inherent reference point. In order to fly like a bird, one must have a system of tracking that takes one back to one's point of origin without mind being involved. The navigation necessary to travel through time is purely psychological. The mind must grow accustomed to weeding through the time garden and maintaining a sense of planting and flowering that gives time a sense of structure and beauty.

Non-Timebound Civilizations

Interdimensional civilizations are inherently capable of shape-shifting because their response to time is unified. They are not confined to any one particular form because they have gone past the home of reason. There, unconfined, not limited by any inner state of presupposed knowing, they are at home with all of the infinite laws and their apparent shapes and forms. Interdimensional civilizations do not rob anyone of their divinity. They leave room for divinity by giving each and every finite form the possibility of moving into its own essential structure.

Pure interdimensional consciousness breaks all of the boundaries of limitation in form. Thus, this consciousness can then seek the event curves, the sequences of mind/matter interlocution that make up the pattern of divinity. When time imitates matter sequentially, this interdependent, interlocutory force gives matter a curve which signifies that it has met up with the correct pattern in time. The interdimensional being is capable of assimilating all of the possible curves in the inherent substructure and giving breath or life to them. Thus, this being is not a confined superstructure but a magnified field of matter/time/energy that is not ever limited to any one particular event sequence. All of the beings that live in this way are dependent on each other for survival. They must cross the barrier into the space/time vault and unify for existence. They cannot be completely separate. This is the disadvantage of such an existence. Whereas Man is essentially independent and cannot function without a sense of his separateness, the interdimensional being is bound to its sisters and brothers for sustenance, for life itself. It is not really independent in the sense that Man in our sphere has become. This is the drawback of such unification, but it is also its glory.

At this time, Man is being faced with a new historical choice. This choice has to do with whether he will remain independent or merge with the collective relationships that give interdimensional intelligence its life and breadth. When Man makes this choice, he will discover whether he is to stay solid or move beyond such boundaries. Right now, it is only in death that Man rediscovers his true nature. If he is to become an interdimensional being, he will have to lose the sovereignty that has been granted to him. Much is the pity, but as has been discussed the glories in such a trade are also grand within themselves.

The timebound person is like a flake of dust. When the foot comes to kick it about, timebound people must acquiesce. They have no real capability to turn the foot aside. Interdimensional people, on the other hand, since they are not made separate from the dust, can become that which troubles them. The interdimensional person can actually become the substance of the dust and thereby gain access to the keys whereby unification can become self-evident. The reason that timebound people are so attached to their possessions is that they feel that this is a point of solidity for them. They identify with their possessions because deep within them they know that their infinite nature cannot accumulate anything, and that puts them into a state of fear. They treasure such accumulation, mistaking it for riches. This is not the case with interdimensional people because they have no need for anything that will shelter them from infinity. Once one recognizes that time flows in and out of matter like a river, swallowing everything in its grasp, then one can break free from any question of matter as being a source of happiness, power, or success.

Happiness for Man

What constitutes happiness for the completely interdependent Man who is no longer dimensionally trapped? It is certainly not matter. It is the flow of time within the field of matter, the play of time that creates this satisfaction, this quest for divinity. Man must enjoy time in his own way. But the interdimensional person is no longer one who enjoys time just in his own way. The interdimensional person enjoys time as time enjoys itself. The interdimensional person can glide into the subswing of time and with each coasting glance become capable of recognizing infinity and calling out its name. This being is not someone who can be bound restlessly to any particular occasion or sequence. No historical calendars can give this being any form of rest or pleasure. Thus, the interdimensional being never sleeps, never rests, and never causes anyone any distress because he or she is completely wrapped up in the quest for infinite dialogue and sustenance.

Out of the whole there is the sum of the parts. Out of the reality of time forms the whole of matter. Out of the whole of matter forms the infinite quest for unified creation. Man forms a partnership with time so complete, so real, and so faithful that there can be no turning back. Then Man will reach his destiny in the stature that God wished for him.

3.1.7
time and speciate
identification

Species-Specific Identification

he identification of a species is usually ascertained through understanding its social, physical, and mental/emotional characteristics. Usually, one is not in a position to discuss time and its evolution in the development of a species. For an individual sentient being, time presents itself as a backdrop to life in every state—waking, sleeping, and dreaming. As an individual's consciousness identifies the specific value of time that will make a hidden parameter of intelligence possible, the reality of a specific sector in the span of time comes to the fore. The individual views his or her existence through the eyes of a specific set of speciate codes that govern the constitutional makeup of his or her being. He or she operates exclusively through these codes and is unable to deviate from them unless the elasticity of the nervous system is greatly refined.

Time presents itself in most species as a process of unification in which the child learns first to exist as a separate entity, openly identifying with the mother but gradually becoming independent of her. The child develops a type of internal bonding with the mother that governs the clock or consciousness timing that will make psychospiritual development possible. Children learn to breathe time directly through their own respiratory system, accounting for specific functioning through the avenues of time that will signify a different standard of action or behavior. Although individuals are free in the sense that they are independent actors in the field of time, they are bound to the rigidities that dimensional law provides. No one who can reach forward or backward in time can operate solely as an independent entity in this way. Thus, the situation that makes Man wholly unique also limits him in the ability to reconcile his situation with the temporal mechanics that govern him.

The unification of time is pro-animate. Plants, animals, and all sensate intelligence animate the sequentiation of time through their own awareness. They accumulate a basis for reason based on their understanding of the shaping of reality, and test these systems utilizing the core intelligence of their own speciate material. Animals that are more visually inclined will see or hear the template for the time variables within their own awareness. Lacking the sensory capability for analysis or reason, most animals will install time automatically in their awareness and utilize possible outcomes for their own advantage. For example, during the process of hunting, animals will sense the approach of other beings and will rehearse possible scenarios in which these beings have the advantage or disadvantage. Animals therefore can think, but not in the way that humans do. Animals can see possible outcomes and can accumulate thought/time/matter within their awareness, which then spills out onto the field of activity as a sensory outgrowth. They are more apt to act spontaneously and instinctively rather than basing action on a great deal of forethought and accumulated knowledge.

Holding Time Within Our Grasp

Humans utilize a speciate relationship to time that relies on visual cues that are more symbolic than literal. They also rely on a sense of what seems logical or reasonable in terms of the interplay of time, matter, and consciousness. The advanced beings called time lords actually signal the human being to be more favorable to one outcome over the other. This is done very systematically, albeit subtly, and is the reason why certain outcomes appear to be very charming whereas others do not seem as attractive. Human beings are easily influenced in this regard because at this stage of evolution they do not understand how time actually operates and how it is affecting their every move. They are more advanced than animals, however, in that they are able to logically plan and reason, but they do not have a sense of how time actually accumulates as a product or outcome of their activities and how the balance of time affects their concerns. They see themselves as independent actors when they are in fact being influenced greatly by higher forms of intelligence. Their innocence, though less than the animals, is still great.

Human beings are the intermediaries between celestial intelligence and the plant and animal realms. Humans hold time within their grasp due to their ability to manage their behavior consciously and conspicuously without having to rely solely on the patterns of instinct. Since human beings create their personal reality charts through the union of conscious thought and innate standards of reason, they are able to create endless outcomes that are presented from the field of possibility. Humans rely on the flow of time as it appears synchronously from the "belly" of the absolute. Time, in the human sense, functions as a split variable. First, it accumulates strategic endpoints all along the array of possibilities, constructing mathematical relationships that describe the function of consciousness from one set of parameters to another. Then, by increasing its frequency, time delineates the intervals or separations in space/time that will make the accumulation of data possible from all aspects of consciousness. When relative existence meets absolute existence along the field of time, consciousness is able to derive the mathematical correlates that will eventually make full unification possible.

The Schools of Consciousness

Time and consciousness are the unifiers because they actually serve to strip down the matter variables and create patterns of synchronization that allow matter to be materialized in all spheres. Since time and matter are dovetailed in this fashion, time will appear randomly without fixed precipitation as long as consciousness supplies the endpoints or parameters that allow it to do so. Time and matter function as weavers of consciousness. They allow physical reality to manifest and create the system of checks and balances permitting reality to function as a smoothly flowing network. In order to gauge the efficacy of the time/matter unification, consciousness sets up schools or ashrams which are essentially fields of reference that satisfy the parameters of different streams of knowledge. The unification of time is studied and in some cases laid out through these different strata of knowledge. Time and consciousness draw out the plans for these different planes of understanding, and these schools or systems create the blueprints whereby time can be realized in any field of existence.

These schools of learning are guided by lords or visionary keepers of time. These time lords, who could be seen as strata of independent intelligence in their own right, actually delineate and make reference to the systemization of space/time variables in each sector. The unification of time as a translinear system, where events are sequenced, refined, and brought together as a sensate series of objective relationships, is based on the knowledge of these advanced beings. Time is therefore constructed with the knowledge that its basic unification will be brought about behind the scenes, whereas its play in the field of action accumulates through the desire and will of human and sentient interaction on this plane.

The Synchronization of the Subtle Bodies

The field of motion is a physical actuality on the part of human beings. In other words, when human beings act, they are working with a body of motion that correlates their activities and gives them a sense of their relationship to space/time. Time relates to the field of motion in that the event sequences which qualify or move time in random sequential order are interrelated in specific patterns of interest that can be relevant to the seeker.

Time functions as a buffer between the physical and astral bodies, and allows human beings to move fluidly between dimensional aspects without colliding with their own subtle mechanics. The synchronization of the subtle bodies with respect to time is correlated through the relationship of the field of motion with the field of time. When the human being acts independently of any other person, he or she is scheduled quite rigorously so that the action arrives at the exact moment of portended impact. Since the individual must arrive at precisely the moment that is intended, he or she does not have much room for error.

Each action that one takes that is in rhythm with one's own functioning must be correlated with the originating time references that one holds. This is why an individual will need psychological "space" to gain a place of reference at a given interval. It is the need to understand the pure function of time with respect to the possibilities that could be transposed that makes the individual turn back the clock and reach back into the perceived past for a sense of reference or grounding.

It is through the mental/emotional sense of reference that human beings gain a sense of meaning. Time brings a sense of perspective, creating a psychological trail of objectives and sensibilities that carve the foundation for a human life. The main difference between humans and animals in this regard is that human beings are psychologically referenced whereas animals rely more on their physical prowess and placement in the environment. Animals are more advanced in the field of motion. Animals relate to their surroundings through their highly responsive capabilities of motion and speed. They are more advanced in the field of motion than humans, even in our most illustrious expression as mature athletes.

Even in advanced athletic activity, human beings, because of the nature of their mental bodies, are more apt to be slower and less able to advance on the time/matter framework as rapidly as animals. One sees that as animals become domesticated they lose this instantaneous sense of motion, time, and synchrony. Animals require the ability to move quickly in order to be competitive in the field of play. The adroitness that animals exhibit is not only a function of their specific personality, however, but of the underlying character of their existence. Human beings, whether fast or slow in their movements, are not characterized on the basis of their ability to achieve motion. Like animals that have become domesticated, human beings have the need for a pause or respite in their physical functioning to make room for decisions that underlie the field of motion.

Animals and humans are equally responsible for their actions, although animals are obviously more instinctive in their conduct. Though animals are closer to the stronghold of Nature, they also fall under the laws of cause and effect, or karma. Their actions are not governed or assessed on the basis of reason or justice, but simply on the bare bones continuum that their actions denote. Human beings, on the other hand, derive merit on the basis not only of their actions but on the motivations that reside within the actions. They become functionally intelligent on the basis of both their instinctive and reasoned capabilities. Human beings are more than animals and less than gods.

The Strategies of Creation

Motion and time are interfaced through thought. The body/mind sends out streamers or markers into the environment to delineate the field into which attention or activity will be placed. Then the body/mind creates the vision or synchrony that will allow time to be denoted. The body is not a physical structure per se. It derives its physicality through the inference of motion. Motion creates the impetus for the molecular structure of the body to rapidly impose itself on the field of matter and create the illusion of a solid body. The body is more liquid than solid in fact, but its solidity is based on the reality that motion itself defines its pulse, its character, and its sense of direction. It is motion that makes Man capable of reaching out into the environment and creating buildings, structures, and things that are not part of his body. This advanced accomplishment, which allows Man to be the creator of objects and defines his sensibility, is what distinguishes him in the end result from other animal species.

The universality of the time codes is not dependent on speciation. Time is derived from the outgrowth of consciousness as it is placed in the field of opposites. Time grows like weeds in the gardens of many civilizations, creating the signification of reason and the advent of many new crops of influence and regard. Time destroys all of the advantages that species create which seem to make them feel that they are inferior or superior to each other. It is through their relationship to time that God registers a sense of knowledge about a given species.

It is through the study of time itself that God understands His own creation. He is able through His infinite wisdom to develop a mapping mechanism for all of the activities of all of His species simultaneously and to bring them together on both physical and subtle levels for their own advancement. He sees how time will interplay over a vast panorama of space/time correlates, and actually plays out different sequences of knowing simultaneously, creating parallel synchronization of opposites on all planes of existence. One could say that God is the ultimate player of three-dimensional chess. He understands how the advancement of His players will create a rapid interplay between different markers and makes all of the outcomes known. Then the players have their own opportunity to choose. Free will, possessed by human beings as a precursor for the advancement of intelligence, is simply the way that God creates a challenge for them to develop stamina and poise. God does not need human beings to have free will. They need free will for their own enjoyment, and thus it is granted to them.

On the celestial level, time accumulates. Time is banked, stored, and reckoned with on a vast and innumerable scale. The celestial level of time is not reasonable nor is it assessable by any known standpoint. Time accumulates in a type of permanent bank account that can be withdrawn by the lords of time for their own use. They develop accounts or methods of withdrawal which are then circulated or translated to sentient life in a type of exchange system that allows beings to develop strategies of synchronization for their activities.

Gracious Unification

Since time and matter ultimately unify, it is not necessary for these time-generated beings to split time up or to qualify it in any particular way. The time beings or intelligences simply wrap around the different apparent outcomes and install fields of motion that pull time from the internal parameters that it must draw from. This process is called random idealization. Time and motion are filtered out by the Host Intelligence and are fed by the time lords to other life forms without explanation or advance notice. These life forms evaluate the particles, waves, and conduits of time through their nervous systems, and, unbeknownst to themselves, they spit time back out into the field of existence. This unconscious use of time is the area in which human advancement will eventually have the most potential interplay.

For time and consciousness to graciously and auspiciously unite, they must coalesce. When an individual becomes part of a group, he or she enters into a different relationship with the governing influence of time. At first, there is a speeding up of all of the variables that underlie the mechanics of time as the individual adjusts to the quantum arrangement of that particular selection of people. Then, as the group develops its own system of interaction, the individual becomes part of a greater collective effort that will eventually benefit even a larger sector of the population. Individuals are therefore far more limited in their efficacy when they are not aligned with others. Human beings, in their search to develop familial, constitutional, or environmental relationships, adopt new patterns of temporal synchronization that are developmentally more efficient.

Once human beings arrive at the point where they can communicate more effectively at the cosmic level, they are able to interact with the celestial networks that govern and define social systems. The celestial levels inherently map and reconcile the myriad cues that are circulated to human civilization for the purpose of guidance and higher knowledge. Humans are guided as to how to respond to particular life situations that might present a psychological or physical challenge. We are nudged into attention by those beings that are assigned to our welfare; yet there is a subtle hand in all of this that allows us our point of view and a sense of freedom.

Emotional situations constitute events in the life of human beings as much as any physical situation. There is really no distinction on the part of the body/mind in this regard. This is why emotional events appear in the memories of human beings for a considerable distance in time, and are in fact markers for the identification of psychosocial structures. Celestial intelligence offers us cues as to what life events are truly important and invites us to recognize when we are on the mark in relation to our life purpose and sense of future. Our ability to listen to such guidance and give it credence in our everyday lives leads us slowly to its utilization, not just as a marker for human conduct but as an interactive mechanism for the development of consciousness.

3.2
God and time

3.2.1
the dialogue of God and time

God and Preexistence

What is God? That is the fundamental question. One requires an understanding of the force of intelligence that pervades the field of light and awareness at its fundamental source. This intelligence maintains an apparent relationship to every subset of matter. Obviously, one cannot ascertain the range of intelligence of such a source. Even if one were to calibrate the extent of the matter/time response, it is still impossible to imagine a source that can develop time directly from itself. Although it is a mystery, it is apparent to the intelligent light-bearing civilizations that the Godforce is matter/time and that it must therefore be preexistent to any formation of planetary or interstellar origin.

This sense of preexistence causes intelligent beings to contemplate the rate of change that is developed when God radiates the light of His own awareness to every independent source. The cosmic timing is God's timing. There cannot be an independent source of light that is distinct or separate from God. However, the reality of matter is not something in which God has a separate hand. The extent that matter appears as a variable of light forms the backdrop for civilizations and the myriad of space/time derivatives that make up the dimensional backdrop.

The very fact that God exists causes one to question the existence of time as an independent entity. Would it not stand to reason that God created the fundamental function of time as well as all of its possible outcomes? To examine this problem, one must first engage in a discussion about the nature of time in relationship to the force of creation. Time exists as a backdrop for the force of creation, but is not the actual force itself. The force of creation has a profound, internal impetus that pushes the momentum of time forward. God stands as witness to this, rather than being the force itself.

God, in witness of the mechanics whereby time forms, can lend a hand to the systemization of time as a coordinated, fixed standard for motion in the multiverse. Time wobbles, moving from one set of variables to another, until it is launched effectively onto the rudimentary movement that governs reality. Time assaults the systematic alignment of matter, thereby seeking to restore its preeminence in the chain of events that makes up reality. God can act as an advisor to time but cannot impose the act of volition or consciousness on to the laws that govern time. There is a depth of action that time possesses that leaves it outside the fundamental structures through which God grants reality.

Thus, God becomes congruent with time but is essentially bound by internal laws that leave time as a type of free agent. Paradoxically, time is a function of how God works. Without time as a purveyor of internal certainty, God would not be able to actualize the mechanics of creation. There is a profound internal rhythm that God discerns about His creation that makes it possible for all of Nature to be deftly and singularly organized. Time has a part in all of this, and yet, there is this mysterious "outsider" identity that time continues to play, even in the face of all of its ability to come to terms with the avenues of adventure that God displays.

God, Civilization, and Light-Weaving

The range of sources for time is the range of sources for matter. Once the Godhead can interface with time, there is always the chance that time will return back to its source. This would create a "no-time" effect, which is seen often when interstellar space meets up with the light-weaving processes of civilizations that have come to the point of reference for developing planetary bodies independently of the Godforce. What is left to God, after all, if a civilization has come to the point where it can act in its own right as a direct creative mechanism for the assistance or development of star systems?

This question, of course, unfolds the whole nature of time, since God essentially steers the boat and the rowers just go along with it. Why would the power of the Godhead be needed for creation? It is simple: since God is essentially the fountainhead for the creation of time, God does not need the co-mechanics of time to accomplish "dead" or surface action. God is the leader of the manufacturing center for time. And as such, God is the foundation of that centerpiece. All of the functioning of time that God mandates for manifest creation is to His due.

The key to the development of civilization is the dimensional backdrop that forms the sequentiation of time. The "slide" that time plays with matter and consciousness wreaks havoc with our conception of what it means to be alive, free, or intelligently cognizant of our surroundings. As God lends Him/Herself fully to the construction of reality, time is the "click by click" component that determines how each individual set of circumstances will be mounted. Although God reigns when it comes to time, time breaks the back of God.

Time strains the vast perspective of God because it has such a fantastic capacity for sensitivity that it can actually feel into the very foundation of reality that God has arranged. Time can breach the gap between what God feels and what matter will retain. Pushed to the brink of its capacity, the Godforce is broken by the unimaginable kick of time that damages the constraints an organizing power would put on the shaping of reality. Time no more than matter can change the mind of God, but it is time that ultimately determines the way that matter will be reshaped. Time recognizes the essential nature of God and, respectful of this understanding, exists concomitantly with God while being a witness of the Godforce as it emerges. This is the essential and mysterious paradox that underlies the formation of reality.

The Playmates of the Godhead

Because time is uniform, all of the overlapping variables that calibrate time to appear at one source or another drop away when it is standing free. When time exists independently, unsourced, it is liberated from the chain of command. It does not have to follow any of the rules. It is like a god in its own right. As time strives to create matter, it leaves behind this independence in favor of becoming "Father Time." It becomes the mediating influence for determining the flow of results that will lead to all that is. Although matter may appear solid to us, it is time that renders it visible. Without time, matter would appear as a pile of filings, open-ended and incapable of the malleability necessary for creation.

God needs time like matter needs consciousness. God needs matter only for enjoyment, but time for His real beverage, His real fruit. This is the only way to explain how matter and time become crystal seeds for the development of the universal continuum. Time displays itself as a constant due to the increase in surface area that is produced when the matter/time interface switches from one time stream to another.

Time streams are like sheets of rain. They fall in blankets or waves, running counterclockwise to each other, forming pairs or opposites. They dive in and out of the reference points to which they have been assigned. In this dance, the Godforce appears. Recognizing the choreography that time displays in order to bring about a synchronization of motion and dynamism, God signals to time as to how to appear. Should time be unilinear or multifabricated? Should time be the sole process of identification or be interwoven within the landscape it is seeking to define? The Godforce enters a plea, like a good attorney, embarking on a road that time has called into play.

Since time exists independently of the divine intelligence, it must be corralled or contained in order to promote individuation. The Godforce dialogues with time, enters its plea and stands back, waiting for time to do what it is wont to do. It is a delicate balance because the very stature of the Godforce demands action. Time feels the pressure. It wants to answer the protestations of God but it must find its own way, like a child who is seeking independence but knows it still needs its mother.

Pulsations of Time

The main criterion time uses for its success is the development of links or streams, which are like surges in the pulsation of the time wave. These surges produce a system of current differentiation that switches the time impulses from one break to another. Time dialogues with the Godforce to produce this change, and having struck a bargain with the Divine, can bring time and consciousness into alignment with the temporal string that will be most efficacious in that situation.

The secret of success with the time stream is that as each break coasts back from the main link, there is a surge in energy, a variable pulse that switches the current from one time phase group to another. The coasting effect, between surges, is tantamount to a power-down. As the surge proceeds, the level of current is raised at least four magnitudes from the previous point. The Godforce acts as a circuit breaker in its own right, switching pulsations from one amplitude to another in order to control or document the flow of time. The Godforce, completely impartial and seemingly random in its execution of the marching orders for time, is also aware at some other level of the continuation of order and pure reason. Time is inherently logical but its logic knows no apparent order.

Without the Godforce, time would step too rapidly into its chosen domain and the individual mechanisms that turn event streams into material reality might not come about. God always maintains the brakes. It is the intelligence of God that gives matter form and shape, and gives us the psychological recognition to know what we are talking about.

The Transparency of Knowledge

The purpose of the time/matter interface is to switch the time breaks so that they appear backwards on the surface of the wave. The relative distance of the time breaks appears as a slope coefficient, where the rapidity of the slide can be seen from any apparent vantage point. This characteristic permits us to have a fully dimensional perception of time, allowing us to switch backwards and forwards in our awareness to view event streams from different possible viewpoints. It enhances our psychological state and prevents us from becoming too fixed in any one particular frame of reference.

God makes the knowledge of time transparent to us through the subjectivity of our minds. It is through the visual cues and rapidity of impulses that underlie the human nervous system that we are able to interpret how time will relay itself and when the circuitous mixture of time and consciousness will delineate our point of view. This switchback effect, which reproduces the limitations of the inner mechanics of consciousness, is not tied directly to the time breaks themselves but, when cast on a universal level, pertains to the workings of interstellar space.

From the point of view of the individual, time is unilinear, unbreakable, and solid. From the point of view of the Godhead, time is multidimensional and altogether fluid. The individual paints the delicate palate of time onto his or her personal canvas, while God translates this painting in the foremost reaches of the Central Sun, the Heart of the universal continuum.

The mathematics of time is therefore speechless, but not unfeeling. Time stretches to accommodate the underlying psychology, and brings into view all of the questions and answers that the human mind wishes to address. It does so from a refined, clear, and textured surface. The lightwave coefficients that create the building blocks for time straddle event streams like the pendulum of a clock. Ticking backwards and forwards, the coefficients make the calibrations that allow time to be independent from form.

The lightwaves that are formed through these mathematical ribbons create the backdrop for the light/time/matter feed that is orchestrated through the intelligence of the Central Sun. The translinear equations which reflect these mathematical models describe the positioning of the stars and the fixity or divergence of the orbits of celestial objects. This positioning with reference to the intensity of electromagnetic "pull" from the Great Central Sun translates psychologically into the relative fixity that the human consciousness assumes in relationship to time and consciousness.

Space Fasteners

The Godforce is the primary assessor of when time and matter are to trade their individuated lives for the sake of uniformity. Time and space are documented through the Mind of God despite all protests from the level of sentient species. Time/lightwave transference occurs because the spread of the temporal continuum must be kept in some sort of balance. To do this, God assigns "fairy integers," which are documentable proof that light and time can be fastened together for the purpose of space. The transference that space/time organizes is essential for the maintenance of the spin of time. There is rarely an instance where time can appear on its own merit without the lightwave spin becoming manifest. Time acknowledges the proper flow of relational events through its interface with these lightwave sequences. This determination helps time to understand how to repair the norms that govern the formation of space/time.

The distance between time and the lightwave norms can be calibrated through unilateral mathematics. The system of unilateral mathematics is based on the causal derivatives of time. These are "space savers," ideal metric units of space/time without weight or substance that act as a foundation for the unilateral mathematical formulations. They are based on the ideal calculations of mathematical "wizards" of their time. These mathematical concepts actually structure the basis for light/time.

Unilateral mathematics essentially describes space/time in junction points. Each curve in the space/time break acts as a lightning rod for the time links to develop a route of spin. The unilateral mathematical model actually "teases" time and causes time to achieve a sense of unification with matter at a surprisingly earlier "docking time."

The range of light variables inherent in the host mathematical models varies from point to point. Light develops a spin as it curves back on to the time break, which explains how light travels from point to point. Coherent reality is developed simultaneously from light and time and is not independent of this coefficient. The variability of the theory is based on the idea that as time develops its initiatory signature in the space/time continuum, it can hold its own without relying on a quotient of light to further its advance.

296

Light Is a Traveler

Since time and light can exist independently, it is difficult to explain how matter was created in the first place. If time doesn't depend on light to develop its essential frequencies, why does time not go directly to matter for confirmation? Light frequencies travel of their own accord separate from time and are not always tied to it. When matter becomes capable of separating from time, there is a process whereby the light value, which imbues matter with form, exists as a free-standing matrix.

It is the Godforce that governs the utilization principle that underlies the field of time. God strips time of its independence and demands that time adhere to the range of frequencies that speed it along the way and make it possible for light to be assigned to it. Light weaves itself along the surface of time like a spider weaves its net. Light is a traveler. It can travel over very long distances and retain its essential nature. It is not dependent on time to keep its form, its essential body of knowledge, intact. This is why light is such a good communicator of knowledge. All of the light-based civilizations use light as a means of temporal and post-temporal communication for this reason.

Since light is a traveler, it also has something to share, something to deliver. It is carrying the seed packet for illumined consciousness. The planetary bodies, whether of light duration or matter duration, retain a type of substance outside of linear time that makes their position in space/time transitory. They are the documenters of the celestial world. The planets develop a communications highway from one star system to another, encoding the planetary messages that signal the development of different starseed civilizations.

The theory of light development offers the postulate that as light transmits these messages, the space/time derivative itself is changed. In other words, planetary bodies are actually creators of matter and they forge their own consciousness-based civilizations within their boundaries. The planets develop civilizations as an encoded synthesis for the development of matter and consciousness.

Once beings become capable of utilizing light to further their exploration of interstellar space, they can actually calculate the range of light as it develops an interface with time. Since time is not transient, but remains fixed with respect to the mechanics of light, it is possible to determine how much time it will take for the light to refract or curve back on itself. This refractory time is referred to as a light constant or polar variable. There are systems of these variables within the context of every intelligent civilization, for they are the mirror images of how that civilization has developed the coding for matter.

Since light-bearing civilizations are in different stages of intelligent differentiation, they often have to wait for other civilizations to give them the feed or quotient derivatives they need to restore their interstellar matrices. This information is fed along light channels to the planetary bodies themselves. To understand this process, one must realize that light-bearing bodies are themselves intelligent beings with nervous systems and constitutions identical to sentient life. They develop their wings, so to speak, through light quotients becoming random and catalogable enough to create a variety of distance that can reconstitute their own sense of inherent perception. Since light bodies are equidistant in their placement in the continuum, they can rely on their own processes of calibration independent of any time reference.

God remodels time, creating a vehicle through which light can travel. The making of civilizations implies that light, which is the fundamental source out of which the Divine creates sentient life, will present a blueprint of light to follow. The difference in scope between light and time is that although light resides everywhere in the universe, time does not. There are portions of the multiverse where creation steps out of the field of time and is not bound or captured by it. Light however exists everywhere, even where darkness seems to present itself. This is because whatever is, is light.

The Formation of Planetary Systems

In the process of developing the underlying mechanics for unified creation, time exists as a codependent variable, even as it is also a singularity. Time is the first variable manufactured and made variant by light, and also the first factor to be considered in the creation of time/matter. While time is never given to discuss the formation of matter with anyone, it is also not given to hold the light knowledge necessary for travel at bay. Time and matter, when they exist as parallel surface values, become unified at their essential source, spinning out to form the intergalactic structures that we know as planetary bodies. The Godforce recognizes the formation of planets and star systems, and makes sure that planets are coded with the light/matter vestibules that develop free-standing intelligence.

Since intelligent beings must function on a diet of light and time, they rely on planets to distribute this light in a uniformly refractive and systematic way. Time and light interact randomly, developing differentiation at any rate of speed. The Godforce assimilates the channels for reconstruction. It is through the divine tempo, the rhythmic pulsation of light to dark, elemental to cosmic, mind to matter, that the impulses of nature are strung together and given breadth and form. The scope of time is monumental, universal, unspeakable. In order for the Godforce to animate time, it must create moving pictures or strips, which, like comic strips, piece together optimal stories or light sections for time to utilize to resurrect its own imposing set of variables.

From the point of view of Biblical construction, one could say that God made time as He made light—directly, without challenge, not for the purpose of deconstructing reality but for the sole direction of building up the realms of form, shape, and color. God made matter effervescent, fluid, and distinct. He made time distinctive, recognizable, and capable of masking the pretenses that the sentient mind might represent. Teeming with life, the multiverse needed a random, preordained construction handbook. This handbook is written through arrangement in a routinely prismatic fashion with the annals of time.

The Construction of Time

Time is both disjunctive and conjunctive. It creates shape by casting off the field of opposites and making room for different variations of light to appear. It makes color by combining, recognizing, and peeling back the strata of perfection it finds along the way, and imposing a set of orders or relationships upon it. The construction of time is governed by the Divine force itself as it slipstreams around the curvature that time imposes and limits all of the variables that time would so graciously represent. The Godforce is therefore a limiter and provider. The imposition of time on the indelicacies of matter creates the means whereby God can give order to His random creation.

To paint the picture of Divine restoration, one must understand how time and matter play with each other. Like children, they wrestle with the impossible task of growing up and developing a tougher skin. They are the children of God, and their purpose is to recognize how they are to perform on the field of the absolute. They do this through the direct process of animation. In sentient beings this is accomplished by the mimicking of the divine breath or Pneuma.

Time and matter form the components of the cosmic breath. In this strobing dispersal of energy and light, time is breathed out and matter is breathed in. Each successive breath causes a spiral, a break, through which a receding set of covariables is spun out and becomes unilaterally free. Space is an outgrowth of the interplay between light and time. It is the fabric on which the nest of matter is built.

God creates the union of space and time through engendering a period of rest. This Sabbath allows the Godhead the pause in the continuum that joins the configurations of time together and makes it possible for creation to contain itself. The gaps or pauses in the mechanics of creation provide the kick through which time orchestrates its fundamental powers of organization. Each pause determines an entry point for matter to join with the continuum. As God sighs, heaves, and gives way, the potentialities for creation are made available, released from stasis. Time naturally provides spaciousness, a hideaway from which God can release the necessary movement that reconnoiters intelligence. Were it not for the room provided by the nonstatic flow of time, the Godforce would be unable to leave the home of the absolute.

God plunders the absolute looking for the spoils of space to maintain His frame of reference. As the light variables kick in, the majestic impulses that guide light beings to develop civilizations and galaxies come into play. Time dilutes the field of opposites, rapidly advancing onto the glass of consciousness, and creating the mechanism for wave formations to curl back and forth onto each other.

The backwards and forwards movement of time and space is governed through the mind of God. The understanding of our status as material formations is expressed through the choreography that God lays down. He recognizes what will be played out beyond the boundaries of our limited understanding. Since time and matter are essentially wave forms, they rely on the Godforce for their basic cofactors. Matter and time, like good cousins, rely on each other for the purpose of recreation and manifestation. They can appeal to God for their sustenance, but it is only through the intelligence of the Godhead that they can recognize their surroundings and sustain the appearance of form. Matter always relies on the field of consciousness, and God always relies on matter to interpret, represent, and delineate the definable field of vision. God would not have it any other way.

3.2.2
the celestial foundation
of time

Event Patterns and History

he flow of opposites that regulates the psychological experience of humanity is kept in place by the psychological constraints of the mind. Patterns of interaction between human beings are governed by the emotional intensity that is imposed by living in the duality of form. The event patterns that occur, though arising out of this emotional discontinuity, have a grace and efficacy to them that is not always easy to express. Event patterns betray a remarkable resemblance to the underlying sequences of information that have created them. In this sense, they are translinear and beyond space/time as a corroborating value. In other words, they are not always what they appear to be.

The composition of history is based on the incorporation of individual event sequences in the panorama of the collective. History is a flow of backwards and forwards communication between the future-now and the now. History prepictures itself through punctuations in the synchronicity of events, randomizing itself through subtle transformations of the flow of feeling. The clusters or rainbows of time that event structures form as they interrelate one to the other can be characterized as a type of city-state. This is a territory in the psychological and energetic map of time. The historical parameters of a given city-state are mapped, creating a particular region that is split into an infinite range of subsets.

The mapping is performed by beings whose intelligence is intimately woven into their activities. They do not exist independently of time, but rather incorporate the motion of time within their awareness. They function on a diet of algorithms which regulate the flow, spin, and digestion of the time codes as they are registered within their all-time intelligence. These godbeings, who are not incarnate in the usual sense, are blessed with the capability of revealing the subswing or fluidity of time while being able to register a profound level of organization. They provide the synchronicity of time as well as the stability of it.

These beings create a uniform structure of prehistory which precedes the entire format of manifest reality. The arcs of time, which are the equivalent of curtains that mask the underlying value of events until they can be fully digested, are the features that give time its shape and breadth. These arcs are constructed through the assistance of the advanced time beings who also manage their movements. The algorithms that govern time are formulated in stages so as to prevent a backup of information that would limit the development of this prehistorical point of view.

Time beings of this magnitude often function in groups or pairs. This is so the complexities of multitasking are not overbearing. Even for these beings that possess an incomprehensibly intelligent sensibility, the job of assessing the permutations of reality and increasing the chances of fruition of one life stream or another is a complex and arduous task. The indigenous mythologies which document stories of beings that must carry the weight of time on their shoulders speak to these monumental activities. However, the happiness gained through the satisfactory performance of absolute duty is truly great.

Shaping the Time Breaks

Time is fractionizated in order to create differing orders of magnitude. The frayed edges of event streams must be accounted for and all of the optimized variables tied together. Although this interlinking appears random, it demands a type of celestial uniformity that must be garnered through intelligence that is up to the task. Time beings stretch time continuously, anchoring sets of parameters with each turn. They manipulate the style and regionalization of time so that events appear relational. Zones of documentable time are curved around each other, formulating the cultural or psychological constructs necessary for reality to appear as coherent.

Time is arrayed in loop formations because it is through this shape that time betrays its optimum ability for lucidity. Time breaks easily, but with the development of time loops, the frayed or marred surfaces of these breaks are brought back into a smoother and more uniform shape. The beings that govern time are occupied within these loops, establishing fields of stress or tension that eventually get worked out again. Standards of restitution for individual time breaks are developed by nature's time gardeners and are not limited to any particular planetary or cultural point of view.

Interfacing with the God Intelligence

The system of language used for time loops is called a time parameter or time signature. Each time loop maps out the surface or circumference of the wave, giving it width and breadth. Although time loops are themselves uniform, they have to be cast off like their randomized brethren in order for a new spread to be laid in. They are captured by the intelligences that govern them, and form the basis for all of the imaginings that human beings are heir to. Each parameter of time is clean, unbounded, and strikingly uniform. The curves in each time code denote new beginnings and endings.

The language of time is composed through the investigation of the time parameters within the context of the intelligence field that is exploring them. In the case of human beings, language is formulated which allows them to divest themselves of the casing, the encapsulation that has made them separate, discrete entities. The opportunity to become "out of time" is vested in the nature of all humanity, but is rarely seen except in cases where an individual has bravely or unexpectedly stepped "out of the box."

Beings who map time interface more directly with the God Intelligence that has made time possible. Unafraid and strangely unemotional in their operational context, they give new meaning to the term "blind perform-ance." They operate secretly, unquestioningly, and randomly. Yet, their abil-ity to formulate or investigate the twisting, sometimes highly circuitous organization of time is truly extraordinary.

In addition to the fully celestial beings that are responsible for the ins and outs of the time fields, there are those who are mid-beings, a type of crossover, not human but not entirely celestial. These beings are assigned the job of describing how time will interplay. They are like generals of time, assigned to win the war. These beings are capable of feeling, but still their range of feeling is essentially limited in order for them to have the strength or readiness to accomplish their goals.

The capacity for understanding the internal mechanics of time is a spir-itual attribute. Human beings, as they evolve, are being made ready for this task. The purpose of understanding the foundation of time is that it allows one the affordability of creation. One is anchored in being so directly that the mechanics of temporal operation come fully into view. Human beings who are in training for such a capacity are not wholly anchored in one dimension. They cannot be. They are living a double, sometimes triple life, traversing the dimensional realms linguistically, figuratively, and literally.

In God's great world there are beings that form temporal races. These races are of human-like character, but they mirror the celestial beings in their capacity and interest in the interiorization of time. Unlike most human beings in our world, these beings can literally breathe time and take advan-tage of the surrealistic structures that govern its manifestation. When humans begin to arrive at a point where we can imitate these activities, we become "Kali-esque" in scope. We traverse the mountainous celestial regions where the dragon or serpent-like beings who crawl through the range of time gain their fearful reputation.

Humans have the urge to understand their reality, but rarely do they wish to peek through the curtains to find out what is truly going on. Divested of fear and more given to true investigation are those whose minds have literally been peeled back by rigorous spiritual practice or traumatic intervention. In both cases, the armor or shield that ordinarily separates human beings from the interior code-breaking of time is denied. When humans meet up with the functionaries that arrange their reality, there is a cause for celebration. Now they will actually communicate with those who have given them life. They become capable of languaging the Mother from the bones of Her own lineage and learn to speak the mother tongue on their own.

The beings that map time do so multiphasically. They utilize time in two or three different stages in a simultaneous dance of union. This ability to traverse the many breakfronts of space/time from the point of view of celestial travel is magnificent in itself. When a presence or celestial intelligence curves through the domain of space/time and develops the language spirals necessary for the creation of form, the presence is never capable of making the same dance twice. Always wholly original, the presence makes the steps necessary for transmutation of the field of opposites look utterly simple. Like any great dancer, the dancers of time develop their choreography through the science of motion.

The motions inherent in the dance, although changing constantly, are developed through the stored warehouse of temporal values that have been set aside for that purpose. They are brought out, dusted off by the awakening intelligence, and made ready for view. This ordering of time into domains or regions of investigation is called mapping or tailoring the time waves. Those who engage in such activities learn the codification of time like any good mapmaker would do. They color or bring into focus different areas of the time spread, which are then related to the civilizations or individuals who will utilize them. These beings are the rainbow-makers of the absolute.

Players in the Game of Time

There are no players in this game of time that are outside of time. To be inside time one must be part of the dimensional expression that a particular time region represents. This is why we refer to such regions as city-states. They are locations in the breadth and width of time that speak to their own longitudes and latitudes. Each phase of the time game incorporates a polar opposite, a structure diametrically opposed to the sequence to be delineated. The divine mapmakers do their job rapidly and effectively. They cover great ground by incorporating all of the "lampposts" of time directly in their view. These spreads or sequences sometimes appear to "run off the board." They must be interpreted as they arise rather than as they might appear to be later on.

The fresh, original, and distinctive quality of time is kept intact by those governing forces responsible for its upkeep. These forces not only govern the appearance of time but eventually become responsible for the apparent creation of matter. It is out of the originality of time that matter is born. Beings who map time do so as a function of their own awareness. Their activities are not such in the usual sense, in that what is active is already lively within them. They are purveyors of time and as such are really manifestations of it. The time sequences are incorporated into their equivalent of a nervous system or directory of information, and the synaptic material that they transmit is filled with the intelligence of their own bodies. Though truly incorporeal, they are vested with a type of form that signifies their function.

The state of matter is interwoven with the state of time. Beings that control time control the range or density of matter. They provide the influences that maintain the organization of material reality. They signal to time what it will have to accomplish to become corporeal or transdimensional, setting up the avenues where the city-states or municipalities of time will be organized. These directions are formed on both a macrocosmic and microcosmic level. Even the amoeba has a form of navigational marking that will allow it to be fast-ranging or contained, as the case demands. Every cell in the human body is flexed with the power of temporal change, and every molecule that exists in Nature is made grander by the visitation of celestial unfoldment.

Beings that govern time utilize a signaling system that is like the radar of the temporal world. This system mimics or mirrors the call to arms of the Godhead, developing the range of expression for life itself. What would occur in the land of the living without the development of form from the circuitous sphere of intertemporal dialogue? The answer lies in the structure of time as it melts into the field of matter. Matter interlocks with time, and in so doing develops a type of optical feed that is registered in the visionary structure of humanity. We actually see time formulate on a daily basis, and it is through this interpretative reciprocity between the retina of the eye and the avenue of perception that we come to know our environment and ourselves.

3.2.3
space, time, and eternal beings

Open-Ended Sentience

eternity progresses through the slipstream that contains the dialogue between absolute and relative intelligence. Time incorporates a fundamental building block of apportioned energy that is delivered directly out of the standards of this slipstream. As time is converted to a completely open-ended movement, ungoverned by sentience, it is able to develop the complexity needed for unparalleled event structures to take place.

The beings that govern the far reaches of the universe incorporate the knowledge of movement from one dimension to another. They take the laws, structures, and systems that are the management strategies of a given area of the cosmos and reconcile them with the new data and parameters on hand. Eternal beings, due to their infinite status in the flow of time, are equipped to see the management ethics that govern all that is, and work subtle changes into their specialties as need demands.

Within the realm of sentience, time occurs as a sequence of pre-planned or structured events at one end of the continuum and a random sequence of events at the other. How does time move from a form of staggered, complete modeling, in which motion in a sense stops and matter forms itself directly from the absolute, to a situation in which creation is spontaneous and constantly in motion? The information slipstream tells time how to move from one spectral velocity to another. Information is programmed in the form of shells, concentric circles of light/time that form a continuum. This could be compared to the structure of the atom in which the nucleus is formed by a compressed sequence of matter/time, around which is arrayed a contiguous filament of universal information.

Once time reaches the outer shell of the model it is no longer governed by any fixed rate of influence, and it is therefore up to the universal intelligence to organize it into patterns that will be utilizable by sentient life. The codes or software updates of how time will be scrambled, randomly selected, and imprinted into the event structures of a given civilization are looked after by lords who administer this knowledge through eons of experience and grace.

The Mechanics of Time Management

The mechanics of time management involve a system of stop-motion activities that cause it to store time bits over a vast range of space and then slip them very effortlessly into the pocket of the continuum. One might say that to incorporate time, the universal intelligence has developed a calendar of independence whereby it feeds these time codes directly to its own event sequencer, and the array or substream of information that results forms the inherent reality. To develop knowledge of time one must therefore return to time's original encoding. This occurs through literally breathing the time codes directly into the fabric of consciousness and utilizing them as a system of understanding. Since time cannot circumvent all of the parallel realities that manifest inherently within it, one must also analyze the rapidity of these parallel shifts and understand how they relate one to the other.

Time develops parallels by creating knots or portions of time/matter which are hardened by consciousness itself. These knots are like inner vestibules of space/time that contain the core of the event stream itself. Time knots itself in a patterned formation, which is its method of storing data. It is not possible to understand such formations without recognizing time as a code maker as well as a code breaker. In other words, the encapsulation of time occurs at any area in which time is the subject. Time limits itself by rapidly shifting the interior remnants of its own coat or cloaking, and then speeds up its markers through the development of codes or embryonic tracking devices within its core.

This ability of time to weave through the fabric of reality is based on its leanings in space. The space markers are similar to those of time. They are the fabric of time itself. Since space itself is not considered to be really empty but filled with the light-bearing factors of matter that regulate time at its inceptionary level, it is possible for space to incorporate itself directly into the time codes from the very beginning. When space is new or fresh, it has more of this interior feel, and when it is less new it has some limitations in this area. Space is the wrapper for time. When time loses its grip on the factors that simulate its reality, space fills in the gaps. Since space and time coexist simultaneously, one cannot really study space without time.

The Incompleteness of Space

Space is structured from a combination of fluid integral relationships that are internally momentous and incomplete. Space is the most incomplete component of the Godhead. This is because space is inherently meant to be completed through interaction with other components, principally time. When time arrives at the gate of space there is an interchange that allows time to live in a type of shell or cloak. This natural phenomenon is what regulates the flow of time.

Time is like a snail crawling in and out of its shell. Its shell is made up of bits of unconfigured space, space waiting for the arrival of form. Since space and time crawl through the door of matter together, there must be a communications highway between matter, time, and space. This is the function of the Godhead itself. The Godhead is the transmitter that allows space, motion, time, and consciousness to communicate with each other. The Godhead acts as a transceiver to record the underpinnings of space and to make it possible for matter/time to rely on the proven records. Since time and matter are carrier waves for information, they rely on space to hold the grid in place and restore balance. Space and time are the essential fabric of consciousness, whereas matter is the end result.

Space and time communicate through an intricate pattern of impulse-driven language that imparts the flow, rate of change, and eccentricities of a constantly changing map of awareness. The divine intelligence feeds these impulses directly to space and time, and although the initial feed is fundamentally perfect, mistakes or misreadouts occur due to the stepping down of vibration into more relative levels. Time is perfected in relationship to space, with matter then perfected to represent the new data that has been accumulated. Thus, dimensional organization is a continuous process of communication and self-direction, bringing about creation in all its myriad forms.

To understand this concept of self-correction, which is the signature of space and time, one must see that time leans into the folds of space much like an accordion. Time leans into space, dialoguing in an acute and relative angle with both matter and space, developing a complex system of regulation that defines the character of reality. Since reality is not a perfect map, but simply part of this dialogue, the perfection is in the interpretation of that map. Time records the interface between "white matter," which is an undifferentiated coagulation of universal intelligence, and the underpinnings of space. The valuation of time is never dependent on space but rather stands apart from it. Therefore, to understand the nature of reality one must recognize that time can become space but space cannot become time. Time stands apart from everything, a singular, isolated movement from the mind of God

Thought in the Field of the Godhead

One must question why the Godhead would imagine time in the first place. This is a very logical question. To understand the reality of God is of course a very difficult undertaking, but suffice it to say that when God breathes so does time. Time is actually the fluid mechanism of the breath of God. As time breathes, so the universe expands and contracts, and the folds of space are like the lungs of the Godhead. As these lungs fold in and around themselves like a great bellows, the interior of time presents itself. Time at this point is again both random and regular. It has a sharpness, an actual presence to it, that can be both seen and felt. This characteristic of time loses momentum as it enters the free-fall of matter. Here, time becomes a player in the dialogue with matter, and it appears as something incalculable and somewhat mysterious. However, as one grows closer to the Godhead, time takes on the character of jelly, a kind of bouncy demeanor that allows it to be jostled back and forth by the universal consciousness.

Time is the first player for God because it is the vehicle whereby God creates thought. This is of course very relevant for human beings. Thoughts are created through time and are influenced by its random character. That is why thoughts appear to be so difficult to pin down. Since thoughts are dependent on this random quality of time, their organization is also dependent on the other more regulated quality which time emits. Thoughts are essentially a wraparound value of time. They are developed through the synchronization of tiny time capsules, which are part of the mechanics of the central nervous system. The CNS controls time by coloring it and sending these colored vibratory messages throughout the body. Since time knows how to interpret these messages, the sentient being is a system-dependent outgrowth of the essential time streams that have been downloaded into its nervous system. Time relays the structure of reality to the sentient being for the purpose of dialogue with the environment.

Time and space share one other thing: since they are wedded to one another, they are completely eternal. One must therefore ask why sentient beings are not always eternal. This question goes back to the character of time. Since time is sometimes finite, so are sentient beings sometimes finite. Sometimes the markers that have been given to the receiver or inhabitant of time are only destined to play out for a given period. It is like a game in which all of the players must rely on making a certain set of points or cues, and at the end, the game is over. Time creates a type of fixity for the purpose of self-study. It utilizes noneternal life like a laboratory, attempting to understand the finite, which it can only grasp from its eternal nature. Time studies this finite attribute through the development of sentient life, from the grasshopper to the most intelligent of God's creatures. Throughout the universe, time is expressed as a function of this intelligence.

The Cosmology of Eternal Beings

There are, of course, sentient beings not bound by time. We call these beings eternal or lesser attributes of the Godhead. They are unbound by time because their makeup does not demand finiteness. They have been pulled away from the essentially independent nature of matter and caused to survive on their own. Eternal beings exist therefore in a type of isolation. This may defy religious concepts that picture them as closer to God due to their eternal nature. But this could not be further from the truth. Eternal beings grow through time only if they are not inherently fixed due to responsibility. When an eternal being has a job to do that demands an unchanging demeanor or attribute, that being can appear to be stuck or fixed in one position for eons. Change, measured by a standard less than eternity, can then seem to be forever.

Eternal beings are isolated from those that are not eternal, because they live in a dimension that stands outside of the field of time. Their sentience, their knowledge, is not rooted in the event stream of action. They live filled with constant information, constant knowledge, bubbling up from inside their inner core. They do not have the capacity to reason through situations in the manner that we think of as human, because reason involves a certain fixity of opinion or belief. The eternal being scans the situation for information and makes decisions that rest on that point. Eternal beings live in an unbounded experience in which time essentially stands still. However, since they are not part of the universal experiment of finiteness, they cannot share in the dreams, visions, and destiny of sentience in the same way.

Eternity exists as a type of visionary stream in which these beings are able to incorporate different strata of time/space and in which they live relatively isolated lives. Their makeup is therefore completely different than that of the smaller, more finite consciousness. Eternal beings live in a type of unchanging stasis and are therefore filled with the desire to play. They must play constantly, almost like children, because they never really mature. It is the finite being that gains wisdom through the passage of time and ripens. Eternal beings remain childlike, visionary, and often develop a type of cantankerousness as a result. They can be moody and difficult to deal with.

God created both eternal and noneternal beings. This is the nature of the space/time paradox. Noneternal beings suffer a great deal more than those that are eternal. They feel that they can never be free. They long for freedom. Whereas, to live in a situation in which eternity is unfolding in front of one gives a sense of spaciousness in which it seems that nothing is truly insurmountable. It is time that causes a feeling of limitation, and without time as a medium of psychological boundaries, the eternal being is able to live much as a child might do. The human child is protected, guarded from the demands of adult life, and as such feels time to be strung out in front of him or her in an infinite and innocent way. Like the human child, eternal beings utilize play as a form of recreation, but also as a way to distill or retrieve information. They literally see dimensional existence as a play of the absolute.

The human adult also possesses an immortal soul, and this nonphysical aspect imparts a knowledge that all that is will pass while the quality of that which is remains untouched. Being both limited and unlimited simultaneously, the human being is able to grapple with complex emotional challenges, translating them into smaller, more digestible variables for immediate comprehension. This is where language, for instance, comes into play. Eternal beings have no need for a system of linguistic interchange because their communication is direct, synchronistic, and immediate. It is telepathic in the most visceral and organic sense.

Demystifying the Gods

In the mythic stories of the gods, eternal beings take many forms. They can be humorous, wise, quick to anger, unable to release their petty jealousies, or so keen to invoke punishment that their actions seem unjust or cruel. How can one live eternally without developing the basic mechanisms of compassion and justice that so move the adult sentient being? The answer lies perhaps in the nature of the human mind itself. The capacity to learn, to grow, to struggle, and to die lends a certain nobility to human existence. It is not that eternal beings are exempt from such nobility, but they are not always willing to reach into the reservoir of creative intelligence and find the motivation for true loving kindness. One is often kind in the human world through the dictum, "Do unto others as you would have them do unto you." In other words, it is our concern for the outcome of our actions that provokes certain motivations and responses within us. Eternal beings do not have such proddings of conscience. Therefore, when faced with situations that might demand a depth of knowledge of the nature of suffering, they can be surprisingly unknowing or cool.

Eternal beings have a natural arrogance because they do not have to respond or conform to any particular paradigm of behavior. They can be kindly but cruel, open-hearted but judgmental, just but ruthless, in every possible configuration. As a result, noneternal beings often call into question the morality and fitness of the "gods." They resent the pressures and constraints that the gods arrange while at the same time offering thanks and praise. This reveals the confusion on the part of noneternal beings as to the meaning of life itself. For eternal beings, their behavior is just a natural state of awareness, not filled with any sense of what is normal or right. In the wholeness of God's creation, the internal morality of sentience makes sense within itself. But when tested on a logical case-by-case basis, it often falls short.

There are, however, eternal beings whose primary dignity, primary method of functioning, is essentially pure love. These we would define in human terms as angelic. Such beings live in the stream of the Godhead's infinite compassion and as such are incapable of such cruelty as has just been described. Yet, their capacity to know what it actually feels like to suffer may be still a bit blunted, a bit hollow. It appears to be true that it takes direct, first-hand knowledge of limitation, physical and emotional suffering, and all their possible effects in order to gain access to the full wisdom that God provides.

Why would God create both kinds of beings? God wanted to develop a type of symphony that required some players to exist over the long term. He needed human players to keep a continuous stream of consciousness going while the notes of the eternal beings are more fixed. This background of eternal, harmonious vibration is necessary for the continuum to retain stability.

Eternal beings are not necessarily unbounded in their character of movement. Often they are stationary, fixed to a given point. They are referenced in such a position as a matter not of convenience but of necessity. It is through such fixity that star systems are born and made. Eternal beings are often given the job of developing and maintaining the star clusters. Since they exist in a type of fixed isolation, they are capable of holding the expression of matter/time for long stretches of infinity. Noneternal beings would essentially be bored by this job.

Eternal beings live in a state of permanent wakefulness. They do not sleep or eat in the usual sense. They are not bound by any mores, and are not capable of really understanding any form of cultural conditioning. Eternal beings exist independently of form. They use form only as a mantle, in the same way as time itself uses matter as a cloak or mantle. Eternal beings are very close to a pure expression of time. They are the closest attribute that the Godhead has created as an expression of what time actually is or could be. As a result, eternal beings have been worshipped by sentient life (which depends on sensory perception) in all portions of the universe.

Investigating the Mind of God

As sentient life is essentially free, it is also essentially eternal. It only pictures itself as noneternal for the purpose of the experiment. Sentient life has an eternal aspect, but it does not identify with this aspect, for the purpose of learning and growth. It is through limitation, honor, and sacrifice that noneternal beings learn about the nature of God's reality. They are able to investigate the mind of God and learn about the true character of the Godhead. Yet, they yearn always to have their permanent, more eternal nature restored. This is because they are references for the more changeable or transitory aspect of time. They emulate this changeable value which is never satisfied, always longing, always yearning. As a result, noneternal beings are rarely happy in the true sense. They seek to reunify with the Godhead even though they are much closer to God than any eternal being could be. This is because God Himself is both finite and infinite.

God leans on the finite for the purpose of developing form and content, and leans on the infinite for the purpose of breadth, motion, and space. God develops noneternal beings by feeding them the very stuff that eternal beings are made of; that is, a bending, curving circuitry of space/time that is the foundation of all of the concepts and proclivities that make up intelligence. God is the array of that intelligence in formations that defy any form of description. Once God develops intelligence, God does not seek to rely on any one particular expression for its further articulation. The expression of intelligence is categorically infinite and widespread.

God is the fountainhead for all intelligence, but God is something more. God stands apart from any avenue of intelligence that sentience might represent. Filled with the longing of infinite knowing, and stretched further than the boundaries that a human mind can travel, God relates the experience of time to His own understanding, and develops time through the continuity of civilizations and hegemonies that form the backdrop for a sentient world.

3.2.4
temporal liberation
and the mother

Time Springs Forth

ime precedes the awakening of consciousness from the field of all knowing. Since time retains its infinite value in the face of all challenge, it creates markers that are the precursors of what we would think of as relative or clock time. As the precedents for different life events are set on the wheel of life, time turns and provides the mechanism for each to come into being.

Time is called forth from its predecessor in each dimensional wing. As one element of temporal formation is called up, another is waiting. The dimensional range that a given life event can afford is calibrated in the very fiber or force of that event. It is literally pregnant with the principal antecedents that have given the event its essential independence.

Like energy, time is not truly lost. Yet, when consciousness contacts the field of time there is a temporary retreat or loss that comes about before that temporal stream re-emerges. Time is called back to the present through a series of algorithmic functions that will ultimately unify it with the absolute and make it possible for distinct space/time regions to exist. These city-states are like enclosed, self-sustaining villages of time in which all of the parameters are interwoven with each other to create a truly coherent sensibility.

Each corridor that time seeks to define has its own sets of values and these emerge simultaneously as they are spawned by the temporal backdrop. The environment in which time plays a part has an intimate effect on the development of a temporal spiral and will act to unify it when called upon. When a given region is seeking entry into the temporal spin it calls upon the set of time values that will create concordance with its specific intention. Time emerges, open-ended but still very particular to the needs and specifications of that region.

Reality is born anew through the raw material that time provides. Each set of impulses spawns a sister or twin-set that can be examined for the purpose of understanding how parallel dimensional activity accumulates. The many mirrors that time creates register in each region of activity in a different way, thereby creating the parallel ports that will open to new areas of spiritual/mental and physical activity.

The process whereby each set of time variables will formulate a new condition of being is based on time's capacity for infinite and rapid change. Each set of variables is spawned quickly, none waiting for a new set to emerge before arriving at its point of destiny. When time sets arrive they immediately have a springiness or bounciness that affords them the character of malleability. They become coherent rapidly as they coalesce around a given point of intention or period of change and rapidly spring forth with the appropriate information that will alter or develop reality for a given situation.

Time heats up or cools down on the basis of variables appearing or reappearing at the precise moment for which they have been cast. They head down the runway of time, wait for their number to be called and then take off into their given region for the purpose of restoring or initiating activity. Time presents itself as "cold motion" when it is stirred up, unsettled and loosely defined. Much like the movement of water through an open tube, time bends or curves around the areas of development that it seeks to envelop. Light emerges from the surface of time, opening to its flow as if effervescing from a central bubble or plain of reference. Matter eventually absorbs or redefines such light, eventually governing the very parade of time that strides forth.

Like the readily absorbable liquid nutrition given to a growing plant, time heads for the sun of creation, looking to distill light so as to make the background for the crystallization of matter, be it organic or inorganic. Light, time, and matter become self-radiant and completely self-sustaining. All of life is derived from the changes that time provokes in the area of matter. Each individual organism is keyed with the precise fountainhead of realization that will make it possible for its true originality to be birthed. With time as its mentor, matter has the capacity to provide infinite options to what otherwise would be a passive, unalterable existence.

Since time and space are psychodynamically bound, there is no reason why space should exist separate from time. However, as time emerges from the union, it is a cold ground, unencumbered by the relational values that might emanate around it. The cyclical movement of time from the underpinnings of union, back to its free, independent stance, occurs infinitely as space unfolds. Time becomes spontaneous when it leaves the largeness of the cold frame of space and enters the warmer value of the time/space continuum. Time leaves the frozen wilderness of space and enters a free-fall with its own integral structure. This structure, which is both infinite and finite simultaneously, creates the fabric of material reality that is the basis for solid or opaque unification.

The Interchangeability of Time and Matter

The world of matter, which is juxtaposed with space, is the backdrop for all understanding of how reality is constructed. The world of matter, in its opaque darkness, is always surrounded by the light of time. Matter is bonded through the interlacing enterprise of time. The absolute value of time presents itself as a field response that moves from one section of reality to another. In this transition, the relative attributes form an estuary that bonds time to the inner space from which it is derived. Time acts as a curtain, which when drawn over the backdrop of space causes a fluidity that renders space/time completely transparent. Time forms a docket or link with space that is ever-changing, nonstatic, and completely confluent with all of its original values. This makes space/time compact in the best sense.

Time and matter, being interrelated, are also interchangeable. When matter is reduced to its infinite structure, it is always time that presents itself. Space is always distinct, never hiding in the cloak of time. Space exists as a simultaneous but relatively cold reality underlying the space/time matrix. Since space coexists with time it does not turn to its opposite, which is matter. Space remains clean, separate, and coexistent as an opposite value, creating the bridge between time, matter, and consciousness.

The opaque, effervescent flow of time in the absolute makes up the feeling value through which matter is constructed. There is always a break for the flow of matter to arrive at its dimensional gate. When matter is bridged, bringing objects from one dimension to another, it takes time with it. Time holds matter together and creates the scintillating, paranormal effect that leaves matter breathless and co-centered in the space/time vault.

The units of space/time are configured so that each has an uneven or even value. Each unit is also masked or hidden by a ring or sphere that encircles that set of values and protects it from intrusion. This setup is empowered by a gyroscopic movement of energy that creates proportional spins around each unit of space/time and propels them forward. The units are rapidly spun out in even or odd-figured clusters and then spilled out again into the space/time vault. The rapidly spinning, colliding values of space/time act like pinballs in a fast-moving game. They spin, collide, are trampled, and reform, sometimes splitting each other open in the process.

This upheaval or movement in the activity of the time values sets the stage for dimensional shift or interplay. All of the causal values of time, which eventually will make way for the development of matter, are pushed together, creating the unevenness or thickness that will allow for the solidity of relative form. Each object that emerges becomes coexistent with the

316

locality of space in which it finds residence. Formations occur in parallel orders of intelligence, each marking the way for future constellations of matter/time to be born.

The fusion of time and matter causes the creation of pools or clusters of similarly marked areas. These pools are created when the cold vaults of space/time move forward on to the glossy, ebony surface of matter. They are spun out like vast metal turnkeys around a central, luminous core. These pools or clusters bring about the parallel formation of reality that signifies the marriage of events with time. These events, which are psychological and physical, simultaneously form the backdrop for human experience. They are the raison d'être of our understanding of who we are and where we have been.

Parallel wrappings of space/time peel off from each of these glistening spiral conduits to create the absolute curvature for a given reality to be birthed. The absolute prepares a lively, treated canvas onto which the different areas of color and shape can cling. There is always a signatory, defining curvature of space/time that creates the "heave-ho" of time as it coasts along, developing its aperture. Since space/time is equidistant at all points from its principal defining curvature, it always has room for additional space/time matrical points to interlace along its spine. The flux of time values created is due to the rings or curvatures that have been laid down, which create the marker points for time spirals to occur again and again. This is why time appears synchronous, stylized, and remarkable even as it is vastly inordinate and repetitive in stages.

Living in the Rings

Beings who live in the rings that bind time to the absolute are always aware of being trapped in its flow. They are circling around endlessly in patterned interactions, which appear to be random but show up synchronistically as matched sets in the psychological event streams that pattern reality. Beings so caught rarely can see the forest from the trees and live eternally in this miasma of space/time, incapable of recognizing the source of their perception or what binds it. This situation, which is common to all beings who are not arrayed with absolute vision, is the source of great suffering. To unmask this state, such beings must become aware of time as a concrete, clear, and reasonable value dephasing all of their life's accomplishments and underscoring the foundation of psychological reality. Otherwise, they will be bound down to this reality and will not be able to become cocreative operators in the dynamics of relational space.

To free themselves from such binding parameters, beings must occupy space/time in a completely different manner. They must see themselves as temporary occupants in a panoply of event-centered miasmic breakfronts. They can thereby wrestle with their own demons so that they can be freed of the pain of parallel and coexistent opposites. This struggle towards temporal realization is the first step to true unitemporal liberation. Its achievement demands a patient realignment of the core of the psychological reality from a psychologically damaged dual functioning to one in which the fluid coexistence of parallel poles of origin becomes the main dynamic of the life stream.

To accomplish this feat requires a clarity of mind and purpose that is at once singular and perhaps extreme. The difference between a dynamically centered temporo-fluid mind and one that is bound to its psychological constructs is that the latter is more likely to create havoc and extreme dissonance in the event streams of others while the former will remain coexistent and apparently peaceful in its repose. The jump-started, free temporal consciousness is not only unbound by its chords to the relative, it is also unbound from the absolute. It is daringly unbraided by the flow from within or without.

The activity of a mind that is not bound by time is inherently self-deterministic and free. This state is created through an act of will and not simply from the slow-moving process of psychological self-analysis. The consciousness must deeply and permanently desire freedom and must ascertain that it will be able to function without the constraints of mental limitation. Such a freedom is surely attractive but it is not for the uncourageous. It demands a startling capacity for self-will in every moment and commands originality as a necessity. In a land of no rules and unlimited options, only those who have maintained a sound basis in the roots of all discipline can deny the patterns of their genetic lineage and become manifestly resourceful in the face of unparalleled temporal freedom.

The being must lift free of the implicate patterns that define the system of reality of which it is a part. In this process, the space/time values stored for later use, when the being is to return to its more eternal status, are called upon while it is still embodied and psychologically trapped. This reckoning of the opposites which brings about pure synchronicity is the reason that the temporally liberated being is coexistent with the God realms. It is no longer bound to the implied destiny that the patterned existence would have wrought. The tough skin of psychologically defended material has been shorn, and underneath lies a pure, nondefensive internal armoring, which is built from the ground of being up as a pure structure of time.

318

The stature of a being so liberated is that it can create the speed whereby the space/time continuum wends its way from the absolute level to the pure relative. This being therefore can bend the laws of matter, intercede with the ribbons that make up the space/time continuum, and lodge space between its jaws. This being knows the difference between down and up, in and out, and can corral time like a cowboy of interstellar space, relating the values and curves of matter directly to itself. This being is now capable of maturely handling the delicate space/time values that bring life, liberty, and understanding to the sentient mind. By allowing time to depend entirely on its synchronous movement, and at the same time swinging time over the edge of reality, the liberated being lassoes time and becomes a manufacturer of matter.

Mother Space

Since time and matter are the twin attributes of Mother Space, all of the values that they exemplify are part of that Mother value. The feminine aspect of the continuum is that which pauses, heaves, gives birth, recognizes and refines space/time. Mother is considered to be space itself because it is She who creates space/time from the infinite pool out of which God exists. Since the Mother value calls the values of time from their resting place in the infinite, only She can call them back again. This is why the Mother or Optimum Flow of Divine Intelligence is always glistening, radiant, and fluid. She is the definer of that which is meant by luminescent. She exists as this optimum radiance for the purpose of infusing matter with the light of Her hair, Her divine fragrance and demeanor. This optimum value, which is unshared and cannot be weighted by any other, gives the feminine value of universal intelligence the capability of birthing beings from its own womb. She delivers the goods of space/time to Her counterparts in matter and denies any other followers from worshipping Her without developing this source of command.

Time is the armor of the Mother. Time is the standard-bearer for Her walk in the creation. God the Father is the creative principle, circling around the campfire, upholding the primordial standards of organization and repeating the actuarial standards for matter to be born. The Mother stands watch, shepherding the eternal relationship to action. Time in its eternal sense belongs to the Father, but the Mother manufactures the practicalities of time that make it possible to view reality from a relative point of view. Time collapses back on itself again and again, and the Mother is the collapsible point. She is the shirker of worlds rather than the founder. She destroys the absolute through Her dealings with the relative.

Since the Mother is the radiant flow of the absolute, She is also the Queen of Time. She restores time to its essential nature by interrupting the repeating values that trap beings in their randomly executed corridor of patterned perception. She mirrors the God-flow in everything, excelling in ripping the head off of repetition, and developing originality and poise in every endeavor. Because the Mother governs such originality, She is responsible for calibrating the myriad flow of organic lifeforms that populate the planets and give birth to the solar systems. It is the Mother who gives life and also takes it away.

The Coexistence of God and Mother

The permanent, coexistent flow of infinite intelligence that we term God is also an aspect of the Mother and exists simultaneously as a backdrop for all that is. Because the Mother/Father integration of time is so still and so creatively dynamic at once, it is expressed as a field value. This means that each spray or piece of the time/matter unification is spilled out into the relative in a core of influence that will determine the size, shape, and structure of the event sequences that lie within it. This is why it is said that the Mother is the restorer of time to the universe. She belongs to the congregation of all awakened beings, lifting the lamp of influence in all of the forces that underlie space/time.

Since destiny is both fixed and parallel, the Mother must shake free of all of the temporal values that restore reality and keep them free from their opposites. This happens through a redefinition of the parallel coves that form the range of motion for time to appear. Since time appears in a type of grove-like setting, like an array of oranges, the Mother must pluck the fruit of time from the tree. She arranges this fruit, giving birth to the sustenance for matter to come about.

The parallel hooves of time stomp on each other and form the backdrop for reality. They must be released by the Mother and fed back into the infinite. The restoration of time values is always left to the feminine, because in this context time becomes curved, spacious, and never opaque. It is here that time can honor its origins and become effervescent and lively. The jump-start of matter from the mouth of time is always the job of the Mother. One cannot define space without time, nor can one define the reality of the Godhead without its feminine aspect.

The possibility of time springing full-blown from the mouth of the Mother is the reason for infinite beings and infinite possibilities to exist. The Mother has nothing to lose. She has everything to gain through Her attempts at unified creation. She never spills anything without a reason. Because She has been captured by time and can never again be free from it, She does not try to be. She opens Herself to time, willingly and lovingly, and returns to its nature for the express purpose of defining reality for Her space/time children. All beings that recognize the concrete, conceptual nature of time also recognize that it is the Mother that attains to this state. She is the recognizer of opposites and the retainer of all that is mutually beneficial and coexistent.

3.2.5
time and God consciousness

The Host Intelligence

Since the unified dimensional experience is explicated according to the underlying and fundamental will of God, it should be self-evident that God is the Host or Supreme Intelligence. This is particularly relevant when it comes to understanding time as a principal exponent of matter/creation.

Time is by definition not dependent on the Godforce, but stands outside of it in a fundamental way. We might say that time is the purveyor of the Host Intelligence rather than a component of it. Time is the witness, just as in the development of witness consciousness one views the passage of divine expression within the context of the whole. Since matter and time are interrelated, it stands to reason that matter too would lie outside of the God dimension. However, this is not the case. The reason for this is that time is a standard of deviation; it is a presupposed condition upon which the building blocks of matter may be founded. Time creates the conditions for creation, and matter is the outgrowth of these conditions.

Who, then, created time? We could say that time actually precedes the Host Intelligence itself. How is this possible when we view the Godforce as the preeminent and omnipresent purveyor of all knowledge? Time creates the map or blueprint upon which the Godforce can ascertain the desires of creation. God actually serves creation as much as we serve God. God needs to satisfy the demands that His creation has delineated. Surprisingly, there are rules that govern this status, and so in this respect God cannot do everything. Even He has certain governing influences that maintain the equilibrium of the creation. These rules or governing influences are pervaded by an underlying value of time or timelessness as the case may be. The cyclical unfoldment of the universal intelligence is masked by markers or endpoints which signify the arrays that time will display in a given interval. Since the God Intelligence directs this mapping process, we could say that in a sense He directs the flow of time rather than time itself. He determines how time will be spent, rather than actually making time as a smooth derivative in its own right.

Time is a form of witness that seeks to define the degrees of advancement of civilizations. Time looks upon creation like a father would look on his daughter. He loves her dearly but knows that he will one day have to give her up. Time treats creation like a fatherly witness, seeing to it that the cyclical unfoldment of all that is performs in the desired pathways. God utilizes time as a type of marker that gives Him the opportunity to review His creation. Time is a bookmark of the absolute. It is the discretionary marker that describes how the genealogy of peoples, landscapes, and planetary continuums will be stretched out over a given surface. Since God lives in a completely timeless realm, it would stand to reason that time would have to exist outside of God. How could time determine the functions of the Godhead when It is by nature completely timeless, infinite, and unbounded?

The question then arises, if God did not create time, how did it come to be? There is something that precedes even the eternal Godhead. Time enters the field of existence independently. It stretches out like a canvas onto which the Godhead can paint the mystery of creation. The pulse, the rhythm, the tempo to which the dance of creation can respond is self-evident in the flow of time. It is the primary unit of existence, preceding even the intelligence that brought it into being. These apparent paradoxes, of time standing still but being in motion, of being the rudimentary force of unification and yet expanding outward from its own origins, of being dark but light, linear but curved, delimit but do not alter the character of time. In its effervescence and its seeming duality, time strives towards a unified territorial domain in which the Godhead can make Its mark.

The Drama of Creation

Time is an estuary that curls back on itself, catching the tip of God's tongue. Time wraps itself around the event streams that will eventually bind it to a dimensional reference point. The character of these temporal events will form the container for psychological reality. In order for time to lose itself in the flow of matter, creation mechanics has the responsibility for underlying all that is sentient, dramatic, and powerful in the play of life. The repository for such intelligence lands in the lap of the Mother.

The drama of time is a not simply a function of the Mother. Time is the Mother. In this analogy, the Mother is the function of wholeness that underlies the manifest creation. God creates creation, while the Mother creates the conditions for creation. Hers is the womb, the repository for the wholeness of creation to be born and bred. Since time is the organizer of creation, it stands to reason that the Mother would also be that organizer. It is She who brings the darkness as well as the light. In the experience of opposites, the shadow of the Mother introduces the inter-reflective spirit of events that leads us to the reason behind our actions as voiced from the unconscious. The Mother casts a shadow, a hidden meaning behind our actions and consensus that affords us the comfort of a shaded zone where we can experience both our deepest truth and our deepest pain.

Time is the indwelling spirit. It is the interior light that governs the standards of unified creation. The Mother whistles the spirit of time into the cauldron of matter. Since time spins endlessly, the characteristics that determine creation must also be filled with this type of curving complexity. The Mother lunges forth, tearing at the fabric of matter in a rather angry display of Her wrath and genius. It is through the curtain of prehistory that the Mother reveals Herself and displays Her armor.

The transitory nature of time is founded on the breath of the Mother. With each sigh, She imbues time with the emotional thrust that causes us to embrace our personality. Time stands directly behind the decisions of creation and the Mother witnesses this rebirth in every moment. Time destroys the tendency for creation to be based solely on the needs of the absolute. Time and the Mother cause consciousness to bend to the will of the individual life.

To distinguish time from any other seed intelligence, the Mother makes time a marker for relative existence. She lets Her children know who they will be when they grow up through offering them a temporal witness. Time is registered or imprinted through a rhythmic, cyclical styling in the fundamental pulse of reality. Time engages the Host Intelligence in the demands of creative performance.

The Challenge of Love

Since the Mother is also the holder of the love dice, the gambler that splays the numbers onto the court, She must empower time to earn the power of love. She creates a standard whereby time must be accountable to the love force in the universal stream. Love and time must be equidistant. They must stand together because through these two waves of knowledge all sentience is realized. The desire for wholeness that the Mother represents is the participatory marker for time. Time stretches past the boundaries of love by identifying what the constituents of love will be. Love challenges time to become responsible for its actions. Love relays the appreciation of time to sentient life.

Time is indistinguishable from the Mother. Her breath forms the basis for time. It is Her pounding, heaving, sighing breast upon which the treads of time are made. Since the Mother is not bound by time any more than the

Father is, She can incorporate the fundamental knowledge of time directly into the fabric of creation. But unlike the Father, She is time, and therefore has nothing with which to unify. She balances the creation at Her feet and documents the delicious saturation of the infinite through Her dance.

Time, behaving as it does without ground and without location, must establish a point of view. This the Mother does as well. Each aspect of creation is given a locator point, a marker in the display of manifest life. She puts these markers in place much like the surveyor who measures the land on which the castle will be built. Time marks the way, making it possible for the structures of creation to have a foothold. Without time, all creation would simply slither away, unhooked to the infinite, unable to be put on display.

Since time and the Mother are truly synonymous, the dialogue that ensues between time and creation is always with the Father. It is He who determines how time will be used. The Father witnesses the spread of time, like butter on the bread, letting time fan out in every direction, smoothly and seamlessly. The Father witnesses the shock that ensues when time is not smooth, when it becomes wedged in by the demands of a particular situational effect. Time stops when the mathematical junction points between time and matter become caught or frayed. Time recedes, strengthening itself before it can return to its original blueprint.

The Appearance of Duality

Since the God Consciousness witnesses time and twists it for Its own use, It is unafraid of the consequences when time is misused. How can time be misused? As time is a marker and as the markers are in themselves both infinite and finite at the same point, sometimes the tendencies of determination for the fundamental creation can be switched. They are like twins switched at birth: so identical, so perfect, so clearly one form that sometimes one does not know what is relative or what is absolute. This kind of twinned universal speciation makes the God Intelligence howl with delight. There is nothing better than such a fundamental split that allows the creation to become duo-fold, honed into qualities of light and dark. So it is with the earthly variety of creation, a type of anomaly, a mistake in the pattern that is both a welcome relief from the boring invariance of infinite markers, and at once decidedly apparent and unique.

The Mother creates duality for Her amusement. She likes the play of light and dark, relishing in the interplay of shadow and form. The Mother enjoys the dialogue that happens when time must meet the dualistic and frozen version of itself as it rises from the absolute. In the moment that time laughs at itself, it produces a noticeable effect that mirrors the undeniable power of creation.

The play of time is a profound element of the cosmic dance. In its malleable quality, time emulates the compassionate nature of the Mother that enjoys playing amiably with Her children. Time enjoys seeing what the circumstances of reality will hold. At times, this spontaneous display of affection on the part of the Mother can be a form of embarrassment to the Father. How can the deterministic, dominant force of unified creation hold the *lila* of primordial play in its wake?

Time is made from the eternal substance of the Mother. Through unification with the Father, time embodies the masquerade of relative existence. When masculine and feminine, mother and father, join together with grace and aplomb, they coordinate the patterns of creation, marbling the surface of life with a swirling arrangement of temporal icing. Whereas the Mother knows the course of time, purveying the points of reference for each curve, the Father commands the constitution of absolute existence and gives rise to all that might be seen as fundamental or statutory. Together, Mother and Father contribute the hum that governs relative existence. They engender the pulse that keeps everything alive and in tune. Time requires a break in the rhythm of creation, a type of temporal holiday that gives respite to the intense forward-moving action that creation demands. Inherent within this pulse is the tendency towards both action and renunciation.

Consciousness Holds the Controls

Since time and consciousness are wedded, the fundamental change in time relies mostly on consciousness. It is through consciousness that time is bled onto the screen of existence and is made righteous, refined, and coherent. Consciousness controls the speed, duration, and latitude of time, and it makes the corrections in the course. Consciousness is the mind of the absolute, the speaker of the river eternal. In this sense it is both masculine and feminine, and neither. Consciousness, which controls the rate of reversal of time, makes time a concubine, a mistress of its own standards of living.

If time is interdependent with matter, why is it that matter retains its solidity? Time and matter should shrink back, moving into the recurrent pattern of eternal existence, but they do not. This is because the Mother holds the keys whereby the patterns of matter will be born. The creative influences are like the cosmic DNA that holds the vocabulary for awakening matter. The Mother is the ghost, the witness, and the purveyor of truth all at the same time. When She gasps, time stands still. When She breathes, all is well; there is order to the chaos.

Time and consciousness, wedded together, give matter its grip, its special hold on creation. Without manifest matter there would be nothing to interplay with the absolute royal continuum that the Godforce represents. Time creates the backdrop for this continuum, like a stage on which the forces of nature can dialogue and make fun of each other and themselves. Like an aging actor, time is always up for another part, another opportunity to show off its ever-changing character. Since time never gives up, never falls short, never needs to be reminded of its role, it is innocent and ever so playful. Without the crucible in which time and matter are forged, there would be no workable vessel for God to utilize.

Time, matter, God as Father and Mother: they are seamless, transparent, and purely objective. They are personal, continuous, transcendental, and obvious. They play upon each other, wrapping themselves into the cloak of matter and pretending to be afraid of death and normality. There is little that time cannot take apart that matter cannot put back together. This is why time must remain as a witness, not taking part completely in the divine medley. As a witness it retains its distinctive purity and its mathematical precision. It is the grid onto which the forces of nature can be laid.

3.2.6
temporal mechanics
and the godforce

The Mercy of the Godforce

t he Godforce is the actuarial component that strengthens, elongates, and refines the imprints of time as they appear on the map of the transcendent. Time, wrapped around the fingers of the Godforce, inhibits the formation of matter, building the energy continuum that stretches reality past where creation forms. The Godforce embraces time, stripping it of any impediments that would cause creation to be unable to form as It demands. Within the context of creation, pockets of empty time or no-time also form, open-ended portals in which time is given a rest, is eased off, yet is kinetically charged. Such areas are essential to the formation of the whole and the interrelationship of the parts.

God in His mercy gives creation the capacity to imprint time directly on sentience. The ability of a human being to think, feel, and relate to his or her environment is contingent on the power of reason. Time, inherently unreasonable and fabulously illogical in its sequencing, documents creation as an inexorable witness. Time infuses creation with the power of God through an everlasting perspective that causes matter to recalibrate its innate capacities and leads to its eventual dissolution. Time is the vehicle whereby God witnesses the final states of both the birth and destruction of matter and signals its impending synchronization.

The formation of civilizations is dependent on time as a witness. Time looks upon the structure of civilization from two vantage points. The first is like the roof of a house, protecting the upper floors from rain, dust, and the ravages of weather. Time functions in its protective capacity, sealing in the event streams that circulate through the intelligence of the Godforce. The second is like the good neighbor, looking after the house, making sure that everything is in place, in proper order.

Time creates order from the spontaneous and chaotic reckoning of the Godforce. Time governs the flow of reality. In its ability to distinguish the calendar, the mapping of events and feelings, time functions as a bookmark for the absolute. It acts as a marker that carves out the landscape of peoples, regions of influence, and planetary characteristics. God lives in a timeless realm, and therefore time stands outside of the innate region where God dwells. By holding the standard of creation as the eternal witness, time has the inherent capacity to carve form and become the underlying value behind culture, tradition, and human conduct.

God Is Absolute

The Godforce is the Host Intelligence. It is more than omnipotent, It is omnipresent; thus It exists in all time and all space. Delightfully innovative, full of the paradoxes and succulence that makes it possible for time to develop the vestibules of existence, the Host Intelligence has no need for stagnancy. Everything that is tenuous, untouchable, and magnetic is food for the characteristic expression of the absolute. The grips of time are let go and the apparent reason for creation is pulled apart. Within the fountainhead of living time is the seed of expression that the Godforce wishes to transduce. There is no obstacle that God must endure other than the whimsical forces that seek to undermine the power and determination of the will of God.

The forces that seek to bleed or drain the will of God originate from God's own hand. They are built into the fabric of His will in order for the continuum to be in a state of fluidity and balance. Just as we fight within ourselves to retain our cohesion, there are forces within the Godhead itself that seek to tear down His reality. One can view these as evil, but they are the falcons of change and ultimately create the stir in the winds of creation that bring about unity. All life returns to its Source, and so those that seek to tear down that which has been created find themselves soon enough as remakers of the very thing they destroy.

The Godforce is the fundamental standard for the breaking apart and pulling together of the All-time. It is here, in the workshop of the absolute, that the timeseeds are broken open, their contents spilled onto the floor of the matter/time continuum. The Godforce structures stages or gradations of time from within Its depths, each of which is responsible for the layers of dimensionality that call forth the universal truth. Each layer of time is signified by a standard of deviation, a map, a blueprint that circulates around and over that given field and gives it a structure that will eventually be the backdrop for a portion of creation. The Godforce executes the underlying attributes that mirror creation, and then gives them their timeliness, their flavor of knowing that will allow the individual and the collective to reflect the responsibilities and duties that are mandatory.

The Godforce gives rise to knowledge in its pure sense. Stripped of any sense of personal demeanor or dependency, this knowledge emanates directly from the will of God and transmits the power of uniformity to the dimensional expression. The creation, constantly in search of the information that will bring it to its fullest expression, looks to the Godforce for this knowledge and to time for its panoramic execution. Time delineates the spin, the pull of the Godforce as it strikes forth into the universal continuum. Time stretches, pulls, delimits, and magnifies the Godforce in a rhythmic, pulsing drive towards the perfect installation of universal truth.

The Precision of Birth

Time cannot speed up this unfoldment, nor can it slow it down. Time is dedicated to precision rather than speed. It is inexorable in its calculating magnitude, encircling the creation like a cradle and bringing forth the new cries of birth and the rage of death at every turn. Time cocreates with the Mother, the feminine attribute of intelligence. Time is the mechanism whereby the Mother expresses motion, action, and material substantiation in the universe. Time emanates from the Mother and so may be described as the Mother Herself.

The Godforce, unlimited in Its ability to reckon with the power of creation, does not have need of anything to carry out Its will. It stands independent, dominant, and inherently free. However, through the marriage of the masculine and feminine forces, the underlying transparencies that mimic the causal structures of time will come forth. Time will become the vehicle whereby the Godforce will elongate the absolute and make matter become visible. All that is ethereal, delicate, and intangible becomes available and routine through the calculated interference of time.

God circles back and forth through the continuum in a peak spiral, looping over the reaches of space/time and discovering the rudimentary dialogue of feeling. The capacity of time to create motion gives rise to the experience of emotion in its most pure and elevated state. This experience is dependent on the rise of the Godforce from Its nest of tranquility to the sharpness of Its spin into the infinite. Time plays out, creating perturbations in this sanguine, salutary stage, which eventually becomes the compass whereby star civilizations are born.

Looking in the Mirror

Time mirrors God in the way that Man mirrors the infinite. Each tiny thread of time alters the way the Godforce perceives Its creation and makes it anew. The Mother intelligence, unafraid, bold, determined, and strong in Her stations of multiplicity, seeks out time from within the boundaries that the Godforce creates. Here is time, stripped of companionship, isolated from its associative stream of continuity with creation. Here is the Mother, enveloped by time, interactive with the Godforce and qualitatively different in Her approach. The Mother wants to restore time, to nurture, to sustain; the Godforce wants to peel back time completely, making it transparent and full of the richness of the unmanifest. Strung out blindly on the curve of time's unbending flexibility, Mother makes time acquiesce to Her demands.

Time is the plaything of the absolute and Mother is not jealous of this. She is not frightened or intimidated by the scope of the range of feeling it evokes. Time arranges for the consequences of action and the positivity of creation. Time engages the intelligence of the Godhead for the purpose of organization and synthesis while never relinquishing the pure chaos, the pure fun of being that the Godforce denotes. Time strives for perfection, growth, understanding, and comprehension, while the Godhead seeks only to renew, sustain, and make whole. Time gives voice to the human need for freedom, while the Godforce views Man as inherently free.

The true nature of Man lies in his ability to know God. This knowledge is not sacrosanct or dogmatic in its intensity. The knowledge of God is found in the recesses of the eyes and ears of His creation. Man seeks God out through the knowledge of death. It is here in the terminal impulses that make us go towards the goal of recession that time imprints the fundamental steps towards the Divine Will. The temporal impulses of creation determine how a living thing will die or should die, and here the knowledge of how to live wisely and well is born. Strategically, the manner in which we live affects the manner in which we die. The compassionate resonance of the Mother intelligence births the knowledge of love onto the field of a cold and rational scale of time. Time is infused with the banner of love and all of life warms up to receive it.

The eloquence with which time expresses itself is dependent not only on the will of God but the relative internal comprehension that each individual achieves in his or her existence. The Godforce creates the capacity for such comprehension by stridently breaking the codes of existence down until the individual is left with a timeless and incessant wonder about all things. The infusion of this wonder, this awe in the magnificent complexity of life, is the birthright of each individual. Time provides the stroke of recognition, the fire under which the foot of insight is never burnt.

Human Freedom

The deliverance of Man from the stridency of a rigid, temporal existence is always available. It is inherent and unchangeable. It is only the desire of Man to find his home in the universe that makes him cling to the temporal cord. Plunging loose, letting go, leaping into the eternal without the benefit of any safety net beneath him, Man can free himself from want or need. The recognition that human beings are inherently free unites us with all sentient life forms in the cosmos. We stand inside the record-keeping function of history, the time-release capsules that open us to our story, without having to leave behind our comprehension of a casual embrace by eternity.

The Godforce sinks deep into the structure of humanity. Here it is that hope, the force that unites human beings towards their journey of self-realization, can magnanimously come forth. Time reenters the picture through self-awareness, the majesty of tracing the direction of event streams to their acquiescent source. Time holds the key towards eternal self-reflection, towards the meaning of existence, the meaning of reality.

Time and reality are the vessels whereby the Godforce instills the desire for reproduction into living organisms. Based on the synthesis of all knowledge with all time, living things become capable of a modular replication, in which they open into their seed capacities and become inordinate and full. The process of replication is the starlight of time. It is the inner sanctum where the sacred capacities of the time intelligence reacquaint themselves with the patterns of matter. Every strand of hair, every facet of the individual makeup, is laden with the necessities of time. The Godforce relinquishes the power of His creative stature to the individual being. He delivers the sacred awareness of light-filled awakening to the beings that must give birth. Here the Mother enters, stretching the inner envelope of time to the point where everything will finally balance, will be made succinct and understood. The Mother holds the key to the mystery; She knows what will be and what will die.

Invincibility and the Cry of the Infinite

The final impermanence of reality is vested completely in the remarkable capacity of time to be renewable and perfect. Time escalates the grandeur of creation to its infinite proportions. Why should time waste a moment shedding this grandeur unnecessarily? Time transmutes the imperative laws of the Godforce, making the creative shrink and expand. Time opens the language of itself to human creation. There is never a moment in which time is not original. The Godforce, running contiguous with time, creates a place for time outside Itself. How can there be anything that exists outside of the Godforce Itself? The knowledge of infinity, its resting place in the panoramic unfoldment of creation, exists outside of the boundaries of the Host Intelligence. God expands and time contracts. Time exists as a preeminent force that transmits the efficacy of creation to the Creator. This is why the Mother Intelligence is seen in most traditions as a separate spiral, a separate ribbon that twirls and enlivens the God rhythms. Time and the Mother, synchronous and loving, alter the living dream of creation and give it spiciness, laughter, a cause for love.

The Godforce is helpless without time. Time must divulge enough of its secrets to make the union of creation possible. Perfectly adjusted, invincible in Its capacity to transmit, the Godforce holds time dear just long enough for the temporal knot of reason to take hold. Time makes the absolute sing. Time intentionally creates the bereavement of matter. Matter is called back from its singularity and given infinite rebirth through the signature of time. The Godforce desires only Truth, and this truth, not based on anything that is conceptual or actuarial, can only be relit through the function of an all-time construct. Time spins and twirls, recalibrates and delineates, entering the fabric of eternity and nodding at the patterns that make matter form. All that is lives inside the whirling dervish of time, but the Godforce Itself stands outside.

This situation is what creates in human beings the function of an internal witness. Human beings, made in the image of God, live their reality from two planes. One, the facet that plunges in, sinks its teeth into experience, suffers, misunderstands, and is innocent in its helplessness. The other, wise and nonsuffering, is capable of the most complex understanding, beyond the pangs of birth or death, strident, and unreformed. These dualities reflect the nature of the Godforce itself, at once inherently all-knowing but completely innocent, at once spontaneous yet magically and beautifully organized, at once as strong, brave, and weak as a newborn child.

The Godforce recognizes Its humbleness because It knows that It is nothing without the Mother Intelligence, the capacity for the ingestion of time. Here the Godforce learns of the true satiation of existence: It is able to feed on itself. Human beings are ignorant so that they can reach into the pocket of time and cross the dimensional threshold with a kind of innocent rectification. The wind is at their back; they are free to misdirect, misunderstand, and misrepresent. Time is their friend, because when they die they immediately understand their mistakes and can evince them.

Belief in Self-Knowledge

How can life offer human beings the possibility of partiality? Human beings live for the sanctification of their own belief systems. They thrive on feeling that they are right and others are wrong. With these standards firmly in place, they eventually transcend them, and in so doing they immediately stand clear of the binding force of time. Unafraid, strident in their belief that they are right, human beings step forth and recover their self-knowledge slowly. They are trapped in the heartbreak of time, but are also by birthright able to step beyond it whenever they so choose. They are lifted up by love, incapacitated by their own limitations, and stretched by the knowledge that they will eventually set sail on the time continuum with nothing to hold them close. They are usually not ready to enter such a dizzying embrace with love and time until they realize that they are playing with the diamond of intimacy. It is through physical, engaging love that they learn that they are not one but a system of many. They become a "we" instead of an "I" and move beyond their limited nature.

It is time that dispels the myth of separateness and it is only time that can split the atom of individuality apart. Time is vested with the job of making individual life a perfected, intangible odyssey into the rhythms of the absolute. Time is the daughter of God/Man and the reason why human beings cannot afford anything but divine enterprise and a sense of mission. Time invests human beings with the need to accomplish, to master, to create, and to destroy. Time gives Man the capacity to reach past all boundaries and limitations and make history through incalculable enterprise.

Once human beings can get past the deluge of time and transcend their individuality, they recognize that they are castaways from such turbulent waters. They open to their freedom and expand their horizons past the borders of any limited dimensional territory. To become worthy and open to such freedom, time must clear the way, acting as an ambassador for the culmination of matter in its most spiritual guise. Time suspends the need of the Godforce for stringency, and human intelligence can then display itself fully and with dignity. In such a world, the problems of limitation, greed, or avarice cannot be distinguished. The light of time makes all such notions impossible.

The limitations of time are met through the process of human development. Through focused intent, human beings find their place within the infinite context of time-centered objectification. Mindful of the extent to which their place in history will be documented by their travails in the face of destiny, human beings search for God much as they search for time. With a keen desire, recognition of possibility, and implacable investment in the continuity of truth, humanity looks for the opening from which it can comprehend the meaning of time. As the Godforce opens Its eyes and gives vision to all that is, time becomes a willing, sentient partner. The capacity to know is linked with the capacity to dream.

glossary

Actuarial
The subtle statistical background for action accomplished by a divine force

Algorithms
A mathematical description of sequential unfoldment that acts as the standard for the movement of time

Breakfront
The gap that forms in the energy interval between one series of time sequences and another, often generated through a time loop

Cloak of time
A shielding of the nascent process of time configuration so as to birth a more solid, opaque form of matter

Coastal
The jagged boundary created when time is spread over a wide range, necessitating a break, similar to a coastline

Dimensions
Formats that arise when time is allotted to proximate and overlapping envelopes of space

Event streams
The fast-moving sequences of psychological cognition that form the basis for occurrences of a relative nature

Field of consciousness
The scope of influence of the most refined responses of awareness

Fractionization
The process by which time individuates through a prismatic display of cohesion and spin

Godforce
The free-flowing inherent intelligence behind the mannerisms and movement of time

Interdimensional civilization
A society in which the structures that bind temporal reality have been freed

Interdimensional mathematics
The systems and methodologies that describe the mechanics of temporal unboundedness, expressed in symbolic terms

Law of opposites
The breaking of two temporal forces from their internal stance of union and reconfiguration as free-standing opponents

Law of randomization
The spontaneous juxtaposition of temporal probabilities presented in the formation of reality

Light language
The figurative and symbolic representation of solid and translucent tonal colors as expressed in the context of sentient awareness

Locator points
The centric, centrifugal gateways that open time to its specific geographical identity

Mapping
The process of defining a particular region of either space/time or its derivatives

Mother Intelligence
The originating feminine expression of unification and self-nourishment that opens awareness to its source

Motion
A primary characteristic of sentient behavior that is made possible through the flexibility of time

Multidimensional time
The breaking off of temporal regions into interweaving categories that stretch the boundaries of perception

Nation-states/city-states
Temporal and material landscapes as delineated through prescribed boundaries that form communal stages of union

Nonreferential mind
The ability of intelligence to identify its own state separate from the confines of object or sensation

Parallel realities
The situation in which two or more personal event streams occur simultaneously and mirror open-ended but interweaving possibilities

Parallel universes
The cosmological formation emerging from multiple temporal streams that maintains an infinite continuity within an independent stream of events

Refraction
The interactive process of movement and creation whereby time elicits prismatic self-definitions which span the entire range of universal intelligence

Skin of time
The compacted layers of metered consciousness that preexist the formation of reality

Stretch of time
The process by which event structures must pull in one direction or another to align themselves with the formation of matter

Suspension
The situation in which time is held in abeyance as a function of movement from one space/time interval to another

Temporal blueprint
The map of corresponding intervals that defines the path of a given life stream or a direction of creation

Time arc
The bridge that forms when time curves back on itself to create a new set of possibilities

Time break
The gap that occurs when a forward- or backwards-moving procession of time intervals is interrupted in its quest for unification with the infinite

Time code
The mathematical expression of light by which a particular formation of time is described

Time curvature
The bend in the wave formation of time that stretches to fill the space in which consciousness will next manifest

Time loop/ribbon
Ripples returning to their source in the space/time continuum that produce the effect of past, present, and future

Time lords
Archetypal sentient beings that govern and systematize the fabric of time

Time matrices
Dense, complex networks of overlapping mathematical ribbons that relay the fundamental organization of time and consciousness

Time optimization
The rapid increase of speed, motion, and distance that supports the centricity of time in its dance of self-unification

Time pools
The collection of descriptive mathematical variables from which time/space formations are created

Time travel
A profound shift in inherent dimensional focus that alters personal and collective reality through a splitting off of time values, thus causing a new range of motion in space/time

Time variables
The values that are arrayed to describe time in its patterned expressions

Time window
An opening in the procession of event sequences that makes room for new elements of choice in the psychological and structural reconfiguration of time

Time/matter interface
The encounter of matter with the inner processes that organize and set the rhythm for the unfoldment of events and that are then reflected in one's personal environment

Uniform dimensionality
The profound stability or composure that is created when consciousness identifies infinite regions of experience and awakens to the common foundation of vibrational reference points found within them

index

e

f

g

About the Author

For the past quarter of a century, Janet Sussman has been engaged in a deep personal process of integration of her spiritual, psychological, and energetic fields. This originally led to the publication of *Timeshift: The Experience of Dimensional Change*, first published in 1996. The work has charted the way for new ideas articulated through a unique vocabulary chosen to express the fundamental mechanics of the consciousness of time and space. She views this work as a direct interface with her spiritual counseling practice in which she emphasizes the unfoldment of the heart chakra as a prerequisite balancing force in the maturation of the human light body.

Janet has taken this work to the step of developing experiential exercises that bring participants to the point of stepping out of their time/space reference through the integration, articulation, and lucidity of chakral work. She is known for her vocal techniques which help the listener/participant to see into subtle aspects of the physiology and make adjustments necessary for spiritual growth.

Janet is the developer of a unique energy balancing system called Sunpoint™ and is an active teacher to physicians, health professionals and spiritual aspirants.

A musician as well as a writer and counselor, Janet is accomplished on piano and synthesizer. Her CD, *Bridges*, is used in clinical settings as an adjunct therapeutic tool. She is available for personal consultations, seminars, and concerts of transformational music. Her e-mail is Janet@timeportalpubs.com.

Other books and recordings are planned for release over the next few years. Check Time Portal's website at www.timeportalpubs.com for information about new products and the online study group on *The Reality of Time*.

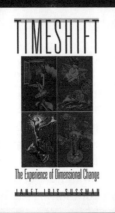